EGOTISTS and AUTOCRATS

the Prime Ministers of Canada

GEORGE BOWERING

VIKING

VIKING

Published by the Penguin Group
Penguin Books Canada Ltd, 10 Alcorn Avenue, Toronto, Ontario,
Canada M4V 3B2
Penguin Books Ltd, 27 Wrights Lane, London W8 5TZ, England
Penguin Putnam Inc., 375 Hudson Street, New York, New York 10014, U.S.A.
Penguin Books Australia Ltd, Ringwood, Victoria, Australia
Penguin Books (NZ) Ltd, cnr Rosedale and Airborne Roads, Albany Aukland
1310, New Zealand

Penguin Books Ltd Registered Offices: Harmondsworth, Middlesex, England

First published 1999
10 9 8 7 6 5 4 3 2 1

Copyright © George Bowering, 1999

Th excerpt from *Anne of Avonlea*, by L.M. Montgomery, is reproduced with
the permission of Ruth Macdonald and David Macdonald, trustee, who are
the heirs of L.M. Montgomery.

Anne of Avonlea, Anne of Green Gables and other Images of "Anne" are trade-
marks and Canadian official marks of the Anne of Green Gables Licensing
Authority Inc.

The Collected Poems of F.R. Scott by F.R. Scott. Used by permission, McClelland
& Stewart, Inc. *The Canadian Publisher.*

"Lament for the Fourth of June 1963." is a translation of "Deuil" by Paul
Chamberland, translation by F.E. Sparshott. Used by permission of author
and translator.

Printed and bound in Canada on acid free paper ∞

CANADIAN CATALOGUING IN PUBLICATION DATA

Bowering, George, 1935–
    Egotists and autocrats: the prime ministers of Canada

ISBN 0-670-88081-7

1. Prime Ministers – Canada – Biography. 2. Canada – Politics and
government. 3. Canada – History. I. Title.

FC26.P7B68 1999   971'.009'9   C99-931262-6
F1005.P7B68 1999

Visit Penguin Canada's website at **www.penguin.ca**

For Tommy Douglas

CONTENTS

A prime minister under the party system as we have had it in Canada is of necessity an egotist and autocrat. If he comes to office without these characteristics his environment equips him with them as surely as a diet of royal jelly transforms a worker into a queen bee.

—John W. Dafoe, Laurier

CHAPTER I

THE RED EMINENCE

———•◆•———

HERE IS THE MAIN difference between the democracy of the
United States and the democracy of Canada. In Canada
we elect our cabinet ministers and appoint our dog-catchers.
In the US they appoint their cabinet ministers and elect their
dog-catchers.

That is an old joke. But it is not a bad place to start looking
at the differences between the two governments.

In Canadian theory the various federal ridings send a member to the House of Commons, and then the party that has
most members in the House looks around its elected ranks and
chooses a head of government, called the prime minister. In
reality, everyone knows long before the election which man or
woman has been chosen by their party to act as prime minister
if that party comes in on top. That candidate can be defeated
in his riding's poll, in which case he has to direct things from
outside the House until he can find a safe by-election.

In the US and other republics, such as those in South America,
the president is the head of government and the head of state.

In the parliamentary democracies, especially those in the former British Empire, the prime minister is the head of government, while the head of state is the monarch or her representative (in Canada the governor general). Thus when a session of Parliament opens, the British monarch or the governor general in Canada will read a speech that is all about what will be attempted in the coming session by "my government."

Of course the vice-regal position is nowadays mostly ceremonial, but not always: in 1975 the governor general of Australia dismissed the prime minister and called an election.

But, even when Louis XIII was sitting on the throne in Versailles, France and the French empire were being run by his prime minister, Armand du Plessis, Cardinal Richelieu.

Most people agree that the first real prime minister in Britain was Sir Robert Walpole. He had to learn on the job, and during his twenty-one years in the position, he and his friends worked out the duties and perks of the position.

In 1720 the South Sea Company made an amazing offer to King George I: it would take over the entire national debt in exchange for certain preferential advantages in the world of trade. Walpole's specialty was the world of trade. He sat and watched. As soon as the deal went through, shares in the company soared by a thousand per cent. The King and his ladies were getting wealthier by the minute. Walpole sat and watched. In very short order the bubble went splat, and thousands of shareholders had to start selling their shoes. A good portion of the nation was highly miffed at the government and the King. Walpole stood up and offered his help.

A grateful King handed him the keys and went on a business trip to Hanover. Lord Stanhope, the secretary of state, got up to make a speech in the House of Lords and keeled over dead. Walpole was the man.

So in 1721 Robert Walpole became, in effect, the prime minister of Britain. He was always to reject the title, but until his resignation in 1742 he set about inventing the structure of the position. He gathered prime power by surrounding himself with less powerful men in other ministries. And his record of longevity would set the standard for prime ministers until William Lyon Mackenzie King stayed and stayed two centuries later.

The King was grateful to him for saving his Royal Derrière, and the King's son and the King's son's wife were to remain supportive. Walpole would never have a real majority in the House of Commons, but he would be skilful enough to keep on winning elections until 1741. He had no rivals of any strength in the cabinet. He cracked the party whip and demanded loyalty to policy. He found a way to dismiss anyone who opposed his principles. When Royal Patronage was to be handed out, it found its way through Walpole's hands first. He had the power to make hundreds of appointments in the civil and foreign services, a prerogative that remains to the prime ministers today.

His successors did not gather as much individual power to themselves until William Pitt the Younger ran the country for almost as long a period, starting in 1783.

The Treaty of Utrecht had left Acadia, Newfoundland and Hudson Bay in English hands. If we can say that power in Westminster was power in North America, maybe we can, by way of footnote that is not footnoted, say that Robert Walpole was the first prime minister of British North America, and therefore of the parts that would become Canada.

The idea catches on

It was really William Pitt the Younger who got the British people and the British Parliament used to the idea of a prime minister. He filled the job and used the title from 1783 to 1801, and again from 1804 to 1806. In France the guillotine was the fashionable invention in politics, followed by Napoleon's new empire. The latter, along with the new republic that menaced the remaining British holdings in North America, supplied Pitt with a foreign policy.

Pitt would set an example for the prime ministers of the nineteenth century. Enjoying the confidence of George III, who chose him at age twenty-four, he would, except for a short hiatus, remain PM until his death. His tenure was only one year shorter than that of Walpole.

Canada went through an interesting change during Pitt's time in office. In the east, the former New France was cut into two halves, a predominantly French-speaking Lower Canada, and a predominantly English-speaking Upper Canada. The Canadas, people said. In the west Captain Vancouver showed the flag and made friendly noises to the Spanish, securing the fur-trading place the British called Nootka, on the west coast of the big long island, thus ending the old papal notion that the whole Pacific Ocean belonged to the Spanish travellers.

In any case, after Pitt, the job description of the British prime minister became regularized. The PM would supervise all government departments, and coordinate them, insisting on seamless government policy. He would appoint all the ministers and diplomats. He would name the leaders of the Anglican Church. His approval would be needed for all cabinet measures. If he felt that Parliament had to be dissolved, he would go to see the King or Queen. He would hand out military and civic decorations and honours. He would have official residences established at 10 Downing Street and Chequers, his country mansion in Buckinghamshire.

As colonies in the British Empire attained some sort of parliamentary government on the model of the old country, they got their own prime ministers, often immigrants from Britain. Lucky us.

The first du Plessis

But it was in France that the term *premier ministre* was first employed, and it was used in reference to that figure known to old-time movie-goers and schoolchildren, the frightening Cardinal Richelieu.

Armand du Plessis de Richelieu was born in September 1585 into provincial gentry, a family that had some influence on the court of Henri III, but which had known better times. When his father died in 1590, the family was, except for its estate called Richelieu, just about broke. They were not poor in the sense that diseased paupers in rags were poor along the river in Paris; they were poor the way country gentle-folk might be said to be poor. They still had connections. The oldest son became the seigneur, of course, and the second son went away and became a monk. Because of an old family dispensation, Armand became, at the age of twenty-one, bishop of Luçon, and a year later after some quick parchment-shuffling, he was ordained, having charmed the clerical vestments off Pope Paul v.

Armand was not much of a man to look at. He was small and he coughed a lot. But he was very ambitious and snotty. When Henri IV was assassinated by a knifeman for being too accommodating to Protestants, Marie de Medici became the regent of France in 1610, and Armand started cozying up to her, as later he would to Anne of Austria when she became Queen. By 1616, when he was thirty-one, he was a member of the Royal Council, and soon the secretary of state for foreign affairs. Europe was an arena of rivalries, as usual, and du Plessis took advantage of all the conflicts, establishing a system of secret agents all over the continent. He was always looking ahead.

In 1617 when Louis XIII cleaned house after a revolt of the princes, Marie de Medici and Richelieu went into political exile. But in three years Richelieu was back. He still had his spies and he still had his connections in Rome and Paris. In 1622, at the age of thirty-seven, he was made a cardinal. Two years later he was on the King's council. This rapid rise in the establishment made Marie and her group turn against him, but no one was going to stop Cardinal Richelieu. He was going to bring his family back to a proper level of respectability, and he was going to make his country pre-eminent in Europe and overseas. He was going to act at all times in the name of the King, re-establish the power of the monarchy that had been threatened by provincial upstarts for half a century, and he was going to get rich while doing so. Louis XIII was frightened of Richelieu, but he was grateful for his support. Richelieu ran France from 1624 until his death in 1642. In 1628 the title of prime minister was invented. A du Plessis could not be king, but he could be cardinal and now he could be prime minister. That was as close as one could get.

He believed in order. Rebellion was disorder. The state with a king at the head was the epitome of order. Conspiracies against Richelieu were rebellions against the designs of God. Richelieu's spies were the agents of the moral order. The forces of disorder were not to be ignored. The King's mother, after all, took his brother Gaston to Spanish Holland and set up a rebel kingdom. Louis XIII needed his prime minister to protect him against family and foe.

Meanwhile, Richelieu got really rich. He owned property

here and there in France. He gathered dividends from agricultural, Church and company activities. He knew how to turn political power into coin of the realm. He set a precedent for prime ministers to come. You did not want to run afoul of his secret agents, because people who did tended to have their heads removed. The King knew that Richelieu was ruthless and ambitious, but he and Louis XIV would see that the prime minister had managed to hold off the Hapsburgs of Austria and Spain, and prepare France to take over as the leading power on mainland Europe.

If Armand du Plessis, Cardinal Richelieu, the most powerful individual in the western world, was prime minister of France, and France possessed land that would more and more often be called Canada, could we say that he was the first prime minister of Canada? In Quebec these days, one see his name all over the place, in advertising and administration. He may have been pleased to see, for instance, a listing for "Richelieu Biotechnologies," supplier and manufacturer of coupling reagents, solvents and amino acids for peptide synthesis, or "Air Richelieu," which offers flight training for private and business pilots. Every year the town of Saint-Jean-sur-Richelieu is the home of a hot-air-balloon festival. When he died, the Richelieu River was named after him. Running from Lake Champlain to the St Lawrence River, it became an important route in wars between the French and British. Later still, with the help of a canal system, the river makes it possible to ship stuff between New York and Montreal. Richelieu's spirit survives.

The prime minister never visited Canada, of course. But that should not surprise anyone. When I was a boy growing up in the Okanagan Valley, I never saw a prime minister. In fact, to this date I have never seen a prime minister while he or she was prime minister. I have seen a few governors general, but that was in the line of duty. No, Richelieu never set slippered foot on the soil of his North American province, but New France was on his mind.

By Richelieu's time the French had been operating along the St Lawrence for a century, but not many of them. It was very expensive to sail across the ocean, and French people have a high opinion of their own country. Thus there may not have been two hundred of them on the St Lawrence when Richelieu began to manage that poor place.

The Thirty Years' War kept most of the government's attention so that total exploitation of the American continent did not fall into French hands. As to his personal business affairs, Richelieu was kept so busy amassing his fortune in France that the colonies were simply a bonus. He did not bother to send his spies to the New World. His magnificent art collection would have no room for the masterpieces of aboriginal origin.

There were beavers in the forests, though, and there were trading companies looking for them. The trading companies were not interested in bringing settlers over, because settlers did not gather beavers and fish. There was not a plough in Quebec until 1627. There were no horses or oxen to pull one anyway. There were very few immigrants, and they did not hack away much of the bush along the river. Meanwhile, to the south, English pioneers were teeming.

There was already a trading company in New France, but it was run by some Protestants. Richelieu employed patriotic reasoning to disenfranchise them and set up a monopoly for the Company of New France which was allowed to operate from Florida to the Arctic, from the Great Lakes to Newfoundland. No one would have to pay any duties. As president of the company, Richelieu could influence policy pleasing to his King and advantageous to his pocketbook. The company was founded in April of 1627, and approved by the King a year later.

The Cardinal decreed that this company would be in the immigrant business, and that all immigrants would be Catholics, with Jesuits and Récollets to guide them in their adventure. The president had vast dreams. He would people the continent with French Catholics. With those immense forests stretching past the limits of the imagination the company could not help but pay enormous dividends, both in pelf and souls.

But since 1621 the Scots had been sending folk to the New World coast, where they soon outnumbered the French inhabitants. By 1627 Britain and France were engaged in one of their customary wars. Early in 1628 a fleet of French ships was surprised by three British merchantmen at the mouth of the St Lawrence. Everyone fired off all the shot they had, and at the end of a long day and a longer night, the French ships had become British ships.

Champlain and his hundred French people at the fort tried to get through a Quebec winter. They did not know how to fish and they did not know how to hunt. They traded their clothes to the Native people for eels, and hiked into the snowy forest, looking for nuts. Richelieu was in Paris, dining on French cuisine. By July of 1629, British pirates had managed to kick Champlain out of Quebec, not knowing, probably, that the French and British had decided to stop the war three months earlier. The pirates were very polite to Champlain, and gave him a ride to England.

In England Champlain went to see the French ambassador, then went across to France and had talks with the prime minister and the King. Champlain was a great explorer and colonist. Now he pleaded for a renewal of poor little Quebec's Frenchness. France's reputation was at stake. The forests were full of pagans and furry animals. There was a place called New England, and it was filling up with priestless Puritans.

Luckily, Charles I was facing a civil war and needed money.

Richelieu was in favour of kings, and of money. Luckily, too, Charles owed a lot of money to France for his wife's dowry. Richelieu, Prime Minister of France and President of the Company of New France, was ready to deal. In the March 1632 Treaty of St Germain-en-Laye, Quebec and Acadia came back to France. Now Richelieu could try to save the company, which had never yet paid any dividends. He decided on streamlining.

In 1633 Samuel de Champlain and the head Jesuit Father Brébeuf were back in the company town. Champlain was a sophisticated and transcendental man. He was happy to have what he thought to be a theocratic colony. He announced that attendance at Mass was compulsory. He even managed to die on Christmas Day of 1635. He once wrote: "The salvation of a single soul is of more value than the conquest of an empire." Cardinal Richelieu may have concurred, on the Lord's day.

But his great North American company went from bad to really bad. The French Catholics were greatly outnumbered by the people they called the Iroquois, and the King did not send troops to protect his prime minister's resources from these people. In 1645 the company let out its business franchise to local operators, but retained political power. In 1663, that was revoked by the French government, and Canada became a Royal Province, *comme les autres*.

CHAPTER 2

THE PROVINCE
OF CANADA

———◆●◆———

I KNOW THAT SOME people will say you cannot call Cardinal
Richelieu or Robert Walpole the prime minister of Canada.
Stop fooling around, they will say. The first prime minister of
Canada was John A. Macdonald, the man on the purple ten-
dollar bill. The majority of Canadian high-schoolers may not
know it, but Sir John A. was our first prime minister. Period.

Well, parentheses. In 1867 Sir John A. Macdonald was the
first prime minister of Canada (when Canada was made up of
four provinces, one of which, Nova Scotia, had a population
that was 65 per cent opposed to Confederation).

But on February 10, 1841, at Lord Sydenham's glorious house
in Montreal, there was proclaimed an earlier act of confederation, although that was not the original plan. There was a lot of
snow outside, and horse buns were freezing as soon as they
landed in it, but the date was auspicious with optimism. It was
young Queen Victoria's first wedding anniversary. It was also
the christening day for her first child, who would be called "Little Vickie." It was also the third anniversary of the cancellation

of Lower Canada's constitution. What a day, the loyal English businessmen of Montreal rejoiced.

Lord Sydenham was presiding over an act that responded to the recommendations made in Lord Durham's famous report. Lord Durham's Report was a staple of Canadian history in high schools in the middle of the twentieth century. I went to high school in the Okanagan Valley. The only things we ever heard about Canadian history were the Plains of Abraham and Lord Durham's Report. In British Columbia schools Canadian history was mainly about the way to handle the French problem.

Lord Durham was sent across the ocean to figure out why there had been rebellions in the two Canadas, and what to do about them. Durham spent five months over here, mainly in Montreal, where the streets were cobbled and the restaurants were pretty good. The rebellion in Upper Canada had been pretty well taken care of by the locals, who were eager to protect the province from any kind of US invasion. The rebellion in Lower Canada had been more threatening to London, because of the French problem. But Lord Durham was rather liberal as an emissary of the British Whigs, and some people went so far as to call him a champion of the local Reformers, which in those days meant a progressive party.

And he was an Englishman. He believed that the British Empire had been granted the nineteenth century as a stage upon which to act out its progressive destiny. The great inventions came from British imagination, including, for example, the steam engine and Hong Kong. The British were especially proud of their enlightened system of government, and saw their industrial and imperial successes as consequences of it. Thus the benign Lord Durham felt a moral compulsion to rescue the nostalgic French-Canadian community from its unproductive seigneurial torpor. The union of the Canadas would bring British progressiveness along with a new British majority population, and put an end to costly strife between the two peoples.

Radical Jack Durham *was* progressive. He suggested that the Canadas be united and granted responsible government on the British model, with a fully elected assembly rather than colonial power groups shaping law and commerce. Almost all his views were opposed by the fat cats, of course, and the fat cats had their own ideas about the French problem. Because of them a fateful compromise was reached in the British Parliament.

Durham wanted to see one homogeneous province. The fat cats, as fat cats will always do, were looking for short-term gains, and showing more interest in their investments than in the future of their country. When the Act of Union was proclaimed, a compromise was put into effect. The "united" province was made up of two parts, a confederation in effect. Lord Durham dropped dead. Lord Sydenham fell off his horse and perished. The Canadian pattern was established. Apparent equality would be bound up with resentment on the part of a people that came to know itself a minority, one that could survive only by insisting on its difference and parity.

In February of 1841 British troops spent the short daylight hours nailing the proclamation of Unity to posts and walls in Montreal, and every morning the posts and walls would be bare. When Lord Sydenham threw a big party to celebrate the Union, the only French-Canadians who came were government types and some priests.

But now the English-speaking Montreal businessmen and their newspaper the *Gazette* were looking forward to seeing the French Canadians outvoted on measures enacted to assist English business. They were encouraged by the gerrymandering that was being done to make sure that there were safe English seats in Canada East. The French-language papers in Quebec had another view.

In the new eighty-four-seat Assembly the French language could be used in debate, but English would be the only official language, that is the language used in documents.

Responsible government, sort of

When Britain allowed this new form of representative government in the Province of Canada, her motives were not entirely altruistic. There was the question of outvoting the French Canadians. There was also the question of responding to the energy of the self-congratulatory United States, from which raiders and traders were always entering Upper Canada. If history seemed to be indicating a relentless growth of freedom, perhaps a way to forfend revolutions in the countries marked in red all around the globe would be to set up an alternative in Britain's remaining North American colonies. Another threat to be considered was the pressure in England to repeal the Corn Laws that protected the well-off growers in the colonies.

Lord Sydenham, even while hosting the big party at his house that snowy night in February 1841, was not a man to be carried away by radical democratic reform. He tended to think of the coming elections as exercises, as rehearsals, perhaps, as opportunities for the locals to imitate the parliamentary procedure in London, the seat of progress and enlightenment. He looked upon the legislative assembly and all its speechifying and voting as a source of advice, a way to keep track of what the people were thinking and what counsel they had for the governor general. So did his successor, Sir Charles Bagot. So did *his* successor, Sir Charles Metcalfe.

They kept reporting to the Colonial Office back home that the people of Canada were devoted to British institutions.

Sydenham did make a mistake or two. He appointed Robert Baldwin, the prominent Reformer, to his ministry, and Baldwin promptly announced that he did not trust the system. He thought that a political party should win an election and construct a cabinet out of its own members. In his letters the governor general said that Baldwin was an ass.

That first election in spring of 1841 did not pit Reformers against Tories so much as Sydenham men against anti-Sydenham men. Sydenham was not the idealist that Lord Durham had been, but he was very adept at winning an election. Somehow the French-Canadian moderate Reform leader Louis-Hippolyte LaFontaine knew that he did not have a chance against an English candidate in a riding that was 85-per-cent French-speaking.

People who are used to clear constitutional systems of government, especially in a democracy that entails a party system and not too many parties, will find it very hard to understand how the first sessions of the united Canadian House in Kingston worked. Sydenham hand-picked his ministry. The assembly itself was made up of lots of sectarian rumps attached to the bodies of the Reform party or the Tories or the other conservatives. Most questions were entered by one or more of the governor's ministers. One would like to point at one of the assembly leaders and call him the first prime minister of Canada, but the 1841 session was handled by Lord Sydenham, who had set up in a nice house in Kingston, while complaining that the colonials were being spoiled by their fancy furniture.

Sydenham's successor, Bagot, was sent out by the Tories, who had reacquired power in Westminster, and he set about following Sydenham's policy of acting as his own prime minister, while learning how difficult it was to live with men like Baldwin and LaFontaine. He did not last long. Like Sydenham, he perished in Kingston not long after taking over. He was followed by Metcalfe, who had been working in the tropics, and who arrived in Kingston on a sleigh over the deep snow at the end of March in 1843.

Metcalfe thought of himself as the government, but he had some opposition. It was made up of the sixty members of the various factions of the Reform party. In a legislature made up of eighty-four members, that sounds like a majority. Obviously, in 1843 Canada there was a limit to the meaning of responsible government. Metcalfe had a hard time of it, and would feel the curse of the Canadian governor general, as his health and eyesight deteriorated up here in the north.

Metcalfe won the riotous election of 1844 by a slim majority, but now he was going blind as cancer found its way into his eyes. He was retired by the grateful British Tories, and replaced by Lord Cathcart, commander of the military forces. Cathcart's attention was taken by defence, especially out west, where the USAmericans were threatening to take the Oregon country and all its furs and forts. He did not have much time for internal politics, and during his fourteen months in office, he let the Canadian politicians fight things out among themselves. True responsible government was sliding, if not under the door, at least toward it.

Knock knock

Who would expect the son of Europe's greatest thief to be the man who opened that door? Thomas Bruce, the 7th Earl of Elgin, had been in the diplomatic service at Constantinople. As the Turks were holding Athens at the end of the eighteenth century, Elgin was able to make a deal with them, stripping ancient sculptures from the Parthenon and sending them to England. The first shipment found its way to the bottom of the ocean. Ah well. The rest of them made it safely to Blighty. The English poet Lord Byron wrote disapprovingly of Elgin's deal. Elgin said that he had acted benevolently, rescuing the marbles from the possible ravages of war. Nevertheless, the English government was allowed to purchase them in 1816. The only good thing about that deal was that Elgin was said to have spent more for them than he was to recover.

So James Bruce, the 8th Earl of Elgin, had a thief for a father. But he had Lord Durham for a father-in-law. In Canada he could atone for his father's arrogant ways, and try to put his wife's father's policies into effect.

He arrived at a trying time for the Province of Canada. There were stacks of timber on the Quebec docks. The forests of the province were levelled but the market was dead. While logs were not departing down the St Lawrence, the Irish were arriving in ship after ship. The ships were called floating coffins, because the Irish, half-starved by the potato famine, and sent across the ocean by the English, were dying from cholera and typhus. These diseases and others immigrated as well, and soon the doctors and nuns at the overtaxed Canadian hospitals were also dying. If Canada was going to take a long stride toward independence, it would have to step between the unemployed and the diseased.

In late 1846 the sewing machine was invented, and Great Britain decided to cut a few threads. When Elgin arrived in Montreal in January of 1847 he was carrying a letter, a copy of which had been sent to Nova Scotia two months earlier. The letter from Lord Grey at the Colonial Office stated that from now on the governor general would hearken to the decisions of the local legislature, that no longer would the governor general act as his own prime minister: "it is neither possible or desirable to carry on the government of any of the British provinces in North America in opposition to the opinion of the inhabitants."

That meant that in the next election the making of a cabinet and policy would be done by the party that won a majority in the lower house, and the leader of that party would be the prime minister of Canada.

Really, the first prime minister of Canada.

Officially he was called Attorney-General East.

But really, he was the first prime minister of Canada.

In the election the next winter, the British governor for the first time kept his hands off. The various conservative factions, including the English racists in Canada East, could never get their act together. If the English Colonial Office said that the next legislative assembly was going to tell the governor what was what, who was going to stop the reform liberals from becoming that government?

In Canada East Louis-Hippolyte LaFontaine's group took thirty-three seats, including English-speaking ones in Montreal and the Eastern Townships. In Canada West his partner Robert Baldwin upset the entrenched Tories and returned twenty-four members. The Reformers had a dandy majority, and Elgin called on them to form the province's first party cabinet. The first real prime minister of Canada was a francophone born near the St Lawrence River. A pattern was being set in early 1848.

One of the first measures put through by the LaFontaine government was an amnesty for all the rebels of 1837-38. Responsible Canada's earliest action was an act of peace. LaFontaine also made French an official language. Lord Elgin read the speech from the throne in both languages. Canadian progressive smugness began to set in.

But LaFontaine and Elgin would soon face two interesting crises. First was the Rebellion Losses Bill. In 1845 the Upper Canadians whose property had been destroyed in the rebellion there had been financially compensated, but so far the Lower Canadians had not seen a penny. The right-wing Tories, led by Allan Napier MacNab of Hamilton, shouted and fumed and protested that any monies paid to Lower Canadians would be recompense for "treason." He tried to get the governor to act the way earlier governors did—to listen to his Tory advisers and act in the interests of the proper Brit colonials. But Elgin was a new kind of governor, and the bill was passed. There were riots in Montreal. Elgin was hit in the face by a flying egg. The parliament building was burned down. The prime minister's house was burned down. US visitors wondered why people were not being shot.

The other crisis was provoked by a bunch of businessmen and malcontents who wanted to be annexed by the US. An outfit called the British American League held a big conference in Kingston in July 1849 to argue about the problems facing the troubled and "abandoned" province. It attracted conservatives from every party, but mainly Brit Tories. The annexationists, expecting a declaration of pro-US sentiment, were disappointed. Instead, there was a resolution to seek ways to federalize the British North American provinces. Then in October, the Annexationist Association uttered a manifesto in Montreal, calling for a peaceful union with the US. It was signed by 325 businessmen, including a future Canadian prime minister, John Abbott, and a future Father of Confederation, Alexander Galt.

But this manifesto was met by lots and lots of anti-annexation meetings. The English Crown advised that it was not interested in handing the province over to a slave-holding jingoistic republic, and the non-business population of Canada showed no eagerness to give up responsible government to assimilation.

Elgin and LaFontaine got past the crises. Eventually reciprocity happened for a dozen years. Railroads improved trade between the provinces and with the US. Times got slowly better.

The St Lawrence canals were opened. A fish war with the US was averted. Decimal currency was introduced, and Canadian coins rang on counters in Montreal and Kingston. Unions organized, especially in the printing trade. There were still huge forests in the north, and in the southwest someone found petroleum. It would probably be useful for something.

Charles Sangster, the first famous Canadian poet, was pretty satisfied. Here is a stanza from his long *The St Lawrence and the Saguenay:*

And bathe the vessel's brow. Isle after Isle
Is passed, as we glide tortuously through
The opening vistas, that uprise and smile
Upon us from the ever-changing view.
Here nature, lavish of her wealth, did strew
Her flocks of panting islets on the breast
Of the admiring River, where they grew,
Like shapes of Beauty, formed to give a zest
   To the charmed mind, like waking Visions of the Blest.

Allan Napier Walrus

In 1966 and 1967 the regions and towns and high schools and whist clubs of Canada were encouraged to take up "Centennial projects," and so the Love Generation in Canada featured a patriotic cast to their "Summer of Love." In Manitoba one town got sewerage and celebrated by making a big bonfire of outdoor crappers. In Hamilton, Ontario, they restored Dundurn Castle to its 1855 condition.

Dundurn Castle, surrounded by a lovely landscape of green fields, little trees and hedges, was the seventy-two-room manor of Allan Napier MacNab, who is regarded in and around Hamilton as the first prime minister of Canada.

MacNab was sent to school up the road in York at age seven. But when the usAmericans decided that they wanted to fight some more, the lad's schooling came to an end. He was fifteen when on April 26, 1813 a us fleet appeared off Scarborough Bluffs. His fifty-five-year-old father, survivor of thirteen wounds in the earlier war, and fifteen-year-old Allan went down to the lake to defend Canada.

After all the explosions along the waterfront, the MacNabs joined the long retreat, walking the 160 English miles to Kingston. There the lad became a midshipman on the *Wolfe*, commanded by Sir James Yea, who enjoyed watching the cat-'o-nine-tails do its job of whipping the crew into shape. After lots of spit and polish and two naval engagements with the usAmericans, young MacNab decided that he was a landlubber and resigned.

He went to the Niagara Peninsula and joined a group called "The Forlorn Hope," ferocious unforgiving night commandos. The boy got his first blood on December 19, 1813. He and his companions took Fort Niagara in fifteen minutes, scaling the walls, forcing open the gates, shooting their way to the roof, and yanking down the Stars and Stripes. The teenaged commando was learning to be a Conservative-Tory member of the legislature.

But there were other wars to be fought. The MacNabs were loyalists and royalists. This one was a fierce opponent of William Lyon Mackenzie in the 1837 rebellion. In one interesting action, Mackenzie recruited usAmericans, and grabbed Navy Island, about three miles above Niagara Falls, and set up the provisional government of a liberated colony. MacNab's forces included Indians and Blacks and volunteers. He used his commando experience to pull off a daring night-time burning of the steamship *Caroline*, which was being used to bring supplies from the US to Navy Island.

He was making his name. By the time that the rebellion was over and the colony still safely under the British flag, MacNab was a name to remember when it came time to fight political battles against liberals and republicans. Queen Victoria knighted him. He was given honours in the legislatures of Upper Canada, Nova Scotia and New Brunswick. Patriotic and political groups feted him, and he came to enjoy dressing up in his uniform and accepting awards. But he was going to learn that victories are punctuated with defeats. Years after his death someone would catalogue his effects and find that on his citation from the Upper Canada assembly he would write "Not worth a fart," and sign his initials. Nevertheless, he enjoyed hobnobbing with military officers and Indian chiefs at his castle.

Despite his leaving school before he had to shave, MacNab became a great Canadian success as a lawyer and businessman and politician. He cleaned up on real estate, and learned the wisdom of owning land where the government and private companies were interested in laying track or digging canals.

His lifelong enemy Mackenzie actually gave MacNab the start he needed for a political career that would take him to the top. Eight years before the rebellion MacNab got involved in a series of court cases that enacted the hatreds with which Tories and Reformers regarded each other. One of them developed out of an incident in which MacNab and his fellows, masked and trying to disguise their voices, tarred and feathered a Reformer named Rolph, whom they accused of sleeping with his housekeeper. In another case involving a burnt effigy of the lieutenant-governor, MacNab and Rolph clashed again. Things got more complicated and sillier, and eventually MacNab, who was in trouble for refusing to testify, mouthed off in front of a committee from the Assembly. Mackenzie introduced a motion to send MacNab to the clink, and it passed.

From February 16 to March 3, 1829 Allan MacNab sat inside the York Gaol, a stinking putrid place made noisy by the screams of lunatics. MacNab must have noticed how much it resembled Upper Canada politics. A year later he roused the Tories in Hamilton-Wentworth to send him to the Assembly. He spent the first part of his political career consolidating alliances, and trying to get the rightist factions together. In the middle years he grew more and more into the type of the hidebound Victorian Tory. In his last years, limping with gout and short of breath, he made his famous declaration that all his politics were railroad. His associate, John A. Macdonald, smiled.

Speaking of railroads, MacNab's main interest (political and financial) was in the Great Western, which would run through his town. It was during his gouty, railroading days that MacNab became prime minister. In the years between 1849 and 1867 there were a lot of governments in the Province of Canada. Men were running up and down the assembly halls, trying to make alliances. Finally, Lord Elgin tapped old MacNab, leader of the opposition, and asked him to give it a try. Augustin-Norbert Morin commanded more seats than anyone else in Canada East, but he was a liberal. MacNab could keep the Conservatives and Tories together in the west, so with the purring, gentle-handed encouragement of Elgin, MacNab and Morin created a big coalition.

MacNab would lead this coalition in the assembly. MacNab could out-vote Morin. His official title was President of the Council and Minister of Agriculture. For this reason, some people, especially those around Hamilton, Ontario, like to promote Allan Napier MacNab as the first prime minister of Canada.

Two years later he was out of there.

Run-up to Confederation

Even reading about the political scene in Canada from 1856 to 1866 is frustrating. It can give you a headache, such as the one I am experiencing now as I write. In those ten years governments were basted together only to come apart at the stitching. God seemed to have forgotten his British American citizens, and human designs were proving incapable of handling the perils of living in such a rugged part of the world. In 1857 a Great Western Railroad train crashed through the big bridge on the edge of Hamilton, and seventy passengers were killed; a steamer crammed with Norwegian and Scottish immigrants caught fire in the St Lawrence, and 250 more people were killed.

Then Canadian crops failed, markets fell like locomotives through bad trestles, farmers and stores and governments went into calamitous debt. The boom of the Crimean War era was over, and the USAmericans were having their own problems, so reciprocity, finally accepted by the USAmericans in 1854, would also apply to depression. No one would choose to govern during bad times, but politicians are always looking forward to good times. So in Canada East and Canada West there were governments. John A. Macdonald and George Brown were in them.

There was a united province called Canada, but there were still antagonisms between the two halves, and one does have to admire the ability of public men to keep the province together and keep the process of responsible government operating. Things were not so harmonious on the other side of the border, where the USAmericans were going through their run-up to the Civil War. That run-up and that war would have a signal effect on politics in the provinces of British America. It had been only a half-century since the last USAmerican invasion northward, and thirty years since the Yankee-supported rebellion in Upper Canada. People in New Brunswick and Canada felt pretty sure that the big military-industrial complex in the northern part of the US would turn its attention northward after they had handled their problems in the South. Certainly, Britain was seen by the US Union government as an ally of the Confederates.

Thomas Jefferson, the great democrat, and Walt Whitman, the great poet, had both said that it was in the natural order of things that Cuba and Canada would one day be part of the United States.

If your provinces north of the expanding republic are to be threatened, maybe it would be a good idea to see a federation of those provinces, and set about building railroads between them. Now the USAmericans were beginning to play the role that the French Canadians had played earlier—a perceived threat that could be staved off by joining the colonies into something larger and more autonomous.

Besides which, English-speaking citizens would form an even more stable majority. John A. Macdonald was in favour of stability.

CHAPTER 3

JOHN A. FANCYPANTS

John A. Macdonald 1867–73

JOHN A. MACDONALD WAS not in favour of confederation. He was a Scot. He was a Brit. He was definitely not a USAmerican. He detested the structure of the republic that was grabbing up all the good earth to the south and west. He saw states' rights as a feature of ragtag democracy, of anarchism. He often announced his ill feeling toward all the recent "isms." He liked the British model, in which the counties offered no threat to the power of the national parliament. If there was going to be a joining of the BNA colonies, Macdonald was going to push for the British model.

Still, he was a prominent speaker at the booze sessions in Charlottetown and Quebec and London that led to the union of 1867. In the famous painting of the dads in front of those improbable windows in Charlottetown, one might look around and find Charles Tupper and Thomas D'Arcy McGee, but one does not have to look for John A. Macdonald. He is in about the position occupied by Jesus Christ in da Vinci's *Last Supper.*

There he stands, a sheet of symbolic paper in his hand, our father among fathers.

The fathers are sitting or standing still, as if for a group portrait, as if there were a painter where you are. That was very unlikely, given the amount of liquor these men were putting away. In that way, too, Macdonald was the father of fathers.

If it was a wonder that this gathering of tipplers could get anything like nation-building done, it is at least doubly amazing, given the material they had to work with—a daunting spread of wild frontier with bad weather, a few muddy towns, French-speakers who feared English domination, Protestants who hated popery, businessmen who liked the look of the usAmerican dollar, farmers who desperately needed protection against imported produce, a huge federal government to the south that would finish its Civil War and find a large mechanized army at its fingertips, and a mother country that could not be trusted not to sell out its most northerly child in its effort to make peace with Washington.

John A. Macdonald is famous for his drinking and his scandals, but British North America was lucky to have him around. A lot of people consider him to be Canada's first real prime minister. As a matter of fact, we seem to be more sure about that than we are about the country itself. Most of us have grown up with confusion about Canada's independence. Did it start with the granting of responsible government in a united Canada in 1841? Did it really happen in 1847, when the governor general became head of state rather than head of government? Did the bna Act of 1867 do it, and if it did, why was that act's name changed to the Constitution Act in 1981? When I was in school I was taught that the Statute of Westminster, in late 1931, gave Canada true independence. Then why are we still spending money with British monarchs' faces on it? Why are we singing "God Save the Queen" when the movie is over, I asked. Why does *New Liberty* magazine always have the princesses on the cover? All right, Canada got a real flag in 1965, and in 1982 we got to keep our own constitution in our own country. Still, we have nagging feelings. Are we all the way there yet?

Of course there are those, I among them, who like this historical uncertainty. It makes a nice informative contrast to the abrupt USAmerican revolution. Those people cover everything with star-spangled banners, and get their bombs bursting in air on July 4. We Canadians quietly celebrate the twenty-fourth of May and the first of July. Just in case.

That's why I say that Sir John A. Macdonald is our first prime minister—in a manner of speaking. In any case, MacNab would have looked funny standing in the middle of that painting.

Young Macdonald Was Never Near a Farm

"A British subject I was born; a British subject I will die," said John A., shortly before he did the latter. He was also born a city boy, and as a man who was so prominent in a decidedly countrified nation for half a century, he knew very little about people in the boonies. Farm louts were people to buy votes from. Louis Riel was some loony who stood in the way of a nation that would stretch from sea to whining sea.

He was born in Glasgow on January 11, 1815. Napoleon was riding a white charger on the island of Elba. Lord Byron was putting the polishing touches to "She Walks in Beauty." The last official war between the US and Britain had been over for eighteen days.

His father, Hugh, was a cotton broker who just never had any luck. Five years after John's birth he moved with his wife and four children to Kingston, Ontario, determined to try his business skills in the promising colonial town named after the unlucky George III. But fortune in the New World was just as elusive. Hugh Macdonald opened a store, then tried to run a mill, then opened another store. He lost his shirt. Finally he went to work as a clerk in a bank. His son John took on somewhat larger challenges, but he was just as unlucky with money.

Kingston had a population of only 2,500 souls, many of them Scottish, but it was situated where Fort Frontenac once was, at the end of the big lake and the head of the big river, across this water from New York state. It was even the capital of Upper Canada for a while. It was a good place to be a lawyer with an eye to politics.

Some people like to draw comparisons between Macdonald and Abraham Lincoln. Lincoln was born six years before Macdonald was. As boys, they both liked to sit under a tree and read a book. They both started the lawyering trade as teenagers, and they both made much of being guileless lawyers from small towns. Lincoln became president of the US at the age of fifty-two. Macdonald was fifty-two when he more or less became the first prime minister of Canada. They never met. Macdonald was not much interested in talking with USAmericans. He met President Grant once while at a meeting in Washington. They said hello and that was that. Macdonald liked to go to Britain and talk with Disraeli. He looked a lot like Disraeli. A British subject he would die, not an assassinated Republican.

Young John went to school for five years, read every book he could lay his hands on, and at age fifteen went to work as a clerk in a law office. He didn't make much money, but somehow he managed to develop a taste for spiffy clothes. He was tall and gangly, and had a long knobby nose and wild frizzy hair. He thought that he could best set off those arresting features with loud checked trousers. There would be no prime minister that would come close to him as a sartorial adventurer until the arrival of Pierre Trudeau with his capes and March Hare hats of the 1960s.

He also liked to have fun. He had a droll wit and was not averse to yukking it up in the pub. There is a persistent rumour that when he was a student he went with a friend to small towns in upstate New York, Macdonald in checked pants, squeezing a concertina, his pal in a bear outfit, dancing Celtic steps, gathering loud comments and Yankee coins from the rubes. This was Canada's answer, perhaps, to the Fenian raids. It was also the last time Macdonald would do a monkey act for the USAmericans.

At the age of twenty-one he went up to Toronto and took what passed for law examinations in those days, becoming a barrister and a young Tory. While Benjamin Disraeli visited the Inns of Court, young Macdonald spent a lot of time in the inns of Kingston. He was popular with the locals, flippant and bibulous, good at telling dirty jokes, making sure that he knew everyone's name. They should have known that he was learning how to be a successful politician.

A year later he took another step that would not hurt a political career when he joined up in the battle against the 1837 Rebellion. Unlike Allan MacNab, he never got into any valiant armed combat, and unlike MacNab, he was never to get rich. But he showed an imagination his predecessor could not rise to. There was an exciting Polish adventurer named Nils Szoltevcky Von Schoultz, ex-French Foreign Legion, ex-music teacher in Italy, who had thrown in his lot with one of those USAmerican forces that once in a while crossed over into Canada to free the locals from the weight of the British throne. This "general" had been captured along with his men at Windmill Point, and marched through the streets of Kingston in ragged clothes, his hand, like those of his subordinates, tied to a rope. He would be court-martialled, charged with breaking a law forbidding pirates from committing mayhem on Canadian soil.

Somebody knocked at Macdonald's door and got him out of bed. While he fought the knife of his hangover, he was asked whether he would defend the "general," and Macdonald said that he guessed so. Why did he do this? Some will say that he acted out of principle—the people of Kingston hated this double foreigner because some of their men had been killed at Windmill Point, and one of them had been mutilated with a Bowie knife. Some will say that it never hurts to get your name in the papers. In all likelihood they were all right. The pattern was being set for Macdonald's entire political life.

Von Schoultz was hopelessly romantic, a noble heart betrayed by the warty dorks around him. He took all responsibility on his shoulders and pleaded guilty and was condemned to hang. Macdonald spent many hours with him at the lock-up, hearing all about his family's destruction by the invading Russians, and about his wanderings through a Europe seething with revolutionary fervour. The young lawyer drew up the hero's will, and refused to be named in it. Later he attended the execution, perhaps the only troubled soul there.

He had defined his brand of conservatism. He would not be a doctrinaire walrus Tory, but a British subject open to liberal ideas, a progressive conservative. He was not a reformer, and he hated the idea of republicanism. He was a Liberal Conservative, a man who, for instance, shared the usual prejudices about French Canadians, but advised that they be treated with respect. He was no friend of the Family Compact, although he knew how to make deals with rich and powerful Tories.

As a young man he worked behind the scenes, organizing meetings, carrying messages, suggesting alliances, getting himself known to all the Conservative politicos and businessmen along the lake. When in 1843, an Assembly candidature became available, twenty-eight-year-old Macdonald's name was entered almost before anyone noticed. He won, and began his career as a hard-working backbencher with sharp eyes and friendly demeanour. He was making himself indispensable. He was learning compromise and moderation. He was becoming the perfect Canadian politician. In the Assembly crowded with lots and lots of factions from both Canadas and both religions, he began surrounding himself with liberal conservatives. He made an alliance with the anglophile George-Étienne Cartier, leader of the Conservatives in French Canada.

But he was everybody's friend, or so it seemed. You could always expect a wink and a slap on the back from the casual-talking, merrily quipping young man with the long nose and the checked trousers. He might have read every book in print, but he was no snob. He did not go home early from the pub.

He was the opposite of that Irish immigrant poet Standish O'Grady, who had recently died in Canada East, leaving a long poem called "The Emigrant," with this kind of sentiment about the people he had to live among:

> The lank Canadian eager trims his fire,
> And all around their simpering stoves retire;
> With fur clad friends their progenies abound,
> And thus regale their buffaloes around;
> Unlettered race, how few the number tells,
> Their only pride a *cariole and bells!*
> To mirth or mourning, thus by folly led,
> To mix in pleasure or to chaunt the dead!
> To seek the chapel prostrate to adore,
> Or leave their fathers' coffins at the door!
> Perchance they revel; still around they creep,
> And talk, and smoke, and spit, and drink, and sleep!

Irish Protestant O'Grady died in 1841, the year of union. He looked forward to a possible transformation of the colony he hated spending his life in, but like many of those who surrounded Macdonald, he believed that certain things must be left behind. He ends his poem:

> With sanguine sash and eke with Indian's mogs,
> Let Frenchmen feed on fricassees and frogs;
> . . . .
> Still leave their *lower province* to themselves.
> Let patriots flourish, other deeds displace,
> Let adverse men new politics embrace;
> Yet come it will when wisdom may control,
> And one sound policy conduct the whole.

Macdonald would have heard many such sentiments while the new province was taking shape, though perhaps not in such drab verse. Yet he continued to gather his coalition, staying in the middle of the lakeside road, learning the politics of the possible.

Family man

Macdonald liked to hang around in the inn, making jokes and slinging gab, being a hearty man's man, but we don't hear about any excessive chasing after long Victorian skirts. He did his chasing after votes. He learned the relationship between money and elections, and the Conservatives found him to be a productive backroom lad. His rewards would not be monetary, but political. Step by step he rose in the hierarchy, and bit by bit his hard work and administrative skills attracted associates who wanted to be on the winning side.

He did not chase skirts, but he spotted one during a trip to Scotland, and fell into a sad and romantic love with his cousin

Isabella Clark. He brought her back to Kingston in 1843, the year he entered the Assembly, and began family life with a woman who would almost immediately become an invalid. There has been a lot of speculation about Isabella's condition. It has been called psychosomatic, the vapours, consumption and most recently chronic fatigue syndrome. In any case, she was a sickly wife, though she had at first been gay and playful. John A. was consumed by her condition. He overcame his repugnance for the US and took her south, hoping to cure her condition in a warmer climate.

During her first pregnancy he took her across the line, planning to go to Georgia, but fetching up in New York City when she became incapable of more travel. There in August of 1847 their first son, John A., was born. He lived just over a year, and it looked as if there would be no more Macdonalds, but miraculously Isabella gave birth to a second son, named Hugh after his grandfather. He grew up and became a successful politician, premier of Manitoba and inside man in Ottawa. He was the last of the parliamentary Macdonalds.

John the A-type Macdonald was used to working harder than any six men, but now he kept telling himself that he should quit politics. He sat at his wife's bedside in USAmerican spas or in the drab house they stayed in while the Assembly was in session in Toronto. But there was a political party forming around him, the Liberal-Conservatives. They should have been called the Macdonalds. When the British North America Act was passed in London, Queen Victoria pronounced Macdonald the first prime minister of the new entity, but what choice did she have? The moderate centre would define the Canadian state. Macdonald epitomized the moderate centre. At Charlottetown and London he had even used his amazing *bonhomie* to bring his great enemies, George Brown and Nova Scotia, to the bar. Actually, Brown was for Confederation before Macdonald was, but once

Confederation looked like the best bet, Macdonald turned on the energy. No Queen of England was going to make a fiery Liberal newspaperman such as George Brown the head of government in her new Dominion.

As soon as the act was promulgated, Brown took a few steps away from his fellow midwife and began the serious business of loyal opposition. He had the *Globe*, and Macdonald didn't have a newspaper. Brown would bring the old compromiser down.

Hugh Macdonald did not live with his parents much. His father was working and drinking twenty hours a day, and his mother was an invalid. He grew up with other relatives. His mother faded and faded, finally giving up the *geist* in 1857. Macdonald *père* had ten years to devote his attention to the birth of a nation. But in 1856 he had seen a good-looking woman at a hotel dining room, and asked the simple question, "Who might that be?" In 1860 he finally met her. She was Susan Agnes Bernard, daughter of a colonialist who had left Jamaica after the slaves were freed.

They were married in grand fashion in February 1867, during the last stages of the Confederation conference, feted by British and BNA politicians. Macdonald quipped that as an honest minister he was applying the principle of union to his own life. Susan vowed to abstain from alcohol, hoping to set a good example. She also took great interest in the process of nation-making, and in the years to come could be spotted in the parliamentary gallery, stamping her foot or scowling at George Brown or smiling at her husband's wit.

But they too were unlucky in child-rearing. Their daughter, Mary, had an overlarge head, never learned to walk or talk clearly, and though she lived till 1933, remained Macdonald's little child. As he had formerly sat by Isabella's bed, now he sat by his daughter's, an aging man reading children's stories to an unaging girl. Nation-building, for the prime minister, was always seen in perspective.

What'll it be, gents?

In 1856, Macdonald wrote these typical words in a letter to his mother:

> I am carrying on a war against that scoundrel George Brown and I will teach him a lesson that he never learnt before. I shall prove him a most dishonest, dishonorable fellow & in doing so I will only pay him a debt I owe him for abusing me for months together in his newspaper.

That abuse included cartoons showing Macdonald in his checked trousers, with a bottle in the pocket of his stylish jacket. Brown was born in Edinburgh, Macdonald in Glasgow. Brown's father had gone to the United States before coming to Ontario. Brown was the gathering point for the True Grits, for the supporters of rep-by-pop. He wanted Canada West to become huge and mainly Protestant. He accused John A. Macdonald of being the front man for the banks and businesses, for the old Family Compact. Macdonald accused Brown of being the heir of William Lyon Mackenzie.

In truth they were both supporters of business and the British Empire. They were both good compromisers when there was a target in sight. They even took cabs together in London in 1867.

Macdonald would have more dangerous enemies than George Brown. After the first election, when Macdonald breezed in, Brown decided to be a newspaperman instead of a prime minister. He still ran his cartoons, but in an age when just about all politicians were hitting the bottle, the voting public did not seem to mind when they heard of John A. barfing in the House, and they did not always know it when he disappeared for a while.

As Macdonald saw it, his main job was to establish the power of the Dominion government over that of the provinces. To him that meant the ascendancy of the British connection over the bad example of the United States down south. It also meant scooping up all the western and northern territory that had once been the purview of the fur companies. Macdonald did not know a lot about the prairies, and he did not care much, either. He was a city boy, and he knew how to get from hotel to hotel in London, England. But he did not want anyone else gathering up land that Canada could claim. He had been watching what the USAmericans were doing in Spanish North America and Russian North America.

Louis Riel

In his personal letters, Macdonald revealed a common Upper Canada combination of disdain and judiciousness regarding "the French." Just as politicians and landowners in the far west were to assume in their Huxleyan way that the North American Indians were going to disappear in the natural course of things, so, many Anglos judged that the outnumbered French-speaking Canadians would eventually cease to be a problem.

Macdonald made a lot of mistakes about money, North American Indians and "the French."

In October of 1844, while the future prime minister was taking his seat for the first time as a backbencher in a Conservative government, Louis David Riel was born in the Red River Settlement out there in the unimaginable west. He was a Métis, created by the two peoples that Ontario Anglos considered extraneous to the future. Two decades later, while the Fathers of Confederation were putting down whiskies and clauses, Riel was in Montreal, being schooled for the priesthood and studying law. By 1868, after his first short residency in the USA, he was back in St Boniface, preparing to create a country.

Rupert's Land and the North-western Territory were ill-defined, and crying out for lines on the map. The Hudson's Bay Company had been running things for two centuries. Then in 1811 the Earl of Selkirk had got permission to establish the Red River Colony, which he called Assiniboia, around the confluence of the Red and Assiniboine rivers. Scottish people were supposed to arrive and develop the farmland. But the locusts and floods made life hard. Eventually the Selkirk family handed the colony over to the HBC to manage. In fact a lot of the population was made of Scots and French who had worked for the Company, the Scots and French and their Native wives, and the Métis descendants of the Scots and French who had married Native women generations before. By the 1860s there was a multiracial community in the Red River Colony that had got used to thinking of their land and people as a nation, loyal to the Crown, different as hell from the domain of the Family Compact.

But the BNA Act provided that the vast ranges of land west of Canada West would be transferred to the new Confederation. The 300,000 square kilometres of Selkirk's colony were to be included. The French-speaking Catholic Métis people had worked hard through hard times to make a political entity of their own. They were way to hell and gone out there somewhere, but they knew what to expect from the Orangemen of Upper Canada. Someone may have mentioned these unsophisticated sentiments to Macdonald, but it was hard to get Macdonald's attention with rural matters, especially with rural matters expressed by nonentities.

No, Macdonald did not know what to expect from Louis David Riel, but the handsome, dagger-eyed Riel knew what to expect from Macdonald and the Liberal-Conservatives he would eventually annihilate.

Macdonald's government gave the HBC $1.5 million for the prairies, including the Red River basin. The 30,000 people there never heard anything about Canada's plan for the land they had become used to owning. But the Canadians had their own plans for it. Louis David Riel, a twenty-four-year-old orator in Victorian tailcoat and buckskin moccasins, pointed out that no Canadian official had yet stood in their country and declared ownership. Riel and his horsemen rode into Fort Garry, took down the HBC flag, and declared a provisional government, loyal to the Queen and representing the people of Assiniboia.

The news got back to Ontario by telegraph from North Dakota. John A. Macdonald could not believe his eyes. He had always, despite his personal feelings, insisted on cordial relations with the Catholic French-speakers in Lower Canada. In a now-famous letter written in 1856, he had said "If a Lower Canadian British desires to conquer he must 'stoop to conquer.' He must make friends with the French without sacrificing the status of his race and language, he must respect their nationality." But the upstarts along the Red River were not just "the French." They were French-speaking half-breeds. They were inconsiderable rebels against his dream of a nation stretching to the Pacific. He had shouldered a musket in 1837. Now he reached for "Wandering Willy."

This was William McDougall, who got his nickname because he had a habit of jumping from one political faction to another. Now he was a Liberal member of Macdonald's cabinet, and Macdonald decided to solve two of his problems with one brilliant stroke of the pen. He sent Wandering Willy out to be the lieutenant-governor of Rupert's Land. He would preside over the transfer of power and oversee a crew of surveyors.

People who have lived on their little farms for a few generations do not like to see surveyors from some distant land setting up their equipment. The Métis people did not in any way see the approaching McDougall as "their" lieutenant-governor. They were afraid that they were going to lose the farms and language and schools they had been used to. Their Red River country was not officially lost to the easterners until the easterners plunked themselves down and read some sort of proclamation. They decided to stop Wandering Willy from speechifying.

Here was another nifty irony for Macdonald's career. The original Selkirk grant included territory that had now been in the United States since 1818. The Métis people had ties that were older and stronger than any forty-ninth parallel. There were USAmerican spies all over the place, and Macdonald had a perfectly reasonable fear that the USAmericans might prove fond of acquisition. But he had heard the news of the Red River disturbance via US telegraph lines, and when he sent his man McDougall west he had to send him through the northern USA. Wandering Willy was in St Paul, Minnesota, and as soon as he had counted his sixty wagons of belongings, was off north to his new seigneury. It has been said that William McDougall was possessor of a stupidity that could not be made to falter by the most formidable light of reason. But how did he then rise to become a prominent Liberal, you might ask. Keep reading.

When he arrived with his cortège of wagons at the Canadian border, the irony continued as a group of silent Métis men sat their horses and blocked the road into Canada. Wandering Willy decided to stay over in Pembina, North Dakota, for the nonce. There he bided in a log cabin in the snow, and tried to think, meanwhile managing to provide comic relief to US reporters who sent eastward despatches that would eventually reach his prime minister. At last McDougall arrived at what appeared to him to be an idea.

One sub-freezing night he and a few of his men clambered aboard a wagon and rode through a hell-driven blizzard across the international boundary. There they got out and stood in the snow, one side of each man turning white in the drift, bottles of spirits their only comfort. One man was carrying a miniature Union Jack that was nearly torn from his mitten by the wind. McDougall had spent the afternoon writing a Royal Proclamation, and signing his sovereign's name to it. Now, his voice hard to identify in the howl of the storm, he read this proclamation that announced his presence as the legal governor of the Red River Settlement. Then he and his men rode back to Pembina, some of them wondering whether this madman would be the death of them.

The US reporters loved Wandering Willy. The Yankee papers were full of hilarity that week. John A. Macdonald had one hand over his eyes, the other around a glass of strong stuff.

What could the prime minister do? He had to fire McDougall, of course. And he had to put off the acquisition of Rupert's Land for a while. He could not send troops against the twenty-four-year old prophet and hero, because the road north of Lake Superior would be closed until summer, and the USAmericans were not likely to supply a route through their country. Macdonald had to swallow his nation-building pride, and listen to catcalls from the loyal opposition. He sent his old pal Donald Smith, the Scottish (of course) ex-HBC boss and future last spiker, out to the Red River to confront Riel. He was not really afraid of Riel and his half-breeds: he was afraid that the USAmericans, busy killing Sioux in the area, would find some excuse to march northward.

But in sending Smith to speechify and eventually negotiate, he was really recognizing, at least temporarily, an organization called the National Committee of Métis, Louis David Riel, secretary. The promises seemed pretty good: there would be an amnesty, and there would be recognition of property for the locals. There were also a few pecuniary considerations for Métis leaders who were interested in peace. Macdonald was still buying votes. It looked as if things would go peacefully if not completely satisfactorily for Ottawa's adventure in colonialism.

But then some drunken Protestant white guy from Ontario, an Orangeman named Tom Scott, focused the religious and racial tensions that had always been a political fact in the country. He was a surveyor. He saw himself as part of the future. He got into the HBC booze and went around cursing and threatening half-breeds and papists and French-speakers. He rounded up some equally unhappy pals and waved guns in the winter air. There were a lot of Tom Scotts in the country in 1869, just as there are now. But this one was finally arrested by some of the "inferior" people he hated so much. You can imagine the fury building on both sides. Then, according to the police report and later legend, Scott hurled himself at Riel's throat, with the intention of solving the Métis problem. It was not the first incident of racial-religious violence at Fort Garry, but it was tremendously symbolic. What could the people who portrayed themselves as a government do when someone tried to kill the most prominent man in the government?

Scott was court-martialled and shot by a firing squad. The story usually goes that the firing squad had liquor on their collective breath. So did Macdonald when he heard about this. Mr Middle-of-the-Road would not be able to quieten this one down, not with Liberal newspapers seizing what appeared to be an opportunity to throw alcohol on the fire, and Quebec threatening to make a saint of Riel. What could John A. Macdonald do? He disappeared for a while. No one could find him, not even his wife or the governor general. All they knew was that there would be gin in the vicinity.

But he reappeared, as he had always done, and now he resolved to order his first foreign military campaign. When the Canadian road allowed in the spring, he would send troops to conquer the Red River Valley. But this was Canada, not the USA. Before the troops (made up of Canadians and Brits) headed west, the Métis negotiators arrived in Ottawa, much to the fury of Ontario Orangemen and other racists. Ontario troops arrested the western enemies. The Dominion government ordered the release of the western delegates.

The result would be the Manitoba Act, which would go into effect in July 1870. The old Red River Colony would enter Canada as the Province of Manitoba, a word that means roughly God's Country. A little smaller in area than New Brunswick, the new province would be unlike *les autres*. The successor to Riel's administration would guarantee the rights of French schools and churches. Twelve of the twenty-four elected representatives in the provincial House would be French-speaking. Riel the lawyer and very young elder statesman prepared to become an important Manitoba politician.

But he did not believe in the peaceful intentions of the federal troops. When they appeared at Fort Garry, he went out the back way, and headed for his job as a school teacher in the USA. Macdonald's government offered him a thousand Canadian dollars to stay there. Riel said that he could not be bought by the Canadian government. The Hudson's Bay Company offered to throw in six hundred British pounds. Riel said that he would apply himself to his career as a teacher.

But Riel did not disappear. He visited Manitoba often, conferring with his political associates, checking on the delivery of language rights. Then he began his career as a federal politician.

His associates ran him successfully in a by-election and then in a regular election. Riel did not campaign much in the new province, but he did go to Ottawa. There, some Quebec and Manitoba members helped him sign the members' roll in the House of Commons. Macdonald never had to face him across the floor, and it is probably one of the saddest stories in Canadian history that he never sat down for a cup of tea with him. Macdonald might then have known him for a handsome, energetic politician with a gift for gab. It would have, perhaps, gone well as long as they spoke in English. Macdonald did not speak French.

But Macdonald always looked at the youngster as a half-breed who had shown him up in front of the whole country. And, of course, a foe of the prime minister could not be a friend of the nation! Macdonald should have pondered an event that soon transpired. When rumours of yet another USAmerican-based Fenian raid reached Riel's ears, he offered the Métis cavalry to the lieutenant-governor of the new province. Macdonald's simple formulas about his enemies were sometimes at odds with reality—if you can say that there was any such thing during the first five years of the new Confederation.

John A. Macdonald eventually felt that he had to kill Louis David Riel. His son, Hugh John Macdonald, succeeded his father's adversary, becoming the first Conservative premier of Manitoba in 1900. There were, though, two other Manitoba premiers that year.

Show me the money

All right, somehow Old Tomorrow's Canada was filling in the space between the St Lawrence and the Pacific. Little Manitoba was tucked in, but there was still a lot of space out there. Macdonald had hopes.

A key aspiration was the gathering in of British Columbia. The old Hudson's Bay Company preserve west of the Rockies had experienced a gold rush that brought lots of rowdies north, and the population of the place was alarmingly USAmerican. There were newspapermen out there, too, and they were Californians who campaigned for annexation of the colony. There were also disaffected folk who, like the majority of Nova Scotians, dreamed of going it alone.

Macdonald would one day be the Member of Parliament for Victoria, B.C. He thought he knew how to appease the west coasters. Whenever mid-nineteenth-century politicians wanted to gather votes, they would offer a railroad. It had worked for Allan MacNab. It had just barely worked in New Brunswick. Macdonald offered British Columbia a transcontinental railroad just like those threatening ones in the USA. British Columbians were amazed—they had been ready to settle for a dirt wagon road. In 1871 B.C. jumped into Confederation, and Macdonald and the Liberal-Conservatives had the Canada From Sea to Sea they had campaigned for.

But the railroad was too expensive. It was an insane idea. The new Dominion would, sensible people predicted, fall to smithereens if it tried to finance such a monstrosity. Some government people and supporters suggested that it could not be built without USAmerican money and experience. Macdonald was interested in a strong relationship between the Canadian government and Canadian business; he did not like anything about the United States except its climate. So his supporters had to hide the USAmerican money from him.

Louis David Riel, it turned out, had knocked him off his feet. Shortly after getting the Manitoba Act through, Macdonald fell on his face. Fortunately this did not happen in the House of Commons, where his political antagonists might have laughed at the middle-aged man whose body was filled with pain. The months of negotiations and liquor had done their evil work. The doctors diagnosed the great pain and convulsions as gallstone attacks, and alerted the populace to expect a dead prime minister. But this was a man of a hundred comebacks. He went to Prince Edward Island to take the sea air, and left George-Étienne Cartier to handle things for a while. When he got back, he was ready to build a railroad.

The railroad would nearly kill him, too.

It was 1872, and this father of a growing Confederation had to fight a second national election. He had a pretty good record to defend. He had brought in two more provinces, and it looked as if P.E.I. would be joining the family soon. He had staved off the secessionist threat in Nova Scotia. He had snaffled some British money to build railroads and canals. The USAmericans had not invaded.

But he had problems, too. It looked as if his anglophile friend Cartier was not going to live for another session, and Quebec might be hard to hold. The Protestants in Ontario complained against his deal with the murderous savages in Manitoba. The British had sold Canada's fisheries down the tubes in the war reparations meetings in Washington. The Conservative party, though a well-organized machine, was just about broke and a little rundown.

Macdonald tried all his familiar tricks, hinting free trade to the free traders, hinting protection to the protectionists. Noticing that his old nemesis George Brown was having labour problems at the *Globe*, he announced that he was interested in making unions legal. But the main issue of this election was going to be the Canadian Pacific Railway, the huge financial gamble for a continental Canada. The line was supposed to be started within two years of B.C.'s joining the team. There were already US tracks poking northward.

The problem was, of course, the fact that Canada was new and underpopulated, and therefore rather light of tax base. The adventure would not only be the biggest engineering event on the continent; it would also be the most expensive. Hugh Macdonald could not make a go of a store in Kingston. How would his son do with a railroad 4,000 miles long?

The obvious answer would be US money. But Macdonald did not like US money, as everyone knew. His Scottish friend Hugh Allan had made it big in shipping, and was now the head of the Montreal-based Canadian Pacific Railway Company, but there were a lot of Yankee dollars in that company. Macdonald reasoned that Yankee dollars would result in two unacceptable eventuations: Canadian economic and political policies would come under the threat of USAmerican control, and news of the business would result in a lost election of 1872. Get rid of those US backers, Macdonald told Allan, or we do not sign this contract.

All right, said Allan, the US partners are gone.

All right, we will sign pretty soon, said Macdonald.

But Hugh Allan had just shuffled some papers. The US partners were still there, just invisible. We do not know whether Macdonald was fooled or just pretended he was fooled.

There was an election campaign going on, and Macdonald could easily lose his own seat in Kingston, but he did not have time to mend local fences. Businessmen were complaining about the lack of reciprocity, farmers were demanding tariffs, fishermen were ready to shoot at US boats or Tory candidates, and there was a three-year-old hydrocephalic daughter waiting for his kind words. Now his other Scottish friend David Macpherson gave him yet another reason to open a bottle of port. Macpherson had organized a collection to pay off Macdonald's massive personal debts. What a good friend! But Macpherson was also the head of a big Toronto-based railway company. He felt he should have the huge contract that looked as if it were going to Hugh Allan. There were a lot of voters in Ontario, he might have suggested, and they might not take too kindly to the big contract going to Montreal. They had not forgotten the murder of Tom Scott, either.

What a surprise: Macdonald had to reconcile the venomously competitive demands of the two old Canadas! Day after day he used all his Liberal-Conservative wiles to try to bring the two companies together. Night after night he more successfully negotiated a quart or two of the old remedy. Allan said that his company would be prepared to let Macpherson come aboard. Macpherson said that he would not accept an inferior spot. Election day was coming. Macdonald was glassy-eyed. He staggered from meetings to hustings. He had a nip in the carriage.

It was really hard to maintain his famous affability and sly wit. He was really afraid that his career might be at an end. A climax of sorts occurred at a debate in his home riding. Something snapped in Old Tomorrow's brain, and the electors were treated to the spectacle of a fifty-seven-year old head of government lurching across the platform and trying to strangle his Liberal opponent. John A. Macdonald was no Tom Scott, though. He would live to fight another day.

What the electors did not know was that he and his running mates were being heavily financed by Hugh Allan, leading candidate for the big railroad contract. Allan had scads of money, and he put at least three hundred and fifty thousand 1872 dollars into the hands of the Conservatives for this election. As election day neared, the money became more and more necessary. Macdonald was tired and often under the influence; how was he supposed to keep track? He was used to buying votes. He was pretty sure he was not being bought. But a desperate contender can make mistakes. In the last days he sent a hastily scribbled telegram to Montreal. It comprised this famous message: "I must have another ten thousand. Will be the last time calling. Do not fail me. Answer today."

The money was promptly forthcoming. The telegram was locked away in a safe at the office of Allan's lawyer. The Conservatives just barely won the election. Cartier had been defeated in Montreal. The new voters in Manitoba and British Columbia gave the government an edge. John A. had a drink to celebrate.

Joseph Howe, the Nova Scotia independentist, had not been able to beat Macdonald. George Brown had tried and failed. Edward Blake, the Liberal voice, and his stalking horse, Sandy Mackenzie, had not quite pulled it off. Louis David Riel was somewhere on the USAmerican prairie. But Sir Hugh Allan, the shipping tycoon, would do the job.

Macdonald used his experience and his cronies to handle the first few punches. A USAmerican businessman with a Scottish name laid some documents in front of Macdonald, showing that there was a lot of Yankee money in the Allan deal, and a lot of Allan money in the Conservative campaign. He suggested that he would keep quiet if the government signed with Allan. Macdonald called on old Francis Hincks, the slickest politician in Canada, to make arrangements with Allan and the USAmericans. Hincks knew a lot of people from a lot of backgrounds. Pretty soon the USAmericans went home, and Allan was off to Britain, looking for replacement funds.

Macdonald was sobering up. But he was worried. He did not feel as if he were a crook, but he knew that there were certain things in the relationship with Allan that he would prefer remain only rumours. However, here he was with a new mandate, and lots of work to do. He faced the future, unaware that his fate would be decided by a kind of nineteenth-century Watergate. It would be called the Pacific Scandal.

That crazed telegram was still lying among other touchy files in the office safe of J.J.C. Abbott, the shipping tycoon's lawyer.

J.J.C. Abbott had a clerk named George Norris, and George Norris had a key to the safe. He usually worked long hours, but not usually after midnight. One late winter night he was working well after midnight, opening the safe and removing certain files. These eventually appeared on the political market for five thousand 1873 dollars. It turned out that the buyer was a Liberal. Fancy that!

The first session of Macdonald's new Parliament became a national theatre, offering high tragedy and grim comedy. The country's newspapers were shrill with headlines and cartoons. The opposition worked slowly, as if savouring their moment. Chubby Edward Blake sprawled in his chair and smirked across the floor at the prime minister, while a backbencher announced that Macdonald's railroad was a USAmerican organization and Allan had bought the Conservatives with Yankee money. The first problem had been taken care of. How serious was the second? What did those scoundrels know? The newspapers were looking for more.

The Liberals demanded an investigation by committee. Macdonald had the idea voted down. Then some advisers got his ear, and he allowed the investigation to proceed. The newspapers made bigger headlines. The word "Scandal" was used more and more often, and when the big money people in Britain read it, they told Allan to go home. Étienne Cartier, without a seat in Parliament, his secrets in the hands of burglars, escaped the commotion by dying of Bright's disease in the London he liked so much.

One way of looking at the opposition's work is to decide that the Liberals were performing a service, rooting out corruption, protecting democracy. Another would suggest self-interest, dirty politics, character assassination. Well, John A. Macdonald had never denied that he was a good opportunistic practical politician himself. If he were going to wrap himself in the flag, it would be a flag manufactured and supplied by a company that enjoyed Conservative patronage.

But now Macdonald was in his bed, sick and tiddly, crushed by circumstances and fearful of the future. He was thinking about resigning his ministry and retiring from politics. His backers and the governor general talked him out of it; they knew that no Conservative in the House was even the fourth- or fifth-best candidate to lead the new country. Macdonald saw Edward Blake's horrible smile in his dreams. He went to his summer place in Rivière-du-Loup, where he could be with his family, take pleasant walks and view the St Lawrence, and read the newspapers.

One day in July he read the Montreal *Herald*, a Grit newspaper as unfriendly as Brown's *Globe*. There he was quoted: "I must have another ten thousand," etc. etc. Macdonald disappeared again. His cabinet could not find him. Agnes could not find him. No one could find him, and again the newspapers were full of the rumours of his death. But he showed up in Ottawa when the House of Commons was ready to sit again, and he staggered to his office. It was to be the worst parliamentary session of his life. Through a haze of pain and alcohol he saw his allies drifting away from him, saving their own moral images and, in his view, dooming Confederation. Words never failed him but numbers did. At the end of 1873 his resignation was in the hands of Lord Dufferin. He would spend the winter alone, emptying bottles of port and reading French novels in translation. All his work to build a nation from Atlantic to Pacific looked as if it could come down like MacNab's railway trestle.

CHAPTER 4

THE STONE MAN

Alexander Mackenzie 1873–78

THE GOVERNOR GENERAL, Lord Dufferin, went to the Liberals to form the new government. Dufferin had to fight an
urge to hold his nose while doing so. He was an upper-class
snob, and although a Liberal, he felt that the Conservatives
were the normal party to lead Britain's transformed colonies in
North America. The most prominent Liberals were George
Brown, the obstreperous editor of the Toronto *Globe;* and
Edward Blake, premier of Ontario and emotional Caliban of
the House of Commons. But neither of those Killer Bees was
the titular leader of their party. That job was held by Sandy
Mackenzie. The governor general knew what Sandy Mackenzie
thought about a man of breeding with big white feathers in his
hat, sitting on a throne in Ottawa.

What a surprise! The second post-Confederation prime minister of Canada would be a man who had been born in Scotland.
He was a Highlander who had more or less made it to school for
six years, and then learned the trade of stonecutting. When at
age twenty he sailed westward with his teenaged girlfriend's

family, he was carrying his tools with him. Opportunity and love were intimately tied. He went right to work, hiring out as a stonemason on the canals and forts around Kingston, taking on a few small contracts, and then slightly larger contracts, saving as much as he could from his small income, earning enough money to help bring his mother and six of his nine brothers to Upper Canada. He was diligent and honest, and he was not a lawyer. Despite all these drawbacks, he rose steadily through the political ranks.

He had come to Upper Canada in 1842, just after the union of the Canadas. He hung around Kingston for a while, and then made his home on the other side of the province, in Sarnia. There he set about working hard and making himself a useful citizen, his construction company growing in size and influence. He got contracts for banks and jails and other Victorian stone buildings that can be visited today. He may not have been a Father of Confederation, but he was literally building the new nation.

He married his girlfriend Helen, of course, and like any stalwart Scottish-Canadian builder, started a respectable family. But then he was to undergo Macdonald's fate. Helen gave birth to three children, and two of them died in infancy. Then his wife went into decline and died slowly while he sat at her bedside. Here the two Scots differed significantly: whereas Macdonald would handle his grief with liquid spirits, Mackenzie would turn to prayer. He had been born into the Church of Scotland but became a Baptist, taking on the combination of strict work ethic and uncompromising democratic logic a true believer will develop. When he was prime minister, he could not understand why any voter would prefer John A. Macdonald's bibulous pragmatism to his own devotion to principle.

In fact, he was the clear alternative to Macdonald in every way except his place of birth and his family sadness. Whereas

Macdonald saw business as a tool used by a nation in its development, Mackenzie believed in the evolutionary progress of market man as ordained by the *logos*. He thought of government as a kind of totalized business, and business as the natural order of things. He also believed that business could be run honestly. In fact he knew a lot more about money than Macdonald did, and while Macdonald ran more and more into debt, Mackenzie built bigger and bigger buildings. The ten-dollar bill should have Mackenzie rather than Macdonald on its face. But when it came to laying railroad tracks across the prairies and between the western mountains, Mackenzie could not see that there were any factors other than good sound private enterprise business principles involved. Macdonald with his wild-eyed dream had him there.

Of course Macdonald was a famous toper. Mackenzie the Baptist was a teetotaller. He always had the temperance movement lobbying him, and in fact did pass the local-option Canada Temperance Act just before he left office. Macdonald always told the tariff people that he favoured tariffs and told the anti-tariff people that he was opposed to tariffs. Mackenzie thought that it was a good idea to plainly announce his free-trade sympathies (though he was ironically forced to raise the tariff once in office). Macdonald wore checked trousers and a mink hat; Mackenzie wore a well-tailored dark business suit. Macdonald shouted comical insults in the House of Commons, and grappled with opponents on the hustings; Mackenzie liked to argue quietly and logically.

Macdonald the gentleman lawyer and Conservative was famous for saying that he would live and die a British subject. Mackenzie, who had travelled to London and experienced the vapid opinionating of the English upper crust, said to a Tory who had accused him of insufficient Britishness, "Loyalty to the Queen does not require a man to bow down to her manservant, or her maidservant—or her ass." Macdonald would late in life strut around wearing the gaudy decorations that indicated his Order of the Garter. Mackenzie's egalitarian logic led him to refuse knighthood. Before 1921 there were eight post-Confederation prime ministers; Sandy Mackenzie was the only one who died without a "Sir" in front of his name.

His sentiments might have been expressed by the poet Alexander McLachlan, who had emigrated from Scotland in 1840 at age twenty-two. During Mackenzie's time in office, he published a poem called "Young Canada." Here is the third of its four stanzas:

> Our aristocracy of toil
> Have made us what you see,
> The nobles of the forge and soil,
> With ne'er a pedigree.
> It makes one feel himself a man,
> His very blood leaps faster,
> Where wit or worth's preferr'd to birth,
> And Jack's as good's his master.

Look at the usual portrait photograph of Alexander Mackenzie—with his grey Abe Lincoln beard and perfect boiled white shirt he looks like one of those enormous family portraits you used to see hanging on the bedroom wall at your grandparents' house.

The stone parliament

Historians have always made a simple metaphor about Alexander Mackenzie's trade and his character as a man and a politician. So we hear about his words being laid out like granite blocks.

He had principles that were as unyielding as the stone walls of the Houses of Parliament he had once tendered a contract for. He was as humble as the flagstones under his feet. We are talking about one of the great clichés of Canadian political history. Maybe even Mackenzie thought it was appropriate. Canada is lucky that he did not build his house of straw or sticks—and look at all that hair on his chinny-chin-chin!

When Lord Dufferin, with all his condescension, sent his assessment of the newly drafted prime minister to London, he said that the man was a "poor creature" in comparison to his gentlemanly predecessor. He told London that this fellow was a hand puppet for George Brown of the *Globe*. In Sarnia, Mackenzie had been a devoted reader of the *Globe*, and George Brown's most faithful follower. In his retirement he would write a biography of Brown. He wanted George Brown, the free-trading Reformist enemy of Toryism, to be prime minister, and he wanted to serve the Lowlander's cause in the House. During every step he took up the political ladder he thought of himself as Brown's lieutenant.

In fact it is usually thought that Mackenzie would have remained a Reform Liberal organizer if his brother and business partner, Hope, had not died. Sandy wanted Hope to be the brilliant politician of the family, and worked as hard for him as he did for Brown. But he did sort of get drafted. In 1861 he was sitting in the Canadian Assembly, and in 1867 he got elected as a member of the Ontario legislature. In fact he was often left to run the affairs of the latter, whenever the mercurial premier Edward Blake was away on one of his extended trips to England. Blake was born in Upper Canada, but he had an interest in politics across the pond. After his career in Canada he actually sat in the British House as an Irish independence advocate.

Mackenzie the Reformer did not believe that a man should

be able to sit in both provincial and federal Houses, but he was also eager to serve, which he would do while working toward a bill to disallow such activity. It seemed perfectly logical to him. He was a good party man and a philosophical democrat. He won a seat for Lambton County in the federal election of 1867, and while Blake was elected, Brown was defeated.

Who was the leader of the federal Liberals? Most people said that the defeated and newly married Brown was. They waited for a by-election. They saw the Conservatives getting into trouble for the Canadian Pacific mess, and hoped for Brown's return. Brown was not in a hurry to leave his bride and newspaper in Toronto. Edward Blake was making most of the really good points in debate, but he was not the official leader of the Liberals. When Macdonald somehow won the 1872 election, the Liberals decided that they needed a leader. Sandy Mackenzie said that George Brown was his man, but Brown was not interested. All right, said Mackenzie, Edward Blake is my man. But Blake mysteriously deferred. Maybe he did not want to captain a foundering ship. Maybe he knew that the big depression was on its way.

The Liberals turned to Sandy Mackenzie and asked him to carry the flag while they tried to talk Brown or Blake into the job. What about Antoine-Aimé Dorion, suggested Mackenzie. He's a Frenchman, the Liberals said. How can a Frenchman be expected to beat John A. Macdonald? Even Dorion told Mackenzie that he had to do it. All right, said Mackenzie.

Then in November of 1873 the governor general asked him to take over and call an election for 1874.

Bad timing

In the election of 1874 the Conservatives would not replace Old Tomorrow as their leader, and the Liberals clobbered them. Almost all of Macdonald's former cabinet members were thrown out, with only his fellow Father of Confederation Charles Tupper to remain by his side. Macdonald looked around him for a successor and did not like what he saw. He would hang on and at least give a show of opposition.

So Mackenzie carried on the tradition started by Macdonald and Lincoln—he became prime minister at age fifty-two. He believed that he could aim Canada in the direction indicated by his two main beliefs: the Anglo-Saxon race, as it was called in those days, was designed to show the way to human progress, and the competitive world of free enterprise was the natural law of civilized development. Belief in the Anglo-Saxon destiny did not include unalloyed devotion to the way things went in England; while Macdonald still had room for the class system in his vision, plain Mackenzie the stonecutter was appalled by the vapid English aristocracy, and saw a Canada that would step democratically beyond the mother country into the future. He was quite willing to adopt USAmerican models if they looked more practical and liberal than English ones. He was a Scot and a Canadian. The governor general had to put up with him, and in time came to a grudging approval of his work.

But in regard to free enterprise, Mackenzie's luck ran out as soon as he became prime minister. The man who had built his business stone by stone became the victim of the worst international depression of the nineteenth century, or so it was characterized at the time. He needed help. But here he was, the loyal party man who had always done everything he could for Brown and Blake, left to run things pretty well on his own. Blake quit as soon as the election was won, only to come back later as a rival.

Brown would not sit in the Commons, so Mackenzie made him a senator. Other friends coughed into their hands and backed away. Only Dorion came to help, and took over the Justice Ministry, but then he would resign to become the number one lawyer in Quebec. Mackenzie himself took over the Ministry of Public Works. What else could he do?

One thing he could not do was build a railroad to British Columbia. During his administration he constantly faced pressure from B.C. politicos and from the Tories about the promise that had brought the west coast into the union. But the Liberals under Blake had been vehemently opposed to emptying easterners' coffers to lay rails across the west. Some of the greatest insults in the history of Canadian politics had been invented by Edward Blake to describe British Columbia and its inhabitants. As for the railroad itself, Blake predicted that all we would end up with was two streaks of rust across the prairies.

Mackenzie had been against the CPR from the beginning. For one thing, its head office would be in Montreal. For another, it would be tantamount to public enterprise. For a third, it would be a huge boondoggle, stripping the exchequer. The Liberals would suggest a slower method of interprovincial transport, building smaller rail lines to supplement the great opportunities in water transport across the west. The Rocky Mountains? An earlier Alexander Mackenzie found his way across them. This one did not want to hear about them.

He was busy defining Canadian Liberalism. It would combine laissez-faire economics and egalitarian politics. The first would be directed by thrift, the second by honesty. Mackenzie's government brought in a bill ordering that the next election be held by secret ballot. Macdonald, of course, snuffled and spouted and declared that in a democracy a man should be proud of his vote and not feel that he had to slink away and make it behind a curtain. Of course, if one were purchasing a vote, one did want to be somewhat secure in getting value for money spent.

Generally Macdonald, expecting to be replaced as Conservative leader, did not raise much of a fuss during the sessions of Mackenzie's Parliament. He left most of the loud stuff to Tupper. He did jump up and down during debate that led up to the passing of the Supreme Court bill of 1875. Old Tomorrow had been trying to get a Supreme Court since the days of the Confederation meetings. Twice he had introduced Supreme Court bills during his mandate, and twice he had been defeated. Now the Liberals were introducing their own bill, and it looked as if everyone would be on board: Macdonald's men because the court would further establish the hegemony of the federal government, the Reformers and other Liberals because it would be another step in the path toward Canadian independence. The only opponents were those who had defeated Macdonald's bills, the champions of provincial rights.

But then someone threw in a last-minute amendment. The Liberal bill would now declare that Canada's Supreme Court would be the last court of appeal, that one could not then appeal further to the law lords in England, sitting in the Judicial Committee of the Privy Council. But the bill also provided for some appeals to England. This proviso was apparently quite confusing at the time, and may even be so today. Macdonald took the bill to mean that only in rare circumstances could cases be appealed to England, though as it turned out, Macdonald was wrong. In any case, Macdonald ranted against what he saw to be a cutting of British ties.

Those who dislike the colonial connection, he said, speak of it as a chain. But it is a golden chain, and I, for one, am proud to wear its fetters.

If one did not keep a vigilant eye, these Liberals might decide one day to replace the Union Jack with some kind of flag of their own.

But the Liberals had their majority, and the Supreme Court bill was passed. Macdonald was not all that unhappy, and he knew that he would never defeat Mackenzie on the imperial connection. He was banking on British Columbia. He was watching the work of the depression that kept the purse strings tight. He was relying on Mackenzie's two fatal weaknesses— honesty and principle.

His desire not to be bought, and not to be swarmed by supporters and blackmailers who would seek to buy him, led to one of the stone-builder's most famous pieces of architectural remodelling. He got out his drafting tools and designed a secret staircase in the West Block Tower, now called the Mackenzie Tower, so that he could avoid the patronage boys lying in wait for him in the vestibule. Later the passage, which somehow remained a secret from the press, was used by Pierre Trudeau and Brian Mulroney when, for their various reasons, they wished to avoid reporters.

Another of Macdonald's bills had made it through before his departure from office. This was the formation of the North West Mounted Police. The prairie territories now under the federal aegis were likely to fill up with pioneering easterners and the right kind of European immigrants. But there were already two kinds of people out there that needed rounding up and controlling. These were the indigenous groups and the USAmerican whisky traders who aimed to give the former adulterated spirits and old firearms in exchange for stuff that was worth money down south. The USAmericans hated the Mounties, and made fun of them in their newspapers and law courts. Of course: the Mounties offered a model different from laissez-faire Indian-killing and range wars, and were going to get in the way of Manifest Destiny.

When a bunch of USAmericans came up to Cypress Hills and killed some Assiniboine people just the way they were used to doing in Montana, the NWMP went on their trail, introducing their famous ability to get their man. They did find the perpetrators, but USAmerican courts and diplomats managed to assert the US principle that Indian killers were heroes, and the Mounties had to grit their teeth and go about their business of escorting disaffected Natives to their assigned reserves.

But they were there. And now they started building forts near the forty-ninth parallel, and it would be a little more difficult for the whisky men to make their deals. Canadian nationalists liked the bright red Mountie jackets. The Conservatives knew that they had created the force. The Liberals knew that they were in power while the Mounties made their presence known. The railroad might not be there, but the Canadian police were.

But we remember the war about B.C.'s railroad as the main political struggle of the era. John A. Macdonald said that he had made a promise to B.C., and he knew that there were a lot of USAmericans out there; the loss of B.C. would destroy the new nation. Blake and Mackenzie said that the enormous cost of the railroad would destroy the nation. The Fathers of Confederation would lose their offspring and turn into old beggars.

Mackenzie looked around. The depression was becoming more visible all the time. The farmers had no one to sell produce to, and they could not afford to buy seed. There were unemployed men living in crates in Toronto. You could see the floor between coins in the treasury. What should I tell the populace, Mackenzie asked himself. There was no argument for this Baptist idealist. He told the populace that Canada was just about broke. This was before governments hired economists who could fiddle statistics and deficit financing. The Minister of Public Works told his fellow citizens that there was no money to build a grand steel road to the Pacific.

John A. Macdonald sat in his parliamentary chair, the smallest grin under his long nose.

He knew what was happening out there in Victoria. And to the south. In 1869 the US Senate had promulgated these disheartening words: "The opening by us first of a North Pacific Railroad seals the destiny of British possessions west of the 91st meridian. Annexation will be but a question of time." Those sentiments had not changed with B.C.'s entry into Canada. The premier of B.C. was Amor De Cosmos, who had been a west-coast stepfather of Confederation. But he offered the feds a compromise, and before you could say Alexander Mackenzie, a crowd of unionists and drunkards invaded the B.C. legislature and declared themselves the new provisionary government west of the Rockies. Amor De Cosmos hunkered in a backroom. When he came out he was not the premier any more. He decided to represent his province in the federal House. There he waved a piece of paper called the Terms of Union, and demanded that Ottawa live up to Macdonald's bargain.

In a speech in his hometown of Sarnia, the prime minister said that Amor De Cosmos's paper was "a bargain made to be broken." People in B.C. thought that was an odd thing for an honest businessman to say, and an unwise thing for a politician to admit. The new premier, George A. Walkem, was a successful lawyer. He lawyered at Mackenzie for a while, and then said that he was going over the prime minister's head and across the Atlantic.

Mackenzie hated that. He had been devoting his philosophical career to the aim of Canadian independence.

Over Mackenzie's head, nevertheless, was Lord Carnarvon, the Colonial Secretary. He was a kind of grandfather of Confederation himself. Back in 1858 he had persuaded the British government to pass the British Columbia Act which created the unified colony that would become the rowdy province. In 1867 he had brought the BNA Act into Parliament. Now in July of 1874 he graciously offered to mediate the shouting match between Walkem and Mackenzie. His first condition was that both parties would accept the Colonial Secretary's decision. Walkem felt a cold Atlantic wind, thinking that Carnarvon would favour the nation he had carried in his hand. Mackenzie was perspiring in the summer heat beside the Rideau, wary that the British lord had a historical bias for the province he had cobbled together.

Mackenzie's spies told him that Walkem was hanging onto the B.C. premiership by a salt-worn thread. Walkem's advisers informed him that the prime minister was in danger and all alone. Still, they both accepted Carnarvon's first condition, and sent their lobbyists to London to plead principles and economics. Carnarvon came through with a compromise that would give both sides a glimmer of hope for survival. The railroad did not have to be finished until December 31, 1890. Meanwhile the Dominion government would complete the Vancouver Island line from Esquimalt to Nanaimo, and start surveying and cutting a roadway across the province.

The bill to bankroll the Island's E&N Railroad got through the House of Commons, but was defeated by Mr Brown in the Senate. A lot of B.C. businessmen with real-estate dreams started saying the word "separation" out loud. Lord Dufferin hopped onto a USAmerican train and went to Victoria to quieten things down. The first thing he saw was a huge arch over the street, and upon that arch the words "Carnarvon Terms of Separation." The governor general smiled nicely and took a side street to his vice-regal digs. Back in Ottawa, the businessman prime minister shrugged his shoulders and claimed to have tried.

He had a lot of enemies from coast to coast. His friends were even more trouble. But he had a second wife, Jane, to whom he could write mushy letters, before whom he could drop his pose as a stone man. He needed her after his house burned down, destroying all his furniture and books and the tools he had brought with him from Scotland. He got new tools and built himself a new house within a short walk from the West Block. He liked the symbolism.

He wondered why he was not hearing from Edward Blake. He did hear from George Brown, and it seemed to be some fairly good news at last. Brown had come back from his long meetings with the USAmericans, clutching a limited version of a reciprocity treaty. It was a start, Mackenzie decided, and he submitted the deal to Parliament. The Commons passed it, but the Senate had too few Grits in it, and turned the deal down. Mackenzie could not believe that men could refuse the only logical way out of a depression. His hair turned white. Deep lines formed in his face. What else could go wrong?

Well, there was still Edward Blake.

They called him the genius of the Liberal party. He was at times whimsical, at others a volcano of tears and expletives. He was a booster of Ontario's future, calling for huge northern development, complaining every time someone made a dollar in Montreal, suggesting that the country would be better off without those deserts and logpiles out west. He had mysteriously decided not to be part of the country's second government in January 1874. Now he dropped the other well-polished boot. Or rather he wrote one of the great letters in the history of Canadian politics, offering to take all Sandy Mackenzie's problems off his hands.

He claimed that he did not really want any power for himself. He was acting out of a feeling of benevolence toward Mackenzie and the nation. "It might be my duty under certain circumstances to face my difficulties and overcome my personal reluctance to office," he wrote. He was offering to take Sandy's place as prime minister. What a noble heart there beateth! On the morrow he might feed the hungry depressionized masses with an armful of bread and fishes.

Blake told Mackenzie that the latter might remain as Minister of Public Works. It was not a popular portfolio those days. Take it or leave it, said Blake. He hinted that he had a lot of influence among the various factions of the Liberal party. Mackenzie was dumbfounded. Then he was perplexed: what was behind Blake's offer? What was Blake not telling him? There were the usual rumour-shops open for business. Blake was demented. Blake knew that the depression was ending. Blake was seen too often with the crowd that favoured joining the USAmerican republic. Pretty soon Mackenzie was angry and stubborn.

In any case, he did not reply to Blake's letter, not knowing what to say. Blake sent another letter withdrawing the offer and warning that Mackenzie would be responsible for the consequences. The most obvious consequences would appear to be a sundering of the party. Now pride and party loyalty struggled for the Scottish Baptist's mind. He decided to try a little soft soap. He adopted his old pose as the eager student, telling Blake that he needed to talk it over, to see the right way clearly. Blake knew that Mackenzie was thinking of the party first. He told the prime minister to forget about his offer, and then set about arranging the consequences.

He started campaigning in the open for the top job. He went around complaining about the Carnarvon deal and the attempts at reciprocity and the remaining hegemony of the British Empire. He was sounding more and more like Goldwyn Smith and the Canada Firsters, the radical fringe of the Reformists. He was sounding more and more like a Toronto lawyer with no eyes for the concerns of Canadians outside the Ontario borders.

One day in Aurora, Ontario, in the middle of farm country north of Toronto, Blake wagged his head and rolled his eyes and waved his arms and allowed big tears to slide down his cheeks. He loudly declared that the current administration was doing absolutely everything wrong. His targets were many, but he saved his worst words for British Columbia and the British Empire. The former was a worthless sea of mountains, and should be cut adrift. The latter was slavery, and should be changed into a federation. Canadians would elsewise never be free people. Furthermore, Canada needed a new prime minister such as himself to save it from such a fate.

Mackenzie did not say anything in public. Privately he told Blake that he thought the speech was unfortunate, as well-intentioned as it might be. That calm response had Edward Blake chewing the sleeves of his worsted jacket. John A. Macdonald, meanwhile, enjoyed the speech. He considered Blake his ally, the best thing that could happen to the Conservative party. But he was patient enough to hold his tongue. If he were to say anything nice about Blake the Liberals might unite, whereas if he demurred they might break into little pieces.

Macdonald would be disappointed. When Mackenzie acknowledged the Senate's refusal to fund the Vancouver Island railroad, and opted instead for a few piecemeal bribes for the west coasters, Blake came back to the Cabinet as Justice Minister. Mackenzie had to make sure that everyone knew who the real prime minister was, and handling Blake's tantrums took up a lot of his time, but it looked as if the True Grits, Reformers and other Liberals were going to stay afloat.

Greater unity was achieved when the governor general made one of his usual gaffes. Dufferin had learned that Mackenzie was not the bumpkin he had thought him to be, but he still considered the Conservatives the natural link with the old country. In 1876 he decided to step into the vexatious B.C.

waters. His motivations were complex, and they included personal ambition. He wanted to be considered a hero with the Empire's well-being in mind. Petitioned by the cantankerous businessmen-politicians from the west coast, he decided to head out there and offer his own blandishments in exchange for peace. He did not think it was necessary to inform the prime minister of his intentions.

Canada's first important constitutional battle would be the result. Alexander Mackenzie's anti-aristocratic feelings would lead him to action that did more than anything else in the country's first decade to establish Canada as an adult state.

In Victoria Lord Dufferin strutted around in feathers and sashes, playing up the royal connection and promising to do whatever was in his power to get the Dominion government into line. On his return to Ottawa he wrote to London, suggesting that he use his vice-regal initiative to whip the feckless colonial prime minister into shape. Dufferin had made the error that Macdonald had been too clever to fall into. Now Mackenzie and Blake became robust allies. Night after night they drove to Rideau Hall and worked on the governor general; Mackenzie played good cop and Blake played bad cop. Dufferin said that he was the Queen's man in Canada and could act arbitrarily when he saw the need. The Canadians told him that he was living in the past, that there was a Constitution, and they knew it by heart.

The battle went on and on. Dufferin wanted to be the Queen's main man in India, the jewel of the Crown. He could not afford to be embarrassed in this rinky-dink colony in the snow. Luckily for him, and perhaps for Canada, Rideau Hall was off-limits to the journalists, even George Brown. Dufferin could finally back down without losing a lot of face.

The end of principle

In all the photographs of Sandy Mackenzie you will see that he has his thin lips clamped shut. His pale blue eyes will reach out and snag your sympathy. Here was an honest, hard-working man with no luck.

The world depression, especially because it was crippling the US market, was driving farmers and workers into idle hunger. And as his people saw their hopes disappearing, Mackenzie's health slipped away. The doctors told him to ease up, so he worked harder. The international debt was reaching unimagined heights. The banks in Montreal and Toronto could go any day. John A. Macdonald had an explanation: he said that Liberal times were hard times. Such exacting analysis went over pretty well with the electorate.

The other disaster for Mackenzie in the latter part of his tenure was Quebec. He never had a real French-Canadian partner after Dorion's defection. Wilfrid Laurier was promising, but his time was not yet come. During his time in opposition Mackenzie had made some rash Upper Canadian statements about Louis David Riel, and now he was the prime minister. He had to make a compromise, knowing that Riel was not only living in Quebec but a symbolic figure for French-Canadian aspirations and resentments. Mackenzie had to find a way to mollify the Catholic French without seeming a traitor to the Orangemen. He was not the last Canadian prime minister to sit inside that vise. He was a man of principle who had to find some space. He arranged an amnesty for all the Manitoba rebels except Riel and two of his lieutenants, and he promised an amnesty to them as well if they would stay out of sight for five years. Neither the Quebeckers nor the Ontarians cheered wildly, but the man who could not be bought had bought a little time.

Bishop Bourget of Montreal was a more dangerous and less sympathetic creature. All over the world there were right-wing Catholic clerics who rallied mobs opposed to liberal secular governments and institutions. Bourget was not in favour of any Canadian political party, and he was hardly tolerated by the Vatican, but he had a bishopric and a mob, and he set about displaying his intolerant churchism as a liberation struggle against satanic forces in Montreal and Ottawa. The Conservative party was not as far right as Bourget, but they knew a powerful anti-liberal when they saw one. Their newspapers and spokesmen made sport of recalling the younger Mackenzie's injudicious attacks on the Catholic Church and its reins on economic and philosophical liberalism. It did not help that once in a while, especially during by-elections, some of Mackenzie's Liberal candidates carried on the old practice of attacking the politics of the Quebec clergy. The Liberals lost all the by-elections in Quebec. Pretty soon they were losing them in Ontario as well.

John A. Macdonald, still waiting for someone else to take over his job, began lining up friends in Quebec. But it was becoming clear to him that he was the Conservative party. Mackenzie probably knew it just as early. No problem: John A. Macdonald would never be able to come back from the Pacific Scandal. He would never make headway with eastern taxpayers if he joined the westerners in their complaints about slow progress with the train tracks. The only thing Macdonald had going for him was the depression.

Well, the depression and its effect on Canadian farmers and manufacturers. These people saw their only hope in a higher tariff. Sandy Mackenzie was a man of principle; he would not give in even to his own members who represented farmers and manufacturers. Mackenzie believed that there were natural forces alive in the economic world that would adjust the market if you just took your time and gave them a chance. John A. Macdonald assigned his ineloquent friend Tupper to pronounce the phrase "National Policy" from time to time, before he used it himself. It was one of the greatest flim-flams in the late nineteenth century. Canadians who resented the inroads of USAmerican business liked the word "National," and the word "Policy" seemed to offer some plan to get us out of this mess.

But, said Mackenzie, the hard times were a result of international forces. Macdonald allowed the word "traitor" to slither into his conversations about the government. As for the "National Policy," which were often words scrawled on a whisky bottle in the cartoons printed in Liberal newspapers, it was said more often than it was explained, but it was basically a call for higher tariffs. Macdonald said that these would be temporary and selective tariffs, highly patriotic in nature.

Macdonald, judging that British Columbia and farmers from Ontario could not get him over the top in the coming general election, also tried to dig up some scandals, at least enough to divert attention from his own. Canada was treated to the phenomenon of old Macdonald standing up in the Commons and asseverating against the evils of corruption and patronage. Honest Mackenzie made his usual mistake, relying on the good judgement and intelligence of the voting public.

Eighteen seventy-seven was a ferocious, laughable, embarrassing year in Canadian politics, and 1878 was worse. The House of Commons was a cross between a bearpit and a tavern. A look at the complexions and demeanours of the two party leaders might have hinted at the near future. John A. Macdonald appeared rosy and sober more and more often, while Alexander Mackenzie looked like a haggard, white-bearded lonely man who had just groped his way out of a sickbed—which he had.

These two combatants went *mano a mano* for the last two

sessions. In the end, one would stride around the ring with hand raised, while the other would be dragged away through the sand. They fought all day and all night, and slept an hour and fought again. Words like "liar" and "coward" and "miscreant" were shouted and recorded in Hansard, which had been operating since Mackenzie's second year as prime minister. Of course he still had his majority, but he had no strong lieutenants. Blake was gone again, although he would have been at home in this loony bin. Young Laurier had finally taken his place as the prime minister's man, but it was by now too late to insert his intelligence into the fray.

Some sittings lasted well over twelve hours. One went for twenty-seven. Those Canadians who believe in the solemnity of parliamentary tradition are fortunate that there were no photographers allowed in the House. But Brown's *Globe* painted remarkable word pictures. There were members snoring with their heads on their desks. Others were hurling parliamentary publications across the room. Amateur marching bands assembled, with bagpipes and bugles and improvised drums. Compatriots put their arms around each other's shoulders and bellowed rude songs. Even sixty-three-year-old Macdonald continued a personal tradition, trying to get through a restraining crowd and hurl himself on the giant Donald Smith, swearing that he could lick him. When the prime minister, aghast, tried to summon the sergeant-at-arms to restore order, the latter could not be found.

Mackenzie called an election for September. He thought that he had a good chance for a second term. There were signs that the depression was ending. A higher tariff was unnecessary as well as historically incorrect. He had a Quebec lieutenant to save that province. The Maritimes were on side. After this election he would take the rest that his wife had been insisting on, and get some colour back in his face.

On election day John A. Macdonald lost his seat in Kingston! Mackenzie won his in Lambton by only 150 votes. Both weary leaders had been well pummelled. But the reversal of 1874 had itself been reversed. Macdonald's party swept the farmlands and won the election. Sandy Mackenzie was not only disappointed—he was amazed. How could historical necessity be ignored by an enlightened populace? How could corruption win over integrity?

He did not want to be leader of the opposition. He said that the Liberals needed a fresh leader, and in a letter to a friend he wrote that this leader would not be tolerated by the public unless he had "graduated as a horse thief." The idealist had never understood the power of myth. That is why his face is not on the ten-dollar bill.

But his party and George Brown asked him to sit as leader, which he did for two years, until his party and Laurier persuaded him that they needed a new head, and this time Blake took the job. Mackenzie would watch him fail to dislodge Old Tomorrow and finally skip the country. Sandy stayed at home writing books and reading about the troubles of the transnational railroad.

A person has to feel affection and sympathy for this unlucky Baptist idealist, even if he was a market man. He brought us the secret ballot and Hansard. He refused to wear the gaudy rewards of the British Crown. His actions sprang out of democratic belief rather than political opportunity. He chose loneliness over image-building. He gave his fellow citizens more credit than they knew what to do with. He had the grace to be a bad politician in the end.

CHAPTER 5

OLD GANDY DANCER

—◆◆◆—

John A. Macdonald 1878–91

I N JANUARY OF 1861, New York's William Seward, who had just
missed the Republican party's nomination for president the
year before, made a speech in St Paul, Minnesota, in which he
brought up the topic of Canada and Rupert's Land. He said he
could see "how an ingenious people, and a capable, enlightened government are occupied with bridging rivers and making railroads and telegraphs to develop, organize, create and
preserve the great British provinces of the north, by the Great
Lakes, the St Lawrence and around the shores of Hudson's Bay,
and I am able to say, 'It is very well; you are building excellent
states to be hereafter admitted into the American Union.'"

The US and Seward bought Alaska from the Russian czar,
who thought that he had owned it, in 1867. People such as
Blake and Mackenzie may not have taken much notice. In the
US the purchase was called "Seward's Folly" by the Democrats,
and as we know, Blake felt the same way about Canada's adventures out west. But John A. Macdonald was interested in myth,
and in myth superhuman events take place. The USAmericans,

with their social Darwinism and their "manifest destiny," may have thought that they had history with them. Canada would have to counter with myth.

The Liberals called Macdonald's "National Policy" a piece of legerdemain. Close enough. They said that the CPR was a fantasy. That's almost the same thing. Every time it looked as if Edward Blake was in an election that was his to win, he would campaign by making careful speeches well documented with facts and figures, well reasoned with legal nicety, argued with impeccable English prose. If Sandy Mackenzie had overestimated the good sense and sensitivity to morality in the voting public, Blake overestimated the public's appetite for fact and reason.

John A. Macdonald had learned that the public wanted a mythical character to vote for, not a party platform, and certainly not logic and documentation. This gangly man with the runaway hair and the checked trousers would shout bluff threats at his opponents, charge across the stage with clutching fingers, disappear around a corner with a bottle in his hand. He was funny and loud. Once he puked into a wastebasket while Blake was pontificating in the House. "Every time that man starts talking I want to throw up," he said. He was larger than life, and people sitting on farms at the edge of civilization in a giantific land mass thought that they needed such a leader.

Mackenzie had thought that Macdonald would never recuperate from the Pacific Scandal. Macdonald could have been found drunk, his fancy trousers around his ankles, with a gallon of gin and three naked chorines festooned with expensive jewellery purchased by railroad tycoons, and he would have walked away with a few quips that would get George Brown's cartoonists howling and the voters laughing fondly. As he advanced into old age, he polished his imitation of young Mac, and once in a while there would be a shout from the rear of a campaign hall: "You'll never die, John A.!"

He was still looking for a worthy successor in the party. Once in a while he would write a letter to a colleague, mentioning that he and Tupper and the rest were old, that the party looked like old leftovers from pre-Confederation days. But by the late eighties he had come to know that he would never leave office alive. And he came to expect that he would never again be ousted from office. There would be no more purloined telegrams. It was common knowledge that he met in poolrooms and manufacturers' clubs to receive campaign contributions from the folk who would benefit from the National Policy. But now the old man stayed sober more often, and never put anything incriminating on paper. Sure, the CPR was getting a lot of money from the Canadian government, but the party that formed the Canadian government was also getting a lot of money from the CPR. It was the CPR and the Conservative party that would save the nation from the grasp of the US.

The western world was becoming modern. More and more countries were outlawing the slavery of Africans. There were electric trams on the streets of Paris, and ships propelled by steam turbines in the Atlantic. Karl Marx died in 1883 while big unions were being formed, even in the US. The British bombed and occupied Egypt, and paid attention when gold was discovered in South Africa. European imperialism sped up on the African continent and Southeast Asia. It seemed that just about all the real estate in the world had been "discovered," and there was a rush to gather as much as possible. Even the US, that great experiment in democracy and modernity, was reaching across a continent and out into large bodies of water.

On the edge of disaster

In 1878 Macdonald had found himself a safe by-election, and from then until 1891, he would be beset by threats from smaller men who aspired to lesser greatness. The neo-Howe movement in Nova Scotia captured a premier who asked his citizens to vote for secession. Ontario wanted to expand magnificently northward, and so did Quebec. In Manitoba and Rupert's Land they wanted north-south rail links owned by US interests. The yahoos in British Columbia were still bitching about their railroad and mentioning that they had good US neighbours to their north and south. There were Protestants in Ontario who hated Catholics, and Catholics in Quebec who resented the power of Ontario Protestants. Macdonald had better not get himself between the French and English again, as he had in the Riel crisis of 1870.

He fought against all efforts of the provinces and regions for greater autonomy. He was still a Brit who hated all the new isms in the United States, but he did create the position of Canadian High Commissioner to London. The Brits rankled at this apparent step toward independence, but accepted it. The appointee was the Eastern Townships gadfly Alexander Galt, who had been a Liberal and a Canada Firster, a supporter of confederation among the Anglo countries and of Canada's joining the United States. He would seem an odd choice by the loyalist Macdonald, but Galt was also a strong railroad man, and Macdonald needed a railroad man close to the English banks.

Macdonald still hated republicanism, and he was wary of the growing size and ambition of the two original provinces. He felt that centralism was the only way to face threats from outside the country and excessive democratization within. He had lost the battle against the secret ballot, and now he was facing the movement of some provinces toward universal male suffrage. In 1885, he would suggest, however, that women and aborigines might be extended the franchise—as long as they were property owners.

There were obvious differences among the regions. Some were almost modern. Others were outposts in the mud. Some were enormous and others were tiny. From some, especially in the east, people were moving in droves to the United States. People who rubbed up against each other got into wicked fights about the connection of schools to churches.

And it appeared that the country was getting poorer and poorer, especially when it came to being able to pay for the greatest engineering feat in the New World.

Immediately after Macdonald's return in 1878 the big depression lifted, English banks had money for railroads, and the prime minister could announce that Conservative times were good times. Honest Alexander Mackenzie brooded on the vagaries of fortune and the disconnection between honesty and progress. He could no longer afford his nice house in Ottawa, and had to sell it to his enemy Tupper, of all people. The businessman pursed his lips while inking the deal. John A. had, of course, been defeated in Kingston, so he got himself elected in British Columbia and Manitoba. He opted for the Victoria seat, although he had never seen any of the west that he fought so hard for. The idea was that the fractious Pacific province would fall for the same hail-fellow bluff that had worked so well in Ontario, and stay in the union because "one of their own" was its leader. They would get not just a railroad, but its chief engineer in fancy duds.

Good times did not do much for Macdonald's health. He was often laid up, and not just by the hooch. He got almost all the diseases of the Victorian age, and his pending death, as in the old days, was from time to time rumoured in the papers. When he got cholera, even his doctors told him to make his will and designate his successor. The latter prospect probably contributed to his recovery.

But now financiers were lining up to offer deals on a railroad. Macdonald's government signed with Donald Smith's cousin, George Stephen. The new CPR would have steel all the way to Vancouver Island in ten years, and all the government had to do was hand over $25 million 1880 dollars and twenty-five million acres of land along the route. There was plenty more where that came from, Old Tomorrow reasoned. The CPR hired the robust and noisy William Cornelius Van Horne, who declared himself a fervent Canadian, but retained his USAmerican optimism, and started plunking rails westward at a happy rate. The great epic was now underway, and grateful Canadians can read about it in the comic poem by E.J. Pratt and the sincere tome by Pierre Berton.

When it came time to campaign for the 1882 election, Macdonald had half a railroad to run on. The Pacific Scandal was history. Macdonald was in the Imperial Privy Council. The prime minister was glad that his successor had not shown up after all. His health picked up. He drank a little less medicine. Everything seemed to be running smoothly until George Stephen gave him the news—$25 million just seemed to fly away. The ever-threatening difficulties of keeping the lenders optimistic could become a crushing blow. But Macdonald was a man whose obituaries were always being updated. If he could get through the election, he would find some money somewhere; he had been scamming big boys for decades.

He got through the election with guile and luck. The guile involved gerrymandering the Ontario electoral map and calling it electoral reform. The luck involved the fact that Mackenzie had been eased out of the Liberal leadership and Blake was given his chance. Blake's meticulous speeches put the bumpkins to sleep, and Macdonald, running in a safe Ontario seat, carried the day. Now to work.

The provinces were pushing their autonomy, distracting the chief from his attempts to save the broke railroad company. Macdonald could not have been blamed for wondering whether he had won anything with this election. He could not deny that his National Policy, his railroad and his country were on the far edge of visibility. The huge republic was waiting to save the day. The depression was back, and these were not even Liberal times. The gandy dancers out west were not being paid. Smith and Stephen had emptied their enormous coffers. The US and British banks decided not to pour good money after bad. Blake and his boys were hooting in Parliament. Even the Conservative cabinet was showing cracks. They might not support Macdonald's plan to throw another $25 million at the iron horse. He had a lot of enemies. He needed a friend.

Guns on the prairies

After their old home along the Red River had been turned into a Canadian province, a lot of the Métis people had joined their fellows along the Saskatchewan River. In December of 1884 a group of Métis and other settlers sent a petition to the governor general of Canada, informing him that the Indian people who had been persuaded to sign treaties in the 1870s were now dying of starvation, that the Métis people had not been offered the assurances of land that were extended to their people in Manitoba, and that the 60,000 people in the territories wanted responsible government granted to the far fewer people of Manitoba. They were talking about "old settlers," people who had been on the land longer than the US miners who had come north after gold and persuaded the Canadians to make a province out of British Columbia.

The treaties with the Native peoples on the prairie had said, to put it simply, that the white people were allowed to come into Cree land, and that the Indians were to become farmers. The Canadians would teach them to farm, and provide food and other supplies while the farms were being developed. Then other distractions persuaded Ottawa that the Indians could be ignored, that they had been taking care of themselves for a long time and could continue to do so. The trouble was that now the USAmericans had killed all the buffalo that used to come north, and the Indians were not equipped to feed themselves as farmers. When the great leader Poundmaker went to Fort Walsh to suggest to the Canadians that hungry and dispossessed Cree might be forced to fight for their lives, he was told to go home and stay out of trouble.

Some government people had been reading Charles Darwin. They believed that the North American Natives were not the fittest, and that their race would be pretty well gone by the middle of the twentieth century.

Still, the Indian leaders always counselled peace among their people, telling them to rely on the promises made in the name of the foreign Queen. When the Métis rebels tried to enlist the Cree in their cause, they usually had to resort to force and threats.

Informed by his western people that the conditions on the prairie were the kind that could lead to desperate measures, Macdonald acceded to one of the Métis requests—he authorized the disbursing of a scrip among the Saskatchewan settlers, hoping that though it would be yet another expense for a beleaguered treasury, at least it might buy time till the government could come up with some sort of advantage. The Métis, meanwhile, set up another provisional government at Batoche, on the Saskatchewan River near what is now Prince Albert. It was not the first such government in Saskatchewan. In 1875 Gabriel Dumont, grandson of a voyageur, had been head man of a commune organized to help his people make the transition from hunters to farmers. He was an expert agitator in the defence of his people's old land claims against the speculators who were arriving and hoping to strike it rich because of the railroad.

Dumont spoke six languages, and with his father had proven a superb statesman, making various armistices with the Siouan peoples. He was also a great rider and rifleman, a boatsman and military planner. When he asked Louis David Riel to come to Batoche and head the new provisional government, Riel made him his military chief.

But Riel was now a middle-aged family man. Macdonald thought that 1870 had seen the last of any serious trouble with this man. He did not know that Riel was now more spiritual than political, that now he was to lead a crusade rather than a national defence. They say that Riel saw visions, including a vision of his own hanging. He had broken with the Vatican, and saw a Christianity that would join rather than separate Catholics and Protestants, and embrace Jews who were interested in Jesus. As to worldly visions, he wanted the west to be divided among the nations of Europe, Catholic and Protestant, with a section for the Jews to create their new Jerusalem.

But he was involved with Duck Lake. Duck Lake is not far from Batoche. In March of 1885 some Mounties were stopped there by Dumont and his snipers, who were protecting the territory against foreign military. The Mounties rode away and came back with a bunch of white civilians, a hundred men in all, and tried to talk Dumont into some kind of surrender. Then someone got nervous and a fire fight broke out. Dumont's Métis and Indians won the fight and would have won it even more had Riel not told them to let the invaders go.

This battle was great news for the CPR. Van Horne loaded General Frederick Middleton and his angry Protestant volunteers onto his train and headed west for Batoche. While he was getting there, the westerners were winning little skirmishes here and there. By May 9, Middleton and 800 soldiers with cannon and Gatling gun and John A. Macdonald's son, Hugh, were approaching Batoche, ready to do battle with 175 defenders. For a while everything the easterners did was expertly resisted by the defenders. But on May 12 Middleton's army, charging against fusillades of nails and stones, overran the Métis, and the Ontario newspapers would crow about a victory in what they called a civil war.

Dumont escaped to the United States, but the family man Riel, carrying a wooden cross, was apprehended. A century of Quebec-Ontario spats was about to be inaugurated. Orangemen in Ontario screamed that it was time to make up for the mistake that Macdonald had made in letting the traitor go into exile in 1870. In Quebec one would find an image of brave romantic French Canadians once again doomed by overpowering Anglo forces.

The religious antagonisms focused attention on Riel and the other Métis. But right after his grand victory at Batoche, Middleton rode around the northwest, bullying Native peoples, arresting the ones he thought most advantageous to arrest, and sealing the poor reserves. How are we going to eat this winter, the Native people would ask. You should have thought of that before you became rebels, was the army's answer. A lot of the Native people turned themselves in, expecting to be treated as prisoners of war. Instead they were hauled into court and sentenced as criminals against the law. This sort of thing was to occur in British Columbia, too, where there were hardly any treaties. Now an Indian who had captured a foe's horse was sentenced to six years for horse theft. Eleven men were sentenced to death. Eight of them were hanged at Battleford on November 27. Consistent with normal practice, the white people rounded up Indians from the surrounding area and forced them to watch the execution.

The west was being won. The train would be through here in no time.

Gabriel Dumont wanted to ride north out of sanctuary and rescue his chief of state. But in the symbolically renamed Regina, Louis David Riel was guarded by hundreds of Protestant men who hated him. In Regina they tried him in English. The jury was made up of six Protestant men. They were focusing a lot of hatred. Riel had been in a nuthouse in the United States and a loony bin in Quebec. His main activity during the Saskatchewan fighting had been to run around with a crucifix, petitioning the Trinity for assistance. But neither Riel nor the prosecution was interested in pleading insanity. Dr Daniel Clark, who was superintendent of the Toronto asylum for the insane, was there. In January of 1886, he would offer this opinion in the *Globe*: "Had he been an obscure man there is not an asylum in Christendom but would have committed him on the evidence, and legally so; but because he had been an indirect cause of a deplorable outbreak, his mental condition became of secondary importance, as political exigencies arose paramount."

There are still right-wing columnists, in the newspapers owned by Conrad Black, who maintain the image of Riel as a criminal, but a little over a hundred years after Riel's trial, statues of him are being erected in front of government buildings, and he is being described as a Father of Confederation. In 1885, Riel and Macdonald had quite different concepts of his place in history. Riel's view was stated, in English, in his speech at his trial: "I know that through the grace of God I am the founder of Manitoba . . . I believe by what I suffered for fifteen years, by what I have done for Manitoba and the people of the North-West that my words are worth something . . . I will perhaps be one day acknowledged as more than a leader of the Half-breeds."

Despite the many petitions sent by those people to the Dominion government, Macdonald could not take those racial degenerates seriously. He said that if he were to give them any money or material they would "drink it or waste it or sell it." This from a man who swallowed an ocean of alcohol and was always in debt because of financial mismanagement.

The jury, of course, found Riel guilty of treason. He, too, was hanged in November, and his frozen body was taken to St Boniface on a CPR train. History is, luckily, full of symbolic acts.

Macdonald could have commuted Riel's sentence of death. Even the jury had recommended mercy, after all. Apparently he was feeling more political pressure from Protestant Ontario than from Catholic Quebec. But when Riel was hanged in Regina, the Conservative party lost its Quebec base. Macdonald the British subject was no wiser about French Canada than he was about Métis Saskatchewan. He said that French Catholics were flighty and emotional, and that in a short time another issue would attract their temporary attention. Macdonald was burned in effigy at Dominion Square in Montreal, where he had once been pelted with eggs. Riel was hailed as a martyred saint. Young Wilfrid Laurier declared that if he had been born beside the Saskatchewan River he would have aimed a gun at the land speculators from the east. His career was made.

But so was the CPR. Parliament had seen the National Policy in action out west, and it came onside. So did the London banks. In the mountains of British Columbia some fancy-dressed old guys from Montreal inexpertly drove the famous last spike on November 7, 1885, nine days before the hanging in Regina. We historians addicted to symbolism wish they had waited just over a week at Craigellachie.

Next summer Macdonald and his wife Agnes took a fifty-day return train ride to the west coast. The seventy-year-old prime minister would, for the first time, see the west that he had staked his career and place in history on. When the train reached the Rockies, the couple got out and took their firm seats on the cowcatcher of the train and felt the mountain wind whizz by their ears. Sometimes the boss had to go back to his private car, but Agnes stayed the route. Again they mounted the cowcatcher for the night-time zoom down the Fraser Canyon, where the most expensive and dangerous part of the epic work had taken place, where the Chinese labourers that Macdonald did not meet sometimes fell into the gorge. The couple stayed two weeks in elegant digs in Victoria, the prime minister's former seat, and then made whistle stops all the way back to Ottawa.

Can you imagine Sandy Mackenzie sitting on the cowcatcher? Edward Blake? Louis St Laurent?

The last few elections

Macdonald was in trouble with his Quebec voters, but he had Edward Blake over a barrel too. Blake could not attack him for killing Riel, without alienating his Orange base in Ontario. In any case, Blake had proven himself pretty well unelectable beyond a certain level, and he had probably overstayed his tenure as Liberal leader. Laurier was forty-five years old in 1886.

But luckily for Macdonald, who by now was looking for an heir rather than a replacement as Tory leader, the Liberals stuck with the multisyllabic Blake in the 1887 election. Old Macdonald put on a pretty good imitation of young

Macdonald, and the usual electoral process took place. The *Globe* reported that he was dying from brain paralysis. Blake brought out his statistics. Macdonald winked and joked and talked with the boys in the backroom. He lost most of Quebec, partly to the separatists he had created, but he got a slim majority. The myth of John A. would prevail for another four or five years, unless an amazing Tory rival to the waiting Laurier could be found. Macdonald persuaded John Thompson to leave the Nova Scotia bench and join his cabinet, but Thompson was not Amor De Cosmos.

Whenever Macdonald got up to speak in the House of Commons he thought to himself, "Who are all these young folks?" And "Why isn't one of them a young Tory genius with flyaway hair and plaid trousers?"

Outside the House the patterns of Canadian animosities were being developed. The French Canadians were voicing their displeasure at uppity Protestant ways, and English Canadians were complaining about concessions made to the defeated "race." Westerners were griping about Catholic schools and other eastern iniquities, and Ontarians were fussing about all the money poured into the western railroad. Soon the westerners would be bitching about the freight rates laid on those tracks.

Meanwhile times were getting bad again. Money was drying up. The tariffs called the National Policy were not saving the country. The cartoons in the newspapers were getting ever more vicious. What a country to be prime minister of! But the USAmericans still wanted it, Macdonald was convinced. The last half-decade of his reign heard him give speech after speech about the threat of US rapacity. The new Liberal leader, Wilfrid Laurier, was a frank continentalist. He spoke of a North American economy and even "commercial union." Macdonald was proud of the country he had sired and bred, and he knew that the term was another way of saying Yankee takeover. So if he was to live to campaign again, he saw the terms of battle clearly: his British Canadian patriotism vs. Laurier's road to annexation.

Sure enough, 1891 arrived, and Old Tomorrow was still alive. Now he would take on the young man who had an eerie resemblance to him in his youth—similar dramatic hair, familiar flair for the fancy duds. But Laurier was twenty-six years younger. He had been born the year the two Canadas were united. Macdonald decided that he needed two strategies: act the part of a myth identified with the country itself; and dig up some dirt on the Liberals.

A seventh election campaign since Confederation!

Macdonald did not offer a lot of particulars to the voting crowd; he had seen Mackenzie and Blake make that mistake over and over. He wrapped himself in the Union Jack and argued that his Liberal opponents were USAmerican agents. His search for a scandal came up with pretty lean pickings but he picked them, rolling his eyes and inwardly smirking about the ironic justice. It happened that a *Globe* writer had consulted with US secretary of state James Blaine about the USAmericans' view of the North American future. It happened that the secretary of state was the spokesman for Washington's ideas about other countries, and it happened that the *Globe*'s man, Edward Farrer, prepared a pamphlet laying out Blaine's view of Canada-US relations. In a manoeuvre reminiscent of events of 1873, a friendly Tory printer stole the proofs of the pamphlet and delivered them to his friends.

Treason, said Macdonald. The Liberals are preparing to sell the country out from under you. He stumped until he could not speak, and then retired to Earnscliffe to die or win the election. Of course he once more pulled it off, by his slimmest majority so far.

But it was his last campaign. He knew that the Tories were on the way out, and he knew by May that he was, too. Like his parents before him, he became more and more paralyzed. At his last political consultation he told young Thompson to do everything he could to keep J.J.C. Abbott out of his PM's chair. Once again the doctors and newspapers warned the public to prepare for Sir John A.'s demise. Someone in the back of the crowd would always shout "You'll never die, John A.!" But on June 6, 1891 he did.

CHAPTER 6

THE CARETAKER

———◦◆◦———

John J.C. Abbott, 1891–92

W HEN MACDONALD FELT the onset of paralysis and possibly death, he said that he did not want to hang on the way Mackenzie had. For the last years Mackenzie had sat shaking in his Commons chair, unable to speak, sometimes making indecipherable noises out of impatience and anger. A few months after Macdonald's death, Sandy Mackenzie followed him to the great beyond. Pretty soon it would be the Conservative party, and perhaps the nation, that would suffer paralysis and death.

The old guys were disappearing. J.J.C. Abbott was seventy years old, a senator and a minister without portfolio. No one wanted him as party leader and prime minister. He himself was especially disappointed in the caucus's choice. His most famous words were written to a friend while Macdonald lay dying. "I hate politics," he wrote. "I hate notoriety, public meetings, public speeches, caucuses, and everything that I know of what is apparently the necessary incident of politics." He asked why he should want to "gain reputation and credit by practising arts which I detest to acquire popularity."

John Joseph Caldwell Abbott was a politician all his life. He was also a lawyer, a professor and a railroad tycoon. It was from his office safe that the thieves had stolen Macdonald's begging telegram in 1873, to bring down the second Conservative government.

He was born in English Quebec, the son of an English preacher, and he would marry the daughter of Montreal's Anglican dean. He studied law at McGill, and would become a young dean of law there, and later a governor of the university. His specialty was commercial law. While he learned to make a case he also learned how to make a bundle. Like a lot of people in his community, he held the opinion that the English were the proper handlers of British North America, and that the French had seen their day. Like any ambitious lawyer-businessman, he was a young Conservative, and when in 1849 the British decided to offer compensation to French Canadians who had suffered losses in the Lower Canada Rebellion, he signed a notorious annexation manifesto. This was his first significant political act. All his life thereafter he would try to explain that the manifesto was meant as protest, not a real hankering to welcome USAmerican hegemony. Intelligent, practical John A. Macdonald believed him.

At the age of thirty-six he won his first election to the Canadian Assembly, where he would begin his many years representing Argenteuil, the largely English riding on the Ontario border between Montreal and Ottawa. Before 1867 he spoke out against Confederation. He was canny enough to know that Macdonald's strong centralist views designed the new country to keep French Canadians a minority. And the English Canadian in Quebec would be doubly marginalized. But when Confederation came, he saw how useful an English-Canadian businessman in Montreal could be to the Tories in Ottawa. He got himself involved with the first Canadian Pacific Railway Company, as both lawyer and partner.

This man who hated politics would represent Argenteuil until the debacle of 1874, and again from 1880 until 1886. In 1887 Macdonald appointed him to the Senate, wherein he acted as government leader and member of the cabinet. From 1887 to 1889 he occupied his spare time as mayor of Montreal. Meanwhile, in the age of railroads, he got richer and richer. He built a nice big mansion in Ste-Anne-de-Bellevue on the west end of the island of Montreal. In his photographs he looks like a slightly scornful self-made man.

Like MacNab and Macdonald before him, he made himself a little patriotic military record. Perhaps in an attempt to make up for the silly annexation manifesto, he went to the defence of Canada during the US Civil War. In November of 1861 a Union ship intercepted the HMS *Trent* in neutral waters, and captured or kidnapped two southerners, one a Confederate emissary to London, the other a Confederate emissary to Paris. The US knew that British sympathies lay with the Confederacy, but Britain was neutral. A lot of people were betting that Britain would go to war against the US North. There was a lot of nervousness in the Canadas. John Abbott raised a militia, and spent three weeks patrolling the USAmerican border. But in December the Brits and Yanks reached a compromise. The US returned the hostages but refused to apologize for violating British neutrality.

Rent, don't buy

Everyone knew that Senator Abbott was just supposed to take care of the PM title while the Conservatives tried to handle their leadership problem. The seemingly natural choice was old Charles Tupper. He was a Father of Confederation, after all. But Tupper was now the High Commissioner in London, and he liked the posh appointment in the interesting capital. He was not about to come home to be caretaker of a government that everyone knew was on the slippery slope. Macdonald had liked John Thompson, but the man had gone and converted to the Roman Catholic faith. The Orangemen would march and bang their drums and carry their fancy cushions. The French Canadians did not like Abbott any better, but someone had to keep the PM's seat warm.

So Abbott tried to caretaker the government from his seat in the Senate, while the real work in the House of Commons was taken on by young Thompson. Abbott was probably glad that he was among the sleepers instead of the brawlers. The real work had to do, as usual, with some juicy scandals. They could have called the country the Dominion of Scandalia. Thompson was, fittingly, the Minister of Justice. His first important job was figuring out how to get rid of Hector-Louis Langevin. Langevin had been in Canadian politics for forty years, and was first elected to the Assembly in 1857. He, too, was a Father of Confederation, but now he was a problem.

Langevin was usually in Macdonald's cabinet, and he succeeded George-Étienne Cartier as head of the Conservatives' Quebec wing. He had been involved in the Pacific scandal and dropped out of the federal scene. But now he was back. Unfortunately a spy in the Conservative ranks had been digging up old papers and talking with businessmen in the province of Quebec. Langevin had a long history in both provincial and federal representation, and he found it impossible, apparently, to turn down significant gifts from people who wanted government contracts to build things. The system was simple: tell the public that the work would cost a lot more than it actually would, and kick some of the margin back to the party in power. Canadians and Quebeckers were accustomed to graft and bribery in their politics, but even goldfish want the bowl cleaned once in a while.

Langevin had to go. On paper he was the Conservative leader in the House, but he had to go. John Thompson worked a deal for him: someone else would go to jail and the official report would minimize Langevin's involvement if he would agree to resign. John Abbott, the Anglo-Quebecker, listened to Thompson's plans and approved. He hated scandal and all the rest of politics, of course. There were always well-dressed men approaching him and asking for a favour. He didn't even have Sandy Mackenzie's handy secret escape route.

The government's second main problem was the return (again!) of hard times. It can be really difficult to run things when there isn't enough money around, and crooked politicians are snapping up a lot of what there is. Luckily for the government, the Liberals were being exposed too. The Liberal premier of Quebec had to quit for taking back-door money. Blake, the unelectable federal champion of the Liberals, was calling for economic union with the USA. John Abbott, the reluctant prime minister, did not need any trouble from the traditional source of trouble for the Conservatives, the Canadian west. But it came anyway.

Once again it had to do with religion and what people in those days called race. In 1870 Macdonald had approved the Manitoba Act, whereby the Catholic population was guaranteed support for schools operated by their church. But now in the 1890s, Manitoba was a province full of immigrants, and only one person in seven was a Catholic. The act, however, said that no future law could be passed to limit the Catholic schools. But religious fervour and political opportunism are not stayed by legalities.

The leader of the anti-Catholics was a former Ontarian named Clifford Sifton. He was an Irish Protestant, and an ambitious and hard-working man. In 1890 he was the attorney general of a Liberal government in Manitoba, and he passed a provincial law declaring an end to French as an official language and an end to separate schools. If Louis David Riel was a messiah, Sifton was the anti-Riel. Old man Macdonald groaned as he faced yet another pincer movement. The bishops in Quebec and their fellows out west did more than groan. They were quite loud in their advice that Ottawa slap the Manitoba Liberals down. If it is the last thing I do, said Macdonald, I will see that the Supreme Court upholds my legislation. It was just about the last thing he did.

But now in summer of 1892 Macdonald's old wish that the British Privy Council should be more powerful than the Canadian Supreme Court came true, and the Manitoba anti-clericals had won. The Privy Council said that the Manitoba law would stand, but the Canadian government could, if it so chose, restore the Catholic schools. Justice Minister Thompson was aghast. Prime Minister Abbott hated politics more than ever, and vowed to get out and leave this problem for someone else before the year was out. Blake was gleeful. Laurier sat back and smiled, making sure that a bishop was not watching. Sifton rode around on his fancy horse and proclaimed provincial rights.

John Abbott was renting Earnscliffe from Agnes Macdonald, who had gone out west with Mary. During the fall of 1892 he gave some nice dinner parties, and looked on morosely as prominent Conservatives peeked into corners for Old Tomorrow's ghost.

The ghost had eased itself into Macdonald's chair in the Commons, which looked empty to the members until late 1892, when Langevin had also disappeared and John Thompson went forward and sat in the most prominent spot. That symbolic act was all that Prime Minister Abbott had been waiting for. Let the Catholic from Nova Scotia handle the Protestants in Manitoba. Abbott was just a tired old senator.

As ill as Macdonald or Mackenzie had ever been, and hating politics more than he had thought possible, he resigned on November 25, 1892. Off he went to Tupper's London and to the Continent, to seek health in the restful British air and to consult the excellent English and European doctors. But he came home and died in Montreal in October of 1893.

The old guys were dropping left and right.

CHAPTER 7

How Was the Soup?

———————◆•◆•◆———————

John S.D. Thompson 1892–94

IN 1960, THE USAMERICANS elected their first Roman Catholic
president. Canada got its first post-Confederation Catholic
prime minister sixty-eight years earlier when the Conservative
party came to its senses and chose John Thompson to succeed
the recalcitrant John Abbott. The Conservatives did not have
much of a choice. True, Thompson may have been a papist,
and he may have come from Nova Scotia, a province that was
small but crowded with separatists. In fact Thompson's father
was an adherent of Joseph Howe. As for the danger of religion,
Thompson was not only a Catholic but a person who had
become one a while after marrying a Catholic sea captain's
daughter. In English Canada such people were called "per-
verts" rather than converts.

John Thompson often said that it would be a shame if
Canada's political contests were waged along "racial" and religious lines, but his ministry would be tangled in such rivalries.
As a matter of fact, he was not that much interested in government. He wanted to be a judge, and had entered local Halifax

politics on his father's advice. He started on the school board, but before he knew it he was a Halifax alderman, and then almost against his will he was chosen to run for the opposition Tories in the Nova Scotia legislature. The next thing he knew his party was in government, and he was attorney general. Then the premier resigned, and one morning John Thompson woke up as premier of Nova Scotia. It was 1882. He was thirty-six years old.

But he wanted to be a judge. His father was a Protestant Irish immigrant who worked as a Queen's Printer and had seven children, the last being "Johnny." They lived in a little house under the shadow of the Citadel, and there was not a lot of money around the place. Johnny left school at fifteen, joined a temperance movement, and worked hard at the law. He was articled at age seventeen, admitted to the bar at twenty-one, and married in Portland, Maine, at twenty-five.

He and his bride, Annie, were thin and pleasant looking, but they were Victorians. They started raising a substantial family, and packing on the pounds. By the time John finally made it to the Nova Scotia Supreme Court, they were both properly portly. Thompson looked like a judge. He filled his suit, he had big bushy sideburns, and his facial expression was always a mixture of wisdom and satire. It looked as if he was well settled, and could look forward to replacing Charles Tupper as the loyalist Tory grand old man of Nova Scotia.

But in 1882 skinny old John A. Macdonald was looking for young blood. He knew that the Grits were just waiting for Wilfrid Laurier to get old enough. Laurier was three years older than John Thompson. Macdonald knew that the young Thompson had done a lot of work in 1867 to help the cause, and he had good reports of Thompson's debating skills. Thompson argued like a lawyer, with a wit to match that of Sandy Mackenzie. He was a master of detail, but he did not put people to sleep as

Blake did. As a young party worker he laboured as many hours as the young Macdonald had, and he did not drink. Everybody but the Orangemen liked him.

John A. sent his best wishes, his blandishments, his blackmail; he appealed to the young judge's patriotism because he could not appeal to his ambition. He played the anti-US card. He played the youth card. He played the Nova Scotia card. Finally, he offered John Thompson the position of Minister of Justice for Canada. All he would have to do was win a by-election in the county of Antigonish, whose people he had represented in the provincial assembly. Unfortunately the seat had been held since 1867 by the Liberals, and there was a Liberal named Angus McIsaac there right now. But there was a rumour that McIsaac wanted to be a county court judge. Macdonald knew how to buy votes and other political assets.

You take your place in my cabinet, he told Thompson, and I will move McIsaac. You get McIsaac out of his seat before I resign from the Supreme Court, replied Thompson. Macdonald looked around at his cabinet members. They were all pretty old. He picked Charles Tupper to go to Halifax with an offer for the Liberal incumbent: if he would resign his seat and persuade his party not to run a strong race against his man in Antigonish, the judge's chair was his. McIsaac went for it, and when John Thompson had his agreement in writing, he resigned his seat on the Supreme Court, and took the train to Ottawa.

In Nova Scotia a voter inherits his franchise. There are Liberal families and Conservative families. But then there are Protestant families and Catholic families. The convert judge had as good a chance as any Tory to talk the Antigonish people around. Besides, he had his best political friend, the Catholic bishop John Cameron, smoothing things in Antigonish. The Liberals kept their bargain, but there were a lot of Tories who were incensed by the favour done McIsaac. Despite promises they had made to the bishop, they backed an independent Conservative doctor, Alexander McIntosh, who decided to run against the prime minister's lad. The Liberals rallied behind the town doctor.

Fortunately, the Liberals in Ontario came to Thompson's help. Orangemen and their newspaper, the *Globe*, came out strongly against Thompson, declaring that the Catholic judge would go easy on Louis Riel. If there is one thing that people in Nova Scotia cannot abide, it is interference in their politics from Upper Canada. Thompson himself was reluctant to practise deceit or dramatics; he was more like Sandy Mackenzie than John A. Macdonald. His party and his churchmen had to do the job for him. Bishop Cameron and John Thompson won the seat away from the Liberals by 228 votes. The new Justice Minister expressed his relief that his politicking days were over. The bishop smiled.

In 1887 Macdonald gave Thompson a job that he himself had tried to do in 1871. He sent his Justice Minister to Washington to represent Canada in the Anglo-US discussions about how many of Canada's fish the USAmericans could grab. In 1871 Macdonald had been very unpopular in Washington, and had not been able to prevent US marauding of Canadian fisheries, but at least he had got the Brits to compensate Canada for their losses. Now in 1887 John Thompson did not do any better in explaining to the USAmericans how Canada felt about foreign boats in its waters in the Atlantic and Pacific, but he was at least a nuisance to the Yanks. He came away with Macdonald's opinion of our southern neighbours. In a letter home to Annie he wrote: "These Yankee politicians are the lowest race of thieves in existence." In later years he would counter USAmerican annexationists and their Canadian agents by sending spies into their meetings.

Queen Victoria knighted Thompson for his efforts in Washington, and Thompson always supported the colonial connection because he knew that the Yankees were supporting Canadian independence as a first step to annexation. He was also totally loyal to his chief. When Macdonald decided that Riel needed hanging, his Justice Minister made a brilliant defence of that decision in the House of Commons. This speech confused the Protestants in Ontario, and cut away future support for the Tories in Quebec. Still, Macdonald leaned back in his chair and watched his protégé tear the Liberals to bits with his measured judicial rhetoric. He knew that he had the man who could handle the inevitable Wilfrid Laurier.

The old goats on the Conservative side of the House were wary and perplexed at times. Used to a manipulative, theatrical pol as their leader, they wondered why Macdonald was so fond of this young man from Nova Scotia. Here was a portly fellow who avoided strong drink and backroom deals. He admitted that there were things about his country that he did not know. He listened carefully to his opponents' arguments and took notes. Later, when Abbott became prime minister, it was pretty clear to everyone that Thompson was running the government, but the latter usually refused when Abbott offered him the perquisites of first minister. As Justice Minister he worked as hard as he had always worked, and did a lot of fine-tuning of the young Dominion, especially its Criminal Code.

On September 24, 1892, the following execrably cadenced poem appeared in J.W. Bengough's Toronto weekly humour tabloid, *Grip* [Note: bad poets can be depended on to rhyme "life" with "strife"]:

> Dear Sir Abbott, we implore you, do not leave us in the lurch,
> In the face of rising clamor o'er the influence of the Church,
> Mere suggestion of Sir Thompson for Premiership appears
> Sure to raise the very devil of a storm about our ears.

You are sick, we know, and weary of the toil of party strife,
And you well may seek retirement from the cares of public life;
Gladly would we aid your purpose, but we dare not yet instal
Thompson as the actual Premier—that, we fear, would ruin all.

We will give you leave of absence, and however long you're
    gone
We will do the business for you and your stipend will run on;
Let no public cares annoy you—heed not shouts of praise or
    blame,
We don't want your able counsel—all we ask for is your name.

Sir John Thompson will relieve you when you go away from
    home,
Leave him power of attorney to effect a deal with Rome,
And to hoodwink Orange bigots who his machinations dread,
If you cannot be our captain please remain our figure-head.

But two months later the discouraged Abbott had resigned, and the old goats had to make a decision. They could choose another figurehead and let Thompson continue to pilot the ship. But now Thompson was making noises about himself retiring. He complained that in his seven years in the job he had pretty well had to do all the work himself. Macdonald had laid on him the weight of the Riel question, the Langevin scandal, the fishing squabble, the Northwest language struggle, the Jesuit estates argument, the Criminal Code, and so on. Nova Scotia was looking more pleasant all the time. He would like to have an office in the Supreme Court or Dalhousie University.

He was too nice a person to be a federal politician. He always got shortchanged in shops. Anyone with a good tale of woe would get a tear started in his eye. But Annie wanted to be the prime minister's lady. She told him that his party needed him.

That didn't work. She told him that his country needed him. That seemed to do the trick. On November 23, 1892, Thompson met the governor general. The next day Abbott quit. By the weekend the news was out: John and Annie would take over from the caretaker. Laurier would have a real contest in 1896.

Prime Minister Thompson's first big problem was the ongoing Manitoba schools debate. To recap: the Manitoba Act of 1870 had guaranteed Catholic schools. In 1890 the Liberal government in Manitoba passed a law forbidding public funding of Catholic schools. The Canadian Supreme Court overturned the Manitoba law, but the Privy Council in London restored the legislation in 1892, much to the chagrin of Justice Minister Thompson. Now the new prime minister was taking up residence in a number of vises: Quebec Catholics against Orangemen and other Protestants, west against east, provincial rights against federal law, and Canadian autonomy against Imperial justice.

Whatever the hobbled Conservative government decided to do, they would be watched by the ghosts of John A. Macdonald and Louis David Riel. Someone was going to shout "traitor!" and take their votes elsewhere. Federalists and Conservatives and Catholics and autonomists were calling for remedial legislation. A law should be passed that would reach around the Manitoba law. The Privy Council ruled that Canada could pass a federal law calling for separate school funding anywhere in the Dominion. Prime Minister Thompson thought about it, and decided to employ Macdonald's method: let it ride and hope that something else would come along to distract everyone's attention. The Liberal MPs, of course, made sure that the issue got talked about. They had a good time accusing Thompson's government of inaction. They knew that they would have slim pickings on the scandal tree.

Now what?

As the third prime minister in two years, Thompson may have felt that he should call an election in 1894. Certainly by law there had to be one in 1896, and by tradition in 1895. Looking around him, he noticed two important things missing: one was a cabinet made up of effective campaigners; the other was an issue that might allow the party to retain power.

The USAmericans offered one in the Bering Sea. In 1867 they had bought Alaska from the Russians for seven million dollars, and claimed that they had also purchased the right to every fur-bearing seal in the North Pacific. The British held a different view: they believed that some seals should be left in the water to preserve the species, and that international waters began three miles off Alaska. In 1886 the Alaskans started grabbing British and Canadian ships and imprisoning the men on them. All this was going on while USAmerican fishermen in the North Atlantic upheld an opinion that they could chase fish inside the three-mile limit off eastern Canada. USAmerican fishermen and sealers were devotees of manifest destiny. They believed, along with Thomas Jefferson and Walt Whitman, that the western hemisphere was on its way to a happy inclusion in the USA in any case, so it was logical to apply US laws just about anywhere.

In 1890 Britain sent a declaration to Washington, in which very nice language was used to hint at military action, and the USAmericans stopped grabbing ships. During the next year the sealing countries decided to get together with some neutrals and look into the international situation, especially the agreements between the Brits and the Russians prior to 1867. The USAmericans assumed that the work would entail clarifying the correctness of the US position. The British, French, Norwegians, Italians and Swedes did not necessarily agree. One of the two British arbitrators was the prime minister of Canada. The first big meeting was held in the spring of 1893 on the Quai d'Orsay in Paris.

Thompson worked as hard as usual in Paris, but he also enjoyed the sightseeing. He and Annie left the sumptuous hotel that his aides had arranged for him and moved to a somewhat cheaper one down the street. But the five-foot-seven prime minister had to sit down and work his way through several courses of French cooking. He wore the high collar, big cravat and thick buttoned jacket of a late-Victorian gentleman, and these habiliments seemed to grow tighter during his stay in the French capital.

For a few weeks at the tribunal's table Thompson intelligently plied the little space between loyalty to Britain and neighbourliness with the US. Unfortunately for the latter, it was revealed that the documents the USAmericans had provided to show Russian control of the Bering Sea were forgeries manufactured in the US. The tribunal, with the exception of the two US representatives, voted against the US position. The USAmericans would compensate the Canadian sealers whose property had been grabbed. There would also be strong international controls on the sealing ships in Pacific waters.

For his eloquent efforts on behalf of the British, Sir John Sparrow David Thompson was appointed to the Imperial Privy Council, only the second Canadian and fourth colonial to be so honoured. He had mixed feelings about going to London. He wrote to the parliamentary secretary: "I have been so much impressed by Paris, that I look on it as rather a hardship that I shall have to spend a few days in filthy, brutal London before going home." At the end of the century the imperial capital was smoky and crumbling, whereas the City of Light was full of great painters taking advantage of the colours. Maybe the converted Catholic was thinking about the situation in Manitoba.

Most people who compare London unfavourably with Paris mention the cooking. The arbitrators on the edge of the Seine had been eating eight-course meals with several wines, whereas the most likely thing the visitor to London would find was the notorious grill-room. Chops and steaks and sausages sizzling on the gridiron! Now you are talking, said the Canadian prime minister and his wife. But that high, tight Victorian gentleman's suit would have to go back to the tailor's again. Fresh from victory in Paris, Thompson was well entertained in England. The Queen liked him. When he got home he found that Canadians seemed to like him. When the new governor general, the Earl of Aberdeen, arrived that year, the Aberdeens and the Thompsons hit it off. The five Thompson offspring spent a lot of time with Ishbel Maria Gordon, Marchioness of Aberdeen, and the latter was interested in the prime minister.

The Aberdeens were Liberals, and the Earl had for the past few years been the governor in Ireland, sympathetic to the Home Rule cause there. But any fear that the newcomers were there to usher in a Liberal government in Canada were soon put to rest. The Earl spent much of his time skating and curling, winter activities in which he became an expert. His wife was the real activist of the two. Is it unlikely that she admired the hard-working prime minister more than her sporting husband? The Ottawa establishment was not entranced by her progressive attitude, but she never lacked for support from the leader of the Conservative party. She had his total support when she helped establish the National Council of Women in 1893 and 1894. And she made certain that it was not to be a mouthpiece for the temperance movement or the Ontario Protestants. When she consented to become the first president, she did so on condition that the vice-presidents be Lady Thompson and Zoë Laurier.

It was pretty common for men in 1894 to get a chuckle out of such an idea as a National Council of Women. But when its big inaugural meeting was held in Ottawa in April of 1894, John Thompson left a noisy budget debate in the House and walked to the meeting, where he gave a speech and stayed until the event was over. Wilfrid Laurier had been invited, but had backed out. The wife of the governor general noticed that.

With all this good feeling, Thompson began to think that he stood a chance of saving Macdonald's party in the coming election. In the fall of 1893 he had toured the Ontario ridings, touting traditional Conservative positions against free trade and its resultant annexation. His secretary told him to ease his remarks and try to imitate Macdonald, who had managed to get both free traders and tariff people thinking that he was on their side. But Thompson was a judge, not a politician: he liked to be clear in his opinions. Still, he tried to avoid any discussion of the Manitoba schools question. That is before the courts, he would say. It had been before the courts for four years, and he was satisfied to let it remain there until, say, 1897. He had similar hopes about the movement for prohibition of alcohol. He saw to it that the question would be referred to lawyers who could take their time arguing about whether booze and its banning were a provincial matter or a federal one.

The climax of the tour took place in Hamilton, where on November 1, the prime minister met Sir Oliver Mowat, the long-time Liberal premier of Ontario, to unveil a granite statue of John A. Macdonald. Usually Thompson liked to make up his speeches as he went along, but he had carefully crafted this one. In it he said that Macdonald worked harder than anyone else around him, and that he had died in office because of his devotion to duty and because there was no one around to replace him. It is unlikely that any reporters attending the ceremony missed the point. Then Thompson got onto a waiting train and headed to Montreal to attend the funeral of John Abbott, who had died the day before.

The good die young

In the late-Victorian period it was desirable to look prosperous, and to look prosperous it was normal to look substantial, to have what was jocularly called a "corporation." The stout prime minister certainly filled yards of material, and might appear to be a well-off man. In the years to come, curious citizens might notice that a president or a prime minister seemed somehow to be wealthier at the end of his administration than he was going in. John A. Macdonald had had to dance to keep ahead of his creditors, it is true, but he had no gift for finances. Sandy Mackenzie was a self-made man. But John Thompson was an enigma to a lot of his contemporaries. He allowed millionaires to buy dinner for him, but he did not want to join them otherwise. He always said that he detested the notion of being wealthy. He gave great dinners at his home, but Annie did most of the cooking. The prime minister got lots of financial offers but he always turned them down.

His colleagues scratched their heads. Sir Charles Tupper said that Thompson's refusal to take the money and make his family more comfortable was somehow immoral. The judge from Nova Scotia helped the women form their council. He brought in legislation creating an annual Labour Day. He amended the Criminal Code to get children out of adult prisons, and bring in a parole system. Here he was, taking care of the edges of society, but dooming his family to honest poverty. Here he was, working all the day and half the night, and giving the labourers an annual holiday.

The prime minister was himself persuaded to take a vacation in the summer of 1894. The family went to a little island in Muskoka, and had picnics and boat cruises and photo sessions. Once in a while Thompson would go somewhere to give a speech, or receive his cabinet on the island, where some time could be profitably employed in making political decisions. By Labour Day, though, he was back in his office, working while most Canadians were enjoying their new long weekend.

The autumn was busy. Thompson spent a lot of time in train cars, writing speeches on his way to Halifax or Toronto or Montreal. On October 13 he unveiled another statue of John A. Macdonald, this a bronze one in Toronto. The crowd of 30,000 cheered both prime ministers, and Thompson smiled happily, the picture of robust energy and light mood. He was forty-nine years old. Maybe politics was not such a bad job after all. He had decided that he would lead the party in an election in 1895. If the party should win, he would tidy things up and resign a winner.

His doctors had given his heart a passing grade, but were concerned about his kidneys. They were encouraged when he decided to go to England for a month. The ostensible purpose for the trip was the ceremony for his investiture in the Privy Council. He would also accompany one of his daughters, who was going to go to school in France. Annie would not come along this time because they could not afford it after their trip of the year before. He thought that since he would be alone, with time on his hands, he might just have a few courtesy meetings with the Colonial Office. After getting a medical checkup in London, he started working as usual, preparing Canada's plans for gradually more independent status in the international community.

At Windsor Castle there were two main parts to the Privy Council ceremony—the solemn words in front of solemn lords and ladies, at which the Queen would not let anyone sit down, and the luncheon immediately afterwards, to which John Thompson was probably looking forward with more pleasure. It was a warm sunny British December 12th, there were English roses blooming outside the castle, and the Canadian prime minister was putting up with being the centre of attention. But before he could take his first bite of the expensive food, he fainted. Luncheon was delayed while he was helped to a nearby room, where he recovered, filled with embarrassment. After a while he was escorted back to his place, and now the luncheon could start again, with the Queen's doctor seated beside Thompson. He mentioned to the doctor that he had felt some pain in his chest, and then without touching a morsel of food, fainted again. This time he was dead in the doctor's arms.

The Queen gave her new privy councillor the royal treatment. A special train and gun carriage took the body to Portsmouth, where a British battleship was prepared to sail for Halifax, in which city there was a great funeral, and where the hope of the Conservative party was laid to rest in the little Catholic cemetery.

CHAPTER 8

THE ENIGMATIC
ORANGEMAN

———◆———

Mackenzie Bowell 1894–96

O NE OF THE GREAT puzzles of Canadian parliamentary history ensued on John Thompson's death. How, politicians
and historians asked and still ask, did Mackenzie Bowell
become prime minister of Canada in December 1894?

By any kind of logic and precedence, the job should have
gone to Charles Tupper the elder. He was the old warhorse of
the Conservative party, a Father of Confederation, the most
prominent living Conservative in the land. But he wasn't in
the land. He was enjoying the posh life as Canada's diplomatic
representative in London, and he was in no hurry to give up
that job.

Perhaps we can say that it was normal for Bowell to step up
because Thompson had sailed twice across the Atlantic and
once back, and made Bowell acting prime minister while he
was gone. But the question remains: why did he do that?

There's no mystery to Bowell's rise in Conservative ranks. He
was an ex-militiaman, he was an Orangeman, and he managed
to get elected for Belleville to the Dominion's first government

in 1867. John A. Macdonald looked at the irascible little news-paperman and counted votes.

But Bowell was the opposite of John Thompson in just about every way. Physically, he was a skinny little guy with a big white beard. He was a vehement Protestant, or at least he knew well enough to get his votes from the vehement Protestants. Whereas Thompson did not like politics very much, and liked to use the measured and sober language of a judge, Bowell could be swiftly provoked into the intemperate diatribes commonly employed by the newspaper editors of the time. While most people, even his enemies, seemed to like John Thompson, the feisty little Bowell made enemies among his cabinet confreres.

He was born in Suffolk in 1823 and, like a lot of early Ontario politicians, brought to Canada when he was a boy. He was apprenticed as a printer to the owner of the Belleville *Intelligencer*, and he would later, along with his brother-in-law, own that paper, until he got into violent arguments with the latter and bought him out. He started courting a local girl when he was a nineteen-year-old printer, and married her five years later. They would become the parents of nine children.

He had ink on his fingers and the politics of confrontation in his veins. He absolutely despised Liberals, and he just did not want to know any Catholics. But he was, despite his temper, a pragmatist, maybe even a bit of an idealistic democrat: his first and last real political campaigns would be in the service of rights for Catholic Canadians. He was not going to be a lawyer, so he set about building himself a political record based on patriotism. He founded a militia in Belleville, and patrolled Ontario's border during the time of the Fenian raids. He rose steadily in the Orange order, denouncing any accommodation of Catholics or French Canadians or Grits, until he became Grand Master for British North America. Unlike other politicians who used the

Orange order to get to high places, he kept his membership active all his life. Orangemen (and drumming boys in white shirts) paraded with their fancy cushions and banners all over Upper Canada, and reached the peak of their influence toward the end of the nineteenth century.

His first campaign took place in the 1863 election, when he inherited from his boss the Tory nomination in Belleville. The Liberals and George Brown were waging a tremendous campaign against the Tories' support of French-Canadian interests, so young Bowell sat on his personal feelings and supported his party's position. He was defeated at the polls for the first and last time. In 1867 he won the seat in Hastings North, and held it, even through Mackenzie's years, until 1892, when he was elevated to the Senate by the incoming prime minister, Thompson. John A. Macdonald, who had declared himself progressive, knew that he had to hold on to a coalition within his party, and he needed Mackenzie Bowell to rally the extreme right wing.

And finally the right wing had to be represented in cabinet. When Macdonald returned to office in 1878, he had to recognize Bowell's retaining of his seat in Belleville, and found him a safe job as Minister of Customs, the man who would implement one of the two main segments of the National Policy. When Abbott took over he made Bowell the Minister of Militia, where it did not look as if he could start any trouble. And when John Thompson succeeded Abbot he sent Bowell to the Senate, where he would act as Minister of Trade and Commerce, a new invention. Bowell was soon off to Australia, leading a trade commission without incurring any disasters. But everyone knew that his main job was to keep the Orangemen's votes coming to the Conservative party, even if that party seemed to be soft on Quebec.

Some people say that Bowell's singular lack of success as prime minister was due to his stupidity. Others blame his tendency to blow his little top. Some point to a remarkable absence of humility. Still, there are those who would have us regard the bad luck of somehow attaining the first minister's chair just when the long-smoking Manitoba schools debate burst into high hot flames.

Lord Aberdeen got off his horse long enough to direct Bowell to form the government in late December of 1894. In the last days of January 1895, the Judicial Committee of the Privy Council at last sent down the decision that Canada could overturn Manitoba's law (whereby no provincial funds would go to French and Catholic schooling), and enact remedial legislation. The word "remedial" and its various interesting French equivalents would be heard often over the next year.

The Privy Council's decision was that the Dominion government *could*, if it wanted to, bring in remedial legislation. Mackenzie Bowell could, if he wanted to, use the techniques of his predecessors—do nothing while pretending to be doing something. Certainly there were a lot of voters in Manitoba and Ontario who were not interested in "special privileges" for the 15 per cent of Manitobans who were Catholics. Of course the issue was not what some kid in Manitoba was going to experience in his classroom. It was all about the hatreds and suspicions that had been operating in all the Canadas since General Wolfe had expired so picturesquely in 1759. In Quebec the bishops, still declaring the Vatican more worthy of loyalty than Ottawa, were putting pressure on French-speaking MPs.

Some people say that Senator Bowell's elevation to the number one job in Canada turned his head. A few others might have said that he was an upholder of federal rights over provincial challenges. People with devious minds might suggest that he wanted to steal Wilfrid Laurier's thunder. Whatever the case, he put his name to an Order-in-Council demanding that Manitoba restore the separate schools. Premier Greenaway still had

Clifford Sifton as attorney general, and Sifton was as much a rammer as Bowell. Forget it, he told Bowell. Bowell told the Protestants that it was not his idea, that he was carrying out the will of the Queen and her Privy Council. Well, said a number of people in his own cabinet, that is not quite true—the Privy Council had deliberately suggested the status quo.

Before 1895 had become very old, Mackenzie Bowell lost control of his cabinet. Charles Tupper the younger demanded that the prime minister go to the public with a referendum on the Manitoba schools question. Bowell was not about to suffer demands from his ministers. Pretty soon the members of the cabinet were fighting among themselves and ignoring the prime minister. Bowell, like Abbott, had the disadvantage of trying to govern from the Senate. No normal work was getting done, and the Manitobans were threatening to bring Canada to a hacking, coughing halt. Two Quebec ministers threatened to resign if the remedial legislation did not go through. Even more English-speaking ministers threatened to resign if it was not withdrawn. How was Bowell expecting to get out of this jam?

Once again he decided to come down on the side of Catholic rights. He reasoned that this way he would hold the Quebec voters and force Laurier to side with him. He would try to mollify the Orangemen by saying that London had tied his hands. He was encouraged by Laurier's silence. Laurier could not seem to decide what position to take. He had a problem much like Bowell's, except that he had the luck to be in opposition. If he sided with Manitoba, he would ensure the Liberal votes in Ontario. But what would happen to his Quebec support, especially with the bishops coming down on him?

Laurier liked the party system because it looked as if his party was about to begin another reign. He was afraid that the west-east, Catholic-Protestant, provincial-federal animosities would split party lines and produce some kind of "chaos" across the country. He was a law graduate of McGill. He did not like chaos.

Laurier's Canadian bacon was saved by a Quebec conservative who lived with the Liberals. This was Joseph-Israël Tarte, who had followed Laurier to the College de l'Assomption seven years after him, and had become a crusty newspaperman, a Vatican man and a Conservative MP in the 1891 election. He was instrumental in turfing Langevin, and saw enough scandal among the Tories to move him over to the conservative wing of the Grits. He always had a big mouth and no patience, but now he whispered to Wilfrid Laurier the measured words that would send his chief to safety.

It was simple. Say as little as possible about Manitoba, but when asked, come out in support of the Dominion. This way you will win the Protestant swing vote in the other provinces. As for the voters in Quebec? Don't worry: they want a French-Canadian prime minister, even an anti-Catholic. The people of Quebec have more sentiment than policy. Comb your hair to look like a Gallic Macdonald—he won elections on his personality and aura. But remember: say as little as possible. Keep the Conservatives in the dark.

This was a strange time indeed. Here was Tarte advising his leader to be as little like Tarte as possible. Here was a French-Catholic leader opposing the Roman Church, and an old Orangeman championing the Catholics in Manitoba. Politics, it would seem, is more about winning somehow, less about traditional positions. More about arithmetic than history.

But Bowell had enemy forces on all sides. There was a snap election in Manitoba, and the Liberals won there on a promise to defy Ottawa. This got Bowell's back up. Parliament was about to open. He took the draft of his remedial legislation to his cabinet for polishing. Seven of his ministers stood up and demanded that the prime minister resign. They were led by Charles Tupper the younger and George Foster, the Finance Minister from New Brunswick.

Now Mackenzie Bowell uttered his most famous words. He called his caucus a "nest of traitors." He accepted seven resignations and tried to find replacements. Time was pressing. There was a session and an election coming up quickly. The train station in Ottawa was full of ex-cabinet members who met every train and talked with all the arriving Tory MPs. No one volunteered to join Bowell's cabinet. He was stuck. You do not enter Parliament without a cabinet, especially if you are sitting in the upper house. He had to give in to the nest of traitors. This was the deal they offered: Bowell could stay on as a lame-duck prime minister until the spring sitting of the House of Commons was over. Charles Tupper the elder would run things from his new seat in the lower house. When Parliament was prorogued, Bowell would resign and Tupper would lead the Conservatives into the summer election. This was another strange situation. One can be sure that on the death of John Thompson the nascent rebels had informed the governor general that they would like Tupper to become prime minister. But Lady Aberdeen was a feminist, and she did not like the stories she had heard about Charles Tupper and his extramarital adventures in England. Hence the puzzling Bowell.

But in April the Maritimer with the big heavy head became Conservative leader, and the little fellow with the big white beard tromped back to the Senate, where he would sit, getting more and more waspish, until his death in December of 1917. For the first ten years he was the leader of the opposition in the Senate. He was supposed to be a Conservative, but he once announced that he was so disgusted with party politics that he was representing principles instead.

In 1905 he may have chanced to read Wilfred Campbell's newly published sonnet entitled "The Politician":

Carven in leathern mask or brazen face.
　　Were I time's sculptor, I would set this man.
　　Retreating from the truth, his hawk-eyes scan
The platforms of all public thought for place.
There wriggling with insinuating grace,
　　He takes poor hope and effort by the hand,
　　And flatters with half-truths and accents bland,
Till even zeal and earnest love grow base.

Knowing no right, save power's grim right-of-way;
　　No nobleness, save life's ignoble praise;
No future, save this sordid day to day;
　　He is the curse of these material days:
Juggling with mighty wrongs and mightier lies,
This worshipper of Dagon and his flies!

"Nest of traitors!" the forgotten old prime minister may have mumbled.

CHAPTER 9

CALLING THE DOCTOR

Charles Tupper 1896

IF ONE OF THE GREAT puzzles of Canadian history is Mackenzie Bowell's becoming prime minister, another is the fact that Sir Charles Tupper did not, until those ten weeks in 1896. The main problem was that he was born when John A. Macdonald was six years old. He was one of the most prominent Fathers of Confederation, and Macdonald's chief ally in the long years of Conservative reign. He brought Nova Scotia into the fold, and talked to Louis Riel in Fort Garry. He claimed to have invented the National Policy. He even looked like a model for Toryism, big and bluff, bulldog-faced and wrapped in yards of thick Victorian cloth. If John A. Macdonald had carried through on one of his many threats to perish before 1891, Charles Tupper would probably have been the archetypal prime minister of the rough new Dominion.

He was not a lawyer or a newspaperman. He did not spend his spare time amassing large tracts of real estate. He was a small-town doctor with a social conscience. He was born in the summer of 1821 in Amherst, Nova Scotia, where his father was the Baptist preacher. He inherited the puritan predilection for hard work and social reform that Sandy Mackenzie had learned as a convert. But Sandy Mackenzie was a private-enterprise man. Charles Tupper believed that any government owes something to the future of its country's populace. When as premier he would pass provincial legislation providing free schooling in Nova Scotia, a lot of tax-paying businessmen called him a radical.

When he was nineteen years old, he sailed to Edinburgh because that was the best place in the English-speaking world to learn medicine. He learned enough in three years to prepare him for a physician's job back home in Cumberland County. He could have made more money in Halifax, but there were lots of mines in Cumberland County, and lots of work for a country doctor. Even in that job he proved a good politician. In the years 1867-70, while he gave up his chance to serve in Macdonald's first cabinet, he was the president of the Canadian Medical Association. Mackenzie Bowell may have gathered a lot of votes as top man in the Orange order, but you could bank some moral suasion by being president of the CMA.

Tupper did think that morality and politics were just about the same thing. He and Macdonald made a good pair: Macdonald had the subtle, crafty, devious mind for the ins and outs of fundraising and campaigning; this maritime bulldog always walked in a straight line, and if he came to a door he threw it open and strode into whatever was on the other side. He believed that if you believed in something you should say it. In 1896 Wilfrid Laurier knew better.

But early in his life Tupper pulled off some neat surprises. In Nova Scotia, before and after 1867, he went about extolling Confederation while just about every other politician was against it. Joseph Howe, the Reform champion, was the most famous anti-Confederationist in the colony, and in the election of 1855 he was running in Cumberland County, so the thirty-four-year-old Tupper accepted the Conservatives' sacrificial candidature there. Howe made fun of the young yokel doctor all through the campaign, but Tupper won it. The Conservatives took notice, and when they won a majority two years later they made him provincial secretary. By 1864 he was premier of Nova Scotia.

In 1867 Joseph Howe's Liberals took their power back, but Tupper was Cumberland County's federal man. He had been at the famous conferences, watching Macdonald's back while John A. did the dancing. Tupper dreamed of railroads built by the government, a line connecting the Maritimes to Montreal and Ottawa, and steel running to the Pacific Ocean. In the first session of Macdonald's 1867 Parliament, all the other Nova Scotia members were secessionists, a kind of Bloc Nova Scotian. But he was not a cabinet minister. All the historians make note of that fact—the Bulldog knew that Macdonald owed too much to too many men. He would wait his turn. Meanwhile he had the Canadian Medical Association to organize.

Macdonald needed someone to mollify Joseph Howe. There were too many people listening to the secessionist. Again Tupper pulled off a surprise. He walked through Howe's door and talked straight, like a country doctor. By 1869 Howe was in Macdonald's cabinet. Every time Macdonald needed someone to talk to his enemies he sent Tupper. When Louis Riel grabbed Fort Garry, and Macdonald sent Wandering Willy McDougall out to fly the Canadian flag, McDougall had one of Tupper's daughters with him. She was married to one of his officers. Tupper went through the door at Fort Garry and had a talk with Louis Riel. Riel told him not to worry about his daughter, but to tell his boss there was a new government out here.

Like Bowell in Belleville, Tupper kept on winning elections in Cumberland County, even when other prominent Tories were losing theirs. He remained bluff and confident. He called the events of 1872 the "Pacific Slander," and when the Tories got back in, Macdonald made him Minister of Public Works. Get me a railroad to my riding in Victoria, he said. Over the years Tupper held all the important ministries except the top one. By 1884 he was sixty-three years old and looking for something cushy. Macdonald made him his High Commissioner in London. He was a baron over there now, and he liked the posh ambassadorial life. He worked hard, of course, and when Macdonald needed him to fight a tough election back in Canada he did so and represented Cumberland County for a year. He went back to London in 1888 and began to settle into a comfortable old age. Even when his son tried to get him into the prime minister's chair after Macdonald's death, he demurred. Maybe he had heard about Lady Aberdeen's suspicions.

In 1895 he was back in Canada. The official purpose was to help get the Atlantic shipping project going, but there are people who think that his son had been pleading with him to help get Bowell out of office and save the party. As if anything were going to save the party. Maybe if the world-wide depression were to suddenly end, that would save the party. But the Tories missed their old legend. Charles Tupper was the grand old man of the party, but he was not a legend.

Now the seven cabinet ministers started their strike. Their picket line met all the trains. You cannot go back to England, they told Tupper. I am seventy-five years old, he said, my wife likes it in London. The party needs you, they told him. Look around. Tupper looked around, and all he could see was faithful old George Foster. He accepted their draft.

He may have been the most respected Tory alive, but he was still a loyal party man. All his years as Macdonald's enforcer had taught him to follow the policy. Bowell's policy was remedial legislation, and Bowell had been the prime minister.

Charles Tupper could have hemmed and hawed. He had to call an election that year. No one would have been surprised to see the Manitoba schools question remain a question for another year or two. Wilfrid Laurier was not saying anything. But the party man had the bill read for the second time. He invoked Section 93 of the British North America Act. Now Wilfrid Laurier spoke out against remedial legislation and against the Catholic bishops. The Baptist prime minister stuck up for the Catholic Métis of Manitoba. This is what he said in the House debate:

> I put it to any intelligent man who recognizes the fact that within this wide Dominion you have got over 41 per cent of the population Roman Catholics; I put it to gentlemen who may hold—and I think some have without due consideration held— rather narrow views on the subject; I put it to them: whether for any object that was not of the most transcendent importance it would be right for this Government to refuse, or right for this Parliament to refuse, to grant redress in a case such as is presented on the present occasion, and to leave rankling in the minds of over 41 per cent of the entire population of this country, [blah blah blah] obtain the same consideration that he would obtain if he were a Protestant.

You could get lost in the middle of a Tupperian sentence, but he knew how to end them eventually.

Laurier tended to go for metaphors and other poetic devices. His favourite way into an argument was a little self-praise. In this instance he portrayed himself as a crusader rising above petty sectarian loyalties for the greater good of the whole country. Then he adopted the classic argument that honey is preferable to vinegar:

The demon of discord is in the land, blowing the wind of strife over all and in all directions, awakening slumbering passions, arousing old prejudices. . . . If religious war is to be brought in this country, by whose action will it be brought but by the action of this Government, which, although it had the methods of persuasion in its hands, has chosen to take the methods of coercion in order to redress a wrong.

The Liberal leader was quite aware, of course, that his future lieutenant Clifford Sifton was not going to hang around and listen to any "methods of persuasion."

The Liberals delayed and delayed as much as they could. Tupper kept the House open. An MP could go out to the toilet, but he had to come back and listen. The Bulldog was hoping for a vote, but time ran out. He had to shut the door and prepare for the election of 1896. Wilfrid Laurier was twenty years younger than he. But Laurier had a lot of opposition in his own party, the ultramontane Catholics, the Rielistes. Despite the hard times that Macdonald had claimed came with Liberal regimes, there seemed to be a chance that Canadians would rally to a party that at last had its proper and natural leader.

Retiring the grandfathers of Confederation

He was the fifth Conservative prime minister in the nineties and it was only 1896. Three of the other four were already dead. The century itself was on its last legs. Charles Tupper was a doctor: he knew about old age and death. And now he had to go into an election against a lively young man with Macdonald hair, and what manner of men were going to help him against the Liberal from Quebec? The bishops with their loyalty to a tiny country across the ocean.

Tupper did not twig about Joseph-Israël Tarte's clever gamble. How was he to know that Laurier was thinking more about arithmetic than philosophy when he turned his back to the clergy? In any case, the Constitution seemed to be Tupper's only plank. In these long-dragged-out hard times, it would not be wise to tout the National Policy. He could mention Macdonald's name a lot, but it would not be smart to mention his successors. He had to hope that the 59 per cent of the population that was not Catholic would never elect a French Canadian as prime minister. Maybe the Bulldog would be prime minister for more than ten weeks.

But Laurier was not just a French Canadian. He was a Liberal. One of the advantages of the latter fact was that he was not a Conservative. Tarte's plan would bring results. The editor of the *Globe* had written Laurier a letter in 1895:

I do not want to preach to you but I cannot refrain from telling you that if you can avoid any declaration in favour of remedial legislation it will be an enormous advantage in Ontario. Be sure that this Province will destroy any party that attempts arbitrary interference in Manitoba. The feeling has grown enormously strong. Be sure also that the Liberals are gaining in Ontario steadily and that nothing can save the Tories if you can maintain your present ground, and all depends on you.

Tupper ran in Cape Breton, and he retained his new seat. But young Laurier took forty-eight seats in Quebec and forty-four seats in Ontario. The Liberals had a majority of twenty-three. They were back in power after eighteen years of opposition. It was Louis Riel's third uprising. There were more Conservatives than Liberals elected in Manitoba, but in Quebec they loved their dashing new leader.

Tupper would hang on as the Tory leader. He said that a

temporary changing of the guard was good for the country. Laurier was presenting himself as the man who could promote harmony between the two "races." But it was not a temporary change. In the 1900 election old man Tupper lost his Cape Breton seat and retired from politics. He would be a writer and a grand old man. He retired to Vancouver, but in 1913 he went back to England and became the old Queen's privy councillor. His wife had died in 1912. Tupper may have been prime minister for only ten weeks, but he was married to Frances for sixty-five years. He was a man who set records. Just before his death in 1915 he was proclaimed "Canada's Grand Old Man," which must have made the wizened Mackenzie Bowell sputter one last time.

Tupper's body, like Thompson's, was brought back to Canada on the deck of a British battleship. He was the last of the Fathers of Confederation. He was the last of the sons of British immigrants. There were Canadian troops fighting on the European continent, and they were not just a segment of the imperial forces. The Macdonald era was officially over.

CHAPTER 10

Young Tomorrow

———◆·◆·◆———

Wilfrid Laurier 1896–1911

MENTION SIR Wilfrid Laurier's name, and almost 50 per cent of Canadians will recognize it, and some of the older ones might quote him as saying "The twentieth century will belong to Canada." What he did say, during the 1904 election campaign was the less abrupt "I think we can claim that it is Canada that shall fill the twentieth century." There were a lot of other people saying roughly similar things around then, the times being so good, but Laurier was the prime minister. He was famous for saying things, and not at all reluctant to take credit for the good times.

In the last years of the nineteenth century and the first years of the twentieth century there were a lot of countries that looked upon the twentieth century as theirs. When John A. Macdonald won his last election in 1891, only half a century had passed since the Act of Union had basted the two Canadas together. At the turn of the century you had to have a powerful navy to impress anyone. You had to show up with that navy on the other side of some ocean to look like a contender.

At the turn of the century the white people saw the planet Earth as a globe on which to float their navies toward land to grab. Canada was almost surrounded by oceans, but did not have a navy. It had a railroad that stretched across a sea of grass.

The prime minister would get a navy for Canada, but the navy would be one of the causes for the fall from power of the prime minister.

Young wraith

Je me souviens it says on the Quebec licence plate. The prime minister who made so much of Canada's future was born in a leafy village called Saint-Lin, where the villagers might be labouring and worshipping in a kind of attenuated New France. The Church was in charge of religion, schooling and politics. Montreal was forty kilometres and two centuries away. But not really: four years before Wilfrid Laurier's birth the English had put down Seigneur Papineau's rebellion, and there was still a bit of smoke in the air. A few months before the boy baby came into the winter world, a new country had been manufactured out of Canada East and Canada West.

The governors general of post-Confederation Canada were men from Britain. The first six prime ministers were the sons of men from Britain. The seventh, like most Quebeckers, had an ancestor who came up the St Lawrence in the seventeeth century. It wasn't anyone named Laurier. Augustin Hébert would leave his name to a lot of Quebeckers, but only some genes to Wilfrid Laurier. Hébert was with de Maisonneuve when Montreal was founded as a holy and strategic town in 1642, the year in which Armand du Plessis, the first ever prime minister, was to die. Thirty-four years later Hébert's grand-daughter would marry a soldier who had arrived in New France in 1665. This was a man named François Cottineau, who decided to go by the name of Champlaurier, after the laurel country of his childhood in France.

The family did not move far. After eight generations they were living between Montreal and the mountains, and they were still changing the family name. Wilfrid's grandfather Charles shortened it to Laurier, and Wilfrid's father, Charles, altered his first name to Carolus. How did his ninth-generation Lower-Canadian son get the Anglo-Saxon name Wilfrid? His mother, Thérèse, was a romantic woman. She had several miscarriages before her only son was born, and she had been reading Sir Walter Scott's *Ivanhoe* during her confinement. In that most British of romances, published in 1819, Wilfred of Ivanhoe joins Robin Hood and others in rallying Saxons against corrupt and rebellious Norman knights. The romance was immensely popular all over the English world.

That Wilfrid Laurier should have an English-French name, both halves derived from fictions, was perhaps prophetic. That he should get an English schooling was politic. After a primary education in a French-Catholic school, he was despatched to the nearby Scottish settlement of New Glasgow, where he lived for two years with a family named Murray, and attended a Presbyterian school and evening prayers. During his teen years he got a classical education at the nearby college of L'Assomption. When he was twenty he went to Montreal and studied law at McGill University. He also worked in the office of Rodolphe Laflamme, the most prominent Liberal lawyer in town.

The journey from L'Assomption to Laflamme was geographically short and politically long. At college the gentle Wilfrid would be found reading Latin history and French poetry, but never banging knees and heads on the playing fields. At places such as L'Assomption a classical education meant the priests' version of religion, history and literature. But Wilfrid Ivanhoe had been away from the priests for a few years, and he found his own way into the books he read. He was a boy with a philosophical head and a radical heart. He took to the debating society as a kitten takes to a rug. But when he argued that the Huguenots should have been allowed to settle in New France, the priests decided that L'Assomption could do without a debating society. They should have marked their calendars; they would wait forever for a second chance to shut that boy up.

The twenty-year-old was a romantic, even Gothic figure about McGill and Montreal. For one thing, he persisted in his frail health, spitting blood into a handkerchief and resembling an exquisite corpse that could have been blown away by a brisk December wind. But he was working day and night, while practising the manners of a gentleman, and learning the radical philosophy of the *Rouges*. One should not confuse the Quebec reds with the reds in Europe. In Europe they were inheritors of the French Revolution; in Quebec they were representative of the anti-clerical liberalism found overseas. Laurier would later call himself a follower of Burke. As valedictorian for the class of 1864 at McGill he championed tolerance between Protestants and Catholics, between French and English.

In Canada East it took a lot of energy to go up against the clergy. The bishops were somewhat right of the Pope. There was a majority of country folk who let the priests do their reading and thinking for them. And there were French-Canadian nationalists who regarded the Church as their best bulwark against Orangemen and Imperialists. But the Lower-Canada Liberals, whose relationship with Upper-Canada Liberals was a kind of alliance, had a lot of nationalists of their own. They could forget that Papineau was a medieval landlord who left the country when things got hot. Papineau had become a republican, and the young *Rouges* liked the idea of a republic, whether an independent one or the one already waiting to the south. In

the meantime they fought the bishops, demanding that education be taken out of church hands, that the priests get their
noses out of secular business.

In those years the Catholic Church had become the most
conservative force trying to hold back the great liberalizing
movements of the nineteenth century. The bishops and cardi-
nals preached that anyone leaning toward liberal ideas was a
heretic, and anyone voting for liberals was a sinner. This was
perhaps easier to do in Quebec than in Europe, because nearly
the whole Catholic population was descended from immigrants
who had arrived during the last days of the Church's medieval
dream. So when young Laurier went to the Eastern Townships
for his health, and started a liberal newspaper there, the priests
told their parishioners that reading the paper would endanger
their immortal souls, and the paper folded for lack of readers.

As a newspaperman he did not make it, but as a lawyer he
sailed. He had eloquent command of all three languages—
French, English and Latin. His voice could melt a frozen heart.
He quoted great literature and always used the perfect word
while persuading listeners that they knew what it meant. In 1897
he would insist that he was inveigled into accepting the Queen's
dubbing him Sir Wilfrid, but he was from the beginning fash-
ioning himself into the perfect gentle knight. He used his voice
and manners to persuade political companions to find space
along the middle road. He did hold the nineteenth-century liberal notion of the "perfectability of man," and the wisdom of
the popular ballot. Those tenets would infuriate the Church
and win the young politician a chair in the cabinet of Alexander Mackenzie.

In 1871, at age thirty, he entered the Quebec legislature, where
he made everyone sit up with his gorgeous rhetoric. In 1874 he
resigned and got himself a federal seat. Everyone in the Liberal
hierarchy noticed him. Too bad that he is so young, they said.

Too bad that he is a French Canadian, they said. But Laurier set about getting older, and he made himself the leading expert in British governance and jurisprudence. He became a kind of anglophile. Later, at imperial conferences he would try to save the idea of British progressive civilization against its enemies in the British establishment.

He may have been young, but he became Edward Blake's Quebec lieutenant when Blake succeeded Mackenzie as leader. He did not speak much in Parliament. Blake put people to sleep with his long detailed legalistic arguments. On the occasions when Laurier would utter some sentences, there were ears that knew they were hearing the Liberal future. Macdonald was carrying two of those ears.

Macdonald had made himself into a myth, and he must have known what he was seeing across the house. Like him, this young man was a dandy. He even had Macdonald hair. He had gold-rimmed *pince-nez* glasses that dangled beautifully on a silk ribbon. He was as hopeless as Macdonald about dollars and cents. But he was also the old man's antithesis. He never slapped another man on the back or uttered homely bar-room jokes. He was not a man among men. He preferred to discourse lightly about popular fiction with the ladies. One could not imagine him lurching across a stage in an attempt to throttle his foe. He had a certain *hauteur*, but he knew how to join in an argument, and unlike Macdonald, he kept track of details.

He was learning how to become prime minister of a dominion in the British Empire. As a young *Rouge* he had gone along with that group's various attacks on the Church and Britain and even Confederation. But he was not a Quebec Liberal; he was a classic nineteenth-century British Liberal. In other words, he was a progressive moderate in an age that was beginning to promise violent revolution. In a speech that would soon become famous, he told two thousand people at a hall in Quebec City in 1877:

I am a Liberal. I am one of those who think that everywhere in human things there are abuses to be reformed, new horizons to be opened up and new forces to be developed . . . I hate revolutions and detest all attempts to win the triumph of opinions by violence. . . . There is always room for the perfecting of our nature and for the attainment by a larger number of an easier way of life.

He said that the French-Canadian people and the Catholic Church had been treated better than any other conquered people had been treated, and that the Church, free itself, should not fight an election by threat and coercion.

Laurier was trying to figure out how to be a French-Canadian Catholic and a loyal citizen of the Empire. He was trying to imagine a new kind of country while he was at it. That country needed someone who was progressive without choosing the USA as a model of progress. All his life he would have to face the fact that stiff-necks on both sides of every question would call him a traitor.

So when it came time, for instance, to fight the Tories who were adamant about hanging Louis Riel, he would not resort to shrill patriotism nor to religious rant. His arguments would rest on principles of universal justice. When Riel was dragged from his cell and hanged in Regina, the emotion in Quebec was more powerful than any natural disaster. Laurier was at his most eloquent in his parliamentary defence of the Métis. He said that they and their leader should have been defended not because they were Catholics, nor because they were French-speaking, but because they were British citizens, and they did not get from the Macdonald government the protection and rights that are due to a British citizen. He said that if he had been raised in Manitoba rather than Quebec he too would have grabbed a gun, though that is a little hard to imagine. He said that the administration of the Northwest had been a matter of "Blood, blood, blood—prisons, scaffolds, widows, orphans, destitution, ruin."

Of course his support of Riel lost him some Liberal support in Ontario. He was always balancing losses and gains. It would take him a while to learn that the best way to retain power is to make your party as much like the other party as possible. He did not know that in his first campaign against Old Tomorrow in 1891. He made a mistake that he would not make again until 1911. Macdonald had himself a railroad, and he had his "National Policy." The Liberals were still running on various versions of reciprocity, and some of them suggested US absorption down the line. Still, the decrepit Tories could just manage their slimmest majority, and after Macdonald died Laurier made mincemeat of their other four prime ministers in the next half-decade.

Then came 1896, and the smart Tarte campaign end-run that brought the Liberals to power again. Laurier was fifty-five years old, just barely older than Macdonald was in 1867. He had been the eloquent Liberal leader for nine years, and he would lead his party for another twenty-three. He would reign as the brightest prime minister in the British Empire for fifteen years.

Laurier's first job was to organize a cabinet, and according to the stories the Liberal party tells itself, his first cabinet was the best ever seen. Laurier chucked out the old guys and replaced them with hotshot provincial politicians. One of the most interesting assignments was Mr Sifton of Manitoba, who became Minister of the Interior. This would be an instance of good timing for everyone, because a year after the Grits came to power, the depression was over, and immigrants began streaming into the Canadian west. The CPR was making money. It was just about time to create a couple more provinces out there, to neaten things up.

Meanwhile, there was that main question in Sifton's province: the Manitoba schools act had been the hot issue in the election campaign, and the new prime minister had to address it at last, or at least he felt that he had to address it. He had Sifton on one side of him and the bishops on the other, both sides playing with little string nooses. It was time for a compromise; it was time for the great conciliator to pave the moderate road. Or one might say that it was time to not quite please either side, but to leave either side with not enough fury to cause serious trouble.

Unlike Macdonald, Laurier liked the idea of provincial rights. He also liked the idea of Liberal provinces. The deal that he worked out sounded like good laissez-faire Burkean business. The Manitobans agreed to give the last half-hour of every school day over to religious teaching, not necessarily Catholic, but by "any Christian clergyman." They also stipulated that students were not obliged to stay at school for that last half-hour. Laurier turned to the bishops in Quebec and said well, at least I tried—I didn't get everything I wanted but what I got is better than nothing, isn't it? The Bishops said that it was not enough, and advised their parishioners that buying or reading any Liberal newspaper was a serious sin. Laurier went over their heads. He and forty-four of his MPs sent a message to Rome. Pretty soon Rome sent an emissary to talk with the Quebec bishops, and their attacks were put on hold—until events west of Manitoba.

Now Wilfrid Ivanhoe set about correcting the mistake he had made in 1891. He began to make the Liberal party more closely resemble the Tories who had done so well for thirty years. Stop talking about North American reciprocity, he told his MPs. He did not use the term, of course, but he fine-tuned Macdonald's National Policy, and he was lucky enough to have the good times that made it possible. Then he had his Finance Minister,

William S. Fielding, reduce the tariff on British goods. This action endeared him to the Brits and frustrated the Canadian Tories, who saw their bombs being defused.

Oh, they seemed to love him in Britain. When they looked around at the map of the world and saw all the red-coloured countries, they could not find a prime minister or governor as beautiful. He was a handsome man with impeccable clothes. His voice could induce peaches to fall from the trees. He spoke the most elegant sentences heard in any parliament at the end of the nineteenth century. He maintained a sunny disposition that seemed to promise a wonderful new century. In June of 1897 he was in London to take part in Queen Victoria's Silver Jubilee and the colonial conference. The hosts put him up in the biggest suite at the Cecil Hotel, and the Queen made him a member of her Privy Council, so that he would have to wear archaic and flamboyant clothing. When the biggest parade in the history of Britain was held, it was led by the golden coaches of the royal family, followed by the coach of the Canadian prime minister, followed by all the other colonial vehicles. Wilfrid Laurier, the boy from Saint-Lin, sat there in his pointy shoes and feathery hat and listened to the Londoners roaring their admiration. It was almost enough to make him forget what he had come to London for.

The British Colonial Office really liked what they saw. They wanted to make this beautiful French-Canadian loyalist their poster boy for empire. He had come out of the Iroquois-infested backwoods of Lower Canada and managed to become an orator to make people remember and forget Edmund Burke. And he hadn't died with his face in the soup. The Durham Report was graciously vindicated. Laurier liked the pomp, but he knew that he was being patronized by Colonial Secretary Joseph Chamberlain and the other stuffed shirts in London.

The immense celebrations for the Queen's sixtieth year on

the throne featured jewel-bedecked Asians, feathered Africans, silk-shoed New Zealanders, and Canadians with dead beavers on their heads. The English-speaking world had never seen anything like it. The people at the Colonial Office saw the festivities as homage from all parts of the globe, and knew that the British Empire was bigger than it had ever been. They did not know that the rose was just about blown.

Laurier smiled and bowed when he was supposed to, and Chamberlain thought that he had a perfect lieutenant at the colonial conference. He did not know that Laurier would soon have it renamed the imperial conference. He did not know that Laurier would spend his fifteen years in power redefining the definition of the Dominion of Canada, addressing the question of how British the Dominion would be. Chamberlain liked to expound on the superiority of the British "race." He said it was "infallibly destined to be the predominating force in the future history and civilization of the world." He had forgotten that the Canadian prime minister, though he spoke better English than anyone around him, was not a member of the British "race."

Laurier smiled and bowed. He listened to the plan that Joseph Chamberlain laid out at the conference. The dominions and the colonies would sit in council with the mother country and work out a world-wide system of economic and military planning. This system would take precedence over measures enacted in the dominions and colonies. But Laurier was a man who listened to ideas about provincial rights within a confederation. He was not about to become a complacent centralist in a world order. As far as he was concerned there was no room in the twentieth century for taxation and conscription on an imperial basis, as suggested by Chamberlain's plan.

Now the Brits were confused. How could such an intelligent colonial not understand what they were proposing? Laurier understood, though, and when the British Colonial Office tried similar notions five and ten years later, Canada still said no, we will not send our money to build a Royal Navy, and no, we will enter any wars we enter not as Brits but as Canadians. At the conferences Laurier would beautifully profess Canada's loyalty, but it slowly dawned on the Brits that this leader of the dominions was talking about loyalty to the idea of a family of nations, not to the country that considered itself the head of the family.

Of course there were anglophiles in Ontario who thought the prime minister was a French Canadian who was out to destroy the family. But there were nationalists in Quebec who did not like to see this native son riding around in London in pointed shoes and feathers. Laurier knew that he would be in this sandwich all his life. In the 1900 election Sir Charles Tupper would campaign in Quebec, where he would say that Wilfrid seemed too English to him, and he would stump in Ontario, where he would say that Laurier was too damned French. Macdonald had made it sound simple: "a British subject I was born; a British subject I will die." Now this intellectual in office would ask: what, exactly does that phrase "a British subject" mean?

What is Canada?

The contents of the sandwich had to show what he was made of soon after his adventures in London. The British were gearing up for a war against the Boers in the Transvaal. It was the end of the nineteenth century, and big world economies were based on gold, and there was a lot of gold in the Transvaal. The way the British told it was that the brutal Boers were not allowing the English people in the Transvaal to have citizenship. This was an outrage. The Colonial Secretary sent messages to the dominions and colonies, advising that he expected money and men to help enlighten the Boers.

Legally, Chamberlain may have been wrong about the war but right about the help he was asking for. In Canada there were obviously mixed feelings about this war, which would break out in 1899. The Tories and other stiff-necked anglophiles huffed and puffed. The French Canadians pointed out that Canadian security was not at stake, that not even British security was at stake, and that from where they sat it looked as if the war would be about the British Empire putting down another people's attempt to express its desire for independence. Some Quebeckers also pointed out that Britain did not have a good record at protecting Canadian interests against foreign depredations, principally USAmerican.

Mr Middle-of-the-Road worked out another of his smooth compromises, knowing that it would not be without problematical ramifications in later years. By Laurier's Order-in-Council, Canada would assemble a thousand volunteers, pay for their gear and transport, and let them fight as Canadian units. They would be fighting under the British command, and they would be paid by the Brits. Volunteers spoke up across Canada, and several more units followed the first batch. Donald Smith, the old railroad man, paid for a cavalry outfit named after him—Strathcona's Horse. Union Jacks filled the air. Eventually seven thousand Canadians fought in Lord Kitchener's vicious war, dodging rifle fire, burning Dutch and African farms, guarding concentration camps filled with Dutch women and children. Eventually the Brits and their colonists would win the war that introduced the twentieth century. They had half a million troops and the enemy had eighty thousand. The Brits did not have to climb any cliff to the plains of anybody.

Laurier's compromise was the best he could do. He used all

his skills as an orator to calm the situation. It was becoming clear to him that he would always have to do this. He hoped that somehow the split between French and English would not characterize all international decisions for the rest of time. On this occasion he pointed out that the majority of public opinion was calling for Canadian troops, and that no government should ignore public opinion. That was not good enough for Henri Bourassa.

Henri Bourassa was the loose cannon on the Liberal deck. He was a firebrand nationalist, a haywire agitator, an uncompromising descendant of the vanishing rebel Louis Joseph Papineau. That is the way the Tories saw him. By today's standards he seems a pretty moderate French-Canadian voice. He did not like the idea that Quebec was one province among several. He said that the French Canadians were one of two peoples, and that all of Canada was Anglo-French. He did not like the notion that Canada should be part of Britain's war machine. He maintained in 1899 and in 1914 that Canada should not go to war unless directed to by the Canadian Parliament as a whole. When Laurier's cabinet issued its Order-in-Council, the thirty-one-year-old political whiz walked into the prime minister's office and loudly announced that he was resigning his seat at Labelle, which Laurier had persuaded him to acquire.

Bourassa would become the voice of anti-imperialist French Canada, and an increasingly irritating thorn in the side of the Laurier Liberals. For now he was content to claim the same attitude toward British Liberalism that Laurier maintained. He said that he was a follower of Burke and Gladstone, and that he would continue to be so although "Chamberlain or other renegade Radicals might choose in their megalomaniac ambition to call these great men blunderers." That intemperate language was to be typical of Bourassa's oratory, and to win him many hothead followers. So now Laurier had the Tories, the bishops *and* the Bourassa camp after him.

Bourassa was back in his MP's seat, on the site of the old seigneury he had inherited from Papineau, for the election of 1900. He was now Tarte's man, not Laurier's. Tupper and the Tories were ready to reacquire their proper power as Macdonald had done in 1878. They began to negotiate another of those strange political alliances as they joined the radical nationalists in Quebec in an attempt to topple the Queen's knight. But it was all to no avail. Times were just too good, the country was enjoying its biggest boom ever, and the Liberals offered the opinion that they were the reason for it. They were re-elected for the first time since Confederation.

The Boer War would come to an ignoble end by spring 1902, and Laurier would go to London for the coronation of Edward VII and another colonial conference. Once again he would rebuff Britain's attempt to create a federated economy and war machine. The coronation was put off for a few months due to the new King's ill health, so Laurier had lots of time to travel around Britain receiving accolades and boasting about Canada's future. By the time the coronation was finally performed in August, Laurier was exhausted and filled with pain. He thought he had cancer. He thought he had tuberculosis. He went to France and Italy to see doctors he knew. They told him he had asthma. He thought he was dying.

Back home Joseph-Israël Tarte thought so too, or at least that the prime minister would resign. Tarte started acting like a Liberal leader, stumping around Ontario and promising higher tariffs. Laurier, looking like the Gothic remains of his sickly college youth, came home and fired Tarte. Then he went to the United States and spent the winter getting better. Tarte had a young friend in Bourassa. As long as he could hold on to Fielding and Sifton, though, Laurier felt pretty safe. He was growing his own myth, wasn't he?

Next he had to test the myth against not the British but the USAmericans. Once again, gold was the cause. The big gold strikes in South Africa and North America had kept roustabouts and nations in turmoil for half a century. In 1886 gold had been found in the Klondike, and as with the strikes in British Columbia a few decades earlier, many of the gold seekers were veterans of the creeks and mines in the western United States. In the United States the gold fields were noisy with the discharge of rifles and handguns, but in Yukon the North West Mounted Police had kept gunplay to a minimum. Across the border in Alaska the gun boys had their usual field day, though. Meanwhile, Vancouver and Seattle were competing to see who could get rich supplying the gold hunters. The fulcrum of the argument was the question of how thick the Alaska panhandle should be. The Russians, who were to sell Alaska to the USAmericans in 1867, had beaten off the claims of the Hudson's Bay Company, and now the USAmericans wanted a panhandle so thick that no inlet would reach Canadian soil. That way Canadian ships and horse-trains would have to pay big duties to US customs houses.

The US president was bellicose Teddy Roosevelt, and his United States were engaged in their latest campaigns of expansion, mainly gathering up islands in the Caribbean and Pacific. Now Roosevelt's attention was drawn by the gold in the Klondike, and he was determined to get that panhandle boundary settled. US plans to acquire the coastline from Baja California to the Bering Sea had not quite panned out, so he wanted as much as possible. He would leave further annexation to the course of North American economics.

There had been several attempts at negotiation in the past but they had all failed. Now the US and Canada agreed on a tribunal made up of three men on either side. But Roosevelt was not patient when it came to settling international contests. He sent troops to Alaska without mentioning the fact to Canada or Britain. He said that if the tribunal did not come down with a decision that he could live with, he would ask Congress to give him leave to settle things his way, "without further regard to the attitude of England and Canada." Meanwhile, he instructed his three representatives to reject all compromises. Let the prime minister of Canada use compromise. The president of the USA would carry a big stick.

The two sides in the dispute were supposed to send jurists noted for their impartiality. Roosevelt sent three men who had vociferously supported the US version of geography. The Canadians did the usual Canadian thing, sending two impartial jurists and hoping that the Englishman, chief justice Lord Alverstone, would not be the agent of yet another British sell-out of Canadian interests in the hope of currying favour with the USA. Alverstone had instructions from his government. He sold out the Canadians, and the USAmericans got their thick panhandle. In Ottawa Sir Wilfrid Laurier thought further about the relationship between Dominion and Crown. He began thinking that Canada should have its own Department of External Affairs.

More and more Canadians were starting to agree with him. Every time the "mother country" betrayed its child in order to suck up to the restless and expanding United States, more voters would reject the Tories' colonial stance. And in the first years of the century the immigrants came pouring in, a great number of them eager to grab the offered 160 acres of homestead out west. A third of them were from Britain, a third from other European countries such as Germany and Ukraine, and a third were from the US. My father's father came over from England, and my mother's father came up from the Ozarks, to finish their childhoods on the Canadian prairies. The USAmericans were usually farm people who had had little success or opportunity in the rural parts of their own country. Many of the rural people in the USA were poor African Americans, but hardly any of them came to Canada. Perhaps the Canadian recruiters, usually so energetic and meticulous, could not find any way of getting the news to African Americans.

In any case, during Laurier's ministry two million people came to live in Canada, which at the turn of the century had had a population of five million. Very few of those newcomers were French-speaking, so the politicians and priests in Quebec saw another threat to their way of life. Louis Riel had said that he wanted to see many nations in the Canadian west. Henri Bourassa insisted that the whole country was made of two nations. Prime Minister Laurier sometimes envisioned what would later be called the Canadian mosaic. He said "I want the marble to remain marble; I want the granite to remain granite; I want the oak to remain oak." He also felt that way about the community of nations that were coloured red on the maps of the world.

He rode the good times and the new votes and the resentment against the British sellout to another victory in the 1904 election, this time against Robert Borden, whom the Tories had chosen to replace old man Tupper after the 1900 election. More immigrants in the west meant more railroads, and the Liberals, figuring that the good times were here for a century, the one that was supposed to belong to Canada, welcomed rail entrepreneurs and sank lots of public money into another line across the country, then another, why not? Sandy Mackenzie turned like feldspar in his grave. But Canada looked like a huge country, and if there was all that gold in the Klondike, there must be enormous wealth out there. The Liberals gave the go-ahead for large new port facilities east and west.

In 1905 it was time to offer new opportunities for provincial rights. Alberta and Saskatchewan were converted into provinces, each the size of Quebec, which was still mainly Laurentian. Laurier had promised such a move in the election. Now he knew that the Manitoba schools question would arise again under a new name. He had time to prepare for any trouble, and lulled by his many recent successes (including the firing of the British head of the militia), he announced that the BNA Act would take care of everything. The act of confederation, he reminded everyone, was a great compromise; it had entailed the giving up of radical positions on either side. It was the twentieth century, after all. We were all grown up. This was not, after all, the US, where the question had been slave states and free states. This was just a question of language and religion— and provincial rights.

In the North-West Territories, there had been a lot of changes in population patterns, and in the rules regarding religion and schools. In an 1875 act the Dominion government had allowed separate schools and in effect separate school systems. In 1901 the separate school systems were abolished, but in practice the Manitoba system was in place—during the last half-hour of a school day there could be optional religious instruction. In addition, Catholics were allowed their own textbooks and teachers, and they did not have to pay school taxes into the public system. Laurier liked the arrangement, and introduced bills in Parliament to formalize it. He thought that this would avoid the problems he had had a decade earlier in Manitoba.

Fat chance. Mr Sifton was ready to ride his noble horse again. He complained that the prime minister was trying to spread the Quebec situation of two separate school systems across the west. Mr Sifton spied the devious hand of Mr Bourassa. He thought he had seen Wilfrid and Henri putting their heads together lately. Everyone knew that Bourassa was in the pocket of the bishops, and Sifton was not going to let those papists spread their influence out on his prairies. The great compromiser could not figure out what was happening— all he wanted was a united Canada with no "racial" and religious strife.

Sifton, meanwhile, heard a dozen languages being spoken on the flatlands. He wanted all these Germans and Ukrainians and Finns—and Frenchmen—to speak one language, the way they did on the other side of the US border. Where did Quebec get off telling the new provinces how to build their societies? Laurier, though puzzled, had an answer to that. How can you be the champion of provincial rights against a powerful Macdonald Ottawa, and at the same time leave the minorities unprotected? Liberals are supposed to protect the least powerful. The priests in Quebec are not the least powerful, said Sifton. They will be teaching what they want Albertans and Saskatchewaners to learn, not what the new country needs.

As Sifton left his chief's office, he saw Henri Bourassa waiting to go in. Sifton went straight to his own desk and wrote his resignation. The knight was facing a palace revolt he had not expected. Bourassa advised him that if he went ahead with his idea, all the French-Canadian members would support him. It's us against them, said the firebrand. But Bourassa was talking to a Burkean who hated factions and dreaded "racialized" politics. Laurier thought of resigning himself, or threatening to resign, the technique that had got rid of the British head of the militia. Instead, he called a cabinet meeting, at which he announced that he had decided to seek another compromise that would keep Sifton with him. The bill in Parliament would be changed and the new provinces would get the same deal that the Manitobans had got—a half-hour of religious instruction per day, period. Now it was Bourassa's turn to put distance between himself and his prime minister. He grouched that French Canadians could expect no home in Canada except in Quebec.

He warned Laurier that compromises with the devil were not in the spiritual plans of the Roman Catholic Church.

Laurier, remembering his own days as the young Liberal hope, regretted the opposition of Henri Bourassa. And he was further disappointed that Bourassa was taking the even younger MP Armand Lavergne with him. Armand Lavergne was Bourassa's cousin and the son of Émilie Lavergne, the wife of Laurier's law partner. Émilie Lavergne always enjoyed putting on dinner parties, and was often in the company of the child-less Zoë Laurier. She had a hand in selecting Wilfrid Laurier's wardrobe, and she was an anglophile intent on dressing the knight in the latest London fashions. She also dressed her son that way, and otherwise enjoyed the resemblance between Armand and Wilfrid. As the boy grew up, observers noted the uncanny resemblance between him and Laurier.

Tory scandalmongers loved that resemblance, of course, and Grit faithful had to be careful where they issued denials. One friend went so far as to say that the allegations were un-founded, and that he knew for certain that the prime minister was impotent. Thank you so much, the prime minister might have said to that spin doctor. But he took what might be called a fatherly pride when he was able to help Armand Lavergne win a by-election and enter the House of Commons in 1904. In the election that followed immediately, Armand kept his seat.

Now in the aftermath of the western schools compromise, Émilie's son was a Bourassa man, helping the pointy-bearded radical stir up trouble in Quebec. In the House, Armand would raise motions for the French language on the prairies, and though he would get some support from some Conservatives, the knight had the votes to turn them down. So Armand, rebelling against his mother and the leader of his party, refused to learn English, much less speak it in the House, and flirted with the rightist priests. He talked about expelling the English from his province. His head was hotter than Bourassa's. Like Bourassa he began to speak of a mission to protect the French language and the Catholic religion, which were the civilization imperilled by secular barbarians. It was becoming clear that one did not have to be liberal to be a Quebec Liberal.

Laurier, who had always showed a strong interest in Armand's upbringing, and who had eased his way into Parliament, grew more and more disappointed in his defection. Eventually he cut Armand out of the patronage system, and watched him join Bourassa in dropping out of federal politics in 1908. Young Bourassa took younger Lavergne into provincial politics, and ran his columns in his new nationalist newspaper *Le Devoir*, but Lavergne began to disappear from the light while Bourassa became a weird Quebec martyr.

La plus ça change

In its fourth term, Laurier's government suffered the fate of every Canadian government, a series of scandals in most of its important ministries. His Minister of Public Works had to resign; Fisheries and the Interior were attacked in the House and the press. Laurier himself, like Macdonald before him, was clean. Like Macdonald before him, he managed to get through session after session without getting rich. Like Macdonald before him, he was innocent of any expertise in matters economic, but given to envisioning great projects.

Clifford Sifton became noticeably wealthy, and despite his disdain for Quebec he employed methods well known there, selling patronage and liquor licences. His collection of fine horses became the pride of the west. If Gucci shoes had been around in the first decade of the twentieth century, he would have owned dozens of pairs. There were a lot of other fortunes made in the west, as federal lands passed into the hands of lucky speculators.

Wilfrid Laurier was a Burkean liberal; he did not like the idea of top-down privilege, and he was not happy with the way the civil service seemed to guarantee wealth and comfort and little observation for its senior employees. He had Fielding set up a commission of investigation, and in the spring of 1908 that commission told the prime minister and the House that in the civil service "it is practically impossible to fix the responsibility on anybody." In June old Sydney Fisher introduced a bill to set up a civil service commission as a watchdog over patronage and corruption. Oh yeah, sure, said the Tories, and probably a lot of the Liberals, and the measure passed easily. Everyone knew that there was another election due later in the year.

Laurier did not get rich, but he did not refrain from playing the game. He got important jobs for members of his family. Unlike Macdonald, he knew how to stay at a distance from the odour of the pork barrel. Admirers knew that he was an expert in the backrooms and that underlings who understood power and privilege would do his bidding, but the prime minister never had a smudge on his high white collar. He used his lovely voice to knit beautiful words around a principle that was not Burkean but perhaps Gladstonian, that government's main task was to get re-elected, while the business of the loyal opposition was to demand reforms.

Between 1904 and 1908 Robert Borden and his Tories presented themselves as the champions of high morals, upholders of purity in politics, enemies of graft and the high life paid for by the voters. Still, they lost the election in 1908, and Laurier had his fourth term. Damn, said the Tories to each other, the Liberals would never be ousted if they kept acting more and more like the Conservatives.

Still, the Liberals' campaign slogan of 1908 had been "Let

Laurier finish his work," and perhaps a little too fancifully, the knight had said "Follow my white plume," whose historical allusion was probably lost on the populace. Laurier's work included his ongoing efforts to redefine Canada's place in the community called an empire. He reminded his fellow citizens that Canada had never fared very well by allowing Britain to handle its external affairs. So in 1909 he created Canada's first Department of External Affairs, although he did not surround it with a lot of pageantry—he rented a few rooms over a shop and installed a local one-armed Irish Catholic, Charles Murphy, as the first Secretary of State for External Affairs. Foreign diplomats must have felt a little strange, hiking up Murphy's stairs.

Perhaps Laurier thought that this little step toward Canadian independence would win a little support away from Bourassa. Maybe he was not surprised when Bourassa would claim that the move simply put Quebec at more peril emanating from Ottawa.

Laurier would raise more reaction to his returned interest in the naval question. The US navy had grabbed a big base in Cuba, all the coastline of Puerto Rico and the waters around the Philippines. German shipyards were slipping warships into the Baltic and the Atlantic at a rate that was at least alarming to the British. Laurier and his wife and satraps had been to another imperial conference in London in 1907, where once again the Brits had asked for money to build a bigger navy, and once again Laurier had suggested that it was time that Canada had its own navy, being as it was surrounded by water and USAmericans. Yes, Britain needed more ships to keep up with the Germans, but if the Canadians were to contribute, they would contribute Canadian vessels with Canadian sailors on them. Now in 1909 he was prepared to do something about it.

Laurier was almost seventy years old. He did not want his naval plans to descend into another tiring fight between the parties or the religions or the "races." So he went to Robert Borden and described the fleet he would build—six destroyers and five cruisers, the usual compromise, this time between the biggest ships and the smallest ones. Borden gave his nod for the time being. He would look for an objection later on. Meanwhile Laurier had his usual two-pronged campaign ready: he told the old Tories that an English war meant a Canadian war, and he told the less pip-pip citizenry that if London wanted help, they were going to have to ask for the help of a Royal Canadian Navy.

What was Ivanhoe expecting? He was sandwich meat again. Borden had said that he liked the idea, but there were walruses in his party who waved the Union Jack and insisted that in such a time of peril there was no room for little shows of national pride. Canada should send Britain the money and let the world's greatest experts in naval dominion build their fleet on Clydebank. One of these walruses was Sir Rodmund Roblin, premier of Manitoba. He is remembered for two remarks. One had to do with the possibility of votes for women: "I think too much of woman to have her entangled in the mesh of politics. She would be stooping from the pedestal on which she has sat for centuries." (Of course the word *ped*estal suggests standing more than sitting, but it is unlikely that Roblin knew up from down anyway, given this remark.) He also gave us the term "tin pot navy," a phrase that would be picked up and used over and over again to describe Laurier's plan.

Now we know that the more conservative Conservatives had been cozying up to the Nationalists in Quebec. Thus it is no wonder that Bourassa's crowd was also opposed to the Canadian navy, albeit for their own reasons. Bourassa argued that the German navy was no great problem. The English would go around the world engaging in wars, and Canadian sailors would be buried at sea off the coast of Asia and Africa. Why should young men from Quebec or Ontario give up their lives for some English adventure?

Bourassa was a royal pain in the ass, the prime minister might have thought. Now his old protégé was forming a new nationalist party, an outgrowth of his earlier *Ligue Nationaliste*. He was waiting for a by-election so he could fight the navy. Laurier decided on a sure-fire method to embarrass Bourassa and get his ships into the water. He fixed it so that the by-election would be held in a perfectly safe Liberal seat, Drummond-Arthabaska. Laurier had once represented the riding, and since that time it had been the fiefdom of Joseph Lavergne and Louis Lavergne, brother of Laurier's partner and uncle of Armand. Laurier and his wife had maintained their summer home near Arthabaska since their marriage. If there was ever a Laurier seat, this is it, said Louis Lavergne. Laurier raised him to the Senate and called a by-election.

Armand Lavergne announced that he was thinking of running for the seat, but the family must have got to him; he withdrew and made way for a farmer named Arthur Gilbert. Ho ho, said the Liberals. Ho ho and ha ha. They put up a lawyer, and sent thirty-five Liberal MPs into the district during the campaign. Were they worried that a farmer could put a hole in the government's bulwark? Well, if the Nationalists could win with a farmer, they would have terrific symbolism on their side when it came to defeating the Liberals and perhaps standing up to England—and Canada.

There was a lot of noise in this campaign, and a lot of dirty tricks. The Nationalists were prepared to lose the election and complain loudly in *Le Devoir*. Bourassa dressed some men up in military clothes and sent them around to people's houses, taking the names of all men eligible for the military. They let it be known that the Liberals had passed a navy act, and they needed a lot of French-Canadian lads to go and fight England's wars all over the world. The naval bill, as introduced in January, had made it clear that the Canadian ships would have no crewman who was not a volunteer, of course, but who reads parliamentary bills?

Arthur Gilbert, a man so obscure now that you will not find him in the index to a book about the period, won the election by two hundred votes. Independentists marched around singing the national anthem, but replacing the word "Canada" with the word "Bourassa." The prime minister got off the best line, stating that it was more honourable to lose some elections than to win them.

Laurier tried to pass the defeat off as a bump in the road, but he knew that it was a bad sign, to be defeated in an old family seat in the middle of southern Quebec. Still, he had a navy to prepare, and in the late days of 1910 a session to convene. At Dalhousie University in Halifax a new naval school was set up, and two British warships were borrowed to be used as training vessels. Soon there would be loud noises in Canadian shipyards, pairs of birds being slain with single stones—a navy built for Canadian pride, by workers well-employed. It may have been a "tin pot navy" but it was to be made of Canadian tin.

Oops, did it again!

Now it was 1911. Twenty years had passed since Laurier first led the Liberal party in a general election. He had learned a lot in those years, but apparently he had not quite learned the lesson the voters tried to teach him in 1891. The Liberals had stayed with their old reciprocity plank that year, and lost to the National Policy. Laurier had then held the National Policy to his own breast, and even out-Macdonalded his predecessor, sending new steel across the west and giving preferential customs considerations to Britain. He had won three elections against the Tories by being a very progressive Tory with good looks. But now a big fat president whispered in his ear, and he went back to being a Liberal.

He went back to being a Liberal without Tarte, Sifton and Bourassa. He was faced with the problem that seems to plague parties that are in power for a while—the prime minister looks around and sees that his original cabinet members are either old farts or absent. He saw one hopeful light, William Lyon Mackenzie King, and he recognized his earlier self, a comer who would have to wait till he seemed old enough.

The fat president was not Teddy Roosevelt but the even fatter William Howard Taft, 350 pounds of Republicanism. Henry Ford's Model T had begun to putter off the assembly line in 1909, and President Taft, who could just barely fit into one, was smart enough to see that the industrial world and its implications for trade were at a crossroads. Although he had, under Roosevelt's wing, been a high-tariff man, he was now a reciprocity president. There were a lot of USAmerican voters out west who hated high tariffs. Taft now had a deal for Canada, which he preferred to talk about in a quiet room. He was willing to negotiate a lowering of duties across the border, without demanding that Britain's preferential treatment be adumbrated. Think about it, he said.

Laurier thought about the traditional economic view of the Liberal party. He thought about the hordes of new Canadians out west, and about the fact that western farmers really like free trade, and about the fact that the number of new votes out there was rising faster than totals anywhere else. He did not know that President Taft had recently explained his switcheroo in a letter to Teddy Roosevelt, in which he opined that lower tariffs would make Canada "only an adjunct of the United States." The same old story.

Laurier had been decorating a fine fence for years. He had pre-empted most of the Conservatives' platform, while edging Canada away from its colonial position. A limited reciprocity would continue that work. He decided that he needed some momentum heading into the election that he intended to call in 1912, so he would send his agents to secret meetings south of the border, and introduce a good-news reciprocity bill in 1911. He fooled Robert Borden again, who thought the knight could pull it off. But he underestimated the reaction of the Toronto and Montreal businessmen and bankers. Van Horne and the other railroad men hated the idea of tracks that ran south. There were men in southern Ontario who had dreams of Canadian automobiles. And there were seventeen important Liberals, led by the westerner Sifton, who petitioned Laurier to lay off the tariffs. Laurier said that they should follow his white plume. Sifton was a friend of big businessmen now. He told his chief what he could do with his white plume, and went to talk with Borden.

It was a time for strange alliances again. Laurier and his loyalists said that Sifton was a traitor for going to the Tory leader. Some Tories said that Borden was a traitor for embracing Sifton. Borden said okay, he would resign. That frightened the Tories. Now Borden had a unified party with promises of deep pockets in the coats of industrialists and financiers, and he had the splendid Sifton, who knew how to make deals. Laurier, on the other hand, would have to swing his cane at both Bourassa and Sifton.

All that spring of 1911 the combatants shouted at each other in the House of Commons. Laurier could not get reciprocity through before closing for the summer. Now he had to go to England, for another imperial conference and another coronation, this time of George v. Again he would set up in the Cecil, and be feted and oozed at by the British. He was now the beautiful white-haired prince of the Empire. This time Zoë was not with him. She waited at home, her eyes and ears failing her, her strength diminished. Before his ship left Quebec for Britain the prime minister wrote a quick letter to her. He sounded a little like Macdonald in 1891:

> [W]hen I return, I will have to go back to work until the next election. When the election is over, whether I win or lose, I will retire. And then, there will be nothing to separate us.

When he got back he found out that he was not going to get the deal through, so he decided to go to the people. He called an election for September 21.

It was a nasty election, but what Canadian election is not? Laurier had to fight against many enemy groups—the Tories, Bourassa's nationalists, the defecting Liberals and the USAmericans. The Tories waved the British flag. Bourassa made sure that it was not behind him whenever he made his inflammatory speeches, although the Ontario Tory newspapers would promote him as a great admirer of British democracy. It did not help that the Speaker of the US Congress said "We are preparing to annex Canada." Robert Borden probably stopped once in a while to throw up behind a bush. But he could clean things up after he won the election and saved the country.

The Conservative candidates in Quebec were a kind of Bloc Bourassa. They were not campaigning for Borden; they were fulminating against Laurier and the British Empire. They did not focus on the deal with Taft; they spent their time attacking the naval act. Bourassa had been for reciprocity until Laurier took it up; then he was against it for purposes of the election. In Ontario and other parts of Anglo-Canada, Laurier was portrayed as a Quebecker who was turning his back on the Union Jack and selling his country to the USAmericans. Tupper's duplicitous attack of an earlier election was now intensified, to the point that Laurier had to campaign on his patriotism:

> I am branded in Quebec as a traitor to the French, and in Ontario as a traitor to the English. In Quebec I am branded as a Jingo, and in Ontario as a Separatist. In Quebec I am attacked as an Imperialist, and in Ontario as an anti-Imperialist. I am a Canadian. Canada has been the inspiration of my life. I have had before me as a pillar of fire by night and a pillar of cloud by day a policy of true Canadianism, of moderation, of concilia-tion. I have followed it consistently since 1896, and I now appeal with confidence to the whole Canadian people to uphold me in this policy of sound Canadianism which makes for the greatness of our country and of the Empire.

It is perhaps an instructive Canadian irony that the man who saw himself as the apt instrument of union—a ninth-generation French Canadian with a love of British Liberalism—should be assailed by extremists from both sides. But surely he must have known that lesser politicians will elevate ambition and oppor-tunism above the common weal. Maybe he was only shocked by the vehemence of the attacks.

That vehemence was felt most directly in the streets of Mon-treal. Politics in Quebec are more direct and energetic than in other provinces. Patronage is assumed as a fact of life, and political differences are often displayed in the form of fist fights. Banners and flags make good weapons in street skir-mishes. During the 1911 campaign the crowds would listen to the long fiery speeches of Henri Bourassa and get mad as hell. There were a lot of young separatists in those crowds, and after a Bourassa speech they would walk along nearby streets looking for something imperialist to hit. On September 19 Bourassa made his climactic speech at a hockey arena, a three-hour tirade, and after the speech the young separatists, teeth grinding and eyes blazing, encountered the prime minister of Canada on a nearby street.

Sir Wilfrid Laurier was just trying to get to the train station. He was on his way to Quebec City to make his last big speech. All at once his automobile was surrounded by angry young punks with big knuckles. They pounded on his car with their fists. They kicked the tires with their boots. They shouted insults and curses. They flung stones and horse buns at the windows of the official vehicle. Laurier's driver edged his way through the mob. They finally got to the train station, and the knight with the white hair got onto his train. But he could still hear the enemies of liberalism singing the anthem: "O Bourassa! . . ."

Two days later he was in Quebec City, receiving telegrams that explained the arithmetic. He won Saskatchewan and Alberta handily. He squeaked through in the Maritimes. That was it. British Columbia and Manitoba turned against him. Ontario and Quebec buried him.

He went to Ottawa, was driven to his home on Laurier Avenue, and tucked dear old Zoë into bed. He ate some cold chicken and a little salad. Then when he was sure that there was no one around to see the old man do so, he had a good long cry.

Into the dark

Laurier had been prime minister for fifteen uninterrupted years. His leadership of the Liberal party would extend more than twice that long. He had had the luck to rise to power while the world and Canada were enjoying boom times, in a new century that looked as if it would offer wonder after wonder. But the world was soon to descend into the horrific dark that was signalled by a pistol shot in the unfortunate city of Sarajevo. Laurier would spend his last eight years in loyal opposition, watching the work he had done for Canadian independence and unity being pulled apart by events in France and Quebec.

At first he did what so many defeated prime ministers had done, offering his resignation as leader. But too many members of his once-brilliant cabinet had lost their seats in 1911. William Lyon Mackenzie King was a man to watch, but he was just getting ready to turn thirty-seven. He would have had to be an idiot to volunteer himself as the white knight's successor. He agreed with the remnants of the former government—the party needed a myth if they had any hopes of getting back into power in 1915 or earlier.

Laurier was a terrific leader of the opposition. He put his wonderful voice and his great English and French sentences to work in the coming years, making an average of one important speech every ten days. He fought Bourassa for Quebec. He travelled the province and spoke to small-town folk, and became their favourite son (or grandfather) again. People crowded into university halls and ice rinks so they could tell their grandchildren that they had heard the words of Canada's greatest man. Robert Borden was prime minister, but Laurier was a hero.

Laurier would work hard in the House too. He would lead the spectacular filibuster against Borden's puny naval bill. The people in Quebec would begin to see that Laurier's Canadian navy was a lot better than Borden's British navy. They regretted turfing the old man out in 1911. They started voting against Bourassa's candidates in by-elections. They saw that Laurier approved Canadian entry into the Great War, but they also saw that he opposed Borden's conscription bill after the war had been dragging on for nearly three years.

During the war the leader of the opposition instructed his party to refrain from partisan politics, to ignore scandals despite the fact that there were avid men who found ways to profit from the war. He would not demand an election in 1915 or 1916, though the Constitution provided for one. He was not a jingoist or a separatist—he was a Canadian. He went around making recruitment speeches, and almost died during one. When Ontario decided to enforce its regulation against French classes in its schools, in order to punish francophone Catholics for their absence at recruiting offices, Laurier fought the Ontario government.

He was a very busy man. His promise to Zoë was doomed from the start. In 1916 he turned seventy-five, and his Gothic frailty was back, but like the seventy-five-year-old John A. Macdonald, he could not for the life of him locate a successor. He had agreed to give the prime minister a one-year extension on his mandate, and it looked as if he would be leading his party into the 1917 election. Borden, noticing his own lack of popularity around the country, offered a coalition instead of an election. But a coalition meant an acceptance of conscription, and that would mean handing the province of Quebec over to the extremists. Laurier still dreamed of a Canada in which important measures would not be fought across "racial" and religious lines.

So the old man went into another election in 1917, and the alliances were even stranger this time. Some of the pro-conscription Liberals joined Borden in what he called the Union movement. Bourassa had no traitor to the church and blood to attack this time. Race hatred became the air people breathed across Canada. On election night Laurier took just about all of Quebec, but the flag-wavers beat him everywhere else. Laurier had opposed conscription because it was not truly a liberal concept, and because he saw it as a knife across Canada. The jingoists saw anti-conscription sentiments as Quebec's petulant revenge for the Plains of Abraham.

Still the frail old man rebounded with energy and spent another year as the voice and myth of Liberalism in Canada. He survived the Great War in Europe and the other in Canada, but like Macdonald he suffered two strokes, and two months after the armistice in Europe he was dead.

The photographs of Laurier's funeral procession in the snow outside the fire-damaged Parliament Buildings suggest a momentous occasion during which an independent Canada gravely and proudly recognized the passing of what one of his biographers would call The First Canadian.

THE GOOD NURSE

Robert L. Borden 1911–20

I F SIR WILFRID LAURIER was a Liberal who attained his greatest political security when he expanded on the program of his great Conservative predecessor, Sir Robert Borden was a Conservative who was quite willing to adopt Liberal ideas if they seemed to make more sense than Conservative ones. He would go for an option on the basis of whether it was good or bad, rather than whether it was Grit or Tory. If ever a prime minister was going to have a cabinet made up of both Liberals and Conservatives, Borden was the man. His family was Liberal, always had been, as they say in the Maritimes. The young Borden became a Conservative because there were too many Nova Scotia Liberals who wanted Nova Scotia out of Canada, and too many Canadian Liberals who did not want to keep Canada out of the United States.

The Bordens emigrated to Canada at least twice. Richard Borden had left Kent and settled in Rhode Island in 1638. But the family bought real estate in Nova Scotia in the eighteenth century, just in case a war of independence should happen along.

Later the Bordens decided to try farming at Grand Pré, three miles from Wolfville. Robert Borden was born in June of 1854, seven years after the publication of Longfellow's *Evangeline*. Borden does not mention Longfellow in his memoirs, but he does mention a lot of other reading during his childhood and youth. Some prime ministers like to hire professional writers to write their autobiographies, but Borden wrote his own. Other prime ministers born in the nineteenth century are known to have been readers, but Borden had the biggest appetite, especially for the classics.

He went to school a little, where he was exposed to those classics, but he would spend fewer years in classrooms than any other prime minister. His father was a reader, and so was his mother, the former Eunice Jane Laird. She may have read *Ivanhoe*, but did a lot of serious reading, too. Robert Laird Borden grew up thinking that it was normal to hear one's parents discussing literature and philosophy. Working on his father's farm, swinging a scythe in a hay field or an axe in a woodlot, left some time for thinking, and the youth spent it in learning Latin and Greek, French and German. He "delved also into higher mathematics," he would tell us in his memoirs, as well as English poetry and history and the Protestant Bible. He knew that he could never afford to go to university, but he wanted to learn to be a responsible citizen. He thought back upon his bucolic gymnasium when he observed teenagers dying in the mud of France during the Great War.

He was so bookish that at the age of fourteen he was hired as an "assistant master" at the school where he had always been known as a serious book boy. His family needed the little money he brought home. He was a man-child, pondering the meaning of existence, and acting the role of the oldest offspring. He was a young puritan, devising a detailed timetable for his daily activities, sometimes the butt of family humour.

When he was nineteen he was invited to Matawan, New Jersey, to teach classics to the children of immigrants there. "I was astounded and horrified to find that in the school calendar I was announced as 'Professor of Classics and Mathematics,'" he tells us, but he took his timetable with him, and fitted in the hours spent with the local literary society.

A year later he was in Halifax, working in a law office and studying for his law examinations at night. Like John Thompson, he looked forward to a career in law, loving the logic that seemed almost to combine mathematics and language, never envisaging himself as a politician. When those law examinations came along, he passed them with the highest marks in the province, and by 1882 he was the junior partner in Graham, Tupper and Borden, which would become the biggest firm in Atlantic Canada. Unfortunately for the young man who just wanted to be a good lawyer, there was a Tupper in the offices.

He did become a top-flight lawyer, and they saw his face at the Canadian Supreme Court. They would see his face in the British Privy Council, which still had the right to offer judgements on Canadian cases. Everyone in Halifax knew who he was, and people in Ottawa knew him too. He was on his way to amassing a personal fortune, as lawyers like to do. But when lawyers get that famous and successful, there are political hacks who want to enlist them. Businessmen think that government should work like a business. Lawyers think that politicians should be good lawyers. Farmers think that the people in government could use a little soil under their fingernails.

In 1886 William Fielding was running for the premier's job in Nova Scotia, promising that his Liberals would do everything they could to raise Joseph Howe's younger ghost and get Nova Scotia out of Confederation. Borden's family had escaped life in the US, and he wanted to do whatever he could to prevent its being included in that republic. He allowed his name to stand in the federal election of 1896, just this once, and he topped the polls in Halifax while Laurier's Liberals sent Prime Minister Sir Charles Tupper's Tories packing at last.

So now he was a backbencher in the opposition. Once in a while, if there was a scandal to be addressed, he made a speech filled with good sense. He was a plain figure and he spoke in plain figures. He had his greying hair parted in the middle, and wore a bushy moustache. He was a loyal party man, and liked to attend old man Tupper on his travels, as when they went to the Tory nominating convention in Cape Breton, prior to the 1900 election. Somehow he was running for re-election instead of being a lawyer full-time. In the 1900 election the good times kept the Liberals in office, and this time Tupper lost his seat. So did old party stalwart George Foster. Sifton had clobbered John A. Macdonald's son out west. Charles Tupper the younger retained his seat, but if he were ever to inherit his father's position as leader, he would have two sets of enemies, and the party might never recover.

The Tuppers took the train to British Columbia, where they were going to campaign for a Tory who was running in a delayed election out there. They had succession to talk about. The front benches were pretty well emptied. The Conservative party needed a bright new hope. By the time they reached the west coast they had pretty well decided on Robert Laird Borden. Charles Tupper the younger, who now lived in Vancouver, sent a telegram to his former law partner.

Borden had two main assets. He was electable. He had not been involved in the unattractive elbowing since the death of Macdonald. But he was still on record as saying that politics was just a temporary job. Further, he had been told by his doctors that his nervous system would not stand the pressure. No one knows for certain what that means. All his life Borden would complain of just about every illness known to the period. He may have been subject to psychosomatic illnesses, though with his carbuncles he would never be as romantic a figure as the frail Laurier. In any case, here is what he said to the Tuppers: "I have not either the experience or the qualifications which would enable me to successfully lead the party . . . it would be an absurdity for the party and madness for me." Maybe he did not want to wind up like John Thompson, with his face in his dish. But he did not say no, did he?

In February of 1901 Charles Tupper convened a meeting in Ottawa, where he announced his retirement. For the first day the party faithful made speeches about the great career of the last Father of Confederation. All the aspirants for Tupper's job were there, and their supporters listened to the Tuppers speak in favour of young Borden. It was a time to make deals and arrange a decent future, to trade off positions and patronage. Borden did not look at it that way. The supporters of Sifton and Foster and the others pointed out that Borden was a little shy of experience. Charles Tupper the elder pointed out that given the circumstances, that might be his greatest asset. Tupper won the day, and Borden was the choice. He spoke about his surprise that they should choose him, dropped in a few phrases in Latin that might translate as "aw shucks," and said that he would do it, but on two conditions: he would hold the job in trust for one year, and during that time there would be a committee charged with finding a real leader with whom to head for the election in 1904 or 1905. Did he wink to himself in the men's-room mirror after the drinks that sealed the deal?

Common sense

Borden did not have any illusions about becoming prime minister very soon. Laurier was building his own myth. Laurier got the job just in time to enjoy the international boom. Laurier looked like a Macdonald with a more attractive nose, and he took over Macdonald's National Policy, complete with tariffs and railroads. What good did it do Borden that he was the first Conservative leader who could speak French? Laurier had the Quebec vote. Borden would eventually make his mark in Canadian history by asserting Canadian independence, but during the first decade of the twentieth century, Laurier was managing to do that too.

In fact Borden and Laurier got along pretty well. They recognized one another as scholars and gentlemen. They argued with one another in the House, Laurier with his flair and Borden with his mathematics, but they did not insult one another. The Canadian parliamentary system looked more attractive than it ever had, both leaders taking the high road. There would be no puking into wastebaskets or choking opponents while these two men faced off.

Borden soon forgot his stipulation that he be a one-year leader. The Conservative party demonstrated with great efficiency the fact that they could not come up with an alternative. After losing the 1904 election, he moved with Eunice Jane Baird Borden to Ottawa, and settled in for a while. Like the Lauriers, the Bordens had no children. They could still visit Grand Pré, but the Nova Scotia law business would have to take second place to the Ottawa opposition business. Robert Borden would read Bliss Carmen's poem "Low Tide on Grand Pré" (1903):

> A grievous stream, that to and fro
> All through the fields of Acadie
> Goes wandering, as if to know

Why one beloved face should be
So long from home and Acadie.
Was it a year or lives ago
We took the grasses in our hands,
And caught the summer flying low
Over the waving meadow lands,
And held it there between our hands?

Mr and Mrs Borden became ordinary citizens of Ottawa. They would be seen in the farmers' market, fingering the tomatoes, haggling over a chicken. The leader of the opposition liked to go to work on his bicycle, his middle-parted hair looking like small wings. He was often chewing tobacco while he pedalled. This was no white knight. He was a modest man who wrote in his diary every night. He had built up a fortune as the best lawyer in Halifax, but in Ottawa he was a plain gent who liked his privacy.

But he was the leader of the opposition in good times. What could he campaign on? Well, good times bring with them people who want to get rich quick. The USA was not the only North American country with robber barons. Borden noticed that the Grand Trunk Pacific, especially, and other companies, kept coming to Laurier and pleading near-bankruptcy. The Liberal government said that this was Canada's century, and kept giving more money to the railroads. The executives in charge of those railroads kept building grand houses to live in. Robert Borden noticed that the Conservatives in Manitoba and Ontario came to power by aligning themselves with the grassroots voters who did not like to see natural resources or tax moneys making a few plutocrats richer. The new Conservative premiers showed their progressive natures by making electricity and telephones and railroads into public utilities. Borden liked that idea.

He did not like it because it was a Conservative idea. He liked it because it made common sense and appeared the most moral of the alternatives available. Whenever a Tory veteran or newspaper suggested that he was deviating from the principles propounded by Tory veterans or purchased by persuasive financiers, he would use logic and mathematics to argue his cause, and a tacit suggestion that if they didn't like it they could scrounge around in their pork barrel for his replacement.

He was not a saint. He was an Anglo-Saxon man born in 1854. He had been taught all his life to assume that the Anglo-Saxon "race" was the apogee of civilization. Events would conspire to have him lead the first federal cabinet with no French Canadians. In August of 1907 he announced a sixteen-point platform of national reform that would be the firm Conservative position for the 1908 election. Its most progressive plank was a call for an unpoliticized civil service. But it also called for more careful screening of immigrants, to keep non-Anglo riff-raff out of the country. That year also he argued in the House that Canada should be careful about signing any agreement with Tokyo that might bring more Japanese immigration to British Columbia. In B.C. all the politicians campaigned on Asian exclusion. Now Borden joined the premier and the unions in employing the usual argument that exclusion was not really racism; it was just a way to "prevent the immigration of persons of a certain occupation whose competition would not be fair to the labouring men of Canada." (I remember hearing that argument from the vigilantes who kept Oriental farm people out of the area in which I grew up.)

Laurier won again in 1908. His white plume drew the voters away from Borden's common sense. And he had a pretty solid Quebec. Neither Laurier nor Borden liked the idea of a country that would fight its elections along lines of race and religion and language. In any case, those lines could be wiggled a little if some leader was going to make a mistake with a navy or a reciprocity deal.

In 1911 Borden had to run for prime minister a third time. But now he had an unstable ally in Henri Bourassa, and a turncoat genius in Arthur Sifton. The Liberals did not have a chance. As soon as he heard that he had at last sent old Ivanhoe down to defeat, Borden hied his way to Grand Pré, where he could think about this new situation without any newspaper people or patronage people around to bother him while he wrote humbly in his diary. Canada settled in for a quiet time, everyone thought. The Conservatives were back in what they thought was their rightful position, and it did not look as if there would be any scandals or fireworks as long as people toed the line for Robert Boredom.

Laurier had come in fifteen years earlier with the great golden cabinet. But in the ensuing years the Conservatives had not attracted an overabundance of bright lights. The prime minister asked Bourassa whether he would join, but Bourassa had a reputation to maintain in Quebec, and declined. In all likelihood he would have to target Borden the Anglo-Saxon sometime soon. So Borden gathered the best of a bad crop and faced the possibility of a Laurier comeback. That possibility became more distinct when, a few months after the election, the boom times petered away and farms and businesses started to suffer. In some European countries bad times were blunted by a buildup of war matériel, especially naval. Canada was not looking for a war, and not preparing for one.

Still, Borden, who had once agreed with Laurier's Canadian navy, now agreed with Winston Churchill, the British First Lord of the Admiralty, that the proper thing to do was to set an example for the Empire and send money to build ships in England. Borden had Quebec nationalists and Ontario imperialists in his caucus, so his gate was strait. When Churchill announced a naval buildup, Borden went to England. While he was there he visited shipyards, discussing the possibility of making dreadnoughts in Canada. But he also met with Churchill. He had to tell Churchill not to order Canada around, or Bourassa would give him trouble. He had to tell Churchill that he would agree to send money instead of Canadian-built ships, or the bulldogs in Ontario would give him ulcers.

So he had meetings with Prime Minister Asquith and suggested that if the dominions were to help build an imperial navy, they should be in on decisions about imperial defence policy, and Canadian officers should command the three ships the Canadians would finance. Asquith set up three walnut shells and a pea, and got the Canadian to agree that the dominions could start as advisers. Borden took whatever he could get, including a peek at Churchill's strategic plans, but let it be known that he would be back for more. At least he had something to show Quebec.

In December of 1912 the Conservative government introduced its naval bill, and Laurier's tin pot navy was scuttled. There was an emergency in Europe, the House was told—thus there was no time to start up a ship-building economy. Canada would send $35 million to England, with the stipulation that it be spent not on the Royal Navy but on imperial defence. And maybe, if the details could be worked out, the ships would someday be returned to Canada, if and when Canada could supply officers and men to operate them. Wilfrid Laurier played the patriot, downplaying the emergency, and calling for a Canadian navy now. Thirteen Quebec members of the government joined the Liberals in speaking against the bill. Never had the House seen such a naval blockade. For two weeks the Liberals waged the Great Filibuster, quoting anything in print to block passage of every article in the bill. Members slept in their offices and on their desks. Dogs and cats could have argued with as little relevance and as much effect. Above the fray amazed gallery visitors could see seventy-two-year-old Laurier's white mane shining as if in the light of his personal moon. The prime minister slumped at his desk, a doctor by his side, his neck wrapped in cloth to hide and treat his carbuncles.

Still, the prime minister and the leader of the opposition greeted one another politely outside the chamber.

For months and months the venomous battle continued inside. Why is Laurier going on in this crazy manner, the Tories and others wondered. Laurier had already begun his last great battle—to become the historical champion of French Canada. Newspapermen and newspaper readers just saw the election fight being continued by other means, and began to wonder whether this humble Nova Scotia man could govern such a seemingly complex country.

But the Nova Scotia man was a very smart lawyer. He turned to his Manitoba man, Arthur Meighen, and they worked out a tricky way to manipulate procedure and bring about closure before anyone had got the morning mush off their whiskers. For two weeks the Liberals debated the motion for closure, of course, but eventually Laurier had to accept the success of Meighen's trap, and he promised that Borden could look forward to similar manoeuvres when the Liberals got back in.

Laurier had been in power for fifteen years. He owned the Senate. And he told the Senate to kill Borden's naval bill. By so doing he won a lot of voters back, and pretty well defanged Bourassa's nationalist party. Borden's first great fight had ended in failure and anti-climax. The other dominions sent their contributions to the imperial war machine, and Canada remained the peaceable federation of the north. Borden's only comfort was that against Laurier's expectations, the battle had not resulted in a broken government and a new election.

The war to end all peaces

But the big empires in Europe decided to have a go at each other again, and war came anyway. As a member of the Empire, Canada would be a combatant. The government had two main problems.

The Canadian military was not ready.

The Canadian military was led by the Minister for the Militia, Colonel Sam Hughes.

The war started long before 1914, and the causes of the war would for decades after the armistice provide a subject for generations of Canadian high-school social-studies student essays. Battles in Morocco and the Balkans had been frightening enough to make the Germans and British spend a lot of credit on battleships and destroyers and rifles. Wilfrid Laurier said there would not be a big war; all that talk was Anglo-Canadian propaganda. Shortly after the 1911 election Borden had started asking the military bigwigs in London to send him information, but it did not arrive. He had to rely on the papers for the news. Still, in 1913 Canada spent a lot more on defence than it had two years earlier, and though there were only 3,000 regular troops in the country, the militia had been growing of late.

The militia was organized by Colonel Sam. Patriotic stories and propaganda of the time make Sam a bluff energetic Canadian hero. But anyone who had ever had to work with him knew him as an annoying blowhard and egomaniacal loony. Borden in his autobiography writes of his reluctance to include Hughes in his first cabinet, and later sums up the man's behaviour:

> In my experience his moods might be divided into three categories; during about half of the time he was an able, reasonable, and useful colleague, working with excellent judgement and

indefatigable energy; for a certain other portion of the time he was extremely excitable, impatient of control, and almost impossible to work with; and during the remainder his conduct and speech were so eccentric as to justify the conclusion that his mind was unbalanced.

Hughes had appointed himself commander of a Canadian contingent in the Boer War, and so much alarmed the British brass that they told him to take his uniform off. Somehow he made it to the front, as a supply officer, and, according to the narratives he would later publish in his own newspaper, the Lindsay (Ont.) *Warden,* he pretty well won the war over the Boers. For years he would announce that his Victoria Cross had not arrived, that there must be some mistake. After Borden assembled his unexcellent cabinet of 1911, Colonel Sam petitioned the governor general, the Duke of Connaught, for his VC. The alarmed Connaught suggested to Borden that he get rid of this madman.

But in the popular imagination Hughes was some sort of hero, and before and after the declaration of war, recruits rallied to his name. He was given to blustery slogans and wild exaggerations and the militarization of male Canada. He demanded that all Canadian boys become dead-eye rifle shots by the age of twelve. His favourite weapon was the Canadian-made Ross rifle, manufactured in Quebec City. Canadian soldiers could have had the British Lee-Enfield, but the Brits refused to manufacture it in Canada, so Canadian troops got the Ross. It was a terrific tool on the rifle range, but it killed as many Canadians as Germans in the war. It was modified a hundred times, but still the back sight fell off and the chamber jammed if you got into rapid fire. Canadian soldiers would die in the mud while attacking their own rifles. Others threw them away whenever they found British corpses with Lee-Enfields in their hands.

Hughes got the volunteers out—except in Quebec. It would be foolhardy to expect a race to the recruiting offices in that province, even with Laurier making his enlistment speeches. But Hughes did not help matters when he sent English-speaking recruiters into the cities and townships of Lower Canada, and announced that all soldiering would be done in the English language. When Quebec youth, some of them remembering the warnings of Henri Bourassa, stayed away from the Union Jack, anti-Quebec feelings were easily manu-factured in Ontario. Here were loyal English Canadians giving their lives on French soil, and the descendants of New France were hiding behind the barn.

Prime Minister Borden did want to drop Sam Hughes, but the man was proving too damned useful in the first year of the war. He had got the first contingent of soldiers across the Atlantic a month after the declaration of war. He had armouries filled and noisy around the country. But while the government had to take some anti-democratic measures during the emergency, Sam Hughes seemed to think that the emergency had made him the most important man in the country. He promoted him-self to the rank of major general. He went from camp to camp, in Canada and England and France, dishing out promotions and a few demotions. He made spectacular speeches and waved his sword in the air. He gave vent to his Orangeman sentiments in Quebec, and it is a wonder that he did not become a wartime casualty there. He disparaged his civilian associates in cabinet, and even suggested that the prime minister was too girlish to wage war. Worse, he bestowed lucrative wartime contracts on his friends in the manufacturing and supply industries.

Hughes's ego grew and grew. Soon he was keeping informa-tion from Borden as well as the British military had. Borden sent the Minister of Overseas Forces to London to find out what was happening. Hughes saw this as the worst conspiracy yet, and sent a series of intemperate letters. At last, listening to a chorus of voices that included his own, the prime minister called for Major General Sam's resignation, and he got it on November 11, 1916, along with an insulting letter. Sam would now begin his own conspiracy to get even with all his enemies.

Union government

Borden the meticulous logician and moralist understood that emergencies such as the Great War made it necessary for a government to take unusual powers. If a fire breaks out you have to send firefighters, not argue about their eligibility. The BNA Act said that there had to be an election by 1916, and common practice would have meant an election in 1915. Parliament had passed a War Measures Act in 1914, whereby power was put into the hands of cabinet in any emergency that might threaten "the security, defence, peace, order and welfare of Canada." The definitions of those nouns would prove interesting in their variation in future years.

Laurier had agreed that the nation could put off the election until 1917. In the first days of the war everyone had been led to believe that it would be over by the end of 1914. But the trenches became deep and diseased, and the clouds of poison gas rolled across Belgium and France month after month. In the summer of 1916, the Allies lost 600,000 men while gaining fifteen kilometres of mud. The insane arithmetic suggested that this war could go on until the twentieth century was over, or there were not any male human beings left in Europe or the British Empire. An election in Canada could not be put off year after year, even if old Laurier agreed. Arthur Meighen, the main strategist of the Conservative side, had been sounding out his chief and the Liberals on the subject of a coalition government to tide the country over and prevent a national emergency that might qualify the country's response to the international one.

But in the meantime, Robert Borden was fighting a war. Most of it was against the Hun. Some of it was against Asquith and the British interpretation of the imperial war effort. The Brits looked upon the soldiers from the dominions and colonies as British fighting men. Men such as Borden of Canada and Jan Smuts of South Africa saw their volunteers as defenders of the Empire, and they saw in the mud of Europe a new definition of Empire. It has become a cliché of Canadian anecdotal history that Canada won its image as an independent nation by its valour and sacrifices in the First World War. Not often enough is it said that Robert Borden, with his insistent plain speech, would drive that lesson home in London.

Europeans can take a long time to learn such lessons, despite the millions of dead. Before the 1989 reunification of Berlin, the old Reichstag on the western side of the Berlin wall housed an exhibit about the two world wars. Large displays showed the totals of human lives lost per country in those wars. Although there were listings for a few Latin American countries, there were none for Canada. Even in 1985 the Germans were confusing Canadians with British. Henri Bourassa never got to see that Reichstag exhibit.

Borden's feelings can be read in a letter he sent to the Canadian High Commissioner in London. He denounced some of the stupidity in the British high command, and he offered his opinion of the old-fashioned imperialists:

It can hardly be expected that we shall put 400,000 or 500,000 men in the field and willingly accept the position of having no more voice and receiving no more consideration than if we were toy automata. Any person cherishing such an expectation harbours an unfortunate and even dangerous delusion. Is this war being waged by the United Kingdom alone, or is it a war being waged by the whole Empire?

All of Borden's letters and speeches were written in such a plain style, a simple elegance that allowed no space for dodging among ambiguities or floridities. The High Commissioner did not publish this letter, but its spirit was made known to the high mucky-mucks. The British finally came around and invented the Imperial War Cabinet. At a 1917 meeting Borden and Smuts were pleased to have made sure of the passing of Resolution IX, by which it was recognized that during and after the war the Empire would recognize "the Dominions as autonomous nations of an Imperial Commonwealth," entitled (along with India) to "an adequate voice in foreign policy and in foreign relations, and . . . continuous consultation in all important matters of common Imperial concern."

In the long effort to develop Canadian autonomy, Resolution IX was perhaps the most important step. Robert Borden, though he has not been accused of glamour, did more for independent Canadian nationhood than anyone else. He did not know how to fashion a personal myth, but he seemed to be able to make a nation.

But could he put together a wartime cabinet? More important, could he assemble the array of candidates that would win him an election that would have to be fought on the most dangerous issue of all—conscription?

Canada had sent an enormous number of fighting men, given its small population. In the first rush of volunteers a lot of recently immigrated British lads were off to defend old Blighty. As the years went by it became clear that the majority of young Canadian men preferred to stay and do important work on the home front. The prime minister saw that there were 300,000 Canadians on the other side of the Atlantic, but he knew how fast they were falling. He saw that the rate of recruitment could not keep up. He had also seen what happened to the young Canadians when they went over to the diseased slime of northeast Europe. He visited exhausted fighting men in the trenches and dying youths in English hospitals. What he saw made him sick, but he drove himself in an attempt to visit every Canadian in the war. He had carbuncles and sciatica and bad nerves, but he hid them as he went from bedside to bedside. He said bluff patriotic pieties, but he was almost weeping. He thought about the young civilian men at home.

In 1916 he had laid down an Order-in-Council that would justify conscription if enlistment fell short, and it had not been debated in the House. When conscription was finally debated in the House, Borden mentioned that Order-in-Council, then he recited the arithmetic about casualties and volunteers, then he mentioned the lads he had visited overseas:

> They have answered the call, they have given glorious service, they have put aside all material considerations; duty alone has been their ideal. Unconscious of every thing other than the supreme task before them, I know from my personal experience that they cannot realize the thought that their country which so summoned them to her service will be content to desert and humiliate them.

He might have quoted from a poem by Dr John McCrae of Guelph, a medical member of the first contingent of Canadian troops. It had been published in *Punch* two years earlier. This is how it ends:

Take up our quarrel with the foe:
To you from failing hands we throw
The torch; be yours to hold it high.
If ye break faith with us who die
We shall not sleep, though poppies grow
In Flanders fields.

But Borden wanted the country to know that conscription would be a Canadian decision: "Some people afflicted with a diseased imagination have asserted that I took my present course at the request or dictation of the British Government. No more absolute falsehood was ever uttered by human lips."

He had in mind the Bourassa separatists, who had been his opportunistic partners in the 1911 election but who would not support him in 1917. He was determined to form a coalition government, and he knew that he would be risking his political life and future reputation on the conscription question. He was aware that he might be building the foundation for a country split along sectarian lines, but he had seen too many dying young eyes in Europe. Of course he and Meighen offered Laurier a seat in cabinet—in fact Laurier was offered what amounted to Borden's job. But Laurier still had Bourassa around his neck, and he was interested in his own reputation in Quebec, and growing more and more obsessed with the idea that the country had rejected him because he was a French Canadian.

Laurier went around saying that Ontario and the Conservatives were trying to make Canada a Crown Colony again. Borden gave up on Laurier, and had Meighen introduce a bill for conscription in the House. Meighen debated Laurier brilliantly, killing off the future careers of the old man and himself. Laurier watched as Liberal after Liberal, English-speakers all, deserted him and went over to Borden and Meighen. Borden watched as his Quebec members slipped away. On June 24 Parliament passed the conscription bill. To conscript wealth as well as youth, Parliament then passed an income tax act. They said that the Income Tax Act would be reviewed in a couple of years, and once the peacetime economy was on its feet, thrown away.

Now there was conscription, and the country was split into two Canadas again, but this time Ontario and the west had more than two-thirds of the votes. Laurier was heartbroken: his dream of a seamless Canada was gone.

Borden and Meighen had to prepare for the election that had been postponed for a year. They knew very well what the issues would be. There were, of course, the money-gobbling railroads, but the war was more important than anything else. Borden was likely to win the election as decisively as he had won the military service question. But there were questions of purpose and loyalty to be taken care of. The Ontario city of Berlin had changed its name to Kitchener, in a time when that second proper noun seemed less problematical. Now the Conservatives passed the Wartime Elections Act, taking the vote away from suspicious people—conscientious objectors and people who had immigrated recently from countries with which Canada was at war. The act extended the vote to women who were the next of kin to enlisted men. Thirdly, it provided that the votes of overseas soldiers did not have to be applied to their home ridings but could be sprinkled where most needed by the government. Anyone could see that while some of these measures might seem necessary or even praiseworthy, given the times, it was pretty obvious that all three measures favoured the Conservatives.

The arithmetic favoured a Borden victory in the necessary election, but the imposition of conscription would be a tougher fight. On the west coast the unions were against it. The sons of those new immigrant farmers on the prairies would rather stook wheat than stand in a muddy trench. In Quebec, where violence and politics are not unknown to one another, crowds thronged the streets of Montreal and other cities, hollering terrible things about the prime minister. A "revolutionary" group found the stately home of Lord Atholstan, the pro-Borden publisher of the Montreal *Star*, and dynamited it. Borden had been visiting Atholstan during his travels around the province, but he was off playing golf with ex-president Taft and some Quebec worthies.

There were conscriptionists in both parties, but Borden found it hard to recruit Liberals into his proposed cabinet. None of the French-Canadian members would dare, of course. Most of the English-speaking Liberals were afraid that they might harm their post-war careers. Borden was sure that the general population, at least outside Quebec, wanted a Union government to show Germany (and Britain) a determined Canadian face. Sifton insinuated that Wilfrid Laurier, who was against conscription and refused to join the cabinet as an example, was next thing to a traitor. Then Sifton started to bend arms among his fellow westerners. He came back with the news that some prominent western Liberals would join if Borden let someone else lead the country. They had political futures to take care of.

Borden said all right, he would step aside.

His party refused to allow that offer. It smelled too much like a combination of common sense and selfless patriotism.

There followed a time of great tension, of despair, of fear and frustration. In northeast Europe the Allies would gain the distance from first base to second base in four months and at a cost of thousands of casualties. Then the Russians would fall out of the war, the Germans would bring their eastern troops to the western front, and the Allies would fall back to first base, dragging corpses with them.

Borden invited the backroom boys to look at the statistics.

Eventually the Liberal party broke, and on October 12, 1917 some nine Liberals left Laurier to join the twelve Conservatives in Borden's cabinet. Only one of the Liberals was from Quebec, and he was an English Canadian. For the first time since 1841 there were no French Canadians in cabinet. This was an ominous situation, Borden knew. He could foresee the situation for his party in Quebec. But he could not forget the eyes of the Canadian soldiers he had visited over there.

So Borden could fight an election, the Unionists against the Quebec Liberals. The election posters tended to look like the war posters people were used to, except that now Laurier was confused with the Kaiser. It was not a subtle election campaign, and Borden's sensibilities would be assailed. He never did want to get into politics, but here he was, running for prime minister a fourth time.

With eleven days to go in the election campaign, Borden was campaigning in Prince Edward Island. At 8:45 in the morning of December 6, some people around him heard a bang in the distance. This had happened in Halifax harbour, and it was the biggest man-made explosion in history. When those two European ships collided in the narrowest part of the harbour, the sparks ignited a mile-high blast that would kill 1,600 people and injure 9,000 more. Downtown Halifax was gone. Pieces of glass cut into people's eyes. That day there were 25,000 people out of a population of 50,000 who did not have a bed to sleep in. That night a blizzard hit.

The prime minister's train eventually made it to the ruins of Halifax, though there was no train station. He was driven around the rubble by a youth whose family had been reduced from eleven to two.

When Borden travelled to Ottawa to make his final speech he was too tired to write anything. He spoke off the cuff there, telling people what he had seen in France and Nova Scotia. On

December 17 he took 153 seats while Laurier took 82. Only two of Laurier's seats were in the western half of the country. Neither Borden nor Laurier liked the look of the electoral map and what it portended.

End of the war, more or less

The German U-boats were sinking British and neutral ships, and Britain was near starvation in 1917. Meanwhile, in the first three years of the war, 8,000 new millionaires emerged in the USA. The British blockade slowed down US profits from trade with the Central Powers, but the Allies were forced to take out enormous US loans. When the U-boats began to sink everything in sight, it looked as if the Germans could win and those loans might never be paid. Then when US ships were torpedoed, it was not hard to rouse the USAmerican people to protect those US loans, and the USA joined the war effort on the Allied side. In December the Bolsheviks signed a peace treaty with Germany, and the European battle lines were redrawn.

Politics were changing too. Lloyd George took over from Asquith as British prime minister. In Germany a military dictatorship took command. One hundred thousand French soldiers were court-martialled for desertion. The Yanks were coming. Germany's partners, Turkey, Bulgaria and Austria, collapsed. The tide, as they say, was turned in the Battle of Amiens. There the powerful Germans were faced with the kind of attack that would be used in the next world war— infantry divisions following massed tank formations and air coverage. The British, French, Australians and the Canadians captured thousands of Germans and hundreds of guns in August, and from then on, with a million USAmericans in Europe, the German people were filled with hopelessness. The

Germans signed the armistice before the Allies could invade their country.

Around the time of the US intervention in the spring of 1918, the Canadian government was starting to enforce the new conscription law. The law provided for exemptions, and most young Canadian men claimed exemptions, which were not all that hard to achieve, especially in farm country. There were 400,000 eligible men signed up, and 380,000 of them claimed exemptions. The nature of the war in the trenches had been made known across the world. Conscription, which would be in effect for less than a year in a war that lasted more than four years, was not a big success. In fact recruitment was lower after it became the law.

In Ontario it was met with a protest march by farmboys. In Quebec it was met by a reaction more fierce. With no French Canadians in the federal cabinet, and with recruitment offices manned by English-speakers, some fiery young men felt that Quebec was an occupied nation. Armand Lavergne, Bourassa's Bourassa, was a colonel in the militia, but he declared that the Canadian army would have to shoot him if they came after him with their draft board. The war came to Quebec City in late March, when a gang of shouting men torched the recruitment office, and for good measure torched the Dominion police station.

Martial law was declared, and the government sent in soldiers from Ontario to put down the riots. Bayonets and old snow gleamed in the spring sunshine. Nasty words were uttered from the sidelines, but the English-speaking troops only guessed at their message. The rioters threw objects at the riflemen, so the cavalry made a charge down the streets. The rioters hid behind chimneys and shot at the Canadian soldiers. The Canadian soldiers had Lee-Enfields and machine guns, and they won the gun battle. At the armistice there were five wounded soldiers and four dead rebels.

One can imagine how Laurier felt on hearing the news. One can imagine how Borden felt. This is the twentieth century. We cannot have a civil war in such a country. As so often happens in such a country, civilized men responded first with shock and then with a determination to keep the decent peace. Wilfrid Laurier and Henri Bourassa both appealed to French Canada's reason. The Church and the press called for calm. The Dominion government vowed thoughtfulness in laying down the new law in Quebec. The prime minister knew that his country was full of people calling each other traitors, but he had a war to end and a peace to handle. He knew that his gentlemanly opponent, Ivanhoe, may have been able to strike him down but chose to preserve the country instead. Borden needed such help. He had to spend most of 1918 and 1919 east of the Atlantic.

West of the Pacific, 4,000 Canadian troops, including some Mounties, went in the summer of 1918 to protect Murmansk and Vladivostok from the Germans and then from the Bolsheviks. There were Brits and USAmericans and Japanese there, too. Really, the only fighting they did was to keep warm as the many winter months arrived. They would stay for a year, marching from time to time, crashing a few airplanes. This was Canada's first expedition in Asia. But Robert Borden was on his greatest expedition in Europe.

He was there to instruct the British and the French and the USAmericans that as Canada had made a major contribution to the war effort, so the Canadians wanted everyone to know that they would be Canadians at the peace conference. USAmericans in particular would find it hard to grasp the concept that the land to their north was not a British colony. But Borden and his entourage first had to remind Lloyd George. He told the Brits that if Canada could not sit at the peace table and sign the resulting documents, if the Big Three expected Canada to be included as only part of the British contingent, Canada would not show up. When Brits would suggest that Canadians were really overseas Brits, Borden would rejoin that there was no room for the English feudal system in his country. To show that he was serious, he enacted a bill that banned hereditary titles for Canadian citizens. He would be the last Canadian prime minister called Sir, and he did not like it very much when people addressed him that way.

Borden shook them up a little at Versailles. While the USAmerican representatives wondered what plot the British were incubating with these pen-wielding dominions, the British worked out a compromise. When it came time for signing the peace treaty, there would be a place allocated for the British Empire. Britain would sign first, and Canada would sign beneath Britain. It was not quite as much as Borden wanted, but it was a lot more than people might have expected before 1914.

The US tried to stop Borden again when it came time to form President Wilson's ideal League of Nations. But once again Borden stood up and began to roar. He made a rather pointed if subtle remark when he said "The dominions have maintained their place before the world during the past five years through sacrifices which no nation outside of Europe has known." Borden got his nation into the League. Wilson failed to enrol his.

When Robert Borden won membership for Canada in the League of Nations, he may have secured a cabin on a ship that was going to founder; but from now on Canada would have dealings with other countries on a country-to-country basis. In the slightly smaller sphere of British-USAmerican relations, Canada would begin more and more to act as a kind of liaison, gaining recognition of its nationhood with each conversation.

Going golfing

Yes, 1919 was a momentous year. Borden's double triumph at Versailles was countered by two dispiriting events at home.

On February 17, Sir Wilfrid said his last famous words to Zoë Laurier: *"C'est fini."* Borden sent a cable to her immediately, and next day issued a press release that began: "It is with the deepest sorrow that I have received the tidings of Sir Wilfrid Laurier's death. Since I became leader of a political party, more than eighteen years ago, our relations have been intimate and never have our political differences interfered with our personal friendship."

An era had, as they say, passed. The soldiers who were fortunate enough to return from Europe alive came back to a country that did not offer them much. There were not enough jobs around, and the jobs that were around were not safe enough, and the pay that was offered for those jobs was not high enough to keep up with the worst inflation anyone in the brave new Dominion had ever seen. In western Canada there were a lot of immigrants, and a lot of those immigrants had ideas about labour reform that they had brought over with them. The One Big Union movement was becoming more and more visible in the cities of the prairies and the coast. The Bolsheviks had finally proven in Russia that the nineteenth-century socialist writers were onto something. Robber barons had the striped pants scared off them. When the Winnipeg General Strike began in May 1919, pants were dropping in Ottawa.

First the skilled tradesmen laid down their tools. Then the unskilled workers, a lot of them from Europe, walked away from their measly jobs. Then preachers in Protestant churches began to show their sympathy. Now to move the crisis into a phase that could not be ignored back east, public workers, municipal, provincial and federal, joined the strike. These were policemen, firemen, post-office and telephone workers, the people who bring water and electricity and locomotives. Thirty thousand people were out on strike, carrying huge signs in favour of collective bargaining. If there was one spectre that struck panic into the heart of a banker trying to pull up his pants, it was that kind of solidarity. The bankers and industrialists decided that they had better get together too. They formed a "citizens' committee," and opened their membership to a lot of local politicians. Then they invited the Dominion government to town.

Robert Borden and everyone else had been hearing about labour unrest for some time. In his May Day speech the prime minister had cautioned that a country trying to achieve recognition among the community of nations could not afford divisive events within its boundaries. It was bad enough that we have the Bourassites; we do not need the Bolsheviks as well. Half a year earlier the cabinet had passed a few Orders-in-Council banning such things as meetings in which "enemy" languages were spoken, pamphlets printed in "enemy" languages, the Industrial Workers of the World, and the Social Democratic Party of Canada. These Orders-in-Council were aimed, said the cabinet, at seditious organizations trying to impede the war effort. They seemed to work. At the end of 1918 the Minister of Labour told the prime minister that labour conditions in Canada were just fine. Good, said Borden from Paris, now let me get on with my peace work.

But now in May the biggest city in the Canadian west was shut down. The hub of Canada's vital railroad system was full of Communist agitators and renegade Christian ministers. Borden got back to Ottawa when the strike was in its twelfth day. The strike committee were maintaining essential services, but the prime minister said that Canada would maintain law and order in Winnipeg. Messages from the respectable citizens of the city averred that the place had fallen into the hands of suspicious foreigners, and one could hear agitators talking in strange languages. The strike committee was acting like a revolutionary government. For a Conservative government in Ottawa, this was sounding all too familiar—were these the ghosts of the Métis upstarts of a half-century ago?

Arthur Meighen went home to Manitoba and looked around. He came back to Ottawa and told his chief that the strike would peter out, and the feds would not have to intervene in the private sector. But the post-office workers could be fired. They were fired. Other measures could be taken to edge the misled labourers back to work. On June 6 the House quickly passed an amendment to the Immigration Act. Any foreigner, including those born in Britain, who suggested the use of force to change government could be deported without visiting a courthouse first. Immediately the mayor of Winnipeg banned all public demonstrations. Then the police started arresting strike leaders and raiding union offices. Much to the surprise of the feds, a lot of war veterans sided with the strikers, and mounted a clearly illegal parade down Portage Avenue. They were met at the crossroads of Canada, Portage and Main, by Mounties on horses. The idea was that the ex-soldiers would be scared witless. But the soldiers had seen worse. They kept coming, though they did not even have Ross rifles. The Mounties fired into the crowd, and one man was killed. Ottawa reminded western Canada of the War Measures Act, invoking it to send federal troops still in uniform to occupy Winnipeg. The demonstrations died down, and the strike was crushed, but the Winnipeg General Strike would do its work to arouse labour organization over the next two decades.

An old Canadian

It makes a lot of sense to read the history of Winnipeg if you want to understand the history of progressive movements in Canada. The Winnipeg General Strike took place on the streets where Louis Riel had campaigned for his seat in the House of Commons. In 1916, twenty-three years after Lady Aberdeen's National Council of Women was chartered, the Province of Manitoba extended the franchise to women. In 1918, while getting rid of hereditary titles for men, Borden's government allowed women to vote in federal elections.

Borden knew that he was not going to run in another election himself, and he wanted to leave as many sensible and honest decisions behind him as possible. He tried to get his cabinet people interested in a permanent Unionist party, as a way of hindering sectarian loyalties and patronage. He did manage to reform the civil service. He made himself the best Conservative prime minister of the twentieth century by adhering to principle rather than party. He tried to attack patronage head-on by creating a non-political commission that would be in charge of government purchases. It was defeated by both Liberals and Conservatives.

The prime minister was like a growing number of people out in western Canada. He was getting tired of Liberals and Conservatives. "Political partisanship," he would write in 1935, "is closely allied with absolute stupidity." He was writing about government contracts.

In 1919 he knew that nineteenth-century politics were gone, that the country he had made people see as sovereign had a new kind of people in it. He had worked hard to get Canada through a great war and into a community of nations. Now he was going to listen to his doctors and his heart. The women of Canada would not get the chance to vote for him. He wanted his Unionists to engage the Liberals in the next election, but that was not going to happen. He faced down some challenges from other Tories and managed to get his man Arthur Meighen installed as the second Unionist prime minister.

When the election of 1920 was over, Sir Robert Borden had cleaned out his office. This man with the long list of ailments would live for another seventeen years, writing well into his eighties. The earnest Robert Borden can be found in his *Memoirs*, for which he had started taking notes at the end of the war. The amusing Robert Borden can be found in the highly enjoyable *Letters to Limbo*. Borden invented an imaginary newspaper called the *Limbo Recorder and Guardian*, and in his last years filled it with things such as political notices, poetry reviews and philosophical musings. Until 1971, one had to travel to Limbo to read this paper. Then it was collected into a book by his nephew and published by the University of Toronto Press.

Just before he died, he told this nephew that his funeral was to have "none of this Sir stuff at the cemetery, just plain Robert Laird Borden."

Like John A. Macdonald, he may have died a British subject. But he had made that term a problem in Canada. That was a great gift to his country.

CHAPTER 12

NO ONE LIKES
A SMART ALECK

———•◆•———

Arthur Meighen 1920–21

I N HIS LAST LIVING room in Toronto, Arthur Meighen had a
bust of William Shakespeare on a pedestal. People said that
Arthur Meighen had a photographic memory. He could recite
a long swatch of William Shakespeare's verse appropriate to any
situation. One imagines that during his earliest years in the
House of Commons, while Robert Borden was trying to edge
Canada out from under Britain's motherly eye, Arthur Meighen
was remembering a cabinet meeting of ancient days:

> Let me have men about me that are fat,
> Sleek-headed men, and such as sleep o' nights.
> Yon Cassius has a lean and hungry look.
> He thinks too much, such men are dangerous.

Arthur Meighen was a tall thin young man who had grown up
in a farmhouse just outside St Marys, Ontario. His parents were
so frugal that none of their six children was given a middle
name.

He was born on June 16, 1874. Six months and one day later, thirty-five miles down the road in Berlin, Ontario, William Lyon Mackenzie King came into the world. He would never be tall and he would never be thin, but he had two middle names. In a couple of decades these two distinct men would start to hate one another. They would each become prime minister of Canada more than once, one of them fleetingly, the other forever.

Laurier and Borden engaged in picturesque swordfights in the House of Commons, but remained fond friends, or so it appeared to the world. Neither Meighen nor King could eat preserved peaches if the other's name were mentioned at the table.

Meighen's grandfather built a school in St Marys, and acted as headmaster. For this he received five pounds a year. His grandson was brought up in poverty by strict puritanical descendants of Ulster. He would learn that hard work and devotion to learning were duty before they were the door to opportunity. Ambitious and competitive, Meighen would make Alexander Mackenzie look effete. He was going to become the youngest prime minister since Confederation, but before that he was going to see how many careers he could excel at. During his lifetime he would be a teacher, a lawyer, a real-estate manipulator and a Bay Street executive. He would prove a master at everything except teaching and politicking.

He somehow got to the University of Toronto, and headed straight to mathematics. In 1896 he graduated with first-class honours. While at university he applied his sharp mind to debating contests. William Lyon Mackenzie King was there, too, and one does wish that there were records of great undergraduate debates between the two, or at least diary entries, but there are not. Meighen did not think that the short chubby fellow with the outgoing manner was worthy of his attention.

Meighen took a year of teacher-training, and then got a job

at a high school. It did not last long. The young instructor got into a dispute with directors and parents about whether he should be allowed to discipline the slackers in his classes. He was not willing to compromise: the example of God and the cause of perfection would not allow it. He would not teach at that school a second year.

Now he borrowed some money and tried investing in gadgets that did not catch on. He was a puritan in debt. But he was a mathematician too. He went to Winnipeg and taught school again, long enough to pay off his creditor. Then he articled in a law firm. In 1902 he went to Portage la Prairie and took over a scratch-wig law practice. During the next five years he applied his logical mind and his photographic memory. He got married and started a family with a son named Theodore Roosevelt Meighen. He put his money into real estate. Portage was a growing city, and the land was flat. Logic and mathematics and diligent work habits and the turning of very sharp phrases brought Meighen the rewards a puritan recognizes as meet. He was a self-made man, and when he went into politics in 1908 he did not owe anyone anything.

In 1902 he had joined the young Conservatives, and in the 1904 election campaign he made his first political speeches in support of a hapless Tory candidate for Portage-Neepawa. Four years later he was out on the hustings for himself, a lawyer arguing in front of a big jury staffed by farmers and farm-implement salesmen. This was free-trade Liberal country, but he won by 250 votes. At the age of thirty-four he was headed for Ottawa. After he made his first speech in the House, Prime Minister Laurier commented that Borden had found his man. From now on the non-sectarian Borden could play good cop and the puritanical Tory Meighen could play bad cop.

No one had ever heard such a sharp intellect in parliamentary debate. Meighen made speeches as a patient sailor makes a ship in a bottle. He appealed to the intellect of his voters and fellow-parliamentarians, and like Mackenzie before him, he assumed that that should be sufficient. He loved language, loved its music and texture. He should have been a poet but he wasn't. Liberals and Conservatives and Unionists in the House recognized that when it came to thinking and speaking he was their superior—and they disliked him for it. Meighen did not know how to make people like him; William Lyon Mackenzie King was never as brainy as Meighen, but he knew how to work on people.

Sir John A. Macdonald knew how to work on people, and he knew how to work both sides of the street. So did Laurier, and Arthur Meighen thought that he was seeing some kind of weakness of purpose or flabbiness of principle there. The thin man just did not get it. But he could sure make a speech! If you were to engage in debate with this rapier from the west, your head would be severed from your body before you could blink. But Meighen had the unfortunate habit of believing every syllable he was uttering. He never hesitated to demolish the argument of an opponent—or rival, because perfection would not allow compromise. He enjoyed his wit and irony, especially when it went over someone's head. Bruce Hutchison, as usual, has a nice phrase for Meighen's demeanour in debate: "supercilious perfection."

This was the boy who would not come out and play hockey, but stayed indoors, reading Shakespeare. Robert Borden had also grown up in an agricultural family that was strapped for funds. He knew what it was to lean against a stump and read the classics. When he had gone with his cabinet to Manitoba and points west on a 1902 tour, he had met the gaze of the young lawyer in Portage. He saw the lean and hungry look, but Robert Borden would never view himself as a Caesar. He took on the young westerner as a protégé, sometimes to the displeasure of older Conservatives. Here was a young man who could get elected as a Tory in an agricultural riding in anti-tariff country. In Borden's government he would rise quickly. He would become Solicitor-General, Secretary of State, Minister of the Interior and Minister of Labour. Most important of all, whenever the plain Robert Borden needed a hatchet-man he would call on Arthur Meighen. Meighen did not look on himself as a sacrificial figure—he was living in a world of right and wrong, and he was interested in legislating against wrong.

When Borden decided that the war emergency required a Union government, he turned to Meighen to round up the Liberal cabinet members. In fact the idea had probably been Meighen's to begin with. So too was the idea of the Wartime Elections Act that took the vote away from recent immigrants and gave it to soldiers' female next-of-kin. Meighen was then given the job of ramming through the conscription act, which task involved rousing support against any Tories who did not like the idea. He sponsored the bill that gave lots of money to the Canadian Northern Railroad, so now he was known as the friend of big business and the enemy of Quebec. His actions and words during the Winnipeg General Strike reveal the strength of his venom and the extremity of his conservatism.

Big business in Winnipeg had been trying to portray the strikers as the dupes of Moscow. In a report in the *Toronto Daily Star*, W.R. Plewman wrote from the scene:

It must be remembered that this [Winnipeg] is a city of only 200,000, and that 35,000 persons are on strike. Thus it will be seen that the strikers and their relatives must represent at least fifty per cent. of the population. In the numerical sense, therefore, it cannot be said that the average citizen is against the strike . . . there is no soviet. There is little or no terrorism.

Plewman's use of the word "citizen" was a gentle irony, in that the "Citizens' Committee" representing the employers ran a newspaper called the Winnipeg *Citizen*, in which the strike was characterized this way:

> It is a serious attempt to overturn British institutions in this western country and to supplant them with the Russian Bolshevik system of Soviet rule. . . . Why is it that one finds many thousands of men and women among the strikers who state quite frankly that they had no wish to strike—that they did not want to strike, and yet, paradoxically, they were on strike?
>
> It is because the 'Red' element in Winnipeg has assumed the ascendancy in the labour movement, dominating and influencing—or stampeding—the decent element of that movement, which desires the preservation of British institutions, yet is now striking unconsciously against them.

Meighen was the acting minister of justice when he sent this now famous telegram to his agent, A.J. Andrews:

> Notwithstanding any doubt I have as to the technical legality of the arrests and the detention at Stony Mountain, I feel that rapid deportation is the best course now that the arrests are made, and later we can consider ratification.

Strange advice to come from the Dominion's chief protector of the law! But the War Measures Act suggested war, and in a war the protection of "British institutions" must come before any "technical legality" that might be claimed by those outside agitators. Justifying his actions to the House of Commons, the acting justice minister said:

It was essential that the greater issue raised by the assumption of Soviet authority—and it was nothing less on the part of those in control of the strike in Winnipeg—should be once and for all decided and be decisively beaten down before they should concern themselves with the smaller and much less important issue upon which certain men had originally gone on strike.

If Canada had so faithfully supplied troops to help the British in Siberia protect the White Russians against the Bolsheviks, should she not also fight the Reds on her own soil? What was the use of Tory tariff walls without similar walls against the attack of Godless foreign communism?

So Meighen called the strikers out west Bolsheviks. During the rage of the conscription debate he had permitted himself to call Quebeckers "backward." Sometimes, when he was making one of his spiralling arguments he would forget that political opponents that were flat on their backs right now might be capable of rising later on. He was a devout right-wing Conservative, but he had a lot to do with the formation of quite different political movements in Quebec and western Canada. Mathematics treats the principles that have held the universe together since its inception. Meighen the mathematician had trouble seeing that the whole social condition of the twentieth century was going to be different from the nineteenth's. He was like the teacher who considered the Modernist writers, Joyce, Eliot and Pound, to be aberrations who should be deported. He knew Shakespeare by heart but he would never memorize "The Love Song of J. Alfred Prufrock," which had been published in 1915. A common phrase in his speeches was "to get back." It was equated with another, "get to normal." Of the Modernist world he said, "It is an age of indulgence, in Isms and theories." As far as he was concerned, these last were rainbows for the idle. His enemies were not only backward and

Red; they were also lazy. They were "anxious to improve their lot and seemingly unwilling to do it in the old fashioned way by hard honest intelligent effort."

No wonder, then, that when Borden decided to retire in 1920 and hand the controls of the government and party over to Meighen, he experienced a lot of resistance from his other ministers and backbenchers. One political figure who was delighted by his choice was William Lyon Mackenzie King, who had become Liberal leader in 1919.

Meighen was prime minister longer than any of the Conservatives that filled up space between Macdonald and Laurier. He beat John Abbott by eleven days. His government was Unionist in name only; Meighen was a doctrinaire Conservative, and an anglophile. When he made his first trip to England in 1917 he felt as if he had come home to the birthplace of civilization. Nevertheless, when he returned for the 1921 imperial conference, he persuaded the British to bring an end to their alliance with Japan, because the USA was not getting along with Japan, and Canada had to live next door to the USA. Canada, Meighen believed, was a British nation, but it was a new independent British nation. It was a lot like Britain and a lot like the USA. It could be a broker between the two.

When Meighen called the first post-war election for December of 1921, there would be no nonsense about Union government. This would be a showdown between young Meighen's Conservatives and young King's Liberals. Perhaps the prime minister had forgotten what transpired with the namesake of his first son in the US election of 1912. Teddy Roosevelt, rebuffed by the conservative Republicans, had formed his Progressive party and split the ballot enough that Woodrow Wilson's Democrats could ride up the middle and win. Maybe the prime minister's *hauteur* had not registered what had been happening in Ontario: in 1919 the provincial Conservatives were shunted aside by the United Farmers of Ontario, who gathered a plurality with forty-three seats, and formed a coalition with labour. Even in the federal scheme, three by-elections had been won by farmer candidates. Then in Winnipeg, that troublesome city, there transpired a convention of agricultural politicians, who announced the birth of the national Progressive party.

The times were changing. They were also suddenly bad. In the second half of 1920 there was a sudden and alarming business depression, just in time for the coming election. But the prime minister counselled hard work and frugality and British institutions. When he went into his election he would face King's Quebec-backed Liberals and a new party arriving from the west, the Progressives led by Thomas Crerar. Like the prime minister, Crerar had been born in rural Ontario but made his career in Manitoba. He was one of those Liberals brought into the 1917 Union cabinet, where he had served as Agriculture Minister until he quit in a huff. Now he was back, a reform Liberal calling himself a Progressive, and he was going to make the arrogant Arthur Meighen say bad words in his bathroom at night.

The new party came from rural Canada. Farmers are a conservative lot, except when it comes to tariffs. The Progressives were made up of old-fashioned farmers, Christian socialists and impatient Liberals. Twenty years later they would split up and reassemble in three other parties. For now they were the end of the Tories, the party that still managed to persuade itself that it was the natural leadership for a country created by Great Britain. But the campaign was waged on the person and personality of the prime minister. The Tories erected billboards with huge pictures of Meighen, and their simple slogan was "Canada Needs Meighen." Meighen's speeches continued his practice of insulting the voters without knowing that he was doing so. He more or less ran on Macdonald's policies of a half-century before, including the tariffs called the National Policy. Mackenzie King, on the other hand, came down lightly on both sides of every issue, not calling for the old Reformist free trade, but for an invention he called "freer trade." King just simply knew better than Meighen how to be a Canadian.

In December of 1921, the Progressives won 65 seats in Canada's Parliament. The Liberals, welcoming back the errant Unionists, won 117. Meighen's Conservatives had to settle for 50, none in Quebec and none on the prairies. The arithmetic did not look good to the mathematician. He had lost his seat, and so had most of his cabinet ministers. He was the youngest prime minister since Confederation to have been dumped from office. Now he probably remembered the words he had used to describe the young Mackenzie King, who had lost his seat in 1917, then succeeded Laurier as opposition leader in 1919: "outside leader in the outside party in this country." Meighen wanted to get back into the House as fast as he could, but he knew that once he was prime minister, King could delay a by-election for months. So he fell upon an ingenious tactic. He persuaded a newly elected Conservative for Grenville in Ontario, A.C. Casselman, to resign his seat and take a little civil-servant job for fifty dollars a year. Casselman resigned his seat, and a day after his new appointment, resigned *that* as well, so that he did not draw a cent of salary (puritan frugality overlooks no little corner). Meighen called a by-election, and then passed the prime minister's job over to the pudgy little fellow in the rumpled suit.

Mackenzie King opined in the press that Meighen was a little slithery. Meighen offered his usual characterization of his rival: "Indeed the senseless utterances of this man pass comprehension and it is indeed difficult to understand how he has advanced in spite of them." That kind of remark was rather mild in comparison with others he would make about King.

Consider this one: "the most contemptible charlatan ever to darken the annals of Canadian politics."

It was bad enough to be beaten by the smarmy two-sided young upstart with the inferior debating skills. It was worse to be the first post-Confederation leader of a third-place party. Thomas Alexander Crerar was entitled to the perks and power belonging to leader of the opposition. But he was, as far as Meighen was concerned, still a Liberal under another name. In fact, both Crerar and King would have liked to assemble a cabinet of Liberals and Progressives, but King's French Canadians and Crerar's conservative farmers nixed the idea. The closest that King could get to an alliance was an agreement by the Progressives not to act as the opposition. With a few smirks that suggested no surprise at the arrangement, Meighen agreed with the governor general's suggestion that the large Conservative rump act as His Majesty's Loyal Opposition.

CHAPTER 13

RISE OF THE
CIVIL SERVANT

———————◆·◉·◆———————

W.L. Mackenzie King 1921–26

As LEADER OF THE opposition Arthur Meighen could use his rapier wit against the Liberals, and especially King, instead of getting less-intelligent voters and Conservative politicians cheesed off at him. He could straighten himself out with the party, and get it ready for the next election, by which time even the Canadian populace would notice that the new prime minister was an oily little stumblebum. He could start by teaching himself French, hanging out in Quebec, reading French books and papers, speaking as often as he dared in his new language. It might come in handy for insulting King without the latter's understanding what he was saying. And he certainly liked to insult King. In the House everyone began to expect a relentless torrent of well-phrased destructive criticism from the new leader of the opposition.

Mackenzie King just kept smiling, and staying three or four steps ahead of the thin man.

In 1922 nothing much happened until the Chanak crisis. Hands up, all those who remember where Chanak is. Chanak, now called Canakkale, is a little port in the Dardanelles, where the Turks had beaten up on the Allies in the Great War. At the Treaty of Sèvres after the war, the Ottoman Empire was declared finished, and the Turks were supposed to stop hassling the Greeks along their Anatolian coast. But now the nationalist young Turks were in power, and they had military hardware. They had chased the Greeks out of the country, and now the remaining British at the occupation post in Chanak perceived the Turks as a threat to them. In September the British high command was up to its old tricks: they sent telegrams to the dominions asking when they might receive assurances that Commonwealth troops would be ready to put down the Turks. Once again the prime minister found out about the affair in the newspapers before he was contacted by the British government.

The Brits should have known by now that Canada would not come bounding in at a whistle from London. Winston Churchill, who would later refuse to talk to some half-naked savage named Gandhi, could not get used to a twentieth century in which God had withdrawn His proclamation that Britain was His blueprint. Churchill was now Colonial Secretary, but he had forgotten that Canada was not a colony. He had forgotten Borden. Yes, there were a lot of people in that country who considered themselves Brits abroad, and many of them rushed to the recruiting offices. But the Canadian prime minister referred to the impending conflict as a "European war." King had a pretty good idea of what the twentieth century looked like. He knew that his Quebeckers and western farmers were not dressed in the Union Jack. He also knew that there were lots of people inside and outside of Britain who did not support Lloyd George's pro-Greek, anti-Turk position. He told the Brits that he could not commit troops to a European war unless Parliament said he could, and he did not think that the Chanak affair was a good enough reason to assemble Parliament. He had taken one step past Borden toward re-identifying Canada.

It was a step that the opposition leader was bound to denounce. Meighen remembered his first trip to England, remembered how his heart had flipped in its cage. He was a British subject, and he really liked the way things used to be. He believed in duty and seeing one's duty. He was the man who had saved Winnipeg from the foreign attack on British institutions. Turks were just as foreign as Russians. He got up in Toronto's King Edward Hotel and to five hundred loyal businessmen he denounced King's step away from mother Britain. Quoting John A., he said: "Let there be no dispute as to where I stand. When Britain's message came, then Canada should have said 'Ready, aye ready; we stand by you'." The businessmen replied with wave after wave of loud applause.

A few days later the crisis at Chanak was not a crisis any more. With all his toe-turning in the dust, Mackenzie King had continued to rebuild the Liberal party. Arthur Meighen had presented himself as a knee-jerk imperialist. It is doubtful that he knew that he had lost this round, too.

A family tradition

Nowadays, when you mention William Lyon Mackenzie King, the few young people who recognize the name say oh yes, he was a weirdo, wasn't he? He should have been a prime minister of British Columbia. Didn't he talk to his dead dog and roam the night-time Toronto streets looking for ladies, or was it gents, of the night? A lot of this vague characterization results from a 1976 book called *A Very Double Life*, in which C.P. Stacey goes at King's enormous diaries and presents a neurotic private life for the prime minister who served longer than any other and led the country during the Great Depression and the Second World War. Since Stacey's book a lot of the writing about King has been in the form of psychological portraiture.

Of course there *was* his mother. She gave birth to Willy the year after Sigmund Freud started his university career in Vienna. One might say that Mackenzie King grew up with Freudian psychology.

Isabel Grace Mackenzie was born in New York because her father was a Canadian in exile. He was William Lyon Mackenzie, whose democratic radicalism had led to the thwarted Upper Canada Rebellion of 1837. When he tried to organize raids into Upper Canada from New York State, the usAmericans threw him into jail for half a year, after which he lived in penury until the amnesty of 1849. Then the family lived in penury in Canada. He turned down offers of jobs from the government because he did not want the image of the rebel to be dulled. But he did win a seat in the Assembly, and served till 1857. Unlike a lot of politicians, he did not get rich.

But he was the great rebel for a country that could use a great rebel. The radical reforms he had fought for would become government policy, but there were more radical reforms needed, and William Lyon Mackenzie's name would stand as a symbol for moral and political progress. In the last days of the nineteenth century the Conservative party did its best to make that name stand for treason, just as certain usAmericans had managed to do with Aaron Burr, and just as the Conservatives tried to do with Louis David Riel. That was not the story little Willy King heard. His mother told him of the heroism of his grandfather every day of his childhood, inspiring the boy to read the history books. He was a chubby little kid who got into a lot of punch-ups with the sons of Berlin's Tory citizens.

He did have another grandfather, of course, but his father

could not tell many heroic stories about John King. This grand-father was a British soldier, and in fact was based at Kingston during the 1837 Rebellion. So even Mackenzie King's DNA, as well as his name, might be said to have descended from both sides of an important issue; his grandparentage prepared him for the later hornswoggling of Arthur Meighen. In any case, John King died of consumption before he was thirty, and his son John was born four months later.

Willy King's father was a lawyer in Berlin, Ontario. While lit-tle Arthur Meighen was growing up as best he could on a mar-ginal farm up the road, the grandson of the great rebel got chubby in a home filled with good furniture and political phi-losophy. Isabel Grace Mackenzie had not moved from penury into luxury. John King was a so-so lawyer, and he never learned the lawyerly knack of making a fortune in real estate or politi-cal patronage. Still, Willy did make it to the University of Toronto, where he took on the nickname "Rex," and figured out how affability and secretiveness could combine to make one's way in the world. He studied hard, and though he did not have Meighen's quick intelligence, he had discipline. He read his class notes as he walked from bathroom to bedroom.

A new boy in the city, he learned something about the society his grandfather had tried to change. He took exploratory walks through the smoke-grimed slums of Toronto. He saw old men hucking gobs of lung on the street. He saw children with rickety legs. He saw skinny women with facial scars trying to sell their bodies. He visited Sick Children's Hospital. He would never tell Canadians to help themselves with old-fashioned hard work. When he went to the University of Chicago for graduate work in economics and sociology, he spurned the residence offered him and moved into Hull House, a social reclamation project in a terrible immigrant slum among the slaughterhouses and factories. He saw the bottom of the money system, "mysery &

wretchedness," as he wrote in a letter of December 1896, "vice & degradation, abomination & filthiness."

By the time of his twenty-second birthday, Rex King was learning that orthodox liberalism was not working. He could not be the descendant of Sandy Mackenzie, and not even the true son of Wilfrid Laurier. He was the grandson of the Great Rebel. When he got back to Toronto, he wrote articles not for the *Globe* which had been George Brown's paper, but the Tory opposition's *Mail and Empire*. He wrote exposés of slave wages in the garment district. He was also writing his thesis on the International Typographical Union. It was his newspaper work that got him into Liberal politics. Mackenzie and King were on their way.

More like a quadruple life

He was also writing his diary, and he would keep it faithfully all his life. Nowadays one could spend one's whole life in the National Archives, just reading that diary. C.P. Stacey lifted his title, *A Very Double Life*, from the 1898 diary of the young man who described his character that way. The psychoanalyzers see the duplicity in the strange difference between the public man with his strained tweed vest and dull speaking style, and the night-time spiritualist with his ouija boards and long strolls among the night women.

But there are many ways along which the doubleness seemed to pass. There is more writing about Mackenzie King than just about any other Canadian, but no one has ever been able to explain Mackenzie King. He was a bachelor whose best friends were women. He was a man who got rich working for the Rockefellers but identified himself as a poor man in sympathy with slum orphans. He spoke to dead people during seances but was not afraid to topple the shibboleths of his party if they stood in the way of scientific social progress. He knew how to slap a back and pop a wink, but he ran a cabinet as if it were constituted of competent marionettes. He read his Bible every morning but arranged his schedule according to superstition. He looked like a chubby rumpled shmoo with thin lank hair falling over his forehead, but he was as practical as a thin timberwolf. He made a later reputation as an international broker, but stayed a Canada-firster as much as possible. His campaign train was smothered in Union Jacks, but he reminded the Brits of how wide the Atlantic Ocean could be.

It is impossible to describe Mackenzie King, impossible to present him. That is why he was so successful. He wrote a lot. He spent a long time at universities. For half a century the university historians and the newspaper historians have been trying to offer a Mackenzie King to their readers and students. Twenty-five of those readers or students are likely to have twenty-five Mackenzie Kings. From 1908 to 1948 millions of Canadian voters would have more than that.

Laurier's lad

If, as Laurier said, Borden had found his man in Arthur Meighen, it might as fairly be said that Laurier found his man in Mackenzie King.

In 1900 the Laurier government, realizing that trade unions were here to stay, decided to publish a *Labour Gazette*, for "the dissemination of accurate statistical and other information relating to labour conditions and kindred subjects." Twenty-five-year-old Mackenzie King was hired as editor. It was not long till he was agitating for an official Department of Labour, and when it was formed, he was appointed deputy minister.

The government had passed Canada's first conciliation act in 1900, and now it was the new deputy minister's job to travel around the country trying to settle disputes between industry and workers. He brought two assets to the job—his experience with the working poor, and his friendly manner. He had a lot of successes, and Prime Minister Laurier was watching.

In 1908 the prime minister asked King to run for Parliament. He had been told that the young conciliator had said that if he were ever in cabinet he would want to be the Minister of Labour, and that was the position that Laurier had in mind for King. Meanwhile, King was writing in his diary about his belief that God had even greater work in mind for the Great Rebel's grandson. In 1908 he threw his hat, suit, shoes and socks into the ring in his hometown riding of North Waterloo, and won easily. He became the new Labour Minister just when Laurier's great cabinet had pretty well crumbled away. Laurier was starting to run his one-man show, and the peppy young King was his man's man. But he had time to insinuate his reformist ideas, arguing for the eight-hour day and a system of workmen's compensation. He got the Combines Investigation Act passed in 1910. It was a good illustration of his social theory: private industry should develop the country, but government should keep a close eye on private industry to prevent abuse of workers and their families. In his book *Industry and Humanity* (1918), he would envisage a partnership of business, labour and government in the enterprise called progress.

In 1911 Laurier was relieved of his job by the voters and Robert Borden, and Mackenzie King lost his seat after only three years. This may have been part of God's plan, as the diarist would write, but it was not good news on the financial front. As a civil servant and minister of the Crown he had been pulling in a good salary. He spent his savings on a rackelly-backelly farm across the river from Ottawa, and sent most of his earnings home to his unfortunate family. His sixty-eight-year-old father was going blind. His sainted mother, also sixty-eight, was seriously ill, and so was his brother, Macdougall. This was going to be an emotional decade for Mackenzie King. By 1921 he would be prime minister of Canada. But his sister Isabel would die in 1915. His father would die in 1916. His mother would die the day after he was defeated in her father's riding in the 1917 election. And his brother would die of tuberculosis in 1922. Only his sister Jennie would be left to marry and settle in Barrie, and visit her old brother in later life.

So Willy King was the breadwinner, and after 1911 there was no time for leisure. For a couple years he worked for the Liberal party, and tried to get Laurier to find him a by-election seat, but the party and the leader did not go out of their way to help out their altruist. He got a little money for a speech here and there. One of his rich lady friends helped out with an allowance. But he was disappointed, sad, lonely and frustrated. He read his Bible and his favourite self-help books. Something had to come along and lift up the champion of the urban poor.

Along came the Rockefeller Foundation of New York. Mackenzie King stepped jauntily into another paradox. Would his grandfather have worked for John D. Rockefeller? Had any Rockefeller ever walked around the slums of Chicago? Well, if Laurier was going to turn his back on Mackenzie King, the USAmerican plutocrat would get the advantage of King's expertise as a labour negotiator. The Rockefellers were having a lot of trouble with unions and foreign agitators, especially in their mines. They were willing to give forty-year-old Mackenzie King twenty thousand dollars a year to advise John D. Rockefeller Jr. on what to do about his workers and their strikes. The prime minister of Canada wasn't making twenty thousand dollars.

In fact the prime minister of Canada was spending his time in British hospitals, talking with legless youths. The us was not at war, but businesses such as the Rockefellers' were making a pile by supplying minerals to warring countries. Mackenzie King could have argued that he was doing post-graduate work in economics, but his absence was noted around Ottawa. Nevertheless, when the 1917 election was called, he ran for Laurier in North York, where William Lyon Mackenzie had won nine times. William Lyon Mackenzie King lost. Almost all the Liberals in Ontario lost. He had argued against conscription, though he felt that it might be necessary. It looked like the end of the political road for the man who had always thought that the secret hand of God or at least fate had been pushing him toward high office.

Still, he had John D. Rockefeller Jr., and now he also had an offer from the Carnegie Foundation. More millionaires, certainly, but the Carnegie job would entail advising on worthy charities. Now Mackenzie King had to negotiate for himself, and somehow he pulled it off. He would be retained by the USAmerican millionaires for $25,000 a year, but he would be permitted to live most of the time in Canada, mending political fences, and checking out old Wilfrid Laurier's health. He spent a lot of time in Quebec, pointing out to French-Canadian Liberals that he had remained loyal to Laurier during the catastrophe of 1917.

Younger than Meighen

King had been defeated in two elections in a row, in two ridings. His family was dying around him. Laurier had not anointed him his successor. He made his living outside the country. He was a bachelor with no identifiable connections. He had just published a boring book in which he said that absolutely free competition in business had brought "desolation to the very heart of the human race." What chance did this man have in the Liberal nomination convention of 1919? He decided to put his campaign into the hands of the spirit world and the Quebec Liberals. While old William Fielding and a few others rounded up their support, King went to England to do some labour research for his man Rockefeller. He got back to Ottawa just in time for the convention. The workers' friend almost didn't make it—his ship had been delayed by a maritime strike.

It was a hot August in Ottawa, but it had been hotter in Winnipeg that summer. Mackenzie King the labour conciliator had been safely out of the country. Borden the prime minister was losing western votes and losing the Liberals in his Union government. In Ottawa there were several leadership candidates with serious faces because of the death of Laurier and the peril facing the country. Mackenzie King was still a bouncing portly unwrinkled glad-hander of forty-five years. Most of the other candidates took one look and quit. Fielding stayed in, but he had two problems: he was seventy years old, and he had voted for conscription. On the morning of the ballots, King put on his best striped trousers and read these encouraging words in one of his favourite inspirational texts: "Nothing shall be impossible unto you." Inspirational books were very popular in 1919. Chances are that the other four candidates were reading them that morning too.

But cherubic young King led on every ballot, and on the last one he beat back Fielding 476 to 438. He was the new leader, but almost half the delegates had voted for the old finance minister who had been in favour of tariffs and conscription. The left and right had nearly split the vote fifty-fifty. Mackenzie King took note of that. Then he got himself a Commons seat, representing the Prince constituency in P.E.I.

The next year Robert Borden let it be known that he wanted to retire and write books. He was going to pass the leadership of his party to a new man. Oh please, said Mackenzie King to his auditors in the spirit world, let it be Arthur Meighen.

The secret prime minister

As the first post-Confederation prime minister without a decent House majority, Mackenzie King had to find space to dance between the conservatives in the Tory party and his own, and the Progressives, who often clamoured for constitutional change, for recall and referenda, for instance. Every once in a while a party from out west will call for recall and referenda, believing that governments are the yens of the citizenry made flesh.

In 1921 Lady Laurier died and left the Laurier house not to the Liberal party but to Mackenzie King. The furniture all went elsewhere, and the plumbing and gas did not work well, but King moved in happily, acquiring Wilfrid Laurier's brass bed to dream in, and beginning to overfill the big pile with quaint Victorian furniture and ornaments. The news got out in Liberal circles that King was not averse to accepting gifts of giant settees and spindly tables. Across the river at his country place, Kingsmere, he would begin to supervise workmen as they uncomprehendingly assembled a small city of stone ruins gathered from noble buildings that had seen their last days in Ottawa and Toronto. Included would be chunks of the original burned-out Parliament Buildings. Stonemason Sandy Mackenzie looked down in wonderment. In later years the prime minister would take foreign dignitaries on weekend jaunts to the much-expanded estate and show off his ruins. Uh huh, yes, they would nod, wondering what a strange place ancient Canada must have been.

For his first few sessions as prime minister, King tried not to make any mistakes. He moved slowly and diplomatically. He even said nice things about the leader of the opposition, which made the leader of the opposition even more browned off. King assembled a cabinet with important posts for Quebec ministers. Having wooed the Liberals back from the Union cabinet before the election, he now started working on the Liberals who were in the Progressive party. He paid attention to the west, building branch railroads all over the prairies.

The post-war slump seemed to be over, and of course King claimed that his four university degrees and experience with the US economy were responsible. His main technique was to do nothing that would make interesting headlines in the newspapers. When once in a while he did, as with the Chanak affair, he played the strings of Canadian nationalism that had been strung by Canada's record in the Great War. He wanted the Canadian people to get used to a Liberal government with King at the wheel. He invited lots of immigrants and told them that this Liberal Canada was their families' fortune. He carefully drew an image of himself as a dull and competent head of government. Meanwhile his main work was to build a nationwide Liberal machine that would know what to do in the future; he would let Arthur Meighen have the past.

But at the same time his earnest Christianity was making way for spookier facets of the supernatural. Through one of his many lady friends he was introduced to table-knocking in dark parlours. Soon he was visiting lots of mediums, and conferring with his dead family. Eventually he would make contact with famous people from all walks of death. It is unlikely that a man who had gone to graduate school at Harvard University was basing government policy on what he heard in a seance, but he had to be careful to keep his ghosts secret from his colleagues. Imagine what Mr Meighen might have risen to say had he found out where his odious rival was spending his evening hours.

It was not that King's superstitions played no part in his political actions. He looked for omens everywhere. He liked to sign bills at the moment when the hands on the clock were aligned. He paid attention to people's birthdates, and looked for some unseen order in any coincidences that happened to occur. He may have looked to his Saviour as his guide and inspiration to "the fulfillment of purpose for which I was created," as he so humbly put it in his diary, but he felt more comfortable if the signs were right.

King's response to the Chanak challenge was one of his steps toward Canadian independence. For another he turned to the USA with which he was so familiar. In 1923 he sent his Quebec man Lapointe to Washington to sign a fish treaty with the USAmericans. There had been lots of fish treaties in North America, but in previous times people such as John A. Macdonald were members of a British contingent. Now the British had to watch Mackenzie King handling his own foreign bargaining without asking London's permission. A year later King was carrying the message straight into the heart of the empire. At his first imperial conference he made a nuisance of himself, shocking the Brits and the other dominions with his confidence. Canada, he said, would not accede to a centralized or even unified imperial policy. The determining cause of Canadian action would be the Canadian Parliament. Old men with white whiskers spluttered and said unkind things about this upstart. He was no white knight, that was certain.

By the time of the Roaring Twenties the United States had learned to consider itself the most powerful and important country in the world, and was portraying itself as isolated from old European problems. Mackenzie King had heard his old chief say that this was Canada's century, and though he had been close enough to the Rockefellers to doubt that, he was equating nationalism with isolationism. We had spent a lot of

Canadian youth in the battle between the European empires. We had earned the right to make a big new country over here, and little by little to make a more progressive one.

Four years after being elected he had most of his wandering Liberals back. He had smoothed things with Quebec. His economic wisdom had raised the standard of living, and he had been able to reduce taxes and balance the budget. It was a good time for an election. King wanted a nice comfortable majority. He called an election for October 29, 1925. He was a shoo-in.

The unseen hand guiding Mackenzie King's fortune must have been playing some joke. When the votes had been counted, the country looked like Laurier's nightmare. The Liberals took Quebec. The Tories took English Canada except for Saskatchewan and Alberta. King's total fell to 101 seats. Meighen had 116. The Progressive rump won 24, and there were a few others. King was thrown out in North York.

Limping on

The voters in Ontario kept throwing him out. He must have had great faith in the Deity's designs for him. Meighen naturally thought that as leader of the most highly represented party, he should be designated prime minister again. But King, though not a few Liberals were beginning to look for another champion, marched over to see the governor general, Baron Byng, and said that he was going to try to cozy up to the Progressives and carry on. Baron Byng, who could be a clueless vice-regent at times, said okay. In later years the rhyming antagonists would give differing versions of the deal they had made.

These would be busy times for King. He had to slow down his pursuit of the ladies, married and otherwise, and tiptoe around constitutional hazards. To the House of Commons he had to submit his proposal to continue as prime minister. He had to arrange a cabinet of surviving ministers, and he added Saskatchewan premier Charles Dunning, his chief rival among the edgy Liberals. In exchange he arranged for himself a seat in Prince Albert, which he would represent until 1945. It looked as if he might be able to rebuild the national party he had rebuilt four years earlier. When the January 1926 session opened, his main tactic was delay and obfuscation. While he waited for his seat in Parliament, he got Ernest Lapointe to show such an interest in the finer points of the speech from the throne that it was debated until every punctuation mark was considered.

Meanwhile, now that the Liberals from the Progressive party had returned to the fold, the wily prime minister went to work on the leftists. His main target was J.S. Woodsworth, the former socialist church minister who had been imprisoned by the Conservatives during the Winnipeg strike. The government's budget speech hinted at the first old-age pensions, a logical development from King's book *Industry and Humanity*. He knew what would happen. The Tory Senate slapped the bill down, and Woodsworth had yet another reason not to abide Arthur Meighen. So far, so good.

King liked this: the Liberals were taking the high moral road. But then a west-coast grocer and Conservative member of Parliament rose and said that he had heard terrible things about the Liberals' Department of Customs in recent times, namely since the USAmericans had passed their prohibition amendment. It was not as if King did not know about the rumours. Before this election he had made sure that his former minister in charge of customs was stowed away in the Senate. Unfortunately his new Minister of Customs did not understand about the high road. There was a lot of money to be made off

US prohibition. In the movies it is always organized crime that cleans up. But good times could be had by Canadian booze makers and Canadian customs employees.

When the Conservatives raised the point, the Liberals and Progressives said that there should be an investigative committee. When it became obvious that the committee had bad news for the government, Mackenzie King thought about John A. Macdonald. Maybe Macdonald was hurt for a while by the Pacific Scandal. Now King had a Pacific Ocean's worth of whisky to explain away. He was a teetotalling man; what did he know about hooch? It was time to pull another fast one on poor Arthur Meighen. Meighen was bouncing up and down in his chair. He thought he had the porky miscreant at last.

Mackenzie King marched over to see the governor general again. I would like to dissolve the House and hold another election, he said. Hold on a minute, said Baron Byng, I think we will give Meighen a chance to govern. King raided the shelves of the law library and threw book after book at the governor general. It was no use: Byng would have his Conservative government. One hundred and sixteen seats, don't you know?

On June 18, Mackenzie King got up in the Commons and announced in a choking voice that the Government of Canada was no more.

Arthur Meighen had pulled off a feat that only John A. Macdonald before him had accomplished. He was prime minister for a second time. It was clear to him that the Canadian people, having seen the alternative, would hail him as their necessary leader.

CHAPTER 14

CURSES, HE DID IT AGAIN!

Arthur Meighen 1926

WHEN KING TENDERED his resignation and heard that Byng
was going to offer Meighen the chance to give it a try, he
was afraid for a while that Meighen would refuse, thus sending
the ball back into the governor general's proxy court. What
would Byng do? He couldn't offer the job to the Progressives.
He would have to say yes to an election. Mackenzie King was
not sure that an election was what he wanted right then, given
what had happened last time and what had happened since.
Please, he prayed, please, let Meighen get a good look at the
cheese. Let Meighen be a hungry mouse.

Meighen was not only hungry. He was still labouring under
the illusion that the Canadian voter knew what was happening.
The Canadian voter, already sickened by the customs scandal,
would see King's devious manipulations of British constitutional practice, and rush back into the arms of the Conservative party, true custodians of noble British traditions, and the
right order's choice for administration of British civilization in
Canada. He accepted Byng's suggestion, and became prime
minister again. The circumstances were not perfect, but it
looked as if we were on our way to things as they were meant to

be. The first thing he had to do was win a vote of confidence in the House. He had had the Progressives he needed during the customs scandal. They would still be there for the vote of confidence.

Now King, who had been frantically trying to keep his job, had the time to do a little thinking. A little thinking and listening to friends living and dead. He had been doing a lot of reading while throwing the law books at Baron Byng. In those books he found himself an angle. Heh heh heh, he may have said, while inserting bookmarks and hiking to the Hill.

In 1926 a man who was appointed prime minister by the governor general had to get elected to the House. If he was already in the House, he had to resign his seat and run again. Any cabinet ministers he appointed also had to resign their seats and run again. This presented two big problems for Arthur Meighen. The numbers would not let him survive a vote of confidence without those cabinet ministers in the House. And he did not have a surrogate with anything like his own debating brilliance to hold the fort while he went somewhere to get elected. He was stuck in a lovely Catch-26.

The prime minister should have been a ventriloquist. As it was, while waiting for a seat he had to hide behind a curtain and listen without speaking directly to Parliament when it opened June 29. Messages passed back and forth would have to do for the moment. But he thought that he had found a way around the cabinet problem. In order to keep them in their seats he had his men operate as an acting cabinet, without the extra pay that would go to normal ministers. Such an arrangement might look odd to any citizens who cared, but it would keep Mackenzie King quiet. In the first few days the leader of the opposition fired a shot here and a shot there, losing by narrow margins. But he was just waiting for the right moment to release the spring that would close the trap he had invented. It is likely that he waited for a lucky number date and a propitious display of the hands on the parliamentary clock.

On the last day of June the portly figure in the three-piece suit with the strained vest rose casually, as if he were prepared to argue for argument's sake, as so often happened during the summer in that place. He said that he just had a simple question: had the cabinet members taken their oaths? If the cabinet members had not taken their oaths, they were illegal, weren't they? King looked up at the Speaker, innocence and curiosity in his little face. Behind his curtain Arthur Meighen's high white collar began to rotate.

A person who happened on some parliamentary history would know that in both Canada and England, cabinet ministers in the past had before this acted without being sworn in. In British parliamentary law there really was no unambiguous statement that would support King. It didn't matter: he began to fulminate against these duplicitous Tories who were rising perilously against hundreds of years of parliamentary tradition. Like Borden and Laurier before him, Mackenzie King would sometimes take time off his independence schedule to wrap himself in the Union Jack.

In any case, he was not speaking to centuries of British parliamentary tradition: he was speaking to twenty-four Progressive members, and a few others. Soon it became too noisy in the House for anyone to hear what he was saying anyway. July 1, on Confederation's fifty-ninth birthday, the Liberals brought down Meighen's three-day government by a single vote. Meighen scored another first in Canadian history. His was the first government to lose a vote of confidence.

All right, thought King. Now Meighen will go to Byng to try for a dissolution, but Byng will once again refuse and will give me another chance. He was not quite aware of two things about Byng: the governor general did not have a firm grasp on the principles of parliamentary government, and the governor general really did not like Mackenzie King. He gave Meighen a dissolution, and the three-day prime minister called an election for September 14.

Mackenzie King was furious, or at least he let on that he was. Byng had just given him a marvellous campaign issue.

CHAPTER 15

IN THE LIGHT
OF TRUTH

————◦•◦•◦————

W.L. Mackenzie King 1926–30

THERE WERE TWO big surprises in 1926. The Montreal
Maroons won their first Stanley Cup, and Mackenzie King
won his first solid majority. The Conservative party, or rather
Arthur Meighen, was surprised that the populace would elect a
bunch who had profited during the customs scandal. They
were surprised that anyone would pay attention to King's point
of view in the obviously concocted constitutional crisis. King
did not make any memorable speeches about Canadian unity
or continental free trade during the campaign; he just kept
reminding people that the governor general and the anglophile Meighen had tried to steal Canada's sovereignty away. He
had faith that the voters would not understand the legalities
but would respond to emotional words, no matter how poorly
they were delivered.

Most of the Liberal campaign was given to door-knocking all
over the country. Meighen thought that he was still in the
debating society. He could not see why ordinary folks would
resent or distrust his D'Artagnan wit. He *could* get off some

good ones. When King tried to present himself as the pioneer of Canadian independence, Meighen alluded to Borden's earlier success. He painted a picture of King energetically crashing his way through a door that had been open for some time. But he was always playing to the witty judges of the school debate, not to the man or woman with the ballot in hand. Just before the 1926 election he wrote a piece for *Maclean's* magazine, in which he announced, "The people of Canada are on trial." A poor choice of words, a grassroots adviser might have told him. Canadians do not like to be told that they are suspected criminals.

The Liberals won 128 seats. The Tories, in trouble everywhere but Ontario, won 91. The other 26 members, being various Progressive and farm voices, would be no problem for King. He could now forget about the Grit movement to replace him, but characteristically he would call on his skills as a conciliator to embrace them in a unified national party. From now till his death in 1950 the Liberal party would be his. And for most of the half-century to come the country would elect Liberals.

Quiet, we're sleeping

The Montreal Maroons rested on their laurels for the next few years. In fact they would not win another Stanley Cup until 1935, the year in which Mackenzie King would manage his next election victory.

In 1926 King was fifty-one years old, a bachelor who enjoyed the company of women who were older than him and married to someone else. He was full of spit and vinegar. He got on his knees and prayed every night, and he read inspirational passages every morning from a book his sister had given him. He wrote assiduously and ungrammatically in his diary, of his high Christian aspirations and his progressive political feelings. He interpreted his dreams and recorded the advice he got from people such as Wilfrid Laurier in these dreams, which he came to call visions. In his study at Laurier House he kept an illuminated pre-Raphaelite painting of his mother. In the painting she looks a lot like William Lyon Mackenzie. In casual chatter people make Freudian implications about King and his mother. They should look at this painting. Mackenzie King valued his mother as the link between him and the Little Rebel. He knew the link as both physical and spiritual, and as far as he was concerned the physical and spiritual were inextricable from one another.

Here is the question about that link: was Mackenzie King here to carry on the work of the Little Rebel, or had William Lyon Mackenzie been placed on earth to prepare the way for King? Another question: was Mackenzie King a Laurier Liberal or a Mackenzie Reformer? Were the rebelliousness and anti-oligarchism of his grandfather mainly a romantic source of identification and inspiration? Or could we expect the prime minister with the nice majority to upset the Family Compact with his radical legislation?

We should remember what Rockefeller had paid him so well to do. King was a very successful conciliator, first in the United States, and then across Canada. When Rockefeller sent him to his mine sites in Colorado, he was sending him to a place of strife that broke out often into murderous violence. The conciliator was talking with miners who had faced guns and horses and dogs, in a western United States in which law and order were often pretty well privatized. But though he was being paid very well by the millionaires, he held onto his belief that national wealth should be a cooperative project. Plutocrat and worker and voter should negotiate a partnership whose purpose was to develop a nation. If they could all do so with Christian idealism, so much the better.

King would spend his whole political life as a conciliator. His vision of the country resembled one big company union. He had a lot of university degrees, and Harvard University even gave him a PhD for one of his government reports in 1909. But he was no theorist, and he would never win a debate with someone like Meighen. While his opponent was scoring points, however, he would be talking with various people on the telephone. When his opponent sat down at last he would notice how cold his chair was because his trousers would be gone.

In the early twenties Canada needed a conciliator. The country had secured its place in the family of nations, but the price at home had been high—the war had exacerbated all kinds of rivalries and factional conflicts. Quebec used to be half of the country; now it was feeling isolated while railroads reticulated in the west. Westerners found more than tariffs to complain about when they got an eastern ear. The provinces guarded their jurisdictions. Unions created by immigrants complained about owners who imported non-union immigrants. King listened to all sides, and tried to negotiate the narrow spaces among them. He tried to do as little as possible. It became clear that he was not going to quickly reshape the country according to *Industry and Humanity*. In fact, during the late twenties he allowed some party spokesmen to voice leftist sentiments while he sidled toward the right wing of the party.

Times were relatively good in 1926. According to the USAmerican image machines, these were the Roaring Twenties, when Yanks kept inventing wonderful gadgets, and slickly dressed Ivy League boys partied all night and wound up with laughing flappers in city fountains. Mackenzie King had himself a good meal, went home, wrote in his diary, kissed his dog Pat good night, said a prayer, and went to bed. At work during the daytime he might not be garrulous, but he communicated with everyone. He was a loner surrounded by human beings. But he knew that though politics is the art of the possible, it is made possible by the unseen world. The unseen world included God and His Son, as well as ghosts and spirits and the magic of names and numbers. He was not alone in these notions. There were a lot of Margaret Trudeau types in the twenties.

Put it this way: Mackenzie King always saw himself in history, and history could be spooky.

A step or two

The Canadian Liberals had always seen themselves as relatives of the Whigs and Liberals in England, but after 1918 the British Liberals fell apart at the seams, and were replaced by Labour when it came to the big battles with the Tories. To a conciliator such as Mackenzie King that meant two things: he would make a truly Canadian Liberal party with no obvious connections with twentieth-century Brits, and he would have to use his great charm to keep his national party from segmenting. He would perfect his tactics of edging. The tariffs would edge downward, but not so swiftly as to alienate his supporters in business. He did not have to worry about alienating anyone in his own riding, because he had so far been successful in parachuting into ridings in the east and west. He could consider the whole country as his constituency.

So once in power again, he reintroduced the old-age pension bill, and this time it passed both houses. This was a tiny step toward the welfare state, and though some Tory moneybags warned that civilization would crumble, the rest of the country seemed to think that it was a step in the right direction. The provinces would help the feds give twenty dollars a month to people over seventy years of age, if they really needed it. Meanwhile, Canada was paying off its war debts, so the bankers did as well as the old folks. The economic boom kept booming, so King's government lowered taxes every year. In fact, there was even talk of putting an end to the "temporary" income tax brought in during the war.

The twenties were not good for everyone. The maritime provinces had begun to fall behind everyone to their west, and asked whether they could get a break from the Dominion. There were a lot of potential Conservative voters back there, so King reduced freight rates in the region, and applied a few subsidies, but warned that he would not be able to make a habit of it. He heard a few gripes from out west, you can be sure. But he was balancing the budget, and guarding the surplus.

This was King's dance floor, and he knew all the steps.

He made a few moves overseas, too. He was representing ten million Canadians when he attended the imperial conference of 1926 five weeks after his amazing election. The Brits did not gush over him as they had over Laurier, but King did not complain. He really liked the big dinners, and took the time to consult with some eminent spiritualists. He also tried out his worldly charm on his fellow first ministers. They were meeting in committee with Lord Balfour, who used to be a prime minister himself and was now a cabinet minister in the host country. This committee continued the work of earlier Commonwealth ministers, and came up with what would for some reason be called the Balfour Report. The Balfour Report would be good news for sovereigntists in Canada, South Africa, New Zealand, Australia and the Irish Free State. They, along with Britain, were declared to be

autonomous Communities within the British Empire, equal in status, in no way subordinate one to another in any aspect of their domestic or external affairs, though united by a common allegiance to the Crown, and freely associated as members of the British Commonwealth of Nations.

Though still ambiguous, and though generally a formal description of conditions already in place, the Balfour Report was another step toward Canadian autonomy. Such events and statements would continue to mark the history of Canadian prime ministers until Pierre Elliott Trudeau's repatriation of the Canadian Constitution in 1982.

Nineteen twenty-seven was, of course, the sixtieth anniversary of Confederation, and Anglo people were still interested in diamond jubilees. For the occasion, Mackenzie King's regular publisher, Macmillan of Canada, released *Message of the Carillon and Other Addresses,* a collection of King's speeches, many of them from that year. Critics have often noticed that King's writing style was not elegant. His predilection during all his university years had been the gathering of information, not the creating of fine prose. The writing in most of the speeches is not all that bad, but it does not have Borden's directness or Laurier's flair. A rather crabbed sentence in the introduction, though, might show that King was not unfriendly toward literature: "For the most part, they [the speeches] are the fruit of an endeavour to be faithful to a tradition of British public life which aims at an association of letters with politics, and an interpretation on the part of public men of events in which they may be called upon to participate."

We know the reading habits of Macdonald and Laurier and Borden, for example. (I don't recall Brian Mulroney, in later years, quoting poetry.) From his diaries we know that Mackenzie King did carry on the tradition, though restricting his reading to the English language. He spent many an evening with one of his women friends, reading Matthew Arnold. He was fond of

Wordsworth's "Ode to Duty," which does not soar as some of Wordsworth's poems do, but which addresses the moral law that pervades all creation. Its last stanza carries a sentiment that says a lot about Mackenzie King's approach to his job:

> To humbler functions, awful Power!
> I call thee: I myself commend
> Unto thy guidance from this hour;
> Oh, let my weakness have an end!
> Give unto me, made lowly wise,
> The spirit of self-sacrifice;
> The confidence of reason give;
> And in the light of truth thy Bondman let me live!

It is not hard to believe in King's belief in that guidance, nor in his willingness to associate it with the dear departed.

In his speeches and letters King would quote Canadian verse, too. Many might find it unfortunate that he liked most often to quote from Wilfred Campbell, who too had been born in Berlin, Ontario, fifteen years before King. Once at a dinner in New York he quoted these lines, which he heard as support for his ideas in *Industry and Humanity*:

> Teach me the lesson that Mother Earth
> Teacheth her children each hour,
> When she keeps in her deeps the basic root,
> And wears on her breast the flower.

> And as the brute to the basic root
> In the infinite cosmic plan,
> So in the plan of the infinite mind
> The flower of the brute is man.

Here we see that Campbell has a glimmer of Wordsworth's gleam, but we can't help hearing "The Cremation of Sam McGee."

"Message of the Carillon" was the title speech in King's book. It was delivered to celebrate the diamond jubilee and the new peace tower clock built to replace the tower that had fallen in the great fire of 1916. Of course, King loved such symbolic moments, and directed that the carillon be started at exactly twelve o'clock noon, when both hands of the clock were pointed straight up. The bells played "O Canada!" The prime minister felt the presence of Wilfrid Laurier, and could almost believe that this was Canada's century after all.

In September of 1927 world heavyweight champion Gene Tunney would defeat Jack Dempsey in the most famous prize fight of all time. That month, too, Babe Ruth would set baseball's most famous record with his sixtieth home run. Ruth had hit his first professional home run into Lake Ontario at Toronto. Tunney would soon retire and be made an honorary director of the *Globe and Mail*. Nineteen twenty-seven was a heady year in North America, and the Canadian prime minister looked forward to continuing fortune.

Meanwhile, in Germany the Weimar Republic was enjoying boom times too, and Hitler's Nazi party had lost almost half of its seats.

In 1928 Mackenzie King would cross the Atlantic again, to have a closer look at the wonderful new era of peace in Europe. For the first time, he represented Canada not at London but at Geneva. King had never been all that much interested in the League of Nations, and he had not pushed for a Canadian seat in the Council of the League, but he did like the international mazdas, so he went to Geneva. On the way there he stopped over in Paris to sign the Briand-Kellogg Pact.

Aristide Briand was the Foreign Minister of France. In 1925 at Locarno the French, Germans and Belgians signed a non-aggression pact that fixed their post-war boundaries. The pact was guaranteed by Britain and Italy. At last the ancient animosity of Germany and France would be eradicated by the flourish of a pen or two. Aristide Briand and Gustav Stresemann, Foreign Minister of Germany, were tight friends. They both had Locarno fever, and went around their respective republics praising peace. In the aftermath of 1918 public speakers said "peace" a lot. They hoped that there was a magic force in words. After Germany was included in the League of Nations, Briand and Stresemann had lunch in the Alps and came down from the mountains holding hands.

Briand was always looking for an angle. In 1927 he proposed to the USAmericans that to commemorate the tenth anniversary of the US entry into the Great War, the two countries should sign a pact renouncing war as an instrument of national policy. Asking the USA to consider that step illustrates the degree of optimism around in the late twenties. Frank Billings Kellogg, the USAmerican foreign secretary, waited six months, then suggested that the whole world should be invited to sign such a pact. In August of 1928, Briand organized a goofy pageant in the streets of Paris, and fifteen nations sat down to sign the Briand-Kellogg Pact. Mackenzie King, despite all his spiritualism, did not believe that world peace would be guaranteed by such a ceremony, but stopped on his way to Geneva to sign.

Eventually the vast majority of world states would sign the Briand-Kellogg Pact. Argentina, Bolivia, Brazil, Saudi Arabia and Yemen would abstain. Many of the others had their fingers crossed behind their backs. As for Prime Minister King—he enjoyed the attention in the newspapers that seemed to take the meeting seriously. While signing "Mackenzie," he would confide to his diary, "dear Mother's spirit seemed to come between me & the paper, to almost illumine it." The pact did not say anything about peacekeeping methods, but it did contribute to the optimism of the 1920s.

King then went as a tourist to Italy, took in all the sights, and completed the obstacle course that led to a meeting with Benito Mussolini. He found *Il Duce* to have a countenance of "sadness & tenderness as well as great decision." As he left Italy he was encouraged by its progress: "the *people* not the classes have come into their own."

Thud!
—

In the spring of 1929 Mackenzie King was feeling rosy. He was going to pass Borden to become the third-longest-serving prime minister; and it was dawning on him that he could go for the record. Why not? Times were great and promised to get greater. There was one little bother: the new US president, Herbert Hoover, had said something about higher tariffs on agriculture. The new Conservative leader was making the customary Tory noises about Canadian tariffs. But Canada was prosperous at last, and it would remain so, as the Liberals promised more tax breaks and tariff reductions.

On October 29, Wall Street came crashing down. Portly men in striped pants flashed by high windows. All at once simple investors began to suspect that capitalism might not work forever if you just left it alone. A reading of Mackenzie King's *Industry and Humanity* might have warned of such a catastrophe. But now it looked as if King had not read the book lately. Yes, there were grandmothers selling apples in the streets, but he swallowed the line that the market was just taking a bigger-than-usual adjustment. He had drifted pretty far to the right of his party, and now he took a classic laissez-faire approach, trying to hold down public spending. He was beginning to sound less like a conciliator and more like an ideologue. If he was not careful, he might pull a Meighen and say something definite and unwise before the next election.

And he did. King's biographers and apologists cannot figure out why he lost his political savvy before the election of 1930. A legend grew in later years that he handed the prime minister's job to R.B. Bennett because he knew that the Great Depression would ruin the career and reputation of any head of government. But usually when he was pulling one of his fast ones, he would brag about it in his diaries. Most historians agree that this man with the degrees in economics and other social sciences just did not understand how to handle a sudden avalanche of unemployment and poverty.

In the western plains people would come to stealing new horse buns from their neighbours to try to grow carrots. Men rode the rods toward Mexico, trying to sneak into US breadlines on the way south. Children's feet would be deformed from wearing rubber boots that became too tight. People tried to eat things they had never thought of eating.

Maybe the prime minister was working too hard. Maybe Bennett was less witty than Meighen and therefore harder to ignore. By early 1930 it began to look as if we were getting a deep depression rather than a momentary glitch. The provinces were having a terrible time handling the threat of unemployed men on the streets. In British Columbia, a veterinarian named Tolmie had glad-handed the Conservatives into power; now he noticed that the USAmericans were not buying logs and fish. He joined the other Conservative premiers in asking the Dominion government for help in relieving unemployment. These premiers were persistent, and mentioned morality a lot. R.B. Bennett, the rich Calgary lawyer, mentioned morality in the House of Commons.

Mackenzie King could not hear his mother. He stood up, and

people all over the chamber could hear a snapping sound. "I would not give a single cent to any Tory government!" he shouted. The ghosts of Mackenzie and Laurier were saying "shut up and sit down," but the prime minister could not hear them—there was a cacophony of voices from the other side of the room. King stood on his toes and dived in. He shouted that the Tories were not really interested in the unemployed. As for people with "policies diametrically opposed to those of this Government, I would not give them a five-cent piece!"

He had no idea how a tired mother up the dirt road from Whitewood, Saskatchewan felt about a five-cent piece. He thought that it was the speculators who were caught by the crash. He was doing all right with his bonds and his bequests from the Rockefellers. If there was a drought, the rains would come sometime.

It was going to rain nickels. There was some change in the weather.

The governor general persuaded King to call an election for the summer, and the combative grandson of the Little Rebel told himself that he had got lucky again—this Bennett was a hysteric when it came to speechifying, and would sink himself as soon as he got onto the radio. Times were tough, but the Liberal party campaign buckets were filled by a grateful power company that had acquired rights along the St Lawrence River.

During the campaign people kept mentioning Canadian coinage.

On the night of July 28, 1930 someone turned the House upside down. Now the Tories had 138 seats, the Liberals 90, and the farm and labour folks 15. Ominously, the Conservatives now had 25 members from Quebec.

CHAPTER 16

ANOTHER MOTHER'S SON

---◆•◆•◆---

Richard B. Bennett 1930–35

S OME MEN HAVE been fated to have their names associated with unpleasant events or times. Richard Bedford Bennett's name has entered the Canadian dictionaries in the term "Bennett buggy." During the depth of the Great Depression and his one term in office, farmers on the prairies would remove the engines from their square automobiles and hitch the latter to a couple of horses, if they had a couple of horses. The farmers could not afford gasoline, and the horses were fuelled by whatever prickly weeds they could find to eat. Going from automobile back to horse-drawn buggy was a return to ways of the past. Both Arthur Meighen and R.B. Bennett often spoke of returning to the ways of the past.

R.B. Bennett and Mackenzie King, it has been noted, were similar in background. They both had fathers with respectable jobs and uncertain futures. More important, they both had mothers who insisted that their sons be aware of their honourable forebears and expect greatness of themselves in the future. Bennett, like King, would never marry, and for five years in the thirties these two sixtyish bachelors would fight one another in the House of Commons created by the Fathers of Confederation.

Bennett was another easterner fetched up on the prairie provinces. He was born four years before King, in small-town New Brunswick, a few miles from the Nova Scotia home of twenty-year-old Robert Borden. His family, like Borden's, came from the USA. The Bennetts were New England Loyalists, staunch Brits and refugees from the violent republic. Like Wilfrid Laurier, young Bennett was a ninth-generation North American, but he grew up in a British community in a province named after the royal family's ancestral home. When he was a youth, he predicted to his patient friends that he would become prime minister of Canada. The next day he predicted that he would sit in the British Parliament. His friends wondered how that would be possible, but they tended to believe him. He was always talking fast and talking long, so they did not get a chance to ask him how he was going to do it.

His father was a builder of sailing ships during a time of steam. In the Maritimes people are romantic about sailing ships, but Bennett saved his romantic feelings for his reading. All his life he would be a sucker for the novels of Robert Louis Stevenson. Yes, in the thirties the prime ministers of Canada were still reading literature, but as we have seen, the level of the literature was gradually descending. The Bennett boy did not teach himself Latin while working around his father's place. A little refinement was advisable, but Richard had an ego and an ambition that did not allow much time for romance.

Like Arthur Meighen, young Bennett would become for a while a teacher, and then a lawyer. Unlike Meighen, he would show some genius in cultivating strategic friendships. In New Brunswick he met two boys who were as British as himself, and who would become millionaires before they were thirty. One was Max Aitken, who was nine years his junior, and who would become Lord Beaverbrook and get Bennett into the House of Lords. The other was the future Sir James Dunn, who would make millions as a stockbroker, and then join C.D. Howe as owner of Algoma Steel. In his last year on Earth, Beaverbrook would marry Dunn's widow, who became the legendary Lady Beaverbrook, queen of New Brunswick.

Go west young lawyer

R.B. Bennett was a Methodist. He was a teetotaller. He was a Sunday school teacher. He was truly interested in the glory of God, and he thought that he could prove it by resting on the Sabbath and cornering the market on the other six days. One of the ways to get rich at the end of the nineteenth century was to head west and grab real estate. In 1896, he went to Calgary in the North-West Territories. The adoring young Max Aitkin went there too, to open a bowling alley. Joe Dunn became a lawyer in Edmonton before heading east to harvest the Montreal exchange.

Bennett was a partner of Senator James Lougheed. The Lougheeds would always know a lot about power and money in Alberta. It was not that long till R.B. Bennett was a millionaire. He had some pretty good clients, the Hudson's Bay Company and the Canadian Pacific Railway and the Royal Bank. In court their lawyer's job was to get money and concessions from governments, land and businesses away from little outfits. There were four thousand people in Calgary. The city was built along both sides of the CPR tracks.

R.B. Bennett—it is significant that he chose to go by that name. It was a little aloof. It sounded as much like the name of a corporation as a person. Speaking of corporations—Bennett decided that in order to look substantial he would eat a lot. He would not drink spirits but he would eat beef, and there was a lot of beef around Calgary. In the late Victorian age you developed a massive figure if you wanted to look successful. In the USA Theodore Roosevelt and William Howard Taft were packing on the pounds. R.B. Bennett saw success as an obligation to his God and his mother, so he built a torso and a political business. Back in New Brunswick he had managed to get elected to the city council in Chatham, with a teenage bicycle boy named Aitken as his campaign manager. A year after arriving in Calgary he got elected as a Conservative in the North-West Territories legislature. When Alberta became a province in 1905, he ran for the provincial legislature and lost. But a few years later he was sitting as an Alberta MLA. He decided to skip a shot at the premiership, though, and headed straight for the federal arena. In 1911, he was part of Borden's phalanx, winning the federal seat in Calgary East.

If he were to become prime minister soon, he needed a cabinet seat now, but Robert Borden already had a young western lawyer in Arthur Meighen. He thought that Bennett had been working too hard for Bennett and not hard enough for the Conservative party. To make his point, he put James Lougheed in his cabinet as minister without portfolio and made him Conservative leader in the Senate. Bennett did not help his cause when he sent a deluge of cranky letters to the prime minister. In 1917, he decided not to serve as a backbencher in the Union government, and went back to making his millions. He decided that when he got to be prime minister he would run the show with no political debts to anyone.

Calgary was a wild-west town, full of hard drinkers and men with missing fingers. R.B. Bennett, the hard-working, teetotalling Methodist, worked long hours at his office and in his room at Calgary's best hotel. Wherever he went in Canada, Bennett stayed or lived in the best hotel. Mackenzie King might have had Laurier House and Kingsmere, but R.B. Bennett did not have a house of his own until Lord Beaverbrook sold him one for his last years of splendour in the old country. While his friends Dunn and Aitkin headed east, Bennett stayed on the frontier and grabbed what was there to be grabbed.

He grabbed as much real estate as the CPR and his law partner let him. Before Aitkin went to England to become a newspaper baron, he went in with his young hero on a lot of enterprises. They cornered the cement business. They got control of electrical power. They built grain elevators and mills. They founded the Calgary Brewing Company. Here was a Methodist Sunday-school teacher who fulminated against the demon rum and made beer out of water from God's Rocky Mountains. I do not know why people find such a situation puzzling. Later in the century a prairie boy would become Vancouver's most famous capitalist while promoting a self-image as a fundamentalist Christian and acquiring a monopoly on the importation of pornographic magazines.

The little match girl

Another of the young Bennett's New Brunswick friendships brought him one of his greatest and most symbolic fortunes. The friends were Jennie Shirreff and her brother Joe. Jennie became a nurse and then she became the nurse for Mr Ezra Butler Eddy, the Vermont match company man who had moved his factory to the Ottawa Valley and got himself elected the mayor of Hull six times. Logs floated down the Ottawa River and got turned into matches and toilet paper at the E.B. Eddy mill, whose smoke funnels would rival the towers of the Houses of Parliament across the river for a century and more. Mr Eddy married his nurse, and when he died, the controlling shares in the company went to his widow and her brother. Jennie Eddy was a religious woman and a smart business tycoon. She remembered her friends, too. She gave R.B. Bennett one share in the company and made him a director.

Jennie died in 1921, leaving two-thirds of her shares to her brother and one-third to R.B. Wilfrid Laurier died that year, and Mackenzie King moved into Laurier House. For six months that year Bennett was Meighen's Minister of Justice, though he did not have a seat. He ran during the election in December, and nearly won while his party lost. He would get back into the cabinet as Minister of Finance (pardon me, *acting* minister of finance) during Meighen's eyeblink rule in 1926. In that year Jennie's brother died and passed his shares on to Bennett. So Bennett could now run one side of the Ottawa River while he waited for his prediction to come true on the other side. He had never told his boyhood friends that he was going to operate Canada's biggest match company. Still, in gathering this big money-maker from a lady friend who was ten years his senior, he had out-Kinged King.

In 1927, that amazing year of Lindbergh, Tunney and Ruth, the Canadian Tories gave up on Arthur Meighen. If he ever got to be prime minister again, he would probably last twenty-five minutes. The Tories looked around for a winner, and their eyes fell on the big stout gentleman in the high silk hat. Here was a man who had excelled in the law (i.e. got rich from wealthy clients) and succeeded brilliantly in business. His oratory did not have the edgy wit of Meighen's, but he could talk three times as fast as anyone else, and never misplace a modifier. His voice, unlike King's, was strong and melodious, and sounded reassuring on the radio. He had been known to be petulant and egotistical, but maybe that was how he had become a millionaire.

He was a new kind of Canadian leader eructed by the

roaring good times of the late twenties. Like a lot of self- (and friends-)made men, he believed that a country should be run the way one runs a business. A lot of businessmen think this way now, but R.B. Bennett, Ltd. was the first millionaire to take over leadership of a national party in Canada. He knew that there were still some Tories around who thought that it might be risky to go into an election with a plutocrat candidate. He countered their fears by suggesting that a rich man would clearly not be controlled by grafters with kickbacks. He would be his own man. The Tories nodded their heads. They would find out that the director of Canada Ltd. would be so much his own man that his cabinet members would be glorified messengers.

When the crash came, and when a year later R.B. Bennett was prime minister of Canada, everyone might have been cheered to realize that the country had a take-charge expert at the top. There were a few picky leftists out west who pointed out that the New York Stock Exchange had been run by businessmen right up until it nose-dived into the waters off the southern tip of Manhattan. In any case, like Mackenzie King before him, Bennett thought that the market was just going through a little correction. Conservatives, as much as Gladstonian Liberals, thought that the free-enterprise money system was locked into the natural order of the universe. In 1930 a lot of voters wanted to believe it. When they looked at Mackenzie King and R.B. Bennett, they did not have to wait long to decide which looked more like those good times of just a couple of years ago. And they thought that Bennett might give five cents and then some to the Conservative provinces that could not afford to bail out their bankrupt cities.

Now Canada, like the USA, would enter its desperately poor years with an optimistic millionaire as head of government. As the Depression deepened it became more and more ironic that photography and the press and the motion picture newsreel made such advances that anyone could see pictures of their prime minister at ceremonies and meetings. There is, for instance, a photograph of Bennett having a chat with the premier of France on a lawn in Washington in 1933. The PM has his receding hair perfectly brushed back and cut short. He is wearing his usual wing collar and a swallowtail coat, a gold chain across the big waistcoat and a crease in his striped trousers. His shoes gleam. In his left hand he is carrying his top hat, and his right hand, holding a pair of elegant white gloves, rests on the ivory handle of his walking stick. Yes, he looks exactly like the capitalist in Soviet cartoons, or a Japanese diplomat. In those Soviet cartoons the capitalist is usually smoking a fat cigar. In fact the French premier in the photo is holding a cigar, and the Canadian prime minister is tolerating it.

Of course our representative could not go to a big wingding in Washington dressed like an Alberta farmer, could he? It would have taken a brave and imaginative statesman to do such a thing.

Never in Canadian history had the gap between the rich and the poor been so graphically recorded. Never had it been so plain that wealth and political power went white glove in white glove. Back in Ottawa, R.B. Bennett was living in a suite at the Chateau Laurier, the magnificent hotel next to the Parliament Buildings. He did not use the bar and he walked right past the tobacco stand, but every night in the Chateau he ate a box of chocolates. So what? He could afford it.

As times got worse, the government got the blame. Mackenzie King lambasted the Conservatives for the relentless downturn in the economy, knowing full well that New York had more to do with it than did Ottawa. The USA was cutting back its imports and demanding immediate payments on its Great War loans. The unemployed in Canada did not care about the national debt—they wanted jobs and real shoes for their children. While the Liberal leader stood with a serious face and excoriated the government, skinny survivors out west fed on irony rather than poultry. Bennett's name was used to symbolize government unconcern. It is interesting to keep in mind the proliferation of the Bennett buggy while listening to one of the stories told in Barry Broadfoot's famous *Ten Lost Years,* a book of memories gathered from people who made it through the Depression. A person who began by calling Bennett "pompous, smug and rich" recalls R.B.'s attempt to drive his own automobile: "He bought a new car, the jazziest in Calgary and while he was learning to drive it he ran it up a pole. He walked away from it, and as far as I know he never got behind the wheel of a car again."

The working poor and the unemployed held the opinion that government was greatly estranged from them, that R.B. Bennett did not have a hope of understanding the ordinary Canadian. In the west, especially, disaffection grew so widely that voters began to look somewhere besides the old eastern parties. The Communist party was still working hard in Winnipeg and the west coast, though their little English leader Tim Buck was in jail from 1931 to 1934. A group of Fabians and United Farm politicians met in Regina in 1933 and issued the manifesto of the newly formed party to be called the Co-operative Commonwealth Federation, with former preacher and now parliamentarian J.S. Woodsworth as leader. The manifesto called for a mixed economy and a welfare state. The Conservatives were too slow at the former, and the Liberals too slow at the latter. And in Alberta, another preacher, "Bible Bill" Aberhart, read Major C.H. Douglas's book *Social Credit,* adding fundamental Christianity and right-wing prejudices to create another party unseen in the power centres of central Canada. Conservative critics referred to Major Douglas's economics as "funny money." In the normal capitalist system, banks were allowed to lend imaginary money to governments and then be repaid in cash by governments who gathered the cash from taxpayers. This was never called "funny money." This was serious economics. It was going through a self-correction for the moment.

Bennett may have been aware of the animosity directed his way, and he may not have. Perhaps with naïveté or perhaps for his own strategic purpose, he often made public remarks, sometimes on the radio, that had jaws dropping inside un-painted houses all across the land. These messages were all about how hopeful the situation was. The banks are full of money, he told his listeners, there is no shortage of money. In a Thanksgiving address sent by cable from England he actually wrote that "Canadians should be especially thankful for the manifold blessings that Providence has bestowed upon them." It was a sentiment that ordinary Canadians could mull over while they sat down to their Thanksgiving magpie.

Bennett's secretary, Andrew MacLean, wrote and published an encomiastic little book in time for the 1935 election, and had it translated into French, German and Ukrainian. He gives a couple pages to his boss's weaknesses, pointing out that they are aspects of his strength. The worst he can say is this: "Bennett finds it difficult to sympathize with the thriftless. So do all 'self-made men.' They have saved and invested and worked hard, and have accumulated material possessions. They develop a philosophy of the 'haves' which finds it very difficult to understand or sympathize with any philosophy of the 'have nots.' He never went through years of extreme privation him-self, and now he is insulated from such a life. This is a political weakness in a democratic leader."

Even MacLean admits that Bennett was less a democrat than he was an aristocrat. In business there is no place for equality, of course, and the great nineteenth-century busi-nessmen were egotists who kept the switch in their own hands.

Every commentator on the period repeats the story of two men who walk past a seated Bennett who is apparently mumbling to himself. One man tells the other that the prime minister is holding a cabinet meeting. More than one cartoonist drew a table with several pince-nezed R.B. Bennetts sitting around it, another "cabinet meeting."

Bennett glared down the slope of his belly at socialists. He liked to amuse himself by handing out little presents to strangers, but though he gave a quarter of a million dollars to his party, he hated to give a raise to his servants. He thought that business with its "competition" and verticality made a fine model for the nation. Sir Wilfrid Laurier had banned hereditary titles of nobility for Canadians. Mackenzie King got rid of titles altogether. R.B. Bennett undid that un-British radicalism and made it all right again for deserving Canadians to be knighted. When Mackenzie King got back in, he would again put a stop to such foppery. One of the last Canadians to squeeze in under the sword was the old-fashioned man-of-letters from Bennett's home province, Sir Charles G.D. Roberts, who was knighted in 1935. R.B. Bennett would later, of course, calling in his debts from Lord Beaverbrook, become Viscount Bennett of Calgary.

Company business

He was a nineteenth-century capitalist but he was also a Macdonald Tory. That is to say, he believed that the Dominion government should show its hand in Canadian public works. While the farmers were pleading for free trade in case they ever found a crop that would grow in sand dunes, Bennett jacked up the tariffs brick-for-brick against the US wall. The National Policy was back, and R.B. Bennett couched it in terms of economic patriotism. He said that continentalism and the Liberals forced Canadians to be hewers of wood and drawers of water:

> We have been content since 1922 to send out of Canada into other lands free the resources of this country and buy back from them the manufactured materials. Thousands in the United States have been given employment fabricating Canadian goods. They've got the jobs and we've got the soup kitchens.

As usual, the alternative to the USA was the British Commonwealth. Unlike his predecessors, Bennett did not sail the Atlantic for his first Imperial Conference. In 1932 he had the Commonwealth come to him. The conference was held for the first time in Ottawa, and Bennett was in his glory. He outdressed Stanley Baldwin and Neville Chamberlain, and he outtalked them. He did not invite his old friend Beaverbrook because Beaverbrook had not campaigned for him in 1930. At the conference he argued for his notion of "Empire Free Trade," a system in which the partners would trade goods among themselves and raise tariffs against everyone else. Everyone signed, but kept crossed fingers behind their swallowtail coats. Everyone would raise tariffs against the Yanks and others, but they would think twice about lowering obstacles among themselves.

In 1931 the British Parliament had applied the Balfour Report to a new law called the Statute of Westminster. When people of my generation were school inmates we were told that the Statute of Westminster was the document that made Canada a fully independent nation. We did wonder why there was still a Union Jack in the corner of our flag, and why the King was on the little pennies as well as the big ones. But we liked the Statute of Westminster, a place, we thought, that must be somewhat east of here. The Statute of Westminster proclaimed independence for the dominions in all aspects except those that the dominions could not sort out themselves. Because the Dominion and the provinces (read Quebec) could not agree on anything so touchy, Clause 7 (1) of the act declares that "Nothing in this Act shall be deemed to apply to the repeal, amendment or alteration of the British North America Act, 1867 to 1930, or any order, rule or regulation made thereunder." So there we were, an independent nation with a constitution owned by another independent nation. Another very Canadian situation.

R.B. Bennett, Ltd. was pretty well satisfied. He did like to carry on the tradition of Canadian prime ministers who talk tough to London, but he remembered that he still had to make it into the British House of Lords.

In the meantime he set about the corporation of Canada, his extension of the National Policy. During the Great War, Borden's government had established a wheat board, regulating the international and interprovincial marketing of wheat. Prices had gone up, and saved a lot of farmers. When prices fell after the war, western farmers wanted a return to high prices, naturally, but the Liberals were laissez-faire folk, and times were supposed to be good. The farmers tried various wheat pools among themselves, but in the thirties wheat was in trouble along with everyone else. In the last year of his parliamentary directorship, Bennett created the Canadian Wheat Board, which farmers could join on a voluntary basis.

A year earlier, Bennett passed the Bank of Canada Act, in an attempt to control money the way the Wheat Board controlled prices. As the Wheat Board was voluntary, so the Bank of Canada was in private hands, though it would be wise not to offend the government. Its job was to operate between the government and the various commercial banks, ensuring a proper ratio between rates for lending and borrowing.

John A. Macdonald
(National Archives of
Canada, c21603)

Alexander Mackenzie
(National Archives of
Canada, c4953)

Robert L. Borden
(National Archives of
Canada, PA117658)

Robert Baldwin
(National Archives of
Canada, C5962)

Charles Tupper
(National Archives
of Canada, PA31002)

Allen N. MacNab
(National Archives
of Canada, C3615)

Arthur Meighen
(National Archives
of Canada, c47340)

Wilfrid Laurier
(National Archives
of Canada, c4960)

John J.C. Abbott
(National Archives
of Canada, c697)

John S.D. Thompson and family
(National Archives of Canada, c9079)

Robert B. Bennett (left) and William Lyon Mackenzie King
(National Archives of Canada, PA148532)

John G. Diefenbaker (left) and Lester B. Pearson
(Duncan Cameron, National Archives of Canada, PA115202)

Louis S. St. Laurent
(National Archives
of Canada, c692)

Brian Mulroney
(Robert Cooper,
National Archives of Canada,
PA152416)

(left to right)
Trudeau, Turner,
Chrétien, Clark,
and Campbell
(Paul Couvrette,
National Archives
of Canada, PA201061)

You see that R.B. Bennett was no Bolshevik. He was a Macdonaldite with an abiding respect for big corporations.

As Macdonald had come to power in the age of railroads, Bennett was now presiding in the age of the automobile and the transport truck. So he started the tar-ball rolling on a national highway. He knew how important moving goods was, and unlike his forebears from Ontario, he knew that places such as the west coast were here to stay. He started negotiations with the USAmericans on a St Lawrence seaway. Every day in the newspapers he saw stories about some new feat performed by an aviator, so he started talking to manufacturers about a proposed trans-Canada airline. As a veteran of radio speeches, he saw a similar potential in a national broadcasting system with government input. It was not an idea that sprang unannounced into his spherical head. The British Broadcasting Corporation was established in 1927. The Canadian National Railway had its own point-to-point radio network. In 1928 Mackenzie King's government had set a royal commission to investigate government's role in broadcasting. Runaway free enterprise in the United States was resulting in an onslaught of USAmerican radio that sometimes jammed wide bands of anyone's radio set. R.B. Bennett listened to his advisers, and heard the whining of an association of private broadcasters, and set up the Canadian Radio Broadcasting Commission.

You can see that, despite his association with old jalopies containing no motors, R.B. Bennett had a hand in the beginnings of a lot of centralized Canadian institutions. He was not exactly a radical democrat, but he wanted to see a country that could regard itself. While Mackenzie King spent much of the first half of the thirties getting acquainted with ghosts, R.B. Bennett was telling his subjects, I mean, fellow citizens, to pull up their socks, if they had any, and trying to establish the national domestic institutions that would prevent the Depression from feeding Canada piecemeal to USAmerican business.

But he would not tolerate radical politics or even bad manners. In April of 1935 hundreds of men who had been getting thinner at federal relief camps in British Columbia descended on Vancouver, where they began two months of remarkable protest activity, organized by Slim Evans of the Workers' Unity League. The crowds grew to 20,000 for the May Day parade, scaring the hell out of city and provincial governments. Unemployed men took over the library and a hotel and the Hudson's Bay store, until they were dispersed by policemen on horses who crashed through windows and flailed about with bullwhips. Slim Evans decided that the story had to be told in Ottawa, so a thousand men got hold of a freight train and headed east to see R.B. Bennett, picking up sandwiches and passengers along the way. On to Ottawa, they urged. Fifteen hundred got as far as Regina, where they were received warmly by the poor and given relief by the Saskatchewan Liberal government. But R.B. Bennett decided that he did not want a trainload of poorly dressed protesters in Ottawa. He leaned on the railways, and there was no more transport for the protesters. Eight protesters were allowed to go east and meet with the government, but the government was not ready to initiate work programs. The great trek was over. The men began to disperse. They would hold a final rally on July 1, the sixty-eighth birthday of Confederation, gather some sandwiches, and head back westward.

That is the day when R.B. Bennett made one of those stupid moves that all prime ministers seem capable of. There were only 300 trekkers left in Regina, but Bennett sent the RCMP and Regina police into the crowd to arrest Slim Evans and anyone else who was making a speech. It was the Winnipeg Strike all over again. Cops and trekkers clubbed each other as the riot spread through the streets of the Saskatchewan capital. By midnight, when the trekkers were confined at the exhibition grounds, there was one dead policeman, and a lot of civilians with broken faces. A few days later the Saskatchewan government came to the protection of the protesters and escorted them to trains for a safe ride home. R.B. Bennett's actions in Regina cost his party more votes than Meighen's actions in Winnipeg had.

Big business might have been encouraged by Bennett's stand on the tracks at Regina, but big business was not happy about his price-fixing and broadcast regulations and such meddling. The czars of enterprise would be even less comfortable when they heard his astounding radio broadcasts of 1935. They could not believe that this was the same Daddy Peacebucks who had made them smile contentedly by firing his Minister of Trade and Commerce, H.H. Stevens.

Stevens, the firebrand grocer from Vancouver, had been Meighen's right-hand man, the busybody who had exposed the rot in King's Customs Department. He had been one of the "acting cabinet members" when King activated his constitutional trap to oust the Tories again. Now he was back, looking for more scandal. He was a pugnacious Englishman who was now representing the worn-out mining country of East Kootenay. He was a free enterpriser, but the Depression had persuaded him that big capitalism was a lot worse problem than graft in the Customs Department. His investigators found lots of evidence that businessmen were getting rich off the backs of the remaining employed, running sweatshops and watering stocks and wringing every crooked penny they could out of the financial disaster.

We have to do something, he told R.B. Bennett. But the big operator had developed a little contempt for the grocer. Don't you dare ask me to throw mud at my fellow club members, he said. All right, said Stevens, who had never set much store in good manners, and he made a spectacular speech to a group of shoemakers in Toronto. He was subbing for Bennett, who had decided to stay over and attend to a little business in Calgary. The next day he was in the headlines of the Toronto papers, and pretty soon there was a lot of noise across the country. Stevens had accused the big department stores of running sweatshops in Toronto and Montreal, and undercutting the smaller clothing stores. He hinted that his government would do something about it. Soon there were letters coming to Ottawa and to the papers, from women who made six dollars a week with their sewing needles and could not afford to buy the special sale blouses in the department-store windows. There were lawyers from the department stores waiting outside the Prime Minister's Office. The prime minister tried to remind his trade minister that there was such a thing as protocol. He told him that minimum wages and such bothersome things were the responsibility of the provinces. He may have reminded him that the people who ran Simpson's and its competitors were natural supporters of the Conservative party.

I feel a responsibility to the poor and an inability to keep my mouth shut, said H.H. Stevens. Bennett set up a select committee to investigate the problem, starting in February of 1934. He hoped that it would do its work fast, so that he could get people to forget about it in time for an election. No such luck. By July it was still hearing evidence, and Bennett had it changed to a royal commission. He hoped that things would thus quieten down. No such luck. For one thing, Stevens was still going around making speeches and publishing pamphlets, and now he was naming names. For another thing, someone was leaking the evidence being heard by the commission. Luckily for Bennett, he had named an honest young Liberal, Lester Pearson, as secretary of the commission, and Pearson had found the leak and plugged it.

The investigation was supposed to be about price-spreads, the difference between costs and profits, the crowding of small shops off the road. When the federal investigators got to open the books of the big stores they found oozing sores. Desperate women were labouring long hours in sweatshops and getting paid far below minimum wages, and minimum wages were around twelve dollars a week. Stocks were being watered so much that you could see through them. Simpson's and the others were making big profits, and poor children were seeing an exhausted mother for a few minutes every morning.

H.H. Stevens may have been impolite, but that was not the only reason that R.B. Bennett was intensely angry at him. He hated the idea of a cabinet split in such a dangerous time. He had always liked the idea of a cabinet meeting in which he spoke to a group of photographs. Now with this Stevens problem, he knew that he had been right. And he could not ignore him. He knew that Stevens had an endless line of informants out there. He had one of his subordinates send Stevens a message to apologize to the honest businessmen of Canada, and then shut up. Stevens sent a resignation right back. He announced the birth of the Reconstruction Party for the next election. They would champion the underdog and see what could be done about changing the capitalist system. In 1935 the Reconstructionists would win 10 per cent of the vote, and elect one MP.

What is he saying?

In 1931, Bennett had written "Half a century ago people would work their way out of their difficulties rather than look to a government to take care of them." All right, said the business crowd, we have a very wealthy Meighen to take care of us. But they got a shock or five in early 1935, the year that had to see an election. Franklin Delano Roosevelt had come to power as a patrician millionaire in 1933, but was soon creating government agencies to fight unemployment and poverty, offering USAmericans a "New Deal." Bennett's brother-in-law, William D. Herridge, was his ambassador in Washington, and he spent many evenings trying to persuade the Canadian prime minister to follow FDR's path. FDR was a Democrat, and Bennett's crowd naturally favoured the Republicans, but now the man who had nudged H.H. Stevens out of the party was saying that Canada needed a "regulated capitalist system," with motivated government watchdogs.

In early 1935 the prime minister announced that he was going to reform society more than any Canadian government had ever dreamed of. First he went on the radio, and then he wrote a speech from the throne for the spring session, proclaiming that if free enterprise could not get rid of the Depression, the country would have to get rid of free enterprise.

Who is this guy dressed in the PM's fancy clothes, asked the plushbottoms in the banking world.

In January Bennett made five radio speeches, explaining that he had been thinking of these radical solutions all along. Thirty-nine radio stations from coast to coast broadcast his words from Ottawa, and the prime minister paid for the time with his own money. "Free competition and the open market place, as they were known in the old days, have lost their place in the system," he said, "and . . . the only substitute for them, in these modern times, is government regulation and control." He must have raised eyebrows and blood pressures when he attacked "selfish men . . . whose mounting bank rolls loom larger than your happiness," and "corporations without souls and without virtue." He warned that these plutocrats would call "us" radicals and socialists. He zoomed right past Mackenzie King's favourite book: "all the parts of the capitalist system have only one purpose and that is to work for the welfare of the people." He promised that "opposition from any class which imperils the future of this great undertaking we will not tolerate."

If there were any bone-thin ex-farmers who could get near a radio, one wonders what words escaped their dry lips at that moment.

Then in the throne speech he announced plans to regulate the capitalists and come to the aid of labour, "to provide a better and more assured standard of living for the worker, to secure minimum wages and a maximum working week, and to alter the incidence of taxation so that it will more directly conform to capacity to pay." In other words, the high-income people were going to see tax hikes. Arthur Meighen, a high-income person leading the Tories in the Senate, would have his party loyalty well tested.

More important, perhaps, Mackenzie King as leader of the opposition was put into the position of opposing all Tory reforms, including the Wheat Board and the Bank of Canada. Now he would have to be against unemployment insurance and the graduated income tax. He knew that a lot of Bennett's reforms would be knocked down as infringements against provincial rights, but he must have been afraid that people would believe in this new crusader. He was rescued by the riots in Regina and the prime minister's ham-handed response to the "On to Ottawa" train.

So when Bennett called an election for October 14, Mackenzie King went back to his own reform promises, and chose to run against big business instead of the new enemy of big business. King had tucked his belly up to the séance table quite often during his days in opposition, but now he worked on that belly. We remember that the young Bennett had fattened up to look prosperous in prosperous times. Mackenzie King in 1935 could read the electorate: he slimmed and trimmed, and when the fat went away his skin took on the kind of wrinkles that made him look experienced. R.B. Bennett, meanwhile, was looking tired. Not thin, just tired.

He ran himself ragged making his reform speeches all over the place, through January and February. He developed a bad cold, then a respiratory infection. On March 7 he had a minor heart attack. In a month he was ready to sail to England for empire pomp and some visits to heart specialists. He threw himself back into campaigning in June, experienced the Regina riot setback in July, and began the formal campaign in September, with another series of radio broadcasts from Toronto, and then a grand tour of the country. During that trip he began to think that he was losing the election. To explain such an eventuality to himself and some associates, he blamed Harry Stevens for breaking up the party.

Sure enough, when the middle of October came around, the Conservatives suffered their worst defeat since Confederation. The Liberals won 171 seats, and every province except British Columbia and Alberta. Seventy-five per cent of the electorate had voted, which is a pretty good sign that the government is going to change. It was not so much that the Liberals swept in; rather, the Conservatives were swept out. The Social Credit party won 17 seats, and the CCF, with the same number of votes, won 7. Stevens's Reconstructionists got nearly 400,000 votes but elected only their leader. There were five non-King Liberals in Quebec. There were two Liberal-Progressives from Manitoba. There was a non-Bennett Conservative from Yukon. R.B. Bennett was the only

Conservative elected from Alberta, and he was one of thirty-nine Tories elected to the House of Commons.

In 1929 he had joined a lot of businessmen in believing that the Wall Street crash was a glitch in the history of the market. Now in 1935 he seemed alone in believing that the Conservative smash was just a momentary setback in his own administrative career. He hung on to the leadership of the party, and when the 1938 leadership decision was to be made, he seemed to have decided to fight on. Arthur Meighen, the wise old man of the Tories, explained the facts of life. That year R.B. Bennett resigned his leadership and on January 28, 1939 he resigned his Calgary seat just as his ship was sailing for England. He was probably waiting for someone to talk him out of leaving the country. But he still had a childhood prediction to make good on.

That would entail another tough political struggle. Bennett got himself his first house, a nice estate with gardens and the rest, next to his old pal, Lord Beaverbrook, with whom he had made up. Unfortunately the British prime minister was Neville Chamberlain, who remembered playing second fiddle to Bonfire Bennett at the Ottawa imperial conference. It took Beaverbrook two years to get his old chum into the House of Lords. There he could carry on his political life, fulfil the hopes of his mother, and catch a nap from time to time.

But he kept getting older and acquiring more health problems. Now he developed diabetes to go with his heart problems. Wartime was tough on him emotionally, too. His only two nephews would die at Normandy, bringing the Bennett line to an end. And he would have another great set-to with Beaverbrook. Beaverbrook made him an independent investigator to determine whether he could continue to pluck German Jewish engineers from internment camps to work on British airplanes. Independent Bennett ruled against Beaverbrook, the Minister of Aircraft Production, and the neighbours stopped speaking over their hedges.

Bennett was a lonely old man in a big house. He was rich enough to get around wartime and post-war rationing, but he had a butler instead of a friend. The butler was the last person to see him alive. On a June night in 1947 he died in his bathtub. His little dog, Bill, outlived him. Across the sea Mackenzie King's little dog, Pat, lay beside the prime minister's bed.

His body was not brought on a British warship to Canada. Soon after taking up residence in England he had said, "I have led my country; now that it no longer wants me, it will be easier for others if I am no longer there." Viscount Bennett of Mickleham, Calgary and Hopewell was buried in a village churchyard in Surrey, the only Canadian prime minister not laid to rest in his own country.

CHAPTER 17

WAR AND PEACE

———◆◆◆———

W.L. Mackenzie King 1935–48

WILLY KING MIGHT HAVE been the grandson of a Little Rebel. F.R. Scott was the son of a radical Christian poet, F.G. Scott. Scott *fils* was born in Quebec in 1899, and in his young manhood became a theorist and planner for several organizations interested in political social planning. He was in on the Regina Manifesto. He became a law professor at McGill University. He was a centrist in the CCF. He wrote anti-esthetic and satirical poetry as an expression of his reformist beliefs. When Mackenzie King died, he wrote an anti-eulogy called "W.L.M.K." It ends with a wry allusion to the prime minister's peculiar monument at Kingsmere:

> Let us raise up a temple
> To the cult of mediocrity,
> Do nothing by halves
> Which can be done by quarters.

In fact late in his life Mackenzie King would advise his follow-ers that a statesman's importance would be found more in the things he prevented than in the things he inaugurated.

Through his career he swayed from left to right in the Lib-eral party, and to this day commentators cannot agree on whether he was the source or the begrudging permitter of the social programs brought into being during his party's reign. He has been vilified as the man who delivered post-war Canada to the USAmericans. He has also been pictured as a silly old fart trying to get his picture taken with the British royal family. In terms of foreign relations he was an isolationist before and after the Second World War, but during the war he was the link between the British Commonwealth and the United States.

Will Bennett buggies be replaced by King krates?

If the legend that Mackenzie King had lost the 1930 election on purpose were true, why would he have wanted to win the 1935 election? Did his familiar ghosts tell him that the Depression was going to end soon?

He had the biggest parliamentary majority since 1867, but he had a lot of opposition from the provinces. The provincial gov-ernments, according to the spirit of the BNA Act, were in charge of essential social questions, and while they were jealous of these powers, they were going broke. Non-traditional political parties were becoming a distraction. The CCF called for social-ization of banking, utilities—and medicine. The Social Credit people were talking about certificates that would draw on natu-ral resources as if nature were an exchequer. The Union Nationale of Maurice Duplessis uttered a vague platform that was mainly aimed at more widely redistributing wealth. All three groups railed against the excessive control of the banks and big corporations. They all associated banks and big business with whatever politicians had been in political power for a long time.

But Mackenzie King was still a liberal. He was not going to socialize medicine or big match companies, but he was going to undo some of Bennett's mistakes. A Bank of Canada he could live with, but not if it were privately owned. By 1938 it was nationalized. Bennett's tariffs had to come down, and a new triangular trade deal made with Britain, the USA and Canada at the corners. Of course there was going to be no way to make the USAmericans conceive it as an equilateral triangle. King would often, in later times, warn Canadians against the appetite of the USA, but he did more than anyone in history to open the doors to continental business.

As soon as he had won the election, he had announced "a new era" to end poverty in a country of such obvious natural wealth. His cabinet ministers and their chief civil servants must have believed him, because they started to compete for chunks of the budget, grasping the notion that federal money could alleviate hardship among the citizenry, often in their own provinces of origin. According to his faithful diary entries, Mackenzie King believed in restraint but felt himself pulled toward spending by the ministers to whom he was in the habit of extending initiative. By 1938 he had been persuaded to try a new manoeuvre, a deliberate planned budget deficit. All the same, he became more and more worried about the spectre of government by bureaucracy. The trouble with civil servants was that they could outlast the elected politicians who appointed them.

Or they could act with vision and intelligence, and thus embarrass the government. Consider the case of Dr Walter Riddell.

While Mackenzie King was winning his big majority and getting his cabinet together, Benito Mussolini's air force was bombing Abyssinia, the only independent African nation within easy reach of a European air force. Here was a prime case for the League of Nations. The League's job was to prevent just such an occurrence. Canada's contribution to the League had not exactly been a matter of pride, and Mackenzie King did not think that the League could ever be effective. He was also not much interested in getting into any scrap on the other side of the ocean.

Besides, King was vacationing in the southern USA with a friend. His Quebec lieutenant Ernest Lapointe sent a message to Dr Riddell, telling him not to make any great decisions until the chief was back in Ottawa. Dr Riddell was stuck with representing Canada in Geneva because the official political appointee there had left Switzerland with the defeat of Bennett's government. Now the European countries were talking about League sanctions against Mussolini and his land grab. But the European countries also had trade agreements with Italy, and a country that was mounting a big war effort made a good customer. What kind of sanctions should we apply, the European countries asked each other. Maybe tea and golf shoes. Dr Riddell suggested steel, coal and oil, and amazingly, the League members agreed in principle. It looked as if Mussolini would have to park his airplanes and tanks.

For some reason one can be surprised to find that Canadian historians turn out to be Liberals or Conservatives or even New Democrats. Liberal historians will tell you that Dr Riddell was ignoring messages from Lapointe that he should pipe down. Other historians will say that Dr Riddell sent lots of cables to Ottawa but got no replies. He decided that if he had no advice about the political course, he would take the moral course, and represent Canada as if Canada were opposed to a dictator who would drop bombs on herdsmen. Dr Riddell just did not know how Liberal politics worked, and how much Mackenzie King needed Quebec. In Quebec the newspapers and politicians assailed Riddell's sanctions. The Italians were a friendly Catholic nation. Canada was almost declaring war on a friendly Catholic nation. Montreal's perennial mayor Camillien Houde was a staunch supporter of Mussolini, as he would later be of Vichy France. Camillien Houde said that French Canadians would support Mussolini in any war. In the next few years Mayor Houde would make Henri Bourassa look like a moderate.

Ernest Lapointe knew Quebec well, and he was Mackenzie King's one friend in cabinet. He sent a message to Dr Riddell, telling him to desist. He told the European countries that Dr Riddell had been speculating, not uttering Canadian policy. France and Britain breathed a sigh of relief and sent oil to Italy. Their foreign secretaries, Pierre Laval and Sir Samuel Hoare, met and formed a policy that would give half of Abyssinia to Mussolini. Mussolini took it all anyway. Sir Samuel Hoare would later agree to give half of Czechoslovakia to Hitler.

It is probable that Canadians in Quebec and elsewhere were sympathetic with King's isolationism. They had straightened out matters in Europe at great cost to Canada once already. Let the Europeans sink or swim on their own now; there were serious problems over on this side of the ocean.

The Spanish Civil War was another bad sign: in Europe it was a sign that the ideologies were going to settle things by military means; in Canada it was a sign that Quebec and English Canada would have sharply differing attitudes toward the wars in Europe. Once again Mackenzie King felt that he had to take a hands-off position. After all, there was no threat to Britain in 1936, so Canada had no obligations over there. Maurice Duplessis and his Union Nationale had just swept into power in Quebec. Duplessis and Houde and Cardinal Villeneuve and the newspapers were on the side of the fascists in Spain, and they wanted the Catholic Church saved against anarchy and communism and the like. So they cheered Mussolini's bombers again, and Hitler's. When anyone tried to hold a Spanish Loyalist rally in Montreal, there were riots in the streets.

But 1,300 Canadian volunteers went to fight against fascism in Spain. They were called the Mackenzie-Papineau Brigade and their motto mentioned that fighting for freedom was as important in 1937 as it had been in 1837. In 1937 Mackenzie King's government made it illegal to fight for foreign armies, even in a brigade named after his grandfather.

He attended the coronation of George VI that year, then went and visited Adolf Hitler. After finishing his work at the London imperial conference, and consulting the best mediums and soothsayers in England, he headed to Berlin for a secret talk. It was easier to get in to see the *Der Führer* than it had been to see *Il Duce*. The Liberal historians tell us that King warned Hitler that Canada would join Britain's side if Germany went to war with Britain. King did not mention that to the gentle journalist with whom he spent a gracious evening at Laurier House while Lapointe took care of business at a late session in the Commons. King told Bruce Hutchison that he reckoned Hitler "a simple sort of peasant" with ambitions that did not go beyond the pre-First World War borders of Germany. In 1938 he confided to his diary that he admired Hitler for his devotion to his mother and for his spiritualism. He compared him with Joan of Arc as a deliverer of his people.

In 1938 Neville Chamberlain and Sir Samuel Hoare came back from Munich, having given part of Czechoslovakia to Hitler in exchange for a promise of peace after that. Chamberlain became very popular in Britain. On September 29 Mackenzie King sent a letter to Chamberlain: "Your achievements in the past month alone will assure you an illustrious and abiding place among the great conciliators." One remembers that a few decades earlier King had been a very good conciliator in the service of the Rockefellers, whose other agents were lighting fires in little wooden structures occupied by the families of miners in Colorado.

Still, though he was a pacifist and an appeaser, Mackenzie King was gloomy about the future prospects for peace. Canada's military preparedness was no better than it had been in 1913. In his deficit budget King managed to get $33 million set aside for defence spending, but King's speeches and remarks showed that he wanted to stay on both sides of the issue when the question of European dangers was raised. He said that Canada need not be looked for to settle squabbles on the Continent. Yet, if Britain were to go to war, Canada would want to help out—as long as it was remembered that Canada's decisions would be made independent of any empire. He was talking to the Ontario Union-Jackers and the Quebec nationalists.

World War Two

We like to remember great presidents and great prime ministers, and we often associate them with great wars. The USAmericans have Washington and Lincoln and FDR. The Brits have Winston Churchill. The French try to make a legend of Charles de Gaulle. We have William Lyon Mackenzie King. Liberal historians say that King proved his greatness during 1939-45. Other historians admit that King handled the war pretty well, and more important, held the country together while conducting it.

That last task would not be easy. Quebeckers liked to see themselves as Canada's Irish, a large Catholic enclave with a threatened language and no great urge to fight under any version of the Union Jack. Over and over again Mackenzie King would promise that Canada could wage this war without conscripted troops. If the Canadian army was going to fight on

European soil again, they had better not be deployed on the streets in Quebec or Montreal. But of course the Canadian army, and the wives and children of soldiers overseas, were not interested in Liberal party political realities—they would look upon the French Canadians with some powerful negative emotions. When the Zombies came along, they would get some icy stares as well.

The "simple sort of peasant" with the comical moustache, having already annexed Austria and parts of Czechoslovakia and Lithuania, invaded Poland on September 1, 1939. Polish horsemen carrying lances made beautiful photographs but no resistance to German tanks. Franco was mopping up in Spain, and the German air force was no longer needed there. Britain and France declared war immediately against Germany, as they had promised Poland that they would. In Canada, Mackenzie King had made his own promise, one that had been prepared by a former prime minister: he would not go to war without a parliamentary vote. He prepared for the vote by telling his Quebec members that there would be no conscription for overseas duty. On September 9th the issue was addressed, and on the next day, a Sunday, Canada was again at war.

Inevitably, Canada was involved in a triangular war at home, too. First the Quebec premier, Maurice Duplessis, called a provincial election, uttering the interesting word "autonomie." Duplessis was not so much a firebrand as Bourassa had been. He was a practical conservative politician who was willing to live with lots of patronage and vice, and he was intent on bringing down the Liberals in Quebec and Ottawa. He knew that the war gave him a great chance to play the "race" card. If the people of Quebec voted for him in the fall of 1939, they would be stating their intention to stay out of the war. Mackenzie King was terrified—Duplessis was already premier of that province. What chance was there that he would lose the election he had called so dramatically? But if Duplessis were to win, how could Mackenzie King lead a one-legged country into battle?

The great western journalist Bruce Hutchison wrote in 1952 that this was the most important election in Canadian history. It would mean the life or death of the country that was supposed to own this century, and the lives or deaths of a lot of human beings in England and nearby countries. If Duplessis were to win he would expect all Quebec's federal Liberals to resign, bringing chaos to Ottawa. Mackenzie King needed help in Quebec.

He got it in the persons of three of his cabinet ministers from Quebec. Chubby Powers, who had inherited his father's seat at Quebec City, had a body severely wounded in the First World War. Ernest Lapointe had gone to Ottawa without a word of English, but now he came home to urge greater Canada on his compatriots. P.J.A. Cardin went to Ottawa to cut into the power of English Canada, and would work himself to death fighting the Nazis. These three men were the great orators that King was not. At first they had catcalls and objects thrown at them, but they wept as they gestured, and their tears turned the tide. They told the province's voters that if overseas conscription ever arrived, they would quit their prime minister. On election night the Liberal Adelard Godbout took Quebec away from Duplessis.

Now, said all the King's men, we can concentrate on building the war machine and saving civilization. Not so fast. Now another premier decided to make trouble. This one was a Liberal. Mitch Hepburn was a Souwesto farmer who gathered the Progressives to him and knocked off the Conservatives in Ontario. He just plain did not like Mackenzie King. In a few years he would throw his support to Arthur Meighen, for heaven's sake! As for now, he did not like the way that King was accommodating the French Canadians; he wanted a good colonial gung-ho approach to the war. So he introduced into the Ontario legislature a resolution to declare that the feds were twiddling their thumbs.

Mackenzie King resorted to one of his favourite tricks. How can I run a country and wage a war with this kind of ambiguity, he asked. I am calling a federal election. The Tory leader was poor old Dr Robert Manion, one of Meighen's "acting ministers" during an earlier end run by Mrs King's son. There was a chance that Manion was going to defeat Mackenzie King in 1940? He didn't have a prayer. He did not even use the name "Conservative" during his campaign. On January 25, the prime minister stood up and read Mitch Hepburn's resolution. I think that we'd better go to the people, he said. The leader of the opposition jumped up, right into King's noose. Manion said that King was too sneaky to be running the country in such dangerous times. Okay, that's it, said King—we're going to the people.

In the 1940 election the Tories managed thirty-nine seats. King now had Quebec and the rest of Canada onside. He could run the country the way only a wartime prime minister can run a country, even a country that had been in a decade of depression. University of Toronto historian Michael Bliss has a wonderful phrase that must be quoted: he wrote that the war was "a kind of ultimate megaproject." The government did not have to worry about justifying big spending and big taxes, or restrictive wage and price controls. Any wastrel or slacker would be asked "Don't you know there's a war going on?" The second most powerful man in the country was the reformed USAmerican C.D. Howe, who ruled like an archduke as Minister of Munitions and Supply. The iron mines and steel mills were in his back yard. The rest of King's ministers took life very seriously, and the civil service grew and grew. Mackenzie King was chary of this development, but there was a war going on. Anyone who did not like the way things were being done would be suspected of subversion.

Little kids such as I got a bit confused between King George and King Mackenzie.

In 1940 the so-called "phoney war" came to an end as Germans hopped over the Maginot Line and occupied northern France. It would be a while before Allied troops got to the Continent. Canadian ground forces would in the meantime be sent to Newfoundland, the Caribbean and Iceland. Some were sent to Hong Kong in time to be blasted and captured by the Japanese. But as the Canadian army waited and trained, the other services were expanded dramatically. The navy grew from seventeen ships to nine hundred, with its main job the convoy of supplies across the submarine-infested ocean. Chubby Powers's air force led the Commonwealth, and established forty-five foreign squadrons. A quarter of the air crews that were to bomb Germany would be Canadian. Canada would become an amazing industrial-military machine during the war, but the volunteers in the army complained about doing guard duty in Labrador.

Young men who did not volunteer and yet seemed to be the model of health might find themselves the recipients of white feathers handed to them by soldiers' sisters, or they might find themselves becoming Zombies. This was the term given to conscripts for home defence. In 1940 Quebec agreed to King's National Resources Mobilization Act. It did not look as if any French-Canadian boys would have to fight Italian soldiers on Canadian soil.

Rockefeller? Roosevelt?

Canada was the only country in the Americas to declare war on Hitler and Mussolini during the first half of the war. Previous to this time the United States invaded smaller countries in order to grow in size, and in later years would bomb lots of small countries for reasons that seemed to have a lot to do with internal politics. But in 1940 the US was technically neutral, and entrepreneurial politicians such as the Dulles brothers made fortunes by trading with anyone who needed war materiel.

But their president, Franklin Delano Roosevelt, was betting on greater US involvement, and planning ways to help the Allies, especially when it looked as if Hitler might be in a position to overrun Britain itself. That matter was taken so seriously in Britain that there were plans to move King George to Ottawa to join the Dutch royal family. England could use some help from the USA, if not in the form of an army, at least in terms of supplies. The USAmericans were glad to oblige—at a price. And if there were deals to be made, Mackenzie King would become the middleman between Roosevelt and Churchill. A good broker would thus help Britain win the war, but at the price of unparalleled USAmerican influence in Canada.

The first meeting was conducted in secret in FDR's private railway car at Ogdensburg, New York, a town across the river from Prescott, Ontario. FDR did not want a lot of Republican senators listening in. He patted the Canadian prime minister on the back and called him "Mackenzie." On a piece of scrap paper the prime minister and the president sketched a plan for the first Canadian-US joint defence treaty in history. The two men agreed that the US would send 50 Great War destroyers to Britain in exchange for military real estate in Newfoundland and Labrador and Bermuda. Not a bad deal for the USAmericans, who were going to scuttle those ships anyway. Roosevelt was a USAmerican, after all—he had a manifest destiny to advance. Perhaps Mackenzie King worried about those US air bases down the line, but there was a war going on.

More and more, King would act as go-between for Roosevelt and Churchill, and in the meantime he would facilitate US industrial expansion into Canada. There was no time for tariffs during wartime, so US parts, whether for the army or the farmers, flooded into Canada. While no one was watching, the imbalance of trade soared, and Canada's foreign debt (read US capitalism) would mean a far different country once this European business was over. In 1941 FDR signed another paper at Hyde Park, his family estate. It supplied lots of US cash for a nearly broke Canada, and arranged the future economic relationship between the USA and its northern economic colony.

But Mackenzie King would not forget to insist on Canada's historic relationship with the mother country. He flew in a military plane to London, to talk with Churchill and visit the bombed capital. While he was there he picked up pieces of London's ruins to carry home and add to his own at Kingsmere. Like Borden in the Great War, he would visit Canadian troops. Borden had seen boys in French trenches and English hospitals. King went to inspect the troops who had been waiting and training at an English base. Unfortunately it was raining and King was late getting there. The Canadian soldiers had been standing in the rain for an hour and more. When the short guy in the nice hat addressed them, they snickered. Tory critics said that they were browned off at the Zombies. Liberal spin doctors said that they were wet and bored.

Things heat up

By December 1941 the Japanese armed forces had gathered on the left-hand side of the Pacific. On December 7 they hit the US empire directly at Pearl Harbor. A few days later Germany and Italy declared war on the US. Canada declared war on Japan without waiting for parliamentary approval. The west coast of North America now looked closer to Tokyo. A result of the US entry into the war would be combined US-Canadian defence procedures, including the Alaska Highway, a project that even worried Mackenzie King. An ominous political result would be more trouble about conscription.

In the spring of 1942 King decided that he needed a national plebiscite on conscription. In 1939 he had promised that there would be no conscription for overseas service, and since then Quebec had been somewhat quiescent. But now with a world war taking place in oceans on both sides of Canada, the future looked scary. Eventually there would be only eight neutral countries on the globe. The forces of evil were huge. Canada looked like a pretty good target. The Zombies would be overrun. It just might become necessary to send a lot more soldiers offshore to hold back the Japanese and their friends. For now there were enough Canadians mouldering away in Britain and its possessions, but the world might burst into flame. The 1939 promise was made on a 1914 model. King needed a cushion.

He was going to tell the nation that he was still adamantly opposed to conscription, but that the situation just might become desperate. Therefore he needed to be released from his 1939 promise. Once again he had to find some knife-edge between Quebec anger and the pressure he was getting from the English Canadians and the military. He had to persuade the French Canadians that he was still an anti-conscription man, and mollify the forces that despised Quebec "disloyalty." Thus the phrase for which he is best known (though he lifted it from a journalist): "Conscription if necessary, but not necessarily conscription."

He knew that the plebiscite would be rejected in Quebec, but he wanted a fair showing of support in that province. There were Quebeckers who wanted Germany to win the war, and thus rid Canada of English governance forever. There were others who objected to the draft less radically. King had been dealt a stroke of bad luck when his champion Ernest Lapointe finally worked himself to death just after Pearl Harbor. Cardin's molten silver tongue would be a great help, but the PM needed a new Lapointe. Chubby Powers recommended a staid corporation lawyer named Louis Stephen St Laurent, and King telephoned him, asking him to come to Ottawa and be Minister of Justice. King lucked out. St Laurent kept the Quebec caucus onside, and discussion of the plebiscite went to the House.

The wording was the model of a simple question: "Are you in favour of releasing the Government from any obligation arising out of any past commitments restricting the methods of raising men for military service?"

The prime minister knew that he would win the plebiscite. He was pretty sure that it would lose in Quebec, but he sent his warriors through the province to assure Quebeckers that Mackenzie King was still an anti-conscription man. His Ontario men would somehow lead English-Canadian voters to believe that the opposite just might be true. The English-speaking provinces came through all right, voting 80 per cent in favour. But Quebec was a considerable disappointment. There was a heavy vote, and 73 per cet of the province's voters rejected any chance of overseas conscription. Laurier's nightmare of a country divided along "racial" lines was alive during times of emergency.

Still, King carried the overall positive vote into Parliament and introduced a bill to change the National Resources Mobilization Act. His beautiful orator, Cardin, resigned as he had promised his Quebeckers that he would. The rift in the country was reflected in King's cabinet. The Defence Minister, Colonel Layton Ralston, kept threatening to resign every time King suggested that he was not gung-ho about drafting young Canadians from all provinces for overseas duty. All prime ministers are pulled in opposite directions by their constituency and advisers, but not always in the life-or-death situation

Mackenzie King was facing. It is no wonder that he spent a while in the evenings talking to his mother and petting his dog.

As if the crisis needed some comic relief, Arthur Meighen arose dripping from the grave just before the plebiscite was called. Meighen was living a comfortable life provided by the coupons he clipped. Since his two-step into the Senate, the Tories had been sashaying leaders onto the slippery Commons dance floor. Bennett was sitting this one out in England. Dr Manion had been dumped by the caucus right after his disastrous 1940 showing, and replaced by R.B. Hanson. In 1941 the Tories looked around and all they saw was Arthur Meighen. Listlessly, they decided to give him a chance for a third try at the top job. But that meant that the old guy would have to win a seat in the Commons. He had been doing his sniping from the Senate, denouncing King's association with Roosevelt, and trumpeting his faithfulness to the British Crown. But he wanted to use his scornful wit in the House; he wanted to get that little pudge who had through some unbelievable luck managed to thwart him all his political life.

The return of Meighen should have brought a smile of reminiscence to King's mouth, but for some reason it caused him to erupt in fury. He took to pounding furniture with his fist and calling Meighen a fascist. He saw the old anglophile destroying the country by confronting the Quebec nationalists. If Meighen were to win the February 1942 by-election in York South, King would have to be in the same room with him for the rest of the war. In his diaries he invented extremely insulting descriptions of his old rival. These two men truly hated each other.

Of course Meighen, who had a son in the army, would run for York South on a conscriptionist platform. Mitch Hepburn, the onion farmer and Liberal premier of Ontario, threw his party workers to Meighen's support. Meighen seemed ready to become the figurehead for all English-speaking resentment against Quebec. Mackenzie King stopped pounding furniture long enough to think of a way to foil and enrage his foe one more time. He instructed the party to run no candidate in the by-election, and to give support to a CCF candidate named Noseworthy. Noseworthy defeated Meighen, and King took a fairly deep breath, danced a little jig, and kissed his dog. But he knew that the conscriptionists were not finished. He could feel the hate vibrations in the air, east and west.

These vibrations shook his own inner circle. Colonel Ralston went around saying that the new legislation meant that the cabinet could declare overseas conscription. But King told him that the measure would take a vote in Parliament. All right, said Ralston, and wrote out his resignation. King refused it, but he tucked the letter away in case he might need it later. He kept Ralston onside with a compromise: if things got really desperate, overseas conscription could be introduced by an Order-in-Council, and *then* ratified by Parliament. If Ralston had walked right then, even if he had not walked to the other side of the House, the prime minister might have met a soothsayer who warned him to beware the march of aides, and Mackenzie King paid more credence to soothsayers than did Julius Caesar. But Ralston was a hero of the Great War; he loved his country, sir.

Still, when King introduced the conscription bill, P.J.A. Cardin and forty-four other Quebec Liberals voted against it. King knew that they were protecting their careers back home, and he expected them back—as long as he did not have to really introduce overseas conscription and order tanks into the streets of Montreal. In any case, with Lapointe and Cardin gone their various ways, he had the firm and quiet St Laurent by his side, and he was coming to like him better and better.

Love me, I'm a liberal

During the thirties King had drifted to the conservative side of the Liberal party. During the war years he sensed a leftward stroll of the populace. The centralizing of power for the war effort made it easier to satisfy the people's expectation that government can take care of things. Ironically, while King bound Canada's economy and defence more and more to the US future, his social programs declared a clear distinction from the cold USAmerican laissez-faire capitalism. Canadians would come more and more to be disturbed by the USAmerican idea that medicine was a business, that poverty was your own problem.

The Rowell-Sirois Commission that began studies during the last years of the Depression, and delivered its report in 1940, suggested that the Dominion government should make equalization grants for social services in the "have-not" provinces. The three "have" provinces complained, but during wartime it was not difficult to start the process. In 1940, King got federal responsibility for unemployment insurance. He seemed to have found a copy of the book he had published in 1918. Now he set up the Marsh commission on social security, and received its report in 1943. He was beginning to think of post-war society and his own legacy. In fact, around the time of his retirement in 1948 he would be describing his plans for a national health scheme. In the meantime, the ballooning civil service would have to start handling veterans' affairs, address the coming housing crisis, and watch over employment practices. Taking a chapter right out of *Industry and Humanity*, the Dominion government certified unions and instructed manufacturers to engage in collective bargaining.

King always weighed his social measures against the political realities. He knew that the Conservatives represented a fair number of people who feared a slide into socialism. But he turned out to be correct in characterizing the majority who voted for a federal government whose job it was to care for the people within the country's borders. He introduced his reform initiatives one at a time. In the last year of the war he introduced the most Canadian of government cheques—the family allowance. When the "baby bonus" was introduced, what could the Conservatives do? Could they denounce it as both a socialist plot and a bribe to Quebec? Did they really want to come out as the enemies of the nation's mothers? How could they attack the bachelor prime minister?

King, of course, knew that the family allowance was a highly symbolic and radical feature of his social program. He pulled one of his favourite tricks: I have to be fair about this matter, he said in 1945. We will go to the people in an election.

He was not an overly enlightened Christian. He complained about the Jews who were interested in property near his acres in Quebec. He was relieved that the atomic bomb was dropped on Asians instead of Europeans. European Jews and Japanese Canadians did not fare well in wartime Canada. He was not happy to hear about India's post-war inclusion in the Commonwealth. But while arguing for the "baby bonus," King said, "I thought the Creator intended that all persons born should have equal opportunities." The Marsh report had said that there were mothers in Canada who could not afford to feed and clothe their children. Some of the walrus group in the Tories argued that fathers would use this kind of welfare for tobacco and beer. The Liberals wrote cheques for eight dollars a child to the mothers. There were a lot of mothers in the country who had never received a cheque of any kind before this. Mackenzie King was a racist, and he had no women in his cabinet, but when he wrote cheques to the mothers of Canada he was doing more than simply honouring his own.

Revolt of the generals

If we are charitable, we will say that we don't know the full reason for Mackenzie King's opposition to overseas conscription. Could it be that he did not want any boys from the working classes to be sent overseas toward death against their will? Did he believe that a volunteer army would be better motivated and sufficient to the cause? Was he looking ahead to the effect of Quebec's support on his survival and the survival of the Liberal party?

Whatever the reason, he was feeling pretty rosy about 1944 when that year started. He went to England and drank tea with Field Marshall Bernard Montgomery, the man who would command the Commonwealth troops in the coming invasion of France. Montgomery persuaded the Canadian prime minister that once the Allies were on the Continent, they would wrap up the war in a few months. King welcomed the news, because it meant that Canadian casualties could be replaced by volunteer soldiers. He started planning an election. Who could lose an election right after VE Day?

The Allied Forces invaded France on June 6, 1944. They had landed on the boot of Italy in January, and now Canadian soldiers were leading their allies northward, except when it was time to enter a large city, at which point US troops would be jeeped ahead to meet the photographers. The Germans had learned to surrender in North Africa and Russia, but Montgomery's prediction had to be modified; the European phase of the war was now scheduled to end in time for Christmas. The Canadian election was put off until 1945. In September of 1944 Mackenzie King was busy welcoming Churchill and Roosevelt to Quebec. They had met in 1943 to plot the invasion, and now they had to start talking about the most practicable way to handle the defeated people and the liberated lands. The meetings were held at the luxurious Chateau Frontenac.

Mackenzie King was not part of a triumvirate at Quebec. He acted as host to the other two heads of government, made a few speeches, and was briefed every day, but the meeting was the business of Winnie and FDR. For the USAmericans it was a time to tell the Brits that the Yanks would be running things in the Pacific. There might have been some British and Canadian prisoners at Hong Kong, but FDR wanted the world to know that from now on the Pacific would be a USAmerican lake. Mackenzie King sent a note saying that Canadians were not ready for jungle fighting in any case. While he was there, he gave a speech to the Quebec Reform Club in which he reminded his audience that he had always been against con- scription and promised that he would never draft anyone for overseas fighting.

(In May of 1998, the Quebec National Capital Commission would unveil busts of Churchill and Roosevelt at the site of the 1943 and 1944 meetings. The British High Commissioner and the US ambassador were invited to give speeches. They both spoke in French, and heard shouts of "Speak French!" when they lapsed into English. The premier of Quebec, Lucien Bouchard, was heckled by federalists in the crowd. The prime minister of Canada was not invited to the ceremony, and Mackenzie King was not represented in the monument, except in a footnote. Back in Ottawa, Prime Minister Jean Chrétien pointed out that King's Canada had gone to war against fascism more than two years before Roosevelt's USA had, and that King had worked hard to bring Roosevelt into the Allied effort. A few days later, a writer named Lawrence Martin, author of a 1982 book on the relationships between prime ministers and presidents, reminded some reporters that in 1942 Roosevelt had written King a letter in which he advocated the assimilation of French Canadians into English-speaking Canada. But by 1998 the sovereigntist establishment in Quebec was treating history as a tool for socio-political engineering.)

While King was thinking of his post-war election, and assuring his Quebec members and their constituencies that the volunteer army could do the mopping up, his Minister of Defence was over in Europe, hearing a different story. Colonel Ralston came back to Ottawa and informed the cabinet that the Canadian army was terribly undermanned, and had been undermanned before Operation Overlord got underway. Now Canadians in Italy and the north were being sent back to the front after being wounded twice. The replacements were not enough, and the ones who did get to the theatre were not well-enough trained. Like Robert Borden in the first war, Ralston heard from embattled soldiers that they needed help. He came back home to demand conscription.

He knew how the prime minister felt about mothers. He was going to tell him about mothers of eighteen-year-olds who were sent into battle before they had been properly trained.

On October 19, 1944, he told the cabinet that the Zombies had to be sent to Europe. The terrible situation was going to get a lot worse in the big battles to come. King replied that the conscription issue would have to be taken to Parliament, and would result in a political crisis that would split the country in half for decades to come. Ralston could not believe that King would talk about politics when wounded boys were running straight at the gun barrels of German tanks. King had never had much faith in the military mind, and despaired of teaching reality to the colonel. Now Ralston reminded King of his promise in 1942. Conscription, he said, is now "necessary." The two men began to argue about the meaning of that word. They decided to ask the opinion of General Kenneth Stuart, chief of the general staff. Before the invasion Stuart had told both Ralston and King not to worry. Now he said that the war was going to be harder and longer than everyone had thought. Better send the Zombies, and do it now, he said.

The cabinet, of course, began to split in two.

The pressure came so hard from both sides that there was hardly room to remain unsquashed. King worked longer hours than ever, wore his tight-fitting suit for longer hours, and hardly had time to teach tricks to his new dog, Pat II. When he spoke about the danger of the government's fall and the country's shattering, people said that they had heard that before, but they did not know how grave the situation was. Bruce Hutchison told us long after the war about the secret revolt of the military that blackmailed the prime minister and resembled the shadow of a coup.

For a month the stressed cabinet fought it out. Mackenzie King looked across the table at the conscriptionists and asked them in his usual conversational voice whether they were ready to take his job. He was bluffing—he knew that Ralston could form a Unionist movement and go to the people and get the vote of English Canada. But Ralston was a commissioned officer, not a prime minister. Mackenzie King's threat to resign was never serious. He knew that this long wrangle had to finish—it would be Ralston or King, and King had his priorities. He had won many a battle with a tricky move—now he would take the most dangerous one he had ever tried.

On Hallowe'en night, King summoned General A.G.L. McNaughton to Laurier House. McNaughton had been a general in the Great War, and perhaps Canada's most famous military man between the wars. He had been in charge of the overseas Canadian army until the British high command had insisted on his removal before D-Day. Now in the middle of the spookiest night of the year, the prime minister asked him to become the new minister of defence. The next day he went to his cabinet meeting with the letter of resignation that Ralston had written in 1942, and announced that he had finally accepted it. Then he issued the news that McNaughton was their new colleague.

McNaughton was such a heroic and magnetic figure that Zombies would be clamouring to get onto the troopships. The war could be won without losing Quebec.

The future of the Liberal party and perhaps Canada now depended on what Ralston would do. Several conscriptionist ministers were already folding their portfolios. Ralston stood up, shook hands with the prime minister, and walked out of the room. Once again character would bow to politics and save the latter's neck.

The crisis was over. Now it was time for the crisis to begin. McNaughton and King made patriotic speeches and radio appeals, but the Zombies were no more eager to rush overseas than were the young Canadians of 1917. Now the prime minister was a figure for derision by the uniformed men in Europe and the safe young gents at home. The autumn of 1944 saw the Allies landing in Greece, the Russian tanks rolling through eastern Europe, and the re-election of Roosevelt. Canadians fought house to house in the Low Countries, and prayed for some rest and recruits. Late in November the army council, made up of the top command in the armed services, delivered an ultimatum to the cabinet and the prime minister. Either the draftees go overseas or the top brass resigns. If the top brass resigns during a world war, the government might as well ship out itself.

Mackenzie King knew two things: (1) conscription was now "necessary" for sure, and (2) this palace revolt had to be kept a secret. Canada must never catch a glimpse of itself as a military dictatorship. The governor general must believe that civilian democracy was taking responsible decisions.

The Liberal caucus and then all of Parliament were shocked to hear that the prime minister was now a conscriptionist. He was a very reluctant conscriptionist, he said. There were dark forces of anarchy on the loose, he hinted, and Canada might be doomed if several thousand Zombies were not sent to Europe. Aside from the top brass, only McNaughton and St Laurent knew the story. King's old Quebec spokesman, Chubby Powers, lying in a hospital bed, sent in his resignation. Louis Stephen St Laurent was King's new Quebec spokesman. He had the prodigious task of bringing the province's MPs into line, to make them accept King's reneging on his promise, to make them act against the deepest emotion in their people. He told them that if King's sudden about-face was rejected, there would be a new prime minister, and he would be an Anglo who had always wanted total conscription and did not give a damn for Quebec. Louis St Laurent could not tell them about the revolt of the top brass. He had to present himself as a conscriptionist from Quebec. Mackenzie King was going to owe him plenty.

Sixteen thousand Zombies were hauled overseas. Thousands of others disappeared into the woods. The usual riots occurred in the streets of Quebec and Montreal. A Quebec tradition was observed as mobs vandalized St Laurent's house. The Montreal Canadiens had won the 1944 Stanley Cup. The Toronto Maple Leafs won the 1945 Stanley Cup around the time that Halifax played host to the VE-Day riot. Conscription had not caused the wholesale rebellion that King had always feared, though he wondered about the long-term effects. Hardly any former Zombies were killed at the front. St Laurent had quietly become a masterful handler of Quebec affairs. What a good time to call that election!

Once more, into the speech

Roosevelt had started his fourth term in January, but he died in May. Churchill resigned that month and surprised himself by losing the resultant election. The heads of state in Germany and Italy had been shot to death. It looked as if Joseph Stalin would win re-election. But Mackenzie King could be the only western leader to stay in power through and after the Second World War.

All he had to worry about was Quebec: would its voters waste their ballots on the splinter groups and independents, or would they come back to their traditional party? The Tories helped him out on that count: their leader was a westerner named John Bracken, who had been United Farmer premier of Manitoba from 1922 to 1942. In 1942 he accepted the leadership of the federal opposition, and changed the party's name to the Progressive Conservative Party. But he declined to seek a parliamentary seat until the 1945 election was called. Mackenzie King had a lot of fun talking about John Bracken during the campaign.

All through the war John Bracken had been an outspoken conscriptionist. Now he wanted to send conscripts to the Pacific theatre. Mackenzie King spent his time joking about Bracken and promising to expand even further the social benefits he had been enacting. He always found time to talk about showing the nation's thanks to its returned veterans. On June 11th, he did what Churchill could not do. The Progressive Conservatives got sixty-seven seats, most of them in Ontario. The CCF got twenty-eight in the west. The Liberals got a safe majority. There was a sour note. When the military vote was counted, King found out that he was still not popular among the fighting men. He was tipped out of his Prince Albert seat and had to win one against an independent in Glengarry in eastern Ontario.

Winding down

When Canada experienced an economic boom (along with inevitable inflation) in the first years of peace, the Liberals followed tradition by taking credit. There was a lot of wartime energy that could be turned into peacetime energy. But Mackenzie King was an old man now—he could no longer work all hours of the day and night. He had no family whose arms he could rest in, but he had an image of himself as the great man his mother had expected. He loved to be photographed with Harry Truman and Dwight D. Eisenhower and Jan Smuts. He was the experienced leader on the world stage, he thought, even though the vast majority of citizens in the nearest country did not know his name. It was time to see about trying to fulfil Laurier's prophecy.

He had a really good cabinet and a big civil service, but he had been around longer than anyone—how could anyone else know as much as he did about, say, Industry and Humanity? He was cranky and tired much of the time, and his workday grew shorter. His ministers knew that it was time for him to go to Kingsmere and admire his ruins, but who was going to bring up the question at a meeting? They would do the work of redirecting industry and resettling humanity, and let the bald man with the eyebags take the credit.

He had gone to San Francisco to help set up the United Nations, but he had no more faith in the UN than he had had in the League. He agreed with the US politicians that the ambitions of world communism would be the greatest threat to western democracy. When file clerk Igor Gouzenko defected from the Soviet Embassy and revealed a communist spy network that had seemed to infiltrate the House of Commons, Canadians reacted like their prime minister, basking in the klieg lights of the new Cold War. King made speeches denouncing communism as "the most subtle of all evils." Canadians began to look at the map of the globe and notice that their country was situated between the USA and the USSR. Mackenzie King had more and more meetings with USAmerican politicians and generals. In 1947 the first meetings of the future North Atlantic Treaty Organization were being held.

Canada was being drawn more and more into the US orbit, or shadow. USAmerican radio stations, movies, musical recordings and eventually television were predominating more than they ever had. Canadian magazines that used to have pictures of the English princesses on them now had pictures of Hollywood film stars. Mackenzie King felt that he had to announce the remaining British connection as often as he could. The Canadian Citizenship Act became practice on January 1, 1947, and two days later the prime minister, just turned seventy-two years of age, became the first Canadian citizen to receive his certificate. He made a point of pointing out that he was still a "British subject." Canadian independence had been proclaimed over and over again for eighty years, and would continue to be proclaimed for years to come.

Now he wanted to welcome 400,000 new Canadian citizens. Newfoundland, which had rejected Confederation in 1867, had become more and more integrated into the North American complex during the war, and had in fact seen so much war business that when it did enter Canada in 1949 it brought a $40-million surplus. The Liberals in Ottawa and the Liberals in St John's worked hard for each other, but the people of Newfoundland, who had once rejected independence for a return to colonial status, had to have two plebiscites brought to them before they chose Confederation by a narrow margin. There are still plenty of Newfoundlanders who maintain that the Islanders rejected the second plebiscite, too. Mackenzie King wanted to be the prime minister who welcomed a tenth province, but he could not hang on quite that long. There had to be an election by 1950, and custom would set it for 1949. The party, he knew, contained too many people who were not ready to give him another go. They would have to have a convention by 1948. It would have been smart to step down in 1947, handing the leadership to a successor who could go into the next election as prime minister.

But the old man with no family except his invisible mother saw himself as history. Non-historians might call it vanity. He had survived his fellow statesmen and become the senior first minister in the Commonwealth. Now he wanted to go for the all-time record. His Lou Gehrig was Robert Walpole, the first British prime minister. Walpole, remember, invented the position while he served, or rather ruled, from 1721 to 1742. Mackenzie King's beginning occurred exactly two hundred years after Walpole's, and we know King's mind well enough to be pretty sure that he saw an omen in that number twenty-one. Of course Meighen and Bennett had made the arithmetic a little complicated, but King had four university degrees. He made a count of Walpole's days—7,619, and passed that number in late April of 1948. He must have been pleased by that last number too, because 1948 would be declared the greatest year in human civilization.

King was in control of the Liberal party convention in the fall of 1948. He voted for St Laurent as the new leader, and indulged his sentimental regret as St Laurent defeated Chubby Powers, who had brought St Laurent to save King in the first place. King had led his party for twenty-nine years. One day he felt as if the party was an institution that was ordained to run Canada forever, the feeling that the Tories had had in the previous century. The next day he envisioned a party that was old and tired, which now had a leader with white hair and an old-fashioned moustache. He was pretty pessimistic about the world, too. He had no faith that the United Nations could forestall the biggest world war of all, an Armageddon of nuclear bombs. When he died at Kingsmere on the night of July 22, 1950, there was a wiry dog sleeping near his bed, and a new war between capitalism and communism in Korea.

Meanwhile, his nation would have to get used to someone else as prime minister. The population of Canada was almost twice what it had been in 1921. The army uniforms in the photographs from Korea looked familiar, but everyone knew that we were living in a new kind of world.

CHAPTER 18

ABIDE WITH ME

———◆•◆•◆———

Louis S. St Laurent 1948–57

IN THE LAST YEAR OF the seventies, when I was trying to hold onto the notion of being a poet, I gave myself this challenge: write a medium-long poem about a subject that would seem inherently dull. So I wrote a poem called "Uncle Louis." In the seventies there was a lot of patronizing of the fifties. There were generally two pictures of Louis St Laurent: he was either a harmless old duffer who patted children on the head, or he was the figurehead for an arrogant government that rode the post-war boom and tucked Canada a little tighter under the USAmerican wing.

Dennis Lee is a poet most readily associated with the Anglo-Ontarian culture and the Toronto of the seventies. He is, like his hero George Grant, a kind of radical conservative. He took the history of central Canada seriously, and his 1968 poem "Civil Elegies," revised for 1972, lamented "the deft emasculation of a country by the Liberal party of Canada." He excoriates Paul Martin, who had been named Secretary of State for External Affairs by Lester Pearson, who had been named Secretary of State for External Affairs by Louis St Laurent, who had been named Secretary of State for External Affairs by Mackenzie King. In Dennis Lee's poem this was a succession of steps away from Canadian sovereignty.

Dennis Lee is quoted briefly in "Uncle Louis." However, the latter poem is written not from the perspective of Canada's presumed centre, but from the perspective of a far-western rural youth who had become a teenager at the exact time that St Laurent had become prime minister. On becoming a teenager, one has a duty to history:

> You did not say Fred Rose, he fell under the shadow
> of the initial fright in the hearts of a certain
>
> Quebec darkness. It was not fair, what they did
> to Fred Rose, & so you see, history is not fair,
>
> it *is* a fair. At a fair you throw rings at
> bottles & you never ring a bottle. You are training
>
> to be a Canadian, a nice blue suit & you too
> can be in St Laurent's cabinet.

Irving Layton, a poet who made a lyrical killing by writing in the vulgate in the fifties, may have suggested that Louis St Laurent made a most apt head of government for the times. One of Layton's most-often anthologized fifties poems refers to Canadians as "a dull people, without charm/ or ideas."

The poets, though, are fond of ironies. So they should reflect once in a while upon the fact that it was during St Laurent's regime that the Canada Council was created. And the National Library. And federal assistance to universities in the provinces. Writers and readers (and other artists) who see the Liberals as total continentalists might recall that these initiatives would lead to cultural self-awareness that expanded until the sudden blades of the Mulroney government in the eighties.

Made to order

When Mackenzie King telephoned Louis St Laurent during his dinner, and asked him to come and be his Quebec lieutenant for the duration of the war, he did not realize that he was summoning a metaphor for the Canadian unity that had eluded all the men who had ever sat in the prime minister's chair.

St Laurent started life in a house next to his father's general store in Compton, Quebec. Compton is halfway between Sherbrooke and the US border, and now the centre of the St Laurent National Heritage Park. At the time of his birth in 1882, the Eastern Townships were populated largely by descendants of the United Empire Loyalists expelled from the US, the Scots expelled by the English, and the Irish who had arrived after the great famine of the mid-nineteenth century. By the beginning of the twentieth century there would be a French-Canadian influx as the lands along the St Lawrence were pretty well filled up.

The general store of Jean-Baptiste Moise St-Laurent had the proverbial woodstove in it, and his son hung out there, listening to townspeople philosophizing in French and English. He would grow up learning that the two peoples got along well together. In the house next door he heard both languages, too, because his mother had been Mary Ann Broderick, formerly a schoolteacher, descended from Irish refugees. Mary Ann spoke English because her husband had laughed at her first attempts at French. Decades later, people said that they could detect a slight Irish accent in the prime minister's English.

Like the Lauriers, the St Laurents once had another name. They were once the family Huot, and one of them, Nicolas Huot, arrived in New France around 1660. It was not long until he was signing himself "Huot-St-Laurens," and then "Huot-St-Laurent." The "Laurens" probably appeared because that was his father's first name. But his father was not a saint. It seems pretty obvious that he took his name from the great river that would have to make his family's fortune.

The Huots and then the St Laurents had their ups and downs, until Louis would make the family's fortune as a lawyer and eventually director for some big important corporations. He argued effectively in two languages and manoeuvred two legal systems, and unlike Richard Bennett, stayed out of politics. He was Quebecois and Irish, but he never identified himself as a member of a defeated and oppressed people. Unlike the man who telephoned him, he was not a spiritualist, though everyone in his family seemed to be named after a saint. His father was named after the patron saint of New France. His mother was named after the mother of Christ. He was in a way named after the martyred St Lawrence, but also Stephen, after a lot of saints and popes. Irish people like that name, and though it said "Étienne" on her son's birth certificate, Mary Ann made sure that "Stephen" would be the usage.

He went to a bilingual Catholic school in Sherbrooke, where he wrote a column for the school paper, sometimes in French, sometimes in English, and graduated first in his class. He had a bachelor's degree at age twenty. It was 1902, and there was a French-Canadian prime minister whose ambition was to unify the country. But Louis St Laurent was not interested in politics. He went to Laval University to study the French Civil Code and learned English Common Law on his own. He took a little time off to follow his father's campaign as a Liberal in the 1904 provincial election, but his father lost, and the son went happily back to Quebec City, where he again led his class and earned the first Rhodes scholarship ever won by a student at Laval. He was too eager to get into practice, so he advised his pal Marius Barbeau to apply for the scholarship, which Barbeau did. Barbeau, of course, went on to become Canada's most famous folklorist, served at the National Museum for forty-seven years, and wrote a hundred books—in French and English.

Barbeau introduced his friend to Jeanne Renault, who had already looked on the young man with the moustache with sympathetic eye. She had been in the audience while he got his academic robe snarled in the armrest of the chair of the wife of the governor general on his way to pick up his awards as Laval's top law student. They managed to get married without a hitch, so to speak, and had five children. "Grow old with me," he told her. "The best is yet to be."

Grow rich with me, he might have suggested. By 1932 he was the first French-speaking president of the Canadian Bar Association. He knew all about constitutional law, and he was a feared opponent in cases dealing with commercial law. Before that telephone call from the prime minister, he had pleaded twenty times before the Privy Council in London, and more than sixty times before the Canadian Supreme Court. When that telephone call came, it came to a big house filled with expensive furnishings, servants and a chauffeur.

Jeanne St Laurent had tears in her eyes when her husband told her what the telephone call was about. But there was a war on; the world needed saving, and Quebec needed saving for Canada. Louis promised her that they would be moving back to Quebec as soon as the war was over. He had no political ambitions. He was just the top lawyer in Canada. Now he would be the Minister of Justice. Logic seemed to be operating. St Laurent always liked logic better than emotion. He was not the first future prime minister to say that he knew no politics and did not care for politics, but he was the first to prove it. When Arthur Meighen had tried to recruit him, he had just smiled politely. When he campaigned for his first seat, he told his potential voters that down the line he would opt for conscription if it became necessary. He truly did not know politics—you were supposed to tell them that you were opposed to conscription, then opt for it anyway.

But now he was in Ottawa. He was smarter than Ernest Lapointe had been. His mind worked more efficiently than did that of Mackenzie King. His moustache was not the only thing that made him resemble Robert Borden. They could have conversed in Latin. Perhaps because of their knowledge of Latin they both preferred to speak precisely and efficiently instead of making long inflated speeches.

Where a politician or a historian might see a crisis, Louis St Laurent saw a situation that needed sizing up and a problem that needed solving. When the 1944 conscription problem came up, St Laurent campaigned around Quebec, not with Laurier's wet eyes and musical tones, but with short sentences and no fear for his political future. He was Mackenzie King's luck and his opposite. King was always quoting a boy scout God and attending table-rappings; St Laurent's Catholic upbringing never got in the way of his submission to the jury. King thought of his cabinet members as the deployers of his power; St Laurent would almost seem to become a second governor general, happily designating power and duty to his ministers. When he got away from Parliament Hill, King holed up in his bachelor digs among the ruins, or enjoyed an evening with a friend's wife; St Laurent went to the country club with his wife.

But Mackenzie King knew a successor when he saw one. He could not quite believe that there would come a time when he would have to quit his job, but just in case he might be mortal, he should have a look around. Certainly there were some accomplished men in his employ, C.D. Howe perhaps the most self-confident. Young Mike Pearson was a bit drab but did his homework. But his Quebec lieutenant would be best at holding on to Jean Lesage and the other Quebec MPs. How could King make St Laurent break his promise to his wife? Well, no one ever said that Mackenzie King did not know how to manipulate his people. He got into the habit of designating St Laurent acting prime minister while the prime minister was in another country. He took St Laurent to San Francisco for the organizing meeting of the United Nations. When the war was over and it was time for Canada to step downstage, he asked St Laurent to become Secretary of State for External Affairs.

The war is over. I am supposed to go back to Quebec and be a lawyer, said the sixty-three-year-old.

This is the first time in Canadian history that a prime minister has asked someone else to run External Affairs, said the devious and sincere prime minister.

I am a corporation lawyer, said St Laurent.

My second father was Wilfrid Laurier, said the prime minister. You owe it to him, to fulfil his prophecy.

In the post-war era Canada would throw in its lot with the United Nations and the anti-communist North Atlantic Treaty Organization. Louis St Laurent was not as pessimistic as King was about life in the atomic age. He welcomed the unravelling of various old empires. He did not hesitate to make alliances against new ones. He had a blind spot for the USAmerican one.

As soon as the war was over, Canada got into big-time Cold War politics with the Gouzenko spy affair, and St Laurent was still Justice Minister. Igor Gouzenko was a file clerk at the Soviet Embassy who decided to grab a bunch of secret communications and make a dash for western freedom. He could not get anyone interested. Justice told him to come back later. So did External Affairs. The newspapers were leery of the story. The Soviet Union was an ally who had just made great sacrifices to stop Hitler. But when Soviet thugs smashed down Gouzenko's apartment door and trashed the place, the Ottawa police got involved, and the Canadian government had to listen to what Igor Gouzenko had to tell them.

Later on, the Conservatives and CCF would say that the affair could have been handled legally. John Diefenbaker, an MP from Saskatchewan, shook his head and defended the Magna Carta. Mackenzie King tried to keep the whole affair quiet. But Igor Gouzenko knew that his potential assassins thrived on quiet. He had material that seemed to prove the Soviets' success in infiltrating External Affairs, the National Research Council, and Parliament itself. The communists were trying to find out everything they could about the atomic bomb the USAmericans had dropped on those Asians. And during Mackenzie King's time in office, the Canadians were the USAmericans' best friends. Ottawa was now full of USAmerican reporters and spies. Louis St Laurent knew that he would not be able to hush this affair, and he did not feel that either the Civil Code or the common law would do in this case. He was one of the first cold warriors.

So the Justice Minister presided over a secret roundup and interrogation of agents and dupes, the main characters in Cold War narratives. Civil servants sat under hard lights and heard hard questions, and did not have any lawyers to advise them on answers. "Reasons of national security" became a very popular phrase. All through history the spy has had to expect rough treatment and vengeance called justice. In Ottawa there were dark nights after September 5, 1945. It would not be long till the USAmericans staged their own atomic spy dramas. Eventually fourteen people would go to jail because of Igor Gouzenko's paperwork.

The Canadian people felt a kind of thrill. Already the USAmerican movie industry was telling the world that the USAmericans had won the biggest war in history. But we had a top-level spy ring in our nation's capital. The RCMP had even arrested a member of Parliament, Fred Rose, the Labour Progressive from Montreal. Rose would spend six years in jail for his part in the conspiracy, and die in his native Poland in 1983. He had been Fred Rosenberg in his childhood. It was a good thing that his parents came to Canada instead of the US. The US sent its Rosenbergs to the electric chair.

Mackenzie King was disturbed by the speed and relentlessness of the anti-spy operation, and somewhat alarmed at St Laurent's efficiency. In the House the Justice Minister explained his choice in signing the orders that led to the arrests: "We took the right course, the courageous course, the only course, to assure the safety of our form of government in this country." This was an explanation that the world would hear from many government spokespersons during the next few decades.

Laissez les bons temps roulez

That iron-fisted spy-smasher was not the man the newspapers had in mind when they called the new prime minister "Uncle Louis" after 1948. The kindly white-haired man in the stuffy clothes never refused a photographer's request to hold a child on his lap. Children, of course, were always called the future, but North America was entering a time in which children would become the present as far as the marketing geniuses were concerned. It would not be long until all the movies would be about troubled youth who could not "communicate," and all the popular songs would be about frustrated young lovers. The teenager was being invented.

Television would become the exciting new furniture in more and more living rooms and store windows during the St Laurent years. Movies would respond by growing wide wide screens, putting speakers at the back of the hall, and throwing three-dimensional actors and javelins into the audience. Nifty little record players would spin 45-rpm disks that even the least coordinated thirteen-year-old could stack on the fat spindle. Stay young with me, the advertisers said, the best is yet to be.

There was a post-war boom, even while war debts were being paid off, and the Canadian dollar scoffed at the Yankee greenback. Canada, for some reason, was growing rich faster than any other country. The party in power, of course, claimed that this was the natural result of sound Liberal policy. That party was a powerful machine that resembled the US automobiles of the era, big, multi-hued, fuel-gobbling—something you did not want to fall down in front of. The prime minister's limousine had enough chromium on it to chrome-plate the façade of the House of Commons. For almost thirty years Mackenzie King had been building and streamlining this vehicle. St Laurent could have coasted for nine years on the momentum. When he declared that he was not a politician, his able cabinet ministers might have replied: who cares?

Uncle Louis posed for his first election in 1949, a year when western consumers were being stirred into mistaken excitement about the approaching mid-century. The confident Liberals offered the slogan "You never had it so good." Thank you, thank you, said the voters, and though many of them in English-speaking Canada were not quite sure how to pronounce the prime minister's name, they gave him an unprecedented majority. In a "pre-campaign" train trip, the non-politician had posed for photographers at whistle stops across the west, benignly bowing to discuss matters with children at every station. It was in Edson, Alberta, that a photographer handed him the nickname "Uncle Louis." With so many newspaper photographers around, St Laurent and his handlers (especially the gnomish Jack Pickersgill) knew that these photo opportunities were as useful as major speeches in Toronto or Ottawa. They also knew that those were children of enfranchised parents.

Of course, while passing through the west, they were passing through CCF country. In Regina, St Laurent showed that he was as quick with a quip as Arthur Meighen had ever been, and certainly quicker than Mackenzie King. In Regina he opined that the CCF candidates and supporters were simply "Liberals in a hurry." The western trip did a lot to promote the cherished national unity and it did even more for Liberal fortunes in the always-problematical west. Big crowds came out to see this French-Canadian fellow, and were reassured when he told them how great it felt to be a Canadian. They were also somehow comforted to see a family man PM for the first time in decades. "Security" was an often-heard word in the post-war era. An editorial in the *Winnipeg Free Press* hailed a truly representative and symbolic Canadian, "a French Canadian who is half Irish, speaks English with no trace of French, has a gallic shrug and gesture, and might have been brought up in Halifax, Winnipeg, or Victoria."

As soon as the train reached Ottawa, St Laurent called his election. Jeanne wept again, as the Grits gathered 193 seats, including 3 Independent Liberals. George Drew's Conservatives were shrunk to 41. The CCF fell to 13. Social Credit managed to hang onto 10. Misfits and local heroes gathered the other 5. In his own riding of Quebec East the prime minister got four times the majority the great Lapointe had ever won.

Not only had he reassured the west—he was also able to calm Quebec's fears of international entanglements. Of course there were hotheads who would call him a *vendu* and point out that he had non-French blood in him, just as their successors would call a later prime minister Pierre "Elliott-Trudeau." But St Laurent was the first Canadian prime minister to station armed troops on other continents without causing a crisis in Parliament or riots in Quebec streets. When he aligned Canada's military with that of General Eisenhower, there were some Tory complaints, to which the reply was always something like: What's that? I can't hear you. Speak up!

In fact, the North Atlantic Treaty Organization was as much St Laurent's idea as it was Truman's or Eisenhower's. It had been introduced at the Couchiching Conference of 1947, and soon External Affairs Minister St Laurent was holding secret talks with USAmerican and British colleagues. St Laurent's mission was to keep the US from fading into its usual self-preoccupation; he knew that France and Britain had been depleted during the war, and he took the Soviet advances in eastern Europe as a bad sign. Italy, for instance, had a huge Communist party, and there were plenty of communists in France and Austria. Once again Canada would act as the linchpin between the two biggest English-speaking nations. St Laurent and his aide Lester Pearson wanted any treaty to be economic as well as military, at least to forbid punishing economic moves by one member against another. In fact, when the treaty came to be signed, the "Canadian article" was included, but would be ignored while fighter jets were exchanged.

In 1948 St Laurent introduced the idea in the House of Commons. He explained that the universality of the United Nations had room for self-defence alliances among some of its members. And "our foreign policy today must, therefore, I suggest, be based on a recognition of the fact that totalitarian communist aggression endangers the freedom and peace of every democratic country, including Canada." Those, too, were words that would be heard often during the coming years. On the auspicious date of November 11, he made a radio broadcast in which he likened his proposed defence treaty to buying house insurance.

In the spring of 1949 St Laurent wanted to get two major pieces of business done before starting the election campaign. On March 28, he introduced the NATO bill, and it was passed that day. Three days later Newfoundland united with Canada. This non-politician lawyer seemed to have a knack for handling big deals. On April 4, the NATO treaty was signed, and it came into effect on August 24. Western European security would be shared by the US, Great Britain, France, Italy, Denmark, Norway, Iceland, Portugal, the Benelux countries and Canada. Timing seemed to be everything: that year the Soviets exploded their first atomic bomb, and Mao Tse Tung's Communists took over in China. There was one other interesting development: the US withdrew its occupying troops from South Korea.

Korea
—

Louis St Laurent had been interested in Korea for a few years. At the end of the Second World War, the mountainous peninsula had been liberated from a Japanese suzerainty that had replaced a Chinese one in 1910. Soviet troops occupied the land north of the thirty-eighth parallel while US troops occupied the south. The United Nations tried to find some way to unite the halves.

James Lorimer Ilsley, wartime finance minister, was in 1947 Canada's representative at the United Nations. He agreed that Canada would join the UN commission to look for a solution to the Korean standoff. St Laurent, the External Affairs Minister, signed the necessary papers. Now Mackenzie King, who had been away on vacation during this business, tried to repeat his reaction to the unfortunate Dr Riddell's sanctions against

Mussolini. Mackenzie King was no more enthusiastic about the chances for the UN than he had been about the chances for the League, and in his mind the failure of the League was probably a logical precedent. Now he shouted and banged things and rebuked Ilsley as he had Riddell, and even tried to get Canada out of the commitment.

But somehow the message got to him that if he pulled Canada out of the commission, Ilsley and St Laurent were both ready to resign. King stroked his designated successor and sweetly argued that Korea could plunge Canada back into war. He did not mention that he had been told so by the ghost of FDR. St Laurent picked his way through the fabulous dinner that King had laid on for him, but refused to give up his new vision of Canada's place in the world. King had to back down. He would keep Canada on the commission for a year.

In 1948 the Soviets withdrew their troops from the north. In 1949 the USAmericans started leaving the south. In 1950 the Cold War began its scariest years. The North Koreans marched into the south, determined to bring their own solution to unification. There was an emergency meeting of the UN Security Council. The Soviets were boycotting its meetings because the UN had not recognized the Chinese Communist government. The Security Council decided to send a multinational force to drive the northerners back across the thirty-eighth parallel. Canada would send naval and air support. The Canadian cabinet made this decision in a railway car of Mackenzie King's funeral train. Here was an amazingly symbolic turn in the country's foreign policy.

Here was the proof of St Laurent's popularity. The Canadian navy, and later the Princess Pats light infantry, went to war across an ocean even wider than the Atlantic, and there was no need for armed troops in the streets of Quebec. Of course this time, for a change, Canada was not at war to defend Great

Britain. The Canadians, especially St Laurent and External Affairs Minister Lester B. Pearson, insisted that though the USAmericans were running things in the Korean mountains, the Canadian military was fighting as part of the first United Nations campaign.

There was a lot more fear around now than there had been during the Gouzenko episode. The US troops, and thus the Canadians and others, were being led by a very popular megalomaniac named Douglas MacArthur. The Canadians were interested in re-establishing for now the dividing line at the thirty-eighth parallel. MacArthur pushed deep into the north and brought "volunteer" Chinese troops into the war. Now MacArthur was talking about using the atomic bomb on some more Asians, and US President Truman had to put his reputation up against the reputation of the corncob general.

The Communists, remember, had the atomic bomb. Unlike the USAmericans, they might show no hesitation to drop it on non-Asians. In Canadian schools, teachers began to teach children how to hide under their desks.

The Canadian lawyer

The history of the USA is a history of wars and consequent acquisitions. The history of Canada is a history of Canadian independence. The history of Canadian prime ministers is a sequence of stories about unity within and the untying of colonial bonds. The prime ministers always declared their fealty toward the British parliamentary and judicial systems, then faced down governors general or British prime ministers. They were still at it in the post-war era.

Louis St Laurent, who had often appeared as a lawyer in London, decided to abolish final appeal to the Judicial Committee of the Privy Council. Over the objections of a few Tories and of Duplessis in Quebec, he maintained that Canada could develop lawyers every bit as good as any in Britain. He was also interested in getting control over the Constitution. Duplessis argued that the BNA Act was an agreement among the four original provinces, while St Laurent said that it was a federal matter. He was a Canadian, not a Brit who happened to be born overseas. He caused a sensation across the country by appointing the first governor general born in Canada, Vincent Massey the tractor company heir. It was a judicious choice; Massey had gone to Oxford, and had been High Commissioner to Britain. He knew his old country stuff. Yet he had been born in Toronto. To show that he was not a hothead rebel, St Laurent still had his governor general dress up in goofy gold braid and glittering sword for ceremonial occasions.

St Laurent got the Liberal party committed to looking for more symbols of Canadian post-war nationhood, such as a distinctive flag to replace the big Union Jack or the little union jack in the corner of the red ensign. He also converted Canadian wealth and confidence into what would later be called megaprojects. He went ahead with Bennett's rudimentary Trans-Canada Highway. He finally cajoled the USAmericans into cooperating on the mighty St Lawrence Seaway by threatening to go it alone. Every lock between the lakes and every mile of pavement made Canada less and less like the mother country and made the non-Liberals in Quebec jumpy. So did the government's attitude toward immigration. In addition to the usual Brits and USAmericans, waves of Italians and Germans and Yugoslavians, and DPs from eastern Europe entered the country, and unlike the Ukrainians of an earlier time, most of these newcomers, unlike the family of St Laurent's mother, headed for the cities, where ethnic neighbourhoods would develop. Toronto and Hamilton, for example, would no longer be outposts of the foggy isle, but places where one could finally get a really good cup of coffee.

The walrussy Tories sometimes felt their dispensation fading away, and even that party was being joined by men who did not weep over old times in the colonial campaigns. But the old New France dreamers were unhappy as well, as outlanders gathered in their midst and made sure that their offspring learned English. When the recommendations of the 1951 Massey Commission were converted to the Canada Council of 1957, there was a careful effort to make sure that French Canadians got at least their share of support and that French Canadians were strongly represented in the council itself. But poets or painters who espoused any kind of Quebec nationalism had to handle some kind of conflict when it came to accepting anything that smacked of federal money in exchange for their imagination.

Old man river

Louis St Laurent was a septuagenarian when he went into his second election campaign in 1953, on the eve of rock 'n' roll. The Liberal machine was full of confidence and pride. The slogan this time was the bland "For the best years in your life, vote Liberal." Grandfather Louis had replaced Uncle Louis, and his message kept hinting at the dangerous (read atomic) times that needed a "strong and stable" government. Voters were offered a lot of parties scrambling for seats, and the message that trickled down to them was: you cannot rely on any of those other bozos to achieve a majority, and you do not want a minority government that hasn't got the power to oppose the Red threat; you had better give your vote to the Liberals to avoid the unknown. Hugh MacLennan, who was then thought to be Canada's eminent novelist, and who lived in Montreal, wrote for

Maclean's: "I wish I didn't have to vote for the Liberals . . . . Yet how else can I vote this summer?"

On August 10th, the voters reduced the Liberal majority by 22 seats, but they did not remove any of St Laurent's cabinet men, and he himself improved on his great personal victory of 1949. The government saw the results as an approval of their policies, and off they went to contain communism and build a sedate nation.

The plan should have been to keep the yokels asleep, or divert them with the neat new gadgets they could buy on time payments. "Money," sang Dean Martin, "burns a hole in my pocket." Patti Page wanted to know "how much is that doggie in the window?" CinemaScope splashed colour and eye makeup all over the story of Jesus and the centurions. Yes, there were Soviet agents in eastern Africa, and the Indian government was presenting a complication for the Commonwealth as a result of the US alliance with Pakistan. But in Canada there were problems such as this: how do you sit in a Chevy convertible if you are wearing a crinoline?

Grandfathers are supposed to look benign and maybe a little dreamy. Now here was an old gent who had missed the celebration party after winning the 1948 convention race, getting ready to go to war with the premier of Quebec. Any French-Canadian prime minister is going to be publicly vilified by rabble-rousers in that province, and one would have thought that the serene lawyer would be as adept as a Laurier in sidestepping a public scrap. Anyone with an ounce of cynicism knows that if Ottawa were to apply 90 per cent of the federal budget to programs in Quebec, there would still be politicians complaining about Canadian oppression. St Laurent knew well enough that Maurice Duplessis, the smart leader of his Union Nationale, would excoriate the prime minister in order to get saliva running back home.

But St Laurent decided to go after Duplessis, to wage a battle for Quebec. He made the same mistake made by Laurier and Trudeau: he decided to go for the mind. In his first campaign he had told the crowd that he might in the future be a conscriptionist, and he told them to vote against him if that made them nervous. Early in his cabinet career he had made his federal vision clear, telling Quebeckers to forget their old illusion about a French country in North America. He was a citizen of a Canadian nation, and he deplored the notion of "ten separate state provinces."

He did not have it quite right. English Canadians see a country comprising ten provinces. Quebec separatists see two nations who have made a contingent deal. During the 1950s Quebec did see some of the progress and prosperity that excited the rest of Canada, but an image of stagnant and folkloric old Quebec prevailed. Duplessis and St Laurent could not agree on the reason for this disparity. Duplessis had the name of the world's first prime minister, the cardinal who made an immense fortune but did not create prosperity in New France. St Laurent had the name of the wide river by which the resources of Canada's heartland could go out to the world. Neither of them could imagine why the other thought the way he did.

Duplessis was not as rich as Richelieu, but his government operated in a fashion that the cardinal invented. The Union Nationale machine was Duplessis's invention. It toppled a thirty-nine-year Liberal regime, and it fell apart after "Le Chef" died. It chipped away at the secular power of the Church, and it eased the lives of the poor and the blind and the sick, but it ruled with unmitigated patronage and indelicate power. Duplessis, like St Laurent, spent lots of public money on big public works projects; it was just that in Quebec friends of people in government did not find their way to government contracts so difficult. St Laurent pointed out that a lot of the public money had crossed the border from Ottawa to Quebec, and that Ottawa would really like to see Quebec's ledgers from time to time. Duplessis hid the ledgers in a safe spot and diverted people's attention to the latest slight suffered by the French-Canadian people.

Like St Laurent, Duplessis had Irish blood on his mother's side, but he did not care much for unity. He had started as a Conservative, but really as an anti-Liberal, and now he was playing the anti-federal card. He never stopped demanding money from Ottawa, and when it arrived he moved it into a bag with Quebec's logo on it. Then he reached into it and disbursed some little gifts to the waifs in the street before stashing it where no federal nose could sniff it out. You have to admire Duplessis's wile and his nerve. He was a raw politician who did not care what the most intelligent politicians in Toronto thought. But St Laurent was a Canadian from Quebec. He could not stand to see his province characterized by a premier and a regime that looked from the genteel outside like a cross between Paraguay and the Cosa Nostra. He went after Duplessis, even while his friends in Ottawa tried to calm him down.

The apparent field of battle was the Plains of Revenue. Whenever Ottawa decided to step directly into a program such as the baby bonus, Duplessis and his people would call it an incursion into their fiscal rights. They preferred a system by which Ottawa sent some funds to Quebec, and Quebec disbursed them in their own package. If the federal government pointed out that the money came from the people in the first place, Quebec would argue that taxes raised by the feds in the province constituted wealth robbed from the province. Tweedledum and Tweedledee wore angry faces.

Once in a while it is a good idea to remind ourselves that these political guys had all known each other for years and years, and we just know them as characters in books. It is advisable to imagine little things such as Madame St Laurent's tears and the adjectives that could be heard from time to time in the bar at the Quebec Reform Club.

In late 1954 St Laurent went after Duplessis's version of the province in a speech at the Quebec Reform Club, site of many important speeches in Grit history. The federal government was in a tussle with the Quebec government about the provincial sales tax that the Union Nationale was pushing for. The people of Quebec were going to have to pay more taxes than anyone else in Canada, and the two leaders had been busy all summer explaining why it was the other's fault. Now St Laurent was at the Reform Club, not with a speech vetted in Ottawa, but some spontaneous remarks from the heart. Maybe he did not know that his sentiments would be presented to the Quebec people as an attack on the society that had nurtured his childhood and career.

There were some honourable nationalists in Quebec, he said, that were pushing the view that theirs was a province that was not like the others. He said that Quebec can be a province like the others; he did not think that French culture had to be coddled to survive. In an unmistakable dig at the Duplessis administration he uttered this sensible-sounding statement: "Between true provincial autonomy and the kind of autonomy which serves as a screen so that the administration of those responsible may not be questioned, there is a margin, and that is what the members of the Reform Club should explain to the people of the province of Quebec."

St Laurent kept after *Le Chef.* He dared him to open his books. He ridiculed his concept of a state within a state. He refused to budge on taxes and public funds. He was an old man with an old man's health problems, but he would not let up. He was a Canadian from the Eastern Townships, but he misjudged the Quebeckers. The people of Quebec knew that Duplessis was running the place with a tough machine and a lot of darkened rooms, but if he was a warlord, he was *their* warlord. He unashamedly pulled the "race" levers, blew wind across old smouldering embers, posed as the defender of the Church and the old farmstead. He was no *seigneur*. He was some kind of Papineau with underworld connections. His people smiled wryly and admired his bravado. More and more they delivered messages to Louis St Laurent: he was not really one of them.

And Grandfather Louis knew how Laurier had felt. Like Laurier, he could not stand to be called a *vendu*. He offered an armistice and a compromise to *Le Chef.* Come and see me, he said. Duplessis would not go to Ottawa while his voters were watching; and St Laurent, though he had a house there, would not go to Quebec. They met without their seconds at the Windsor Hotel in Montreal on October 5, and talked for an hour. St Laurent said that the Quebec government could raise provincial taxes while Quebeckers got a break on federal taxes. Duplessis agreed to go ahead with the condition that similar deals could, if the occasion arose, be offered to other provinces. If Quebec was not a province like the others, the others could be provinces like Quebec. The situation was a little sticky, but it seemed to suggest that Louis St Laurent could still reconcile the two founding peoples.

Howe the heck?

Maurice Duplessis the foe might have poked a little hole in the Liberal dike. C.D. Howe the friend was certainly not the man to stick his finger into it. He was more like a bulldozer man.

He was a USAmerican go-getter who decided to show Canadians how to be go-getters. He first came to Canada as an engineering professor at Dalhousie, but he had a hankering to build big things and get rich doing it. He went west and built grain elevators, just when they were needed, from Toronto to Vancouver. He became the best and richest grain elevator man the country would ever see. The Great Depression persuaded him to retire from that business and go into politics. Pretty soon he was one of Mackenzie King's most energetic cabinet ministers. During the Second World War he was given the job of war production, and he was given special powers under the Defence Production Act. Nobody was allowed to tell him how to do anything, and nobody was allowed to deny him anything. After the war he was put in charge of getting Canada's economic leadership back into the hands of private enterprise, and a preoccupied government extended Howe's power under the act, without changing its name. Nobody was allowed to tell him anything he did not want to hear.

Howe had been very useful when a go-getter was needed to fight the war and reshape the country's industry, and the government put off any limiting of his special power until after the Korean War. King and St Laurent both knew that Howe would never be a diplomat or even a good politician. He had the biggest ego in Ottawa, which would be all right as long as the press and the opposition could be persuaded by necessity to say yeah, go get those Germans, yeah, go get those airplanes. But sooner or later the mighty industrialist was going to stick his elbow into some intelligent politician's eye.

Slowly the post-war government whittled away at Howe's position. St Laurent could use the communist threat to explain it, but it was nevertheless unseemly for a peacetime government to claim emergency powers, and George Drew kept saying so. So did Liberal ministers and backbench members. In a piece of 1955 legislation, Howe's rule was somewhat limited. He got mad at St Laurent, that near-sighted anti-business lawyer, that old softie. The Liberals started taking sides, and most of them sided with the prime minister. This just made old man Howe get his back up even more. If anyone mentioned party solidarity to him, he just called them the kinds of names that go-getters save for the chicken-hearted.

So when the nasty business of the TransCanada PipeLines of 1955-56 transpired, there was the gung-ho industrialist C.D. Howe ranked against the chicken-hearted in the Canadian Parliament. He had got Trans-Canada Airlines going above the country; now the Trade and Commerce Minister was interested in this other great project under the national ground. Since 1949 the oil companies in Alberta had been finding gushers in everyone's front yard. Every time a few billion barrels of oil were sucked up, an enormous amount of natural gas had to get out of the way. Howe gathered a consortium of Canadian and usAmerican oil companies to plan the massive pipeline project; he was not afraid of foreign money, but he wanted a Canadian route. The line would run across the prairies to northern Ontario, into Quebec and down to New York. It was a natural successor to the CPR and the St Lawrence Seaway.

In 1955 Howe came to cabinet with his scheme. Sure, it was really expensive. Of course it would require lots of public money. But so did the railroad. So did the war. The chicken-hearted side of the cabinet prevailed, and Howe stomped off. They expected him to resign, but C.D. Howe was not a politician—he was a go-getter. He came back in early 1956 with a new improved proposition. The consortium would lay the pipe except in the expensive part through northern Ontario. They would guarantee to pay off their loan. Canada needed a Canadian pipeline. The Liberals needed western votes. The families of Toronto and Hamilton needed warm houses.

St Laurent's cabinet agreed. Now came the bigger problem. Construction had to start when the ground was soft. The loan had to be made by the beginning of June so that the consortium could order its steel pipe from the US. Besides, he told his colleagues, it would be great to get the pipeline into the ground and covered over before the election that was likely to come in 1957. Howe managed to get the loan arranged in early May, but now there were only three weeks to get the bill through Parliament. Of course the Liberals had the votes. The CCF members would argue for public ownership of the pipeline. The Socreds would go along with anything that was good for business in Alberta. The Tories would complain about the fact that most of the consortium was made up of the same USAmericans who had snaffled the oil business in Canada.

C.D. Howe knew that these malcontents and nervous nellies were going to pull every parliamentary trick they could think of, to extend the debate past his deadline. George Drew made no secret of the training he was doing in preparation for a filibuster. Howe pined for the days of the Second World War, when he could just sign a requisition and send a convoy over the ocean. All he could do now was invoke the War Measures Act or invoke cloture. Natural gas in Ontario was not a matter of war, hot or cold. He would have to go for cloture. It had got the navy bill through in 1913. Now it could save the pipeline. But it takes at the least two days to enact cloture after it is announced, sometimes three or four. And it would have to be invoked at every reading of the bill. Most politicians would stop thinking about it right here. Cloture was an extreme step, to be taken only in extreme circumstances. It was not a matter of convenience. Nevertheless, C.D. Howe the bulldozer man came up with a solution: he would announce before debate even began that cloture would be invoked for all stages of debate. He gave the unwelcome news that debate would not exceed fourteen days.

He may as well have stuck out his tongue and flashed an obscene gesture. The House became a circus like its ancestor in the days of John A. Macdonald. Wonderful insults were invented. Terrible songs were sung in disagreeable keys. There were whistles and book-banging and floor-stomping and noises impossible to capture in Hansard. Government members may have had a dandy defence for the pipeline, but they did not want to use up precious time in arguing it. So there was no debate, really, just a lot of cursing and accusing. George Drew probably wanted the pipeline, especially for his province, but he had a marvellous opportunity to denounce the Liberals as arrogant dictators. His cohort claimed to have discovered a resemblance between C.D. Howe and Hitler. They were not allowed to use the terms so popular outside the legislative buildings: #!*@!#, etc.

The newspapers, the Tory ones and some of the Liberal ones, were enjoying the furor. For the first time in Canada, a major parliamentary squabble became the material for hours of television coverage. St Laurent spent many hours during those fourteen days reading a book. His gnomic minister from Newfoundland, Jack Pickersgill, was in the background of all the photographs, smiling in approval of Howe's vision. President Sukarno of Indonesia, in town for a state visit, took in the show one day, and experienced renewed confidence in his own country's legislative process. He wrote a note to himself to advise his successors that they should have armed guards on any visit to this country.

As if cloture were not bad enough, and as if pre-announced cloture were not bad enough, the farce would be compounded by House Speaker René Beaudoin's slapstick error late in the second week. Only a devotee of parliamentary procedure, such as M.J. Coldwell, could begin to figure out what was happening, and the usually serene Coldwell was standing in the centre aisle, shaking his bony fist at the Speaker. The reporters in the press gallery had long given up trying to follow events; their jaws were hanging over the balustrade.

The opposition had been bringing up countless points of procedure, calling for adjournments, disputing the Speaker's interpretations of history, and talking about the weather. Now a CCF member named Colin Cameron rose on a point of privilege, asking for a debate on the problems caused by a newspaper's account of the "debate." Distracted, trying to remember hundreds of contradictory rules, the Speaker allowed debate on the newspaper issue, then shut the House down for the night. Pickersgill and Finance Minister Walter Harris slapped their foreheads—the newspaper debate could go on for two days, and Howe's deadline would be missed.

Beaudoin sat up all night, reading blue books. When Pickersgill arrived at his house early next morning, Beaudoin said "Don't worry, I have it under control." Pickersgill worried. In the screeching, roaring House, Beaudoin stood up and announced that things had changed—the pipeline debate would take precedence. Sweat was pouring off his head. He staggered. His face looked like a bar of Ivory soap. MPs rushed to him with water and heart pills. CCFers and Tories climbed over each other to reach the Speaker's chair. Visitors might have been pardoned for thinking that they were observing the legislature in Taiwan or Israel. Reporters in the gallery threw down their notebooks and wept.

They would call this day Black Friday.

But the Liberals got the pipeline rammed through the House and any MPs who were standing in the way. Louis St Laurent never loosened his tie. But he should not have been so calm. There were a lot of television-watchers out there who did not like to see the Three Stooges in the parliamentary news, and there were a lot of voters who were listening when the Tories accused St Laurent's government of sidestepping democracy. Could Uncle Louis be an Uncle Joe?

Could the Liberals at least celebrate meeting the deadline?

Would they pop champagne as the first pipe was dropped into the first trench? Well, the sad truth followed the tragicomic drama: TransCanada PipeLine could not start this year because there was a strike at the US pipe factory.

No more colonial war

If the pipeline "debate" injured St Laurent's party because it brought discredit to Canada's eighty-nine-year-old Parliament, the Suez crisis would prove that no virtue, not even a prime minister's stand against racism, will go unpunished.

Nineteen fifty-six was a notable and disgraceful year for the European empires that thought they had survived the Second World War. In February Soviet leader Nikita Khrushchev made his amazing speech denouncing Stalin and his policies. In June Polish citizens were the first eastern-bloc people to riot against their Stalinists, and by the fall they had a new revisionist government under Wladyslaw Gomulka. But when the Hungarians had their "revolution," Russian tanks rolled into Budapest and shot the place up. Western non-communists were both encouraged and worried, because the US had tested its first intercontinental ballistic missiles earlier in the year. The Warsaw Pact was one year old.

The Cold War was also being waged in the Middle East. The United States was devoted to its notion of communist containment, and had been instrumental in setting up the Baghdad Pact, an alliance among Britain, Iraq and Turkey, soon to be joined by Pakistan and Persia. This pact was supposed to challenge the Russians to the north, but it really upset General Gamal Abdel Nasser, president of Egypt, who did not want any Iraqi challenging his leadership of the Arab world. He was also in need of lots of weapons to aim at Israel, and no one in western Europe would sell him any. Nasser, like a lot of Third World leaders, knew how to play Cold War games. He got his weapons from Czechoslovakia, and everyone knew who was running the Czech arms business. In exchange for such assistance, Nasser recognized Red China. Now the governments and newspapers in the west started calling Nasser a communist sympathizer, and in the 1950s those words were enough to get you into deep trouble. You want to build your Aswan High Dam? Get your money from your communist friends, said the US and Britain, and withdrew their promises of assistance.

Nasser was not a man to back down, and he knew that he could rally the Egyptians, who did not have fond memories of Turkish and English and French rule in Egypt. Nasser had a scar on his forehead that had been created by a British rifle butt. He had chased the Albanian-rooted royal family and its English protectors out of the country, and become the first Egyptian to run Egypt in two thousand years. Now on July 26, 1956, he nationalized the Suez Canal. He told his countrymen that the canal would pay for the Aswan Dam in five years.

Now the western Europeans were afraid that Nasser would listen to his Russians and prevent Persian oil from reaching the Mediterranean. The British and the French got together with the Israelis and planned an occupation of the canal zone. If Nasser happened to get shot, so much the better. The Israelis invaded Egypt through the Sinai Desert on October 29th. Two days later the British and French bombed the canal zone and Egyptian airfields. Nasser first heard about the invasion while he was at a children's birthday party. Louis St Laurent first heard about it while his cabinet was in session.

St Laurent's External Affairs Minister, Lester Pearson, rounded up his friends at the United Nations, and by November 4, the

General Assembly had approved an international military group to enter the canal zone and secure a ceasefire. Canada would send General E.L.M. Burns to command the UN Emergency Force. But the British and French said to hell with the UN, and dropped paratroopers. They were Europeans, after all, and Nasser's people were only Africans. Just look at the map of Africa: most of those countries had been speaking English or French for a century.

It was not that he had never heard the warnings coming out of London. But here was a shock, nevertheless, the bombs and parachutes landing on the Egyptian people. British Prime Minister Anthony Eden, who looked like the epitome of the foppish English blueblood, had been openly hinting that he could use some colonial help—if not European-based warplanes, at least some official words of loyalty. He expected at least that from the USAmericans, too, and would be puzzled when it did not come. But the Brits were up to their old tricks: they jumped into a war without telling anyone in Ottawa what was up. This time there was no prime minister who even contemplated saying "ready, aye ready!"

In fact, his colleagues later said that they had never seen the old man become so agitated. He plainly opposed the invasion and did not have a good word to say for the British. We were a million miles from any conscription problem. The Suez crisis was another great step in the differentiation between Brits and Canadians. A Gallup poll showed that fewer than half of Canadians supported the invasion, and that fewer than half were opposed to it. The next spring a bunch of RAF and RCAF lower ranks were sitting in an airman's canteen at RCAF base Namao, watching the television news from Edmonton. The cameras caught a passenger plane landing at Edmonton airport—the "first planeload of English refugees." There had been numerous planeloads of Hungarian refugees, of course. One of the RAF lads was heard to expostulate "Refos? *British* refos?" The passengers in the civilian aircraft were young men who were escaping the British military draft. The phrase used by the CBC announcer illustrated the independence of Canadian thinking in what was soon to become post-St Laurent Canada.

Finally, on November 6th, the USAmericans spoke up. Much to the surprise of its NATO allies, the US demanded a ceasefire, and Anthony Eden, who had been told by the Bank of England that there was a terrific run on the pound, listened. A little over a week later the UN soldiers, including a Canadian contingent, were in place, and Lester Pearson was on his way to winning next year's Nobel Peace Prize.

But what about all those anglophiles in Canada who would rather be loyal to the "mother country" than to the United Nations? They demanded to know why the prime minister had broken with other members of the Commonwealth and refused to endorse Anthony Eden's war. Newspapers, led by the Toronto *Globe and Mail*, were all over St Laurent and Pearson, calling the peacekeepers a "UN Police Farce." The Alberta papers, of course, condemned the Liberals for coming to the aid of that commie stooge Nasser.

The prime minister had to listen to belligerent yahoos from all across English Canada, to their vilification of Pearson, to their Cold-War insults against his loyalties. Finally, in Parliament, he got up and delivered a wonderful talk in which he defended the UN's dedication to peace and attacked those well-armed countries that would support it only when it was convenient to them. He complained that the big countries were using the veto against the little countries instead of encouraging the little countries to work out their own destinies.

"Why should they?" yelled some deep thinker in the opposition.

Now St Laurent was really worked up. He flushed, and then delivered one of the noblest sentences ever uttered by a Canadian prime minister.

"Because the members of smaller nations are human beings just as are other people; because the era when the supermen of Europe could govern the whole world is coming pretty close to an end."

Now *there's* an optimist, we say, looking back. But what did the next Conservative voice yell out in the chamber of reason?

"Throwing Canada to the slaughterhouse."

Presumably that Tory analyst feared a bloodthirsty invasion by the Venezuelans.

There is a slight chance that the government might have survived the shame of the pipeline fiasco. But when Louis St Laurent and Lester Pearson opted for peacekeeping instead of war-making, the Liberals were doomed. They were used to winning. They had a most honourable leader, but he was seventy-five years old. There were half a dozen men in his cabinet who wanted to be the leadership candidate, but who was going to walk up to Uncle Louis the reluctant politician and ask him to take Mrs St Laurent back to Quebec? The country was rich, but it owed a lot of money, and the riches were more and more in the hands of USAmerican corporations. People were driving new cars with fins on the back fenders. There was a terrible fear of nuclear weapons, but every little town had a soft-ice-cream stand. We usually like to remember a bland US popular culture made up of equal parts Mamie Eisenhower and Perry Como. But in 1957 Jack Kerouac published *On the Road.* Marlon Brando's motorcycle movie, *The Wild One,* was already three years old, and James Dean had been dead for a year and a half. Elvis Presley was scaring the hell out of Mamie Eisenhower.

Young Canadians did not spend a lot of time weighing the merits of Paul Martin and Walter Harris.

Somehow John Diefenbaker had grabbed the leadership of the Conservative party. The Conservative party often goes out west to find a new leader, but this was really strange—the guy did not have a British or Scottish name. Diefenbaker. Wasn't that a German name or something? Well, Diefenbaker pretty well took over the election campaign of 1957. Quiet old Louis St Laurent was not getting much ink in the spring of 1957. Still, the Liberals could not imagine falling into opposition.

The election was held on my father's fiftieth birthday. When your father turns fifty you suddenly know that things will not stay the same forever. I had been born five weeks after R.B. Bennett's defeat; I had never imagined that anyone but the Liberals could be in power.

On June 10, 1957 Louis St Laurent sat upstairs in his big house, watching the returns on television. Jack Pickersgill was right behind him in case there were any photographers around. St Laurent had promised the weeping Jeanne that he would convene Parliament, and then announce his retirement, handing the job over to one of the boys. No such luck. The returns in Quebec were gratifying, but that was to be expected under any circumstances. Now Ontario and the west just disappeared.

For the first time the seats were scattered all over the parliamentary floor. Diefenbaker took 112 of them. The Liberals hung on to 105. The CCF got their usual 25, and the Social Creditists plucked 19. Whoever became the government was going to have to make a deal. Well, Mackenzie King had made a deal with the Progressives a half-century before. But Louis was too old for minority government. He resigned on June 21st, and settled down in the front row of the opposition side, a book in front of him. He sat through the fall session, and then went back to Quebec to practise law. That was his idea of a retirement.

The Liberal party, which had eliminated British knighthoods for Canadian citizens, created the Order of Canada in time for the centenary in 1967. Louis St Laurent was the first person to be made a Companion of the Order by Governor General Roland Michener that July 1st. He died at the age of 91 on July 25, 1973, and was buried beside Jeanne in Compton, Quebec.

CHAPTER 19

PRAIRIE LIGHTNING

———◦•◦———

John G. Diefenbaker 1957–63

J OHN DIEFENBAKER WAS on the backwoods campaign trail. In
one Podunk town the highest elevation that was not a roof
happened to be a manure pile, so he addressed the locals from
its acme. "This," he said, wiggling his head and rolling his eyes
in the manner of Sir Laurence Olivier, "is the first time I have
ever spoken from the platform of the Liberal party."

Of all Canadians who would become prime ministers, Diefenbaker was the wittiest, and he was the most amazing campaigner anyone would ever see or hear. He faced long odds and
a multitude of enemies. He spent his childhood in a home-
made shack on a ten-dollar farm in central Saskatchewan. He
lost election after election before his first victory, a kind of
fluke that saw him get a parliamentary seat in 1940, just when
his party had pretty well disappeared and his party leader lost
his race to a social democrat. Then he lost leadership race after
leadership race, until his turn came in 1957. That year he
demolished the fat old Liberal party and began his reign as
Prime Minister Lightning.

Like Mackenzie King, he had known since childhood that he was an instrument of destiny. But he had a bad name. No one without a name from the British Isles had ever made it all the way to the top. The usAmericans had had a Roosevelt, but the USA was a republic that had broken away from Britain. Canada, for all its steps into independence, was still a place where people sang "God Save the King" in the movie house. Diefenbaker was a bad name. In central Saskatchewan it was a pretty good name. The farms and feed stores and car dealerships were manned by people with German and Ukrainian names. He was an immigrant too, having come with his father and mother to Saskatchewan from a burg in western Ontario with a bad name—Neustadt. Neustadt did not change its name to Newtown during the Great War, and Diefenbaker did not change his name either, though there were informal committees within the Conservative party that actually suggested the move.

His mother was a Bannerman, from a Highlands family that arrived in Lord Selkirk's colony in 1812. But though he thought he had inherited her Scottish values, he was not going to go to the hustings as John George Bannerman. And hyphens were out.

In the 1950s Canadians had finally learned, more or less, how to pronounce "St Laurent." Now they had to deal with this foreign name from the prairies. They would have a lot of fun with it through the years, inventing the "Diefendollar," the "Diefenbunker" and the "Diefendumb" cabinet. More than once during his early career he told associates that his name was going to be the barrier to success. When it came time to write his three-volume memoirs, he called it *One Canada*. Many times during his career he denounced the notion of hyphenated Canadians, pointing out that Eisenhower was not called a "German-American." One Canada from sea to sea, he said, and thought that the phrase should not cause great trouble in Quebec.

Quixote

Diefenbaker called the first volume of his memoirs *The Crusading Years*. If he was a crusader, he was a free lance. There were those who say that he was never a Tory. In later national campaigns the party's name was less prominent than his own on the posters. There were those who say that he changed the nature of the party, taking it away from Bay Street and offering it to the farmers and pensioners and small-town merchants. He was a prairie lawyer, but he was not a lawyer like R.B. Bennett or Arthur Meighen. Unlike Bennett and St Laurent, he did not find his clients among the giant corporations; he defended the telegraph worker who was blamed for a train accident that caused the death of Canadian soldiers during the Korean War. He defended twenty men who had been accused of murder, and only two of them went to the gallows. He used a handcar to pump his way from railroad stop to railroad stop when he was a bachelor lawyer in tiny Wakaw, Saskatchewan.

He was a small-town lawyer, a critic of the system, an advocate for the little guy. He was an outsider with a great gift for rhetoric and a clear devotion to individual human rights. He was a nineteenth-century liberal who lived frugally, and won the sympathy of people who were forced to live frugally. He was a devout Baptist who believed that populism was a natural outgrowth of Christianity. And he had a terrific sense of humour that did not break down when he himself was the subject. Once, when someone pointed out that the shack of his childhood was something like Abraham Lincoln's famous log cabin, he said that it was more like a manger.

When he and his brother, Elmer, now out of their sailor suits and ringlets, were ready for high school, the family moved into Saskatoon, where the brothers both became newspaper boys and set the stage for one of the most famous anecdotes in

Canadian political history. We remember that when Robert Borden took the train west he was impressed by a young lawyer-politician named Meighen whom he met in Portage la Prairie. When Wilfrid Laurier took the train west he met a young newspaper boy in Saskatoon, where he had come to lay the cornerstone of the University of Saskatchewan. They talked for a while, and then the kid said that he could not waste any more time talking—he had newspapers to sell. During a speech later that day at the university, the prime minister complimented the city on its newspaper boys.

Ten years later he was a young lawyer in Wakaw. Wakaw, Saskatchewan was a little town in the lake country between Saskatoon and Prince Albert. For some reason, probably because someone got paid off, it was built a mile west of a beautiful site on Wakaw Lake. In 1920 the young lawyer decided to go into politics, running for town council. It was his first election, and he won his seat by a dozen votes. He would not win his second election until 1940.

In his memoirs Diefenbaker tells us that he never had to be pushed or pulled into politics, that in his childhood he started training himself to become an office-holder. His high-school yearbook made the odd prediction that he would some day be leader of the opposition. But how could one be messianic if one were at the best John the Baptist? In Saskatchewan there was a big Liberal machine in the first half of the twentieth century. Diefenbaker says that the province was created Liberal by Laurier in 1905, and that the machine rivalled anything to be found in Boston or Chicago.

Diefenbaker's father was a Liberal. But John the people's advocate was not going to be part of the big machine he hated so much. In fact once, when he was out of town, the Wakaw Liberal Association elected him their secretary. When he got back to his office, he picked up the minute books they had deposited there and delivered them to the local president. The Liberals could not believe that a young lawyer with a taste for politics would want to throw away the chance to get in on the goodies. In 1924 they tried to get him to run as a Liberal for the provincial legislature. He moved to Prince Albert and stood as a Conservative candidate in the federal election of 1925. He turned thirty during the campaign. He lost. The Conservatives won, but Mackenzie King pulled his famous deke on Arthur Meighen. In 1926 Diefenbaker ran against Mackenzie King in Prince Albert, and of course he lost again. In 1929 he married Edna Brower and ran in the Saskatchewan election against King's man, T.C. Davis. He lost his first attempt at a provincial seat. In 1933 he ran for the position of mayor of Prince Albert, and lost to a man with a good Scottish name. In 1936 he became the party leader in Saskatchewan, and in 1938 he contested the rural constituency of Arm River, and like every other Conservative candidate, he was defeated.

Five defeats in thirteen years! He had just about gone broke financing his campaigns, his wife was ill, and there was not much left of his legal practice. It was time to forget about politics. He would attend the Conservative convention and watch R.B. Bennett resign, and that was that. The voice that had told the hard-reading farmboy that he would be prime minister had gone to the wrong address. It should have been scouting an Anglo-Saxon farm.

But then another dicky little burg played its part in Diefenbaker's life. He was talked into attending a nominating convention in Imperial, which was in the provincial riding of Arm River and the federal riding of Lake Centre. Diefenbaker gave a speech in which he congratulated the Conservatives for finding some good candidates, at which point the convention hall burst into flame. What amazing oratory, the listeners said, and chose Diefenbaker as their candidate. The Conservatives thought that they had no chance to win the seat, so Diefenbaker had to wage the campaign without any outside help. But Diefenbaker was a great orator: he set all the little towns on fire, and won a seat in the House of Commons. Now the Conservatives had two Saskatchewan seats in Ottawa.

For seventeen years he represented the ordinary folks in opposition. He was always on his feet talking, whether in caucus or question period. It quickly became clear to the Ontario Tories that this man with the shock-wave hair and saxophone voice was no silk-tie Conservative—he was always talking about the little guy trying to fight his way out from under the machine. They considered lining the chambers with asbestos. They had a look at those piercing eyes under those scowling brows and made a note never to get too friendly. And that voice! Canadians who are old enough and lucky enough to remember that voice know that they will never hear the like again. It sounded as if the member from Lake Centre had an echo chamber implanted in his throat. And if the tone was startling, the rhythm was masterful, and the body posture was at times alarming. He could stand with one hand on his hip, thumb forward, and slowly rotate his head. He could lean forward and then lean forward some more until he seemed to be ready to swoop down at you with his talons at the grab. The speech was always theatrical. There would be excruciating pauses, during which the glittering eyes told you that a joke or a revelation was coming. There would be grunts and long-held vowel sounds to introduce an insult or a quotation from John A. Macdonald. When in later years Lester B. Pearson's monotonous civil servant Ontario accent went up against the one-man-band from the west, it was no contest.

But he could not get nominated as leader in 1942 or in 1948. John Bracken and George Drew were regular Tories. By the middle of the century the Conservative party had come to understand that it was the voice of the Toronto banks and corporations. It looked as if the disgruntled farmers out west were going to go on opting for the splinter parties. Yet a sort of balance could be faked if they let this rube speak out in parliamentary debate. The Bay Street Conservatives did not make friends with him, and he did not go out of his way to talk them up. In fact he grew more and more to see the members of their shadow cabinet as potential foes. He knew, for instance, that he was a better politician than George Drew. He just did not have the right kind of name and connections.

The Conservatives did not have much of a chance of knocking the government off its perch in the good-times 1953 election, so George Drew got pretty tired of his job, and in 1956, with an election coming up soon, he retired. The party had tried two former premiers in a row; they had a convention in which the leadership aspirants were all members of Parliament: Donald Fleming the Ontario lawyer, Davie Fulton the blue-blood Rhodes scholar from British Columbia and John G. Diefenbaker the fire-breathing advocate from Saskabush. But they didn't have a chance. The old walruses of the party had scoured the country looking for a really good anti-Diefenbaker candidate, and could not enlist one. Diefenbaker had been a long-talking MP for nearly two decades. He won the nomination on the first ballot. It was such a relief finally to clear the second-to-last hurdle of his ambition's race that he did not notice a mistake he made. The seconder for his nomination was not a French Canadian. He was a huge fan of John A. Macdonald. Maybe he should have talked to him at a séance. Macdonald could have told him how important George-Étienne Cartier had been to him.

Pyrokinesis

No one had ever seen a political campaign like the grass fire of 1957. Uncle Louis was used to prevailing by quietly patting the heads of nearby children. Mackenzie King had been a little evasive chubby with an Ontario chirp. In 1957 Dief, at last the Chief, covered 20,000 miles in a few weeks, playing the role he had rehearsed for forty years, announcing that he was going to overturn the tables and hit the money-changers on the head with them. He was on a crusade, addressing the locals from the back of the train, and the country on black-and-white television. The country was used to crusaders on television. Billy Graham had the eyes of a raptor too, and Canadians loved Star-Spangled Billy. They would flock to this Canadian. They would learn to pronounce his name, and they would feel a thrill of excitement and danger in the air. He sounded like a hellfire preacher all right, and the arrogant backroom Liberals with their pipeline scandal were the devil's party.

In the coming years Diefenbaker's face would be the delight of the cartoonists, and his Olympian voice would make the radio and television comedians ecstatic. In 1957 it woke the country up and so mesmerized the ordinary voters that they attended without irony to his inflammatory phrases, his "sacred trust," his "appointment with destiny." He had seen the worst skulduggery of the Liberals in Saskatchewan in 1920, and now he saw them stomping Parliament's sweet face into the mire: "My friends, there is an issue that transcends all others—the preservation of freedom, its maintenance, the restoration of Parliament, and above everything else in that connection, an imperative and immediate necessity of a return to the two-party system in this country if freedom is to be preserved and political democracy maintained!"

All the while lunging his head forward, jabbing his finger

eastward, waggling his jaw, groaning and nearly spitting. He was Sir Laurence Olivier with electrified hair.

This was not an election campaign between the Grits and the Tories, with side-bets on the Socreds and CCFers. This was a campaign by John Diefenbaker against the enemies of Canadian freedom and independence and honesty. It was virtue that could no longer abide quiet. For the first time since John A. Macdonald a personality was running, or rather stomping, against mere humanoids.

He knew what to promise the electorate too. He made an array of promises that contradicted one another. There would be lower taxes and higher spending, a balanced budget and higher employment. He did not know much about high finance—his clients had often paid him with IOUs. He did not know that the post-war boom was ending, but then neither did anyone else. He said that the Liberals had been piling up a huge surplus created by the work of ordinary people, and that he was going to go in with a shovel and deal it back to them in the form of social assistance. He told them that things such as the old-age pension and the baby bonus, which he had broken party ranks to support back then, were not welfare but earned benefits.

St Laurent watched television. He should have known what was coming. The diamond-stickpin fellows in the Toronto businessmen's clubs were paying attention. It would be nice to get the Tories back in power, but with this madman at the controls, what kind of party would it be? This upstart from the west was moving to the left of the Liberals!

Hadn't they let him get the nomination because they expected to lose anyway?

Before the election there were 53 Conservatives who could sit in the House of Commons if they were in town. After the election, and after the death of an elected Tory, they had 111. The Liberals had 105, and the other 48 went to their usual splinters. For the first time in half a century Canada did not have a majority government. Dief did not get his two-party Parliament, but his followers had knocked off almost all the big Liberal cabinet stars. Seventy-five of the remaining Liberal seats were French Canadian.

When Diefenbaker got all the news in Prince Albert the next morning, he went across the street for a haircut and then went fishing, inviting the newspaper photographers along.

On June 17 the Liberals resigned, and John Diefenbaker became prime minister of Canada. The final hurdle had been hurdled—almost. He had to find an excuse to call an election and invite a lot more people onto the bandwagon.

As soon as the members of Parliament sat down in early 1958, Lester Pearson gave Dief that excuse. On January 16, Pearson had defeated Paul Martin at the Liberal leadership convention, the Grits' fourth since Confederation. Four days later, with Jack Pickersgill looking over his shoulder, the leader of the opposition suggested that Diefenbaker hand the running of the country back to the Liberals, so "ending the Tory pause and getting this country back on the Liberal highway of progress from which we have been temporarily diverted." Oh, no, he was thinking in his head, what am I doing? It had been Pickersgill's idea. What a wonderful way to start a new job!

There was an uncharacteristic silence in the room for a second, then a lot of braying and cockadoodledooing. Diefenbaker sat as if he were listening to a late-Beethoven quartet, but that was a hearing-aid wire leading into his ear. Finally, he stood up, as if he were going to continue rising until his leonine head pierced the ceiling. He sweetly thanked Mr Pearson for his speech. Then radium streamed from his eyes, and he seized some papers from his desktop. He shook them as if they were a rattlesnake he was trying to strangle. For two hours he raged against Liberal iniquity. He was thinking of the telegram stolen from his hero John A. Macdonald, and he was out for revenge. The document in his hand was a confidential report from the former deputy minister of trade and commerce, Mitchell Sharpe, to the former cabinet. Its message was that the boom was over and Canada was in big financial trouble.

Diefenbaker grimaced and winked and seemed to foam at the mouth. Why, he asked the Liberals across the way, had they campaigned on promises of wealth? "Why didn't you tell the people these things?" Oh, he could not abide such dishonesty!

A week later he was in Winnipeg, where he was mobbed by thousands of frantic fans. He was the first Canadian politico to have fans. They wanted to hear him, to touch his suit, to shout his name. Elvis Diefenbaker. He met John A.'s granddaughter, and she was a fan.

Five days later he answered Pearson's ridiculous challenge by dissolving Parliament. The great election of 1957-58 was on again. The Chief went back to Winnipeg to kick off the second half, and it was there that he announced: "This is the message I give to you my fellow Canadians, not one of defeatism. Jobs! Jobs for hundreds of thousands of Canadian people. A new vision! A new hope! A new soul for Canada!" He was going to manage this unlikely gift by opening up the north, just as John A. Macdonald had opened the west.

He mentioned the Conservative party from time to time, but this was a great personal crusade. He almost dropped that troublesome last name. All across the country the sidewalks had painted shoeprints on them, and the stencilled words "Follow John!" His last name might have sounded a little foreign to people last year, but he had the most common English first name there is, and it had also belonged to his hero Macdonald. "I like Ike" had worked for Eisenhower. "Follow John" worked for Diefenbaker. The leader of the opposition started to downplay "Lester" and use his nickname "Mike."

These two men duelled one another for a decade. It was King and Meighen all over again, but this time the witty Conservative seemed to be winning, and the efficient but dull civil servant spinning his wheels.

In 1958 a huge army of Canadians followed John, and a lot of MPs followed even more closely, riding into Ottawa on his coattails. He elected 208 Conservatives, then the highest number ever to form a government. All his opponents put together had 151 fewer seats. The Social Credit party came up blank. The CCF was reduced to a rump of 8, which would not include Coldwell or Stanley Knowles. The mighty Liberals managed 49 seats, their smallest total since Confederation. There were Liberals from Quebec, Ontario, Newfoundland and New Brunswick, and nowhere else. In four other provinces Diefenbaker had swept the board. John A. Macdonald had never dreamed of such a volcano. John G. Diefenbaker laughed out loud, and then he scowled at the few opposition members who dared to sully his House of Commons.

The greatest campaigner of all time had won the greatest campaign victory of all time. Now he had to govern Canada. There's always a hitch, isn't there? Unemployment was high, and the Canadian dollar was living beyond its means. Those two things were not supposed to happen together. The former government might have been dishonest about the economic outlook, but the new government, also known as Dief the Chief, did not know enough about economics to be honest or dishonest. All he had ever had to run was a small-town law office. He had had murderers and unemployed railroad workers for clients, not the CPR and HBC.

But now there were an awful lot of Canadians out there waiting to go up north and get paid for bringing about the great northern vision.

Diefenbaker really felt for those people. He had been brought up in a shack on the prairie. He had practised law while the Depression blew away topsoil and shortened people's lives. Now he wanted to fight for these people, and the fight would be against the heartless profit makers back east and to the south. With his record-setting vote, he felt that he had the backing he needed—from the people.

Mackenzie King had included big business as a partner—with government and the people—in the making of a new kind of nation. His Liberals had introduced important features of the welfare state. Diefenbaker did not see King's partnership; he was after social justice. He could never forget the misery of his Saskatchewan neighbours. The welfare state would have to grow faster, and somehow this huge tract of land with all its promise would be able to pay for it. The old-time Tories, who had shared Meighen's belief that social assistance would sap moral fibre, had to face the fact of those 208 Diefenbaker seats. Most observers, pro-Dief or anti-Dief, say that the most popular PM in history was long on rhetoric and short on details. His vision was sincere but hard to see without the rosy spectacles.

How to win enemies and influence people

How did the best vote-getter in the world get so many people outside the country mad at him? Part of the answer is in the old principle that political virtue, even more than any other kind, is just asking for trouble. Another part of the answer is that Diefenbaker sometimes forgot what he had said yesterday.

First he got the British mad at him. After the 1957 election he went to his first Commonwealth Conference in England, and wowed the British. He was not treated as a colonial angel the way Laurier had been, but British prime minister Harold Macmillan, an old-school Tory, patted his back and welcomed Canada back into the Tory fold. Diefenbaker really enjoyed this first foreign stage, and looked for more light on the teeth, please. When he got home he announced that Canada was going to shift 15 per cent of its trade from the US to Britain. He had not noticed that such a unilateral move was not allowable under the General Agreement on Tariffs and Trade. Macmillan said that they could get around the problem by opening up a Commonwealth free-trade agreement. Diefenbaker's economically literate advisers told him that former prime ministers had deemed it wise to stay away from such a situation. Dief did not mention that 15-per-cent deal ever again.

But he would call up the sacred name of the Commonwealth in subsequent years, when it looked as if the British government had finally learned that their islands were part of Europe. It would not be until 1961, the year the Berlin Wall went up, that the British Parliament would vote to seek membership in the European Economic Community, but semi-secret negotiations had been going on in the late fifties. The Canadian government could not help feeling that Britain was involved in making a choice—EEC or the Commonwealth. More particular for Canada was the fear that the US-GB-Canadian triangle would be threatened. The European community would make certain demands that would be bad news for Canadian business, and if one corner of the triangle were to disappear, all that would remain was a straight line—and at the other end of the line was the United States. Diefenbaker may not have been a genius at economics, but he knew his geometry. He and his finance man, Donald Fleming, made sure that Canada was apprehensive and suspicious about Britain's flirtation with Europe. But British power had been falling since the war, and British pride had to be balanced against reality. No longer could a pecksniff say "Wogs start at Calais."

But John Diefenbaker really liked the Commonwealth. And he did not forget the populism that had brought him from Podunk to Ottawa. He did not like Wall Street imperialism in Canada, and he did not like white imperialism around the world. He had jumped all over the Brits and French during the Suez crisis, and now he was ready to jump all over the white masters of South Africa.

In 1961 the Commonwealth prime ministers met to discuss the question of the Republic of South Africa, which was to become independent that year. A republic has no crown to offer any allegiance to, so the country had to reapply for membership under the new conditions. Official apartheid had been in effect for thirteen years. At the meeting in London, all the white prime ministers but one were in favour of approving South Africa's continued membership, and wanted no discussion of the topic. All the non-white prime ministers wanted the topic discussed and wanted South Africa ousted.

John Diefenbaker was that one white prime minister, the one without a British surname. With his characteristic wit, he suggested a reasonable procedure: South Africa would remain in the Commonwealth and sign a communiqué asserting the family's principle of racial equality. Two prime ministers were opposed to the idea—Keith Holyoake of New Zealand and Harold Macmillan of Britain. Diefenbaker showed that in international affairs, too, he could hold the moral high road. His proposition was approved, and the white South Africans slid away. Diefenbaker told them that there was still room for them in the family, as soon as they came up to Commonwealth standards on racial equality.

Now Harold Macmillan and his lieutenant Edward Heath

were really browned off at this upstart westerner who did not seem to know what Conservative meant. They had liked him, all right, but then he had started to mix morality with international politics. What could you expect, though, of a man with an ethnic chip on his shoulder?

Diefenbaker enjoyed breaking moulds. He was perhaps the most reformist head of government Canada has had, and reformists have no trouble making enemies. Traditionally, in Canada, party leaders leaned away from the US toward Britain or away from Britain toward the US, and caught hell from across the floor for the leaning. Diefenbaker leaned away from Britain, all right, but he wanted to lean away from the US as well. What does that mean, he was asked. Independence, he said. The northern vision.

In the late fifties he seemed to get along with Dwight Eisenhower. They both had German surnames and came from the prairies and were married to women who sported homey first names and unbelievably frumpy dresses. Eisenhower knew a lot about fishing, and there was nothing Dief liked better than fishing. But John Kennedy and his brothers were into touch football. Can you imagine John Diefenbaker playing touch football?

On his way to alienating the Kennedys, though, he had work to do keeping a distance between traditional Tories and himself. They always had to know two things: the prime minister was a populist firebrand from the west, and a heck of a lot of MPs had made it to their Commons seats on his countrified coattails. He was a rube who knew more than they did about the new world of image-making. He paid attention to the popularity polls and played up to them. He had hired an advertising company to manage his campaign. He was a whiz on television. At night he liked to watch that child of television, professional wrestling. Gorgeous George and Yukon Eric knew how to manipulate their own images in a way that all the George Drews and Robert Stanfields would never understand.

In the age of television a country's ordinary citizens developed a yen to see their leaders at leisure, to get to "know" them. Television viewers refer to the figures on the screen by their first names, from Lucy to Oprah. John Diefenbaker was the first Canadian politician to understand that the camera needed actors and personalities. R.B. Bennett might have reached out to Canadians via the radio network, but he was still Prime Minister R.B. Bennett. Now the figure on the screen or in the photo magazine was "John" or "Dief" or "the Chief." He had what commentators would later call "charisma." After Diefenbaker it would be hard for a Canadian prime minister to earn a parliamentary majority without "charisma." For all his bow ties and baseball games, Lester B. Pearson never had "charisma."

After a nomination or election Diefenbaker takes the press to a Saskatchewan lake and gets his picture taken. He is wearing an Indian sweater over a checked shirt, and he has a day's catch of trout prominently displayed. He will often have his picture taken with fish, even a marlin liberated from USAmerican waters. Fishing may be mythic and elemental and peaceful and all that, but above all it is something that country boys do during the best days of their lives, and it is something that men do together with their best friends. The ordinary citizen looked at those pictures of Dief fishing and tried to imagine the fish stories that he would tell that evening while holding a non-alcoholic beverage.

In his other favourite photographic image Dief is wearing a Plains Indian war bonnet, all those feathers seeming to be extensions of his lightning-bolt hair. He is being given a tribal name, and one notices that he is wearing a buckskin jacket. He is not just a man of the people—he is a friend of the first peoples. He knows that there is work to do in Canada as there is work to do in South Africa. Back in 1950 he said, "The law respecting Indians is a denial of the principles we accept under the United Nations." Five years later he made his legal position known regarding Native rights: "In treaties that have been entered into as between their respective Britannic majesties and the ancestors of the present Indians, those rights are above parliament." Dief was a big admirer of Grey Owl (despite the latter's drinking habits), and paid close attention to his skill at playing a role while exposing all the modern threats to the Native people's environment and lives.

For all his respect for those old treaties, though, he was less interested in an aboriginal "nation" than he was in the individual rights of Native people. He felt that way about Quebec as well. In 1958 there were fifty Conservative MPs from Quebec, but these were mainly Duplessis people, anti-Liberals. They had not so much ridden into Ottawa on Diefenbaker's coattails as they had chased out bare-naked Grits. Diefenbaker did not manage to get himself a strong Quebec lieutenant, much less observe that old pre-Confederation notion of a vice-PM. Conservatives would always find it difficult to stay in power without a Quebec contingent, and Diefenbaker should have known that. There were Quebeckers with bad memories of the Depression, too.

Economists, like everyone else, were prone to think of the Depression as a decade in history. Things were not going to get that bad again. But during the Diefenbaker years the boom echoed away into a faint rumble in the far mountains, and the possibility of hard times gave us a word of warning. The word was "Recession." It did not sound as bad as "Depression," and it sounded temporary. But it was not something to like. Of course the Liberal opposition, such as it was, blamed the government, playing the old song about Tories and hard times. The defenders of the Chief's flame maintained that monetary problems came across international borders. But while Diefenbaker spent money on the northern dream and protection for farmers against insecurity caused by unpredictable weather and markets, his Finance Minister, Donald Fleming, was forced to introduce budget after budget with a big hole in it. The national deficit would eventually hit $2 billion. Now another of Diefenbaker's enemies stepped up.

This was the governor of the Bank of Canada. We will remember that R.B. Bennett got the Bank going as a kind of private business machine, and that Mackenzie King kind of nationalized it. By 1945 it had started a subsidiary Development Bank. The Bank of Canada stood as a regulator between the chartered banks and foreign outfits. It printed Canadian currency, fixed interest rates to the chartered banks, played the foreign-exchange markets, and in these ways influenced interest rates for Canadian citizens. The Bank of Canada had advice for everyone, including the government. It was not going to put up with wildness.

The governor of the Bank of Canada was a conservative Liberal appointee with a ringing name: James Elliott Coyne. He got tired of Diefenbaker's expansionism and Fleming's unbalanced budgets, and US investments, and eventually spoke up. The general public does not know what the governor of the Bank of Canada does for a living, but the job sounds important, and if that person suggests that *something* is wrong with the government's financial management, the public gets nervous. That nervousness would not have been enough to bring the prime minister to the downslope; but when the prime minister started to bludgeon James Elliott Coyne, he suddenly resembled an oppressor more than the champion of the oppressed.

Coyne's position was peculiar: the government had to tell the story that the Bank was independent of cabinet control. Otherwise it would just be a powerful political tool. On the other

hand, no government could put up with an uppity bank manager and allow the populace to get the idea that the money-
lenders rule them. The first few times that Coyne made
remarks about the dangerous Tory spending and borrowing,
Diefenbaker and Fleming told everyone that such dissent was a
proof of democracy. Mr Coyne was a Liberal appointee, after
all, and something like the Senate that the Liberals had stuffed.
You had to expect such criticism.

Coyne started making speeches here, there and everywhere,
and the newspapers got statements from him whenever they
could. In the Diefenbaker years the newspapers made sure that
everything was a sensation, from Russian A-bombs to Gerda
Munsinger. Normally one would think that the governor of the
Bank of Canada would be a pretty boring story, but the Liberals in opposition knew that their small numbers made scandal
their only weapon. Their man Coyne was an honest tightwad,
but he was a big talker, too, and the newspapers made sure that
people were listening. Some of those people were USAmericans
and other potential investors in the Canadian economy. When
Coyne kept saying that Diefenbaker was throwing scarce money
away and that foreign investors were not welcome, and that the
Canadian economy was headed for the dump, the US corporations were listening, and they said so.

If Coyne was not going to shut up, Diefenbaker would have
to take part in the melodrama. Everyone seemed to forget that
Coyne's seven-year appointment would be over at the end of
1961. John Diefenbaker and Donald Fleming ran out of patience
in the summer. If they were going to have an election next year,
they did not want to have to run against the Bank of Canada
and the fear that it could stir up across the country. Meanwhile,
Coyne sent daily despatches from his office. Enough was
enough: Fleming announced that the Bank was not so independent after all. The governor would have to go. Maybe the

government could then go to the hustings with the story that if there were any financial problems they were all Coyne's fault.

But the Tories needed more than a disagreement about the budget. In the fall Fleming was going to offer a deficit of $750,000. But for the moment he would be exposing a shocking scam involving a few thousand. It happened that Coyne had failed to tell Diefenbaker's cabinet that his pension had been boosted from $11,900 annually to a nice round $25,000. Now the news was out, and Diefenbaker and Fleming looked absolutely shocked! When Coyne refused to quit early, they pushed through an act of Parliament to dismiss him. The Liberal-packed Senate rejected the act, but then, his honour saved, Coyne resigned on July 13. He took his wife's hand and walked out of public life, a heroic individual who had taken on the biggest Canadian government of all time. Uh-oh!

There is a nifty irony to append to this story. In 1967 the Liberals would pass legislation enabling the Minister of Finance to give written instructions about financial policy to the governor of the Bank. The Bank of Canada, the legislation says, "shall comply with such directive." The legislation also states that the cabinet has to approve any pension for an outgoing governor of the Bank.

Cold War scandals

If you mix atomic bombs and fiery-eyed reformers and the adolescence of rock 'n' roll, you are going to bake a sensational cake. Louis St Laurent had had his spy adventure; now the Tories would have theirs. St Laurent had exposed his spy and exploited his toughness to get the job as PM. Diefenbaker covered his spy with a thick blanket in an attempt to hold onto his job as PM. We are not talking about Herbert Norman's body in the Cairo street nine floors below his apartment. This was Canada's ambassador to Egypt, who had been hounded to his suicide by US McCarthyites and RCMP just before St Laurent dissolved his last Parliament. No, we are talking about Gerda Munsinger, a divorced East German who was living in Montreal and playing footsy and other body parts with a Canadian cabinet minister.

On the nineteenth anniversary of Pearl Harbor, the RCMP came to see Justice Minister Davie Fulton, and told him that Pierre Sévigny, the associate minister of national defence, had been conducting an affair of two years' standing with Mrs Munsinger. In fact, those years were not spent in standing, and the beginning of the affair coincided with the immigration of the woman from behind the Iron Curtain. Five years later the Liberals would try to blow the case wide open, and the newspapers would get agitated about a sex-spy scandal, but their photo-displays did not help much—Gerda looked rather frumpy, and the whole event turned out to be more goofy than sinister.

Diefenbaker did not ask Sévigny to resign. He just asked him to quit messing with Gerda. The RCMP went back to foraging for homosexuals in the civil service. All his Cold War problems should have been so easy to take care of. A year earlier he had, his growing corps of enemies said, destroyed Canadian pride, crippled Canadian business and sold us down the pipes to the Yanks, by cancelling the Avro Arrow. In terms of fiscal reality, Diefenbaker had been right for once. But his genius for publicity had deserted him.

In the late nineties people were still getting all sentimental and upset about the beautiful Avro Arrow, the lordly CF-105 jet interceptor. Guys were suing each other over the right to salvage a scale model from the bottom of Lake Ontario. For decades the Avro Arrow had been a symbol of lost Canadian independence and leadership in the military-industrial-political world. When it first flew in March of 1958, it looked like something from the ominous and beautiful future, a delta of speed and rockets that made usAmerican and Russian and British jet fighter-interceptors look like holdovers from the Korean police action. It was the fastest warplane in the sky and capable of carrying enough death machinery to make any cold warrior bust his buttons. In fact it looked like a lot of the warplanes that would crack the air a decade or two later.

C.D. Howe had spent ten years and a gazillion dollars getting the CF-105 into the air. The A.V. Roe Company gobbled up Liberal government contracts. The planes were supposed to cost $2 million apiece, a hefty sticker price, but by late 1958 they were coming in at $7 million. General George Pearkes, the Defence Minister, was proud of this Canadian achievement, but he had an Edsel on his hands. The Arrow would not fly for long unless the air forces of NATO wanted to buy it, and the price was not right. Diefenbaker, who tended to turn his hearing aid off when his Finance Minister complained about extravagance, added up the expenditures and found a figure of $700 million for the plane he had inherited from C.D. Howe. Here was a cost-cutting measure he could understand. He ordered work on the Arrow stopped at the end of February 1959.

Fourteeen thousand aircraft workers were fired by A.V. Roe. Draftsmen and engineers flocked southward to work for Lockheed. The Liberals, trying to make hay in Ontario, where the plane had been assembled, hollered about a sellout to the usAmericans. They did not tell the Toronto newspapers that they were thinking of scuttling the Arrow themselves when they got back into power.

Diefenbaker and his people did not use the economic argument to justify scuttling the dream. Instead, they voiced the prevailing Cold War wisdom that the Russians, just on the other side of the North Pole, were not going to send long-range bombers over Canada on their way to the USA—they were going to be using ICBMs, and the only defence against these horrible new weapons would be defensive missiles to blow them out of the sky. That argument, though, does not explain the government's handling of the CF-105s that had been sitting on the tarmac at Malton air base. Diefenbaker went after them the way he had gone after James Coyne. The futuristic machines were yanked apart and melted down. They were not going to be museum attractions or monuments to a time when the twentieth century might have belonged to Canada. Many years later they might appear on a postage stamp issued during a Liberal regime.

So what about those interceptor missiles? A.V. Roe was not in the missile business. But Boeing of Seattle was, and they were making a winged missile called the Bomarc. It had a range of four hundred miles. If it was to be fired from, say, Montana, it would engage the enemy missile over, say, Edmonton. For the comfort of Canadians it might be a good idea to fire it northward from high in the Arctic. In September of 1957 Diefenbaker and Pearkes approved the charter for NORAD, the integrated US-Canadian air defence organization, and Canadians started to man the radar lines built by the USAmericans across northern Canada.

Now the Canadian government agreed to have Bomarcs situated on Canadian soil. When General Pearkes bought them, he assumed that he would also acquire the atomic warheads that the USAmericans designed for them. Many Canadians had a horror of atomic weapons and did not want them in the country under any circumstances. The peace movement and the anti-nuclear movement expanded greatly during the late fifties. Diefenbaker did not like atomic weapons, and he especially did not like the USAmerican rule that only USAmericans could tend them. No atomic warheads, he said. What will we put in the nose cones of those Bomarcs, he was asked. Sand, he said. And so, as Dwight D. Eisenhower the dove left office down south, and John F. Kennedy the hawk became president, Canada bristled with foreign rockets armed with domestic sand.

More and more, the attacks on John G. Diefenbaker were punctuated with laughter. The political cartoons turned his eyes from vulpine to simply lunatic.

The "Diefendollar" was the favourite joke of the Liberal party. After getting rid of Coyne, the Conservatives started to listen more carefully to their own Finance Minister. Just before the 1962 election, he announced that the Canadian dollar had been wearing a mask, and pegged it at 92.5 US cents. This number bothered a lot of Canadians whose understanding of international finance and Canadian pride was something like their prime minister's. The Liberals had an election gimmick for the campaign that was just then starting. They printed millions of fake dollars with a caricature of the Chief on them and a dotted line 7.5 per cent of the way from one end. It did not take an overly sensitive heart to recognize the fact that the prime minister's "ethnic" name was still being hinted at as an election issue.

The 1962 campaign was quite different from the 1958 one. There were organized demonstrations against the former saviour, marked by a lot of rudeness. Diefenbaker was technically an old man now, but he glared and waggled his head and gave at least as good as he got. But the pegged dollar did not bring a surge of money into the country; in fact the dollar was hit even harder by a lot of unsavoury speculating on its fall. As his opponents threw the green Diefendollars into the air, the prime minister waved a copy of the Canadian Bill of Rights he had enacted in 1960, and at which provincial judges had raised the corners of their lips.

In June 1962 the country had a minority government again. The Conservatives lost a whopping 92 seats to stand at 116. The Liberals now had 98, and this time Pearson did not make the mistake of suggesting that Dief pass the job over to him. The strange Social Credit got 30 seats where they had had none, and the New Democratic Party, a CCF with more clear support of labour, went up to 19. John Diefenbaker now had to operate as a politician rather than a messiah.

Weirder in a weird land

All right. He had the British mad at him. The Quebeckers were not his firm supporters. The super patriots were after his head. The old guard of the Conservative party were thinking of butterfly nets. The bankers and the airframe bangers were upset. Now it was time to really alienate the USAmericans. Young Jack Kennedy was really going to hate him, hate him and scoff at him. Kennedy the testosteronic cold warrior was going to accuse Diefenbaker and Canada of being too peaceful at a time when he wanted to High Noon the Soviets.

It was not fair. John Kennedy was a rich scion of an eastern dynasty and a very young Democrat, and he was going to somehow represent youth against the old ideologues running the Warsaw Pact. It happened that Diefenbaker was an old populist brought up in a prairie shack, and now he had his Tory party to the left of the Democratic party across the line. He had white crinkles on top of his head and wobbly jowls underneath. He had been the image master, but now he had the wrong image.

He was not a stubborn anti-USAmerican. He had borrowed a lot of money from down south. He had allowed an alarming number of corporations to operate in Canada. He was buying USAmerican warplanes and missiles. He had signed the NORAD agreement. But in the post-war period Canada had been developing a reputation as a peacekeeping nation, especially through the United Nations. The USA was a giant that saw the

UN as a threat to its sovereignty. Diefenbaker and his Foreign Affairs Minister, Howard Green, did not want Canada's peace-keeping reputation wrecked by atomic weapons handled by USAmericans on Canadian soil. Over on the other side of the House, Lester Pearson the Nobel Peace Prize winner agreed with them.

In the United States the politicians and the military and the press started exploring means by which they could remove this Diefenbaker problem. Of course Canada was not a banana republic, so the usual methods could not be deployed. But damn it, the man had sold wheat to the communists in China. He was talking about introducing a socialistic hospital insurance plan. He poured sand into Yankee missiles. The last straw came with Canada's response to Kennedy's Cuban crisis.

The USAmericans were mad at Canada for continuing relations with Cuba after the Cubans had taken US property away from US millionaires and gangsters. Now the Cubans seemed to be letting the Russians install missiles on their island, sort of the way the Turks had let the USAmericans install missiles along its border with the Soviet Union. Kennedy, as his predecessors had so often done, invoked the Monroe Doctrine, the 1823 edict that announced to governments across the Atlantic that if there was any expansion to be done in the New World it would be done by the USA. So the US navy chugged out to stop the Soviet ships that were bringing missiles and aircraft to their ally in the Caribbean. People all over the world began to feel as if the atomic war was coming, and watched TV screens in horror. John Kennedy's hormones raced through his body.

It was late in October of 1962. Kennedy was embroiled in an important mid-term congressional election. He had to look tough, and he had to look patriotic. He sent Diefenbaker a copy of the TV speech he was going to make about the dangerous Soviet missiles and the US response. This was not a matter for NORAD or NATO. There was no question of consulting allies. It was *mano a mano* time. Times had changed: it used to be the British that took unilateral action and expected the smaller countries to support them.

But Diefenbaker was either a ditherer, as his detractors always say, or a man horrified by naked aggression. Maybe he was thinking of Suez and Pearson and a Nobel prize for himself. In Parliament he made noises about a UN contingent in Cuba; he did not send an immediate hurrah to Kennedy. Lester Pearson did not complain—he was a UN peacemaker. But Kennedy and his hawks were not much interested in Canadian peacemakers. This was a major-league confrontation, and Canada was one of their farm teams. The Canadian Embassy in Washington received some tough notes for a day or two. If NORAD was a joint defence system, how could it go on full alert if the Canadians were not ready? Diefenbaker said that he would bring it up with his cabinet in the morning.

(This was before Trudeau replaced the cabinet with the Prime Minister's Office.)

Defence Minister Douglas Harkness was gung-ho. He told his chiefs-of-staff to make as many preparations as possible without scaring the prime minister. Meanwhile Diefenbaker was on the telephone with Kennedy. Kennedy was mad as hell that the Chief had mentioned the UN out loud, and demanded support of USAmerican threats against the Russian ships that were carrying missiles toward Cuba. "When were we consulted?" asked Diefenbaker. "You weren't," said the leader of the Free World.

Harkness went to Diefenbaker and begged for an alert. Finally, Diefenbaker said oh, go ahead, and cabinet would find out later. It took a week for the crisis to settle down to a phone call between Kennedy and Nikita Khrushchev. USAmerican pilots were flying with their thumbs poised over the button. In Ottawa, the prime minister and his entourage were all packed up and ready to head to the "Diefenbunker," the fancy bomb shelter from which government would be conducted while the Houses of Parliament were melting. By most accounts, the Chief was frantic during these days, and sometimes predicted a bombed-out world.

Eventually, of course, things blew over. Khrushchev promised to take the missiles back home. Kennedy promised not to invade Cuba. When he could find the time to think about it, Kennedy vowed to get Diefenbaker out of office, and get the damned nuclear warheads into Canada.

A satellite country?

John Kennedy grew up in the world of power, and he did not understand any other kind of world. As far as he was concerned, Canada was his Bulgaria, and he did not have the kind of sense of humour that would appreciate missiles armed with sand in the middle of the Cold War. "I am a Berliner," he had said in Berlin, not knowing that in Berlin a Berliner is a gooey sweet bun. He should have come to Manitoba and said, "I am a Winnipeg Goldeye."

So he sent General Lauris Norstad, the just-retired commander of NATO, to make a farewell visit to Ottawa. Diefenbaker cancelled his meeting with Norstad, and sent Sévigny in his place. A bunch of reporters grilled Norstad on the nuclear question. Talking about the Canadian pilots flying US-built planes for NATO, the general averred that Canada had committed itself to the nuclear missiles that the US pilots were using. The next day the newspapers were running editorials asking whether there was a Canadian government. In a small-city speech, the leader of the opposition changed his position, saying that Canada's commitment to its "promise" was more important than the fear of nuclear armament. Pearson would have a little trouble with his party, which was also split on the topic.

General Harkness thought that he had seen his opportunity to get closer to the prime minister than Howard Green could. Let's get busy and honour our commitment, he said. Hold your horses, said the Chief. In the meanwhile, Pearson announced that the Liberals would now be prepared to accept the US nuclear missiles if his party were to win an election anytime soon. On the day he said that on television in January of 1963, this amateur historian's wife of three weeks gobbed on the second-hand TV screen, and called the man Lester B. Expletive Deleted. National politics roused a lot of visceral feelings in the early sixties.

Some of the NATO countries got a little edgy when Kennedy and the British PM Harold Macmillan scheduled a two-person meeting in Nassau. The USAmericans, by the beginning of the sixties, had taken over from Europe the battles against nationalist movements in Southeast Asia. Now it looked as though they were doing an end run on their allies. Diefenbaker crashed the party, though it was hinted that he was not invited. Worse, when he got home, he made a speech in which he said that Kennedy and Macmillan were planning changes in NATO's strategies, and a franchised Canadian nuclear capability was in abeyance. The USAmericans really got ticked off. They put out press releases in which they sort of said that the Canadian prime minister was either a liar or stupid. Their statements had a few lies in them, and not a little stupidity. Meanwhile, most regular joes in the Royal Canadian Air Force were pretty sure that there were already secret nuclear warheads in places like RCAF Comox.

In Ottawa, only half the cabinet was willing to follow John. There would have been a more open revolt if the restive dozen could have found a real leader. Only George Hees hinted that he could do it, but George Hees, as far as the voting public was concerned, was a clothes horse from some 1935 Hollywood comedy.

The insulted Diefenbaker declared more and more his opposition to domination by the US, announcing that Canada was no Bulgaria. Government dealings with Washington dwindled to distant insults, and business dealings with the US looked as if they might be in trouble. The Liberal party, long the advocate of continentalism, leapt into the pro-US vacancy.

This minority government was not getting a lot done, and a lot of people inside and outside the government were just waiting for the Diefenbaker years to be over. There were even Conservative cabinet ministers who thought about hiring a temporary head while a real candidate was being looked for. Enough of this, said the Chief. He called a February cabinet meeting and opened the issue up: it was a case of traitors against Diefenbuddies. Anyone who did not like what he was doing could leave or try to beat him. All but one of them murmured and then shut up. Harkness offered his quasi-sacrificial resignation.

So Diefenbaker had a silent majority in cabinet, but he had a minority in the House. He had been bailed out of a few non-confidence votes, but now all the opposition parties got together. Social Credit was now listening to Alberta's right-wing premier E.C. Manning, and he said that Diefenbaker the semi-socialist anti-USAmerican had to go. The Liberals introduced a non-confidence vote, and the Socreds attached an amendment. Diefenbaker was in court again, defending the little guy, Canada, against the big corporation, the USA. He made a beautiful speech in favour of the doomed. He once again hauled the ghost of John A. Macdonald into the Commons chamber and presented him as a model of the leader who would dream big dreams while refusing to bend over for US money.

But he got walloped in the House vote of February 5, 1963. For the second time a Conservative government was defeated on a parliamentary vote. The first, Arthur Meighen's, had fallen with a soft sound everyone had expected. The Diefenbaker party, on the other hand, had held 208 seats just five years ago.

Now there would be yet another federal election, and this time the main issue would be the USAmericans. Diefenbaker's cabinet ministers suddenly had something to do elsewhere— they were not interested in fighting an election against John Kennedy and *Newsweek* magazine. Once again it was a one-man party, but this time the young, the city people, the Quebeckers, stepped aside when Dief's coattails came by. The farmers on the prairie still liked him. The Canadian nationalists liked him. The peace movement was ambivalent. He tried to whip up nuclear terror against Pearson. As usual he out-speeched the Liberal candidate for his job.

And he almost pulled off the impossible. In the race to lose the election, the old parties ran neck and jowl. On April 8, his rhetorical machine just winding down, the Chief sat in a railway car in Saskatchewan, stooking the results. The Diefenbaker party had lost 21 more seats, and now totalled 95. If Hees or anyone else had led the party, they would have been left with a rump. The Socreds fell to 24, the NDP to 17. Pearson's Liberals had 129, gathering up the eastern municipalities and Quebec, but they were four seats short of a majority.

This was no time for John Diefenbaker to quit. He looked forward to a great comeback in a 1964 election. The election did not come until 1965, and Diefenbaker chose to spend his energies fighting the new Maple Leaf flag and the concept of two Canadas. Mike Pearson had decided to spring the election that fall because he wanted to run against the old man. The old man dressed himself as Britannia and demonstrated to the Liberal party that they did not have a good enough candidate. The voters increased both their numbers by 2, giving Canada yet another minority government and telling both parties to come up with someone new.

An assassin was already at work in the Tory ranks. This was

Dalton Camp, a New Brunswick advertising man with an Ivy League education. He was president of the party from 1964 till 1969, and made his opposition against the western firehead more and more clear. The Progressive Conservative party needed to get back where it belonged, in the hands of big business and sensible easterners. Camp forced a leadership review, characterized by unseemly open contempt between him and the seventy-one-year-old leader, and came up with a rival for the Chief—an underwear magnate and former Nova Scotia premier. Diefenbaker lost the leader's position before the 1968 election, but he would not retire from Ottawa. He died there during the brief Joe Clark administration in 1979.

He had scripted a magnificent state funeral, and a train ride for his body and the disinterred body of Olive, his second wife, back to Saskatchewan. Television viewers got an update of the Chief's last trip every night on the news. A lot of the farmers past whose acres the train roared would not have had television sets but for his work on their behalf.

CHAPTER 20

PROFESSOR IN THE BULLPEN

Lester B. Pearson 1963–68

E DWIN ARTHUR PEARSON, son of a Methodist preacher, was a Methodist preacher in southern Ontario during the late Victorian period. Maybe he wanted his three sons to become Methodist preachers. Maybe he thought that he could obviate more worldly jobs by giving them the names Marmaduke, Vaughan and Lester. It almost worked on Lester, who was ready to become a history professor before he accidentally became world famous. When Lester had children of his own, he called them Geoffrey and Patricia.

Lester was born in a township near Toronto on Shakespeare's birthday in 1897, when little John Diefenbaker over in western Ontario was a year and a half old. During the youthful rebellion years of the late 1960s, these two septuagenarians would be noted for their indecisiveness as they argued about the form of a country at the centenary of Confederation.

Like so many Canadian prime ministers, Lester Bowles Pearson had a mother, Annie Bowles, who was more decisive and ambitious than his father. (He would later have a wife who was more decisive than he.) John Diefenbaker's family and neighbours were Liberals, so he became (he said) a Conservative. Pearson's father was a Conservative, so he became a Liberal. The populist Diefenbaker sort of *replaced* the Tories for a while, and led a Diefenbaker party. Pearson would become a star in the foreign service, and become a Liberal politician because he was asked. When he was handed the safe seat of Algoma East in 1948, and sworn in as St Laurent's Minister of External Affairs, he was asked at his first press conference how long he had been a Liberal. Since the swearing-in ceremony, he replied, with his usual self-effacing humour.

Like so many of his predecessors, the future prime minister grew up in a home with little money and a high regard for books. He liked books, but he also liked being outdoors, playing sports. His choice of sports is significant. We remember that his successor, the patrician Pierre Elliott Trudeau, showed off his proficiency in individual athletics—canoeing, skiing, diving, extreme pushups. Lester Pearson loved team sports—hockey, lacrosse, baseball. As the years went by he was first a player, then a coach, then a spectator with the moves remembered by his body. During his lame-duck session of 1968, it was deemed endearing that he made interviewers wait while he caught the end of a ball game on his office TV set.

Pearson always objected, perhaps too quietly, that stories of his youthful baseball prowess were exaggerated. But he never forgot that sports and diplomacy are no strangers. During his wartime service at the Canadian Embassy in Washington, the Canadians carried on "boisterous" softball games with a team from the US State Department. In his *Memoirs*, Pearson describes the international niceties of the games:

> Our diplomatic worry was that we might prejudice our good relations with the State Department by beating them too easily.

At the same time national pride would permit no defeat by the foreigner. So we worked out a unique and most ingenious method of handicapping. We placed a jug of martinis and a glass at each base and negotiated an agreement under which, whenever a player reached that base, he had to drink a martini. This ensured a record number of men stranded on third base and, if anyone did try to make home plate, he could easily be tagged. The scores were remarkably even. It is a tribute to the steadiness and good condition of the players on both sides that every game did not end o-o.

In all the schools he went to while his father moved from church to church, Lester Pearson appeared to be an ordinary boy. Unlike Diefenbaker and some others, he never told anyone he was going to be prime minister one day. He started at the University of Toronto the year before the Great War broke out, and opened his books and got to work. If he had any particular trait it was this: he went to work on his assignments and did them as well as he could.

In the spring of 1915 he turned eighteen and decided to go overseas. He trained at an officer's school, and joined a hospital unit, so that he could handle duty and Christian service at the same time. His unit went first to England, then to Egypt, and thereafter to Salonika. Now he changed his mind, opting for the infantry. He wrote to his father, who knew Sam Hughes the flamboyant militia walrus. When he arrived in England again he was a lieutenant, and ready to become cannon fodder in France. Now he changed his mind again, and though he was terrified of heights, decided to become a pilot in the Royal Flying Corps, the most glamorous job in the Great War, and the one that was most likely to get a person killed. His parents must have wondered why they did not raise a son who could make a decision and stick to it.

On his first solo flight his engine stopped while he was banking into a landing pattern, and his kite crashed to the ground. He was given a few days off flying to inspect his scratches and bruises, so he headed to London to have a look at Piccadilly, though he was not supposed to leave the base. He was having fun in the city, when the air-raid sirens started shrieking. During the comical scramble, he was smacked by a bus in the darkened street, and that was the end of his war. After six weeks of recuperation he was sent home, leaving his brothers to fight the war in Europe, one in the trenches, the other in a navy plane. He did not expect to see them again.

But he had a new name. His flight instructors refused to call him by the wimpy name Lester, and dubbed him "Mike." It was to be useful in later life: how far would he have got in the 1963 election with his flacks shouting "We like Lester"?

Sausages and seminars

So he took up his studies at U of T and graduated. Now it was time for another decision. He decided that he would try the meat business. He went to the Armour meatpacking company in Hamilton, where he had finished high school. Soon he was in Chicago, where twenty years earlier Mackenzie King had been an idealistic social worker. Mike Pearson was a sausage stuffer, and then a clerk for a while, before he decided that business was not his *métier*.

He remembered the gentle fields near Oxford, where he had tried to fly a Camel. By 1921 he was back as a modern history student on a scholarship. He was not a Rhodes lad, but he was an athlete, and a pretty good one. He did his assignments and starred in lacrosse and ice hockey. He was the Canadian lad. He was so much better at ice hockey than your average Brit, that he was asked to play left wing for the British team in the 1924 Olympic games, but he was by that time already back in Canada, becoming a professor. He had, though, gone AWOL again, playing for the Swiss team in the 1922 European tournament. His teammates called him "Herr Zigzag." Maybe they were able to see into the future.

He seemed suited for university life, especially if it involved playing and coaching campus sports teams. Photographs from the twenties do not show him in his later professorial outfit— owly spectacles and bow tie. He did follow one tradition: he married one of his students in 1925, this being the rather earnest-looking Maryon Moody from Winnipeg. It is too bad that Maryon Pearson did not get to be a faculty wife for long. She might have shaken the University of Toronto out of its cobwebs.

Falling into fame

The Department of External Affairs had been established under Wilfrid Laurier in 1909, but before the war it had done little besides issuing passports and liaising with Washington. After the war Mackenzie King saw a new world and a new place for Canada in the world, and started building a big diplomatic bureaucracy, making Dr O.D. Skelton the undersecretary. King was determined that the service's personnel should be found through competition rather than patronage. Skelton was an academic, and as these things happened, was seated beside young professor Pearson at a dinner one day in 1925. There he mentioned the competition and said that he could use some bright young history professors. Two years later the Pearsons were visiting Ottawa because scholar Pearson wanted to write a book about the United Empire Loyalists. Just for the fun of it, said Dr Skelton to Lester Pearson, why don't you write the External Affairs examination? Lots of history in it, he said. Pearson finished the assignment.

Back in Toronto Pearson had to get an eye test to see whether he needed spectacles. When the telegram came from Ottawa, he had drops in his eyes, so someone read the news to him—he had finished first in the examination. It was the first time that that had ever happened to him. He decided to leave the UEL book for someone else. He would try diplomacy for a while.

So here he was, in at the start, the recruit who knew most about a job the Canadians did not know much about. He had to learn how to wear the diplomat's uniform—cutaway coat, striped trousers and top hat. But he was a ball player. He did not like stuffed shirts and he did not like hoity-toity language. He became a famous Canadian with a casual, friendly manner. The casual, friendly manner was partly natural and partly a spider web. He would use it years later on his quarrelling ministers, each of whom would go away from a meeting with the prime minister thinking that he had been agreed with.

He was a diplomat during the post-war period, the between-war period and the war period. What a time to be a diplomat! In the late twenties he got his first house and his first car (a second-hand Ford) and his second child. In 1929 he got his first posting—to Washington. For the next while he would go from city to city, learning how to mix cocktails and making acquaintances. He went to a lot of conferences and wrote a lot of reports. He did not make mistakes and though he liked to have fun, he never caused any scandals, the rude entertainment of the business. He formed his style, cutting through pious declarations and getting foreigners to talk realistically. He did not like big-power alliances, and he was not any more enamoured of the League of Nations than Mackenzie King was. When King stabbed Dr Riddell in the back and scuttled the oil blockade against Mussolini, Pearson was left in Geneva to get all the dirty looks from the little guys.

But he made himself a reputation as an honest broker, and no one in the international diplomatic community hated Lester Pearson. A lot of foreigners still thought that Canada was a British country or a less shiny part of the United States, but Pearson finished his assignments and laid the basis for Canada's later reputation as a peace agent. Late in 1934 he accompanied R.B. Bennett to the royal jubilee and Commonwealth talks in London, and on the way across, on the lovely French liner *Paris*, the prime minister showed his secretary the list of people to whom he was planning to present orders, and asked him to approve. There was an OBE for Pearson. Aw shucks, said the younger man, who was a little seasick and wanted to get back to his own cabin. Later he would be out of town during the induction ceremony at Rideau Hall, but a friend would deliver his decoration to a Rockcliffe tennis court where the thirty-eight-year-old civil servant was keeping in shape.

Pearson knew his way around Europe, and he knew everyone who knew anything about the international scene. In 1939 he knew that war was coming again, and he told Mackenzie King so. King, of course, pooh-poohed the idea, but Pearson worked things so that he could be in London when the air-raid sirens sounded again. This time he did not step in front of any buses, but the government brought him home anyway. They wanted him in Washington, where he would be the ambassador's chief aide, and in fact pretty well run the show. His main job was to try to explain to the USAmericans that Canada was not part of Britain and not an extension of the US. His journals are full of remarks about "juvenile Rotarianism" in the US capital. Pearson did not like European stuffed shirts, but he was no more fond of Columbia's main-streetism.

Mackenzie King had been keeping his eye on young Lester

Pearson (and he knew it), just the way Wilfrid Laurier had kept his eye on young Mackenzie King. The Tories liked to look to provincial premiers and successful business lawyers for their next federal cabinets. The Liberals built the civil service as a pool for their ministers. They promoted Lester Pearson faster than anyone else; in 1945 he was ambassador to the United States. By now he was wearing his trademark bow tie, and Maryon was wearing her famous little hats with feathers or ribbons seeming to explode above her forehead.

Why aren't you in politics, asked Prime Minister King.

Not my game, said Pearson. Politicians have to harvest votes from the uninformed. Diplomats get to bargain with well-briefed veterans of modern history.

He spent his forty-ninth birthday aboard a train to San Francisco and the United Nations Conference. It would be his first trip across the continent. The Canadians had a small delegation that included Louis St Laurent. Pearson did a lot of the talking. Most of the people there knew him, and would go away from the conference almost identifying the UN idea with the slick-haired diplomat from Canada. He had a hand in the formation of most UN agencies. He really would have liked to be the UN's first secretary-general, but the Soviets vetoed him, and would veto him when he was nominated again.

In 1946 he got another promotion. He became the Under-Secretary of State for External Affairs, the top job in the civil service. A year later he would be fifty, at the ceiling, an amazing success for an ordinary Methodist preacher's ball-playing son. He could look forward to a graceful retirement, a round of speeches and parties, maybe some part-time professoring at universities around the country. At least that was what he let his friends and his wife think that he was contemplating. He was a little like Mackenzie King that way: people did not know what he was contemplating.

Slipping into politics

Mackenzie King had been thinking of Pearson as a successor. They both had Foster Hewitt accents and slicked-down hair. They both thought that the world had a pretty good chance of blowing up. But when the Liberals held their 1948 convention to choose a new prime minister, Pearson was not one of the ceremonial rivals to St Laurent's coronation.

Louis St Laurent understood how to keep a machine running. King had telephoned him and told him to come on over and become foreign minister. The position was now open, so St Laurent invited Pearson to take another promotion, and that is the way Pearson looked at it. He would advance from deputy minister to minister. In this way he beguiled lots of political-history commentators—they would repeat the notion that Lester B. Pearson more or less became a political success against his will. But Pearson was a student of modern history. He knew that if he followed St Laurent's steps now, the future looked pretty logical. The Liberal party was going to govern Canada from now on, and Louis St Laurent was fifteen years older than Mike Pearson.

All the time that Diefenbaker was losing election after election, Pearson had been doing his assignments and getting promoted. As Diefenbaker fought alone because he could not abide less idealistic company, Pearson stood in drawing rooms, cocktail glass in hand, listening to inanities mixed with wit. He had been or seemed an ordinary man himself, and he was prepared to work in a world of imperfect human beings and imperfect human institutions. His job was to do the best he could and finish his assignments. He made it seem easy. The Soviets smiled and said that he was a tool of capitalism. The usAmericans often said that he was "soft on communism," a popular phrase where they came from.

So, yes, he said to Uncle Louis, and on September 10, 1948, he was sworn in as Secretary of State for External Affairs. He telephoned his mother right away and told her that he was now a minister of the Crown. Mrs Pearson, who had hoped that he would become a Methodist minister, said that that was almost as good. He had learned his self-deprecating humour from Annie Bowles.

Now he had to get elected to the Commons. There was an MP in the riding of Algoma East who was willing to enter the Senate, and the seat had been Liberal since 1935. It looked pretty safe. Where is Algoma East, asked the new Secretary of State for External Affairs. It was east of Sault Ste Marie, way to hell and gone over by Georgian Bay. Never been there, he said. It turned out that there was really no there there. The riding contained twenty-thousand square miles and no cities. The Tories weren't interested, but the CCF and Socreds ran candidates. Lots of luck. Lester and Maryon rode trains around the low woods, talking to little audiences in Legion halls. It was a long way from London and Washington. Pearson won by more than 3,000 votes. The next day he crawled out of the woods in Sudbury and headed for a UN meeting in Paris. What a strange first twenty-four hours as an elected official!

So Lester Bowles Pearson, with his slicked-down hair and professor glasses, spent the next ten crisis-sprouting years as Minister for External Affairs. By tradition his ministry was supposed to be just about non-partisan, and that suited him fine. He was no more a Liberal than Diefenbaker was a Conservative. You could not often find him around Georgian Bay. He had the UN and NATO to tend to. In 1948 the Soviet Army moved into Czechoslovakia, and the Cold War was on for sure. Every international spat and every civil war in the world became part of the Cold War. Such would be the case in Palestine.

Pearson may not have known the geography of northern

Ontario, but since his Methodist childhood he had known the geography of the Holy Land. In 1947 the British told the world that they could no longer handle the place and were leaving it in the hands of the United Nations. Canada had never had any position on Palestine, but now Canada was committed to the UN, and Canada's man, Lester Pearson, saw a situation that would allow for no ideal solution. He had contempt for the positions and motivations of the British, the Soviets and the USAmericans, but he was a diplomat and he signed the partition agreement. When that failed, and Israel declared itself a republic, he advised Canada not to follow the immediate recognition offered by the Brits and Yanks. He talked to everyone a hundred times each. He agreed to a limited recognition of the new country and even its admission into the UN. He did not expect any solution to the Palestinian problem, and said so. "This was no diplomatic conflict," he wrote later. "It was a life and death confrontation between two peoples. It still is."

In the Middle East, in Europe and in Asia, he had always had to argue against the pessimistic isolationism of Mackenzie King. He got closer to St Laurent's ear. He had tried to get King interested in Korea, but King had refused to let Canada serve on the UN commission that would oversee a change from US occupation to some kind of Korean independence. King had pictures of cataclysm in his head, and he did not want any part in it. Now in 1950 the North Koreans invaded the south, and Lester Pearson confessed to being surprised. He overcame some opposition among his party colleagues and got Canada into the Korean "police action," but he was skeptical of US General MacArthur's leadership of the United Nations troops. In his memoirs he quotes MacArthur as saying "There is no other object in war but victory," then adds: "I always thought myself that the object of war is peace." The corncob general was more logical, of course, but Pearson as usual held the high ground.

As MacArthur called for the bombing of Manchuria and an invasion of China from Taiwan, Pearson made speeches in which he opined that the general should stick to his job. In one of those speeches he declared Canadian independence from the new empire: "The days of relatively easy and automatic political relations with our neighbour are, I think, over." Coincidently US president Truman finally relieved MacArthur of his command. Pearson would be accused by Diefenbaker's crew of capitulation to the Yanks, but in actual fact he would always be a man who listened to both sides of an argument and tried to find the most likely position between them.

In the early fifties Pearson's attitude toward MacArthur would get him into the bad books of the US McCarthyites. Joseph McCarthy, the US senator who saw a communist threat under every bed, was not alone. Red-baiting newspapers and radio columnists seemed to compete with one another in the making of outrageous accusations. The Pope and Marilyn Monroe were commies. President Eisenhower would become the object of a whisper campaign. So it should be a matter of no wonder that Canada's foreign secretary would make the crackpots nervous. McCarthy's congressional committee wanted Igor Gouzenko to testify for them, but the RCMP advised Pearson that Gouzenko would say anything to promote the book he was writing, and Pearson decided not to let Canada's favourite spy talk on USAmerican TV. That settled it: Lester Pearson was a communist sympathizer. A Baltimore newspaper announced that "The best that can be said against Lester Pearson and his followers in the Canadian pinko set is that they are dangerous and untruthful." The *Times-Herald* did not tell us what the worst that could be said might be. Colonel Robert S. McCormick, publisher of the Republican Chicago *Tribune*, used to take vacations in Baie Comeau, Quebec, where he would hand crisp US banknotes to a young Brian Mulroney and ask him to sing his favourite old songs. On one of these magisterial trips to the colony, he advised anyone who would listen that the Canadian foreign secretary was "the most dangerous man in the English speaking world."

What? Our man in the bow tie? He's just a Canadian.

But if Pearson could find no friends among the lunatics in the US Senate and press corps, he probably had the best reputation in the western world among the diplomats of Europe and the New World. So when he went to work on the Suez crisis, he shared his prime minister's moral stance against the imperialistic military actions of Canada's two founding nations, and he placed himself between them and the United States. Of course some right-wing US newspapers would suggest that he was acting as an agent of Moscow. As usual, Pearson's object was peace. He had been around long enough and was a good enough analyst to know that the French and English and the Israelis could not hold onto the Suez Canal without getting into a deep war that would spread throughout Egypt and probably across its borders. He also knew that the war would crack NATO and the Commonwealth.

Pearson conceived the UN peacekeeping force and got the measure through the General Assembly in a 57-0 vote, the communist countries and the belligerents abstaining. No one was angry at him. He was a genuine hero of the United Nations. A year later he would win the Nobel Prize for peace. Aw shucks, he said. They loved him in Oslo. But he had to explain himself to some of the old mossbacks at home who liked to fly Union Jacks from their upper-storey windows. Even Howard Green, usually the most temperate man on the Conservative side, would say that Pearson had knifed Canada's best friends in the back. Green would eventually become foreign secretary and learn that there were people in the Commonwealth who would not automatically cheer white paratroopers descending into non-white countries.

Drifting into leadership

An Ottawa-born teenage boy named Paul Anka was proving that Lester Pearson was not the only Ontarian with an annoying voice who could win world-wide approval. In 1957 the scattered people of Algoma East returned Mike Pearson, but the people of Canada ousted the arrogant Liberals, including a lot of cabinet ministers who may have had notions of succeeding Uncle Louis. Uncle Louis, of course, had his eye on Pearson. A lot of people thought that Pearson had his eye on retirement, but they did not know him as well as he knew himself. He was still playing the role of the reluctant draftee until he somehow managed to roll over Paul Martin in the leadership race.

Then as if to prove his lack of skill as a parliamentarian, he took Pickersgill's ridiculous advice and suggested that Diefenbaker with his minority government hand the reins of power back to their rightful holders. Diefenbaker made every theatrical face he could for two hours, as Pearson sank in his chair. "He tore me to shreds," the leader of the opposition would later say. Then Diefenbaker called the 1958 election and won his huge majority. The scattered people of Algoma bucked the trend and returned Pearson. If they had not, he would probably have thought some more about going back to university and maybe finishing that book on the United Empire Loyalists. But he thought he saw a duty to his country, and he did not see any other party leaders around. Maryon Pearson would like to have gone back to campus life. With her usual dour quickness she said about the Diefenbaker sweep: "We've lost everything. We've even won our own constituency." She knew, one thinks, that the high spot of her husband's career had been reached a year or two earlier.

One wonders what she really thought of Walter Gordon. When the party wanted to persuade Pearson to enter politics, they followed an old tradition of making sure that he would not suffer financially. In 1948 Gordon arranged a comfortable annuity for his old friend, and had it made out in Maryon's name. Walter Gordon had known Pearson for a long time, and had always thought that the man needed a push, that he was not tough enough for partisan politics. Gordon was a money man from Toronto, and considered himself the éminence grise of the rebuilding Liberal party. If Cardinal Richelieu could have his *Père* Joseph, the future prime minister Pearson would have his *frère* Walter. They had known each other since the middle of the Depression, and they had done each other favours over the years. Gordon had an eye on first electing his friend, and then succeeding him. In the meantime, he would employ his skills as a rich businessman in streamlining the Liberal party. He would be at Pearson's ear, extolling Canadian nationalism and just a tad of anti-USAmericanism.

As the fifties ended and the sixties began, Mike Pearson knew that there was a prodigious job to be done, to bring good men and maybe even the odd woman into the party, to find cabinet material, and to prepare for Diefenbaker's inevitable self-destruction, to get the country back into the hands of Mackenzie King's outfit. Pearson had always liked team sports, and now he wanted a team around him. He saw Diefenbaker becoming a lonely man with long coattails, and fought down any temptations toward sympathy. When the Kennedy campaign proved that public relations and sheer image-building could get the shiny new Democratic party back in by a donkey-hair in 1961, the Liberals started borrowing techniques from the New Frontier. Gordon hired Lou Harris and his pollsters, and studied the election manual of Theodore White, *The Making of the President*. When the next election came along Gordon would try to top even the Yanks in one of their main tricks.

The USAmericans had a young president with what they called long hair. The golf-playing ex-general had been replaced by the touch-football dad with two little kids. Youth was to be served, and old conservatives put out to fairway. During the Kennedy years Pearson worked diplomatically to try to get the Liberal party more liberal. John Diefenbaker was left of his party, too, but his methods were different from quiet Mike's. Of course Pearson had to attack the government's performance and measures, and so he did, often contradicting himself in the process. Here they were, the last two leaders born in the nineteenth century, trying to oppose one another at the beginning of a decade that fancied itself very contemporary.

By the time that Diefenbaker called the June 1962 election, the country's financial problems were beginning to become visible except to people who never opened the business pages of their newspapers. A politician like John Diefenbaker would have been all over the prime minister, throwing lightning bolts and orchestrated tantrums. But quiet Mike lisped and mumbled and contradicted himself, calling for financial restraint and big spending on alternating days. The country had become disillusioned by the man who had won the 1958 landslide, but no one could see any light flashing off the leader of the opposition. Give us a candidate! suggested the populace. You can have Tweedledum or Tweedledee, replied the political cartoonists.

Some people like to remember that Pearson hauled down the record-setting Conservatives of 1958, making them lose 92 of the 208 seats they had held. He had doubled the Liberal share, sitting now at 99. But there were 50 seats that went to neither dum nor dee. Canada had entered an era of minority or coalition government. What is this, Italy? asked some old pols.

In a few years the situation would seem normal. If John Diefen-baker had not been able to shoot flames from his throat, the Tories would never have formed a government in the sixties.

Canada already had a foreign exchange problem and a 92.5-cent dollar. Now, with no majority government and no prom-ising opposition, it did not seem an attractive place to park one's money. Diefenbaker's dream of northern development was not affordable without foreign investment, and he was not a popular figure on Wall Street or Pennsylvania Avenue. Diefenbaker's nightmare of Quebec was in Pearson's hands. Pearson met with Diefenbaker's supposed Quebec lieutenant Leon Balcer, who assured the Liberal leader that Diefenbaker was not going to get his support in any interesting circumstance—*par exemple*, another election. Then the US magazines and politicos went to work, portraying old Dief as a stubborn nogoodnik. Pearson just needed one newsworthy debate to bring the avalanche down on his foe. He decided to go for nuclear weapons.

Anyone writing a chapter on Lester Pearson will want to spend more time on his diplomatic career than on his domes-tic politics.

It happened that a gaggle of Canadian members of Parlia-ment did a tour of Canadian NATO bases in Europe. One of them was Paul Hellyer, a forty-year-old veteran who was sup-posed to advise the opposition leader on military policy. He came back and told his boss that Canadian pilots were crying in their rye-and-ginger because they did not have nuclear rock-ets under their wings. But the Liberals have always been against nuclear weapons, said Pearson, and so have I. Nuclear weapons could get you, I mean your party, into power, said the little pitchfork guy on his shoulder. Pearson sat up all one night during the Christmas break, and meditated on nuclear weapons. In the morning he had come to the conclusion that Canada's NATO responsibilities had always included nuclear weapons. In his memoirs he points out that the uranium used for the US weapons was mined in Canada anyway. He would opt for keeping Canada's "promise" for now, and negotiating our way out of it later.

A young Winnipeg Liberal, Lloyd Axworthy, was terribly upset. He hated "to see a man renege on past principles." Pierre Trudeau, a Montreal lawyer who had been considering running as a Liberal, called Pearson the "unfrocked priest of peace." His friend Jean Marchand echoed his disappointment. The hawks in Pearson's party and the hawks in Diefenbaker's putative party were cheered. Both parties were splitting like atoms on the issue. All across the country young anti-nuke viewers were expectorating on their television screens when Pearson came on to explain his position. He had decided to take the gamble that he could bring down the House and win an election on Diefenbaker's anti-USAmericanism during Kennedy's Camelot.

So he managed to force Diefenbaker into a 1963 election, and the Liberals set about their version of the Kennedy hoopla. But their Kennedy was sixty-six years old and wore a bow tie. Instead of youth they had to sell stable, practical administration against Diefenbaker's fire and smoke. No wild cheers were forthcoming from the land. Walter Gordon and his chums decided to liven things up by borrowing the Kennedy team's famous promise of a "Hundred Days of Decision." They would make it even more exciting: "Sixty Days," they trumpeted. Wow.

Television followed the two old candidates around the country. Viewers were used to the Diefenbaker show, but now they saw a new Mike Pearson, not the even-handed professor, but a man who had learned to shout to be heard over the catcalls of the anti-nuke demonstrators that appeared in the crowd. Maybe he wasn't so old after all. The Canadian people gave him 4 more seats than they gave the Tories, but they were not about to give him a majority. Social Credit hung onto 20 seats in Quebec and the west gave up only 10 seats. The champagne could come out at last, but there was no chance of getting drunk on power.

Prime Minister Trouble

Okay, what about those "Sixty Days"? Not much happened for the first fifty. Then Walter Gordon brought in his first budget on June 13, 1963. It might as well have been a Friday. Gordon still thought that he was the life of the party; he had little time for his political advisers and lots for his equally nationalistic private consultants. He offered a few tax breaks to little guys, but he made a tactical mistake when he laid on heavy penalties for any transfer of Canadian shares to outsiders. This action would get him into trouble with USAmerican businessmen and with Canadians who wanted to sell out to them. It was as if Gordon had embraced the traditional Conservative position in the old tariff debate. The newspapers, especially those with some patriotic ink, approved cautiously. But the hard-headed, who knew that powerful people like dollars better than honour, were dismayed. Even Maryon Pearson told her husband that his old friend's budget would be a disaster. And, sad to say, it was. The stock market took a dump. Pearson's first-ever government was already gooey. Gordon had to go through a messy withdrawal of his punitive tax, and then offered his resignation. Mike suggested that he switch to some other ministry. Gordon still considered himself a financial genius, and balked. Pearson said, all right, stay on. Gordon's hopes of succeeding as Liberal leader were shot.

At this point the Conservatives could have harrumphed and defeated the government on a non-confidence vote, but (a) they remembered what happened to the Liberals in 1958, and

(b) they thought that the Canadian voters would be so sickened by the whole show that they might punish anyone who forced another election on them. So they decided to ride it out. It looked as if this cabinet would collapse like the Toronto Maple Leafs, anyway.

Pearson knew that he would not be able to take his minority government through four or five years, so he started to work on those twenty Quebec seats held by Réal Caouette, a character who looked like a bad guy in a Dick Tracy cartoon strip, but knew how to use his television show to urge his adherents to follow him into the flames.

In Quebec, Jean Lesage's Liberals had come to power in 1960, Jack Kennedy's year. Post-war Quebec was saying goodbye to Maria Chapdelaine. Television replaced the parish priest as the provider of a model for living. Lesage ordered a commission to investigate the archaic education system and work out ways to modernize it. The Quiet Revolution was on, and the relationship between Quebec and the rest of Canada was going to change, not just in political rhetoric and calls of ancient blood. Quebeckers would not be looking for a place in Canada but a place in the world. Mike Pearson's Liberal party had to find a way to show that Ottawa knew that. Pearson would not have to face Diefenbaker in Quebec; he would have to talk with Quebeckers in their language. But he did not speak French any better than Diefenbaker did. Maybe he could fix it so that prime ministers in the future would.

The job, he knew, was to create a new kind of union. He took a chance on a bright Montreal lawyer named Guy Favreau, bringing him into government in 1963, making him Minister of Citizenship and Immigration. In the following year he made him Minister of Justice and Attorney General. He made him the party's House leader and captain of the Quebec contingent.

By this time Favreau had been in politics for one year. But he was part of the "new guard" from Quebec. Across the country people began to notice that regeneration of the Liberals in Ottawa was to be identified with the hopeful modern young smart guys from Montreal.

As a diplomat Pearson had learned a lot about the symbolism that feeds national feelings. He decided to take another risk. In the 1960s there were a lot of countries in Africa getting new flags with no European images on them. In Canada there had been semi-comatose discussions of an independent flag since the nineteenth century. King George V had granted us our own coat of arms and the official colours red and white. Mackenzie King periodically raised the issue of a Canadian flag. But in 1963 the official flag of Canada was still the Union Jack, though the union in question had taken place overseas. Some people thought that the Red Ensign, with its Union Jack and multinational shield, was or could be Canada's emblem, especially as it was often seen waving above government properties.

Pearson knew that in the next few decades it would not be a good idea to fly a Union Jack over government offices in Quebec, and he wanted it to be remembered that the Liberals had brought in a new indigenous flag before Confederation started its second century. He recalled that Canadian troops had been unwelcome in Nasser's Egypt because of their British insignia. In 1961 he had announced that the flag was high among his priorities. In the election campaigns of 1962 and 1963 the flag was part of his platform. On St Patrick's Day of 1963 he announced in Parliament that Canada would have a new flag within two years. Diehard anglophiles and bigots made loud and rude noises. Pearson knew that a flag debate just might draw attention away from the scandals and failures that were dogging his outfit.

Pearson also went outside the House, trying out his flag idea in speeches here and there. Yahoos in the crowd would often shout aspersions on his patriotism. Pearson did not point out that he was the only Canadian prime minister since 1867 ever to have been in uniform at the front during a war, but he did mention that a lot of the brave soldiers he knew did not have names that came from any place in the union signified by the Union Jack. Pretty soon a postage stamp was issued—blue and white with three red maple leaves in the middle. Dozens of ridiculous editorials were printed in English-language newspapers and broadcast on radio and television. Then the debate entered the House of Commons, and lasted from June till December of 1964. Tommy Douglas, leader of the NDP, asked whether they could pass a pension bill rather than shouting about some cloth. As fall gave way to winter it was obvious that the flag was going to be accepted, but Diefenbaker and his fellows kept shouting that Pearson was dividing the country. Finally, Léon Balcer, Diefenbaker's neglected Quebec lieutenant, suggested cloture. Cloture was supposed to put an end to meaningless debate, and this time it did. The flag proposal flew, and by February 1965, so did the red Maple Leaf.

The prime minister then mentioned that he was interested in making "O Canada" the national anthem, but that he had some problems with the English lyrics. His advisers suggested that they put this question off for a while. I am thinking of patriating the Constitution, he said. Later, later, they advised.

So much for the visual; now what about words? The BNA Act and the Manitoba schools act had done something to protect the French language and its social implications, but since the late nineteenth century there had been a lot of provincial legislation passed to protect the English language and deter the spread of others, especially French. While Quebec politicians could reach prominence in Ottawa, at least while the Liberal party was in power, people who spoke French could not be as influential in the country's law courts or civil service. Lester Pearson, whose primary interest during his tenure was the making of a newly seen union, decided that we needed a big parliamentary commission to investigate the situation of the two languages and to make recommendations about improving it.

Thus the Laurendeau-Dunton Commission, or as it would be more often called, the Royal Commission on Bilingualism and Biculturalism, or as the tabloids had it, the Bi and Bi Commission, or as high-school comedians put it, the "by and by commission." It was appointed in 1963, and charged with asking three main questions: how much bilingualism was there in the federal government and civil service; how much are public and private organizations doing to promote national unity along bicultural lines; and how easily can Canadians find education in both languages? The commission would not report until 1969, but during six years of work, knuckle-draggers in English Canada, and especially in the west, began grunting that the Liberals were giving the country to those "Frenchmen," and trying to ram French down an innocent cowboy's throat. How were they going to yell "yippee kiy yay," in French?

Shadowy figures

Nineteen sixty-three and 1964 seemed to a lot of Canadians to be pretty good years, despite Pearson's problems with his Finance Minister. They had time to get all excited about symbols of national unity, and they were being primed to gush all over during the coming centennial celebrations. Pearson the diplomat should have been able to relax and soak up some late-life adulation. But Pearson the politician soon had to deal with the fact that his country had a lot of good-time crooks in it, and that the underworld had some valuable connections in high places. It did not help his dream of national unity that a lot of those crooks were operating in Quebec.

We were not dealing now with old-fashioned patronage scandals. The events of 1964 and 1965 seemed to have been scripted by some old B-movie hack specializing in black-and-white mob movies, and while nasty rumours swirled around Ottawa, Canadians began to sense that there might be some fecal smudges on their nice new national self-image. Consider the case, first, of a thug with the nifty name Lucien Rivard.

Rivard had graduated from burglary and assault to Mafia-operated gambling and then heroin-trafficking. When one of his mules was nabbed at the Mexico-US border with a car full of dope, he fingered Rivard, and the US attorney general fed the information to Canadian authorities, who arrested Rivard and dumped him into Bordeaux jail. The US wanted Rivard extradited, but the Mafia was not too happy about the idea of Rivard's coming to the US and answering questions about his organization. Mrs Rivard gathered $60,000 in two days and stuck it into a chequing account, where it would be ready if bail or a bribe should become available. Then several Liberal lawyers working the Rivard side made some connections with civil servants in the Immigration Department, and somehow the Mafia folks got the impression that bail had been purchased. Rivard thought that he was going to be able to skip the country and enjoy his foreign bank accounts. The US Mafia executives had other plans for Rivard's disappearance.

The Rivard story is long and serpentine, and would take pages and pages just to outline properly. The RCMP produced lots of pages and showed them to Guy Favreau, but Favreau was not in a mood to do anything bad to important Liberals he had known for years. He hinted to his prime minister that there was an investigation going on, but did not tell him, for instance, that Pearson's own parliamentary secretary, Guy Rouleau, was a prime suspect. Favreau locked the RCMP report in his desk and hoped for the best.

But an impatient RCMP officer, making the wild assumption that Liberals might be protecting each other's asses, dropped a hint to Erik Nielsen, the puritanical Conservative from the Northwest Territories. Nielsen jumped up in the House and started asking questions that Pearson and the rest of the cabinet—except for Favreau—had not heard. The prime minister was in a tough spot. First he squirmed, and then he headed to the prairies for a round of speeches and ribbon-cuttings. The tottering Liberals were forced to set up an enquiry under Justice Frédéric Dorion, and Guy Favreau was one of those people investigated. His hair turned white. He looked awful in press photographs.

While the Dorion enquiry was going on in the fall of 1964, Lucien Rivard asked the Bordeaux guards for permission to go out and water down the skating rink with his pal André Durocher. The guard looked at the thermometer and saw that the temperature was 40 degrees above zero. He looked at the rink and saw that it was already full of water. Why not? Rivard and Durocher used the hose to get over the wall and headed for the hills. Now he did not need bail, but this did not put a stop to the Dorion enquiry. When it was tabled, the Liberals had to face the fact that all Canada would see corruption in the party, from the PM's secretary on down. The US Mafia was as influential as the US Senate. Dorion did not call Guy Favreau a crook, but he sharply questioned his judgement. Favreau offered his resignation as Justice Minister, over the objections of some Quebec Liberals who wanted to keep the pipeline open. He resigned in June of 1965, and a month later reappeared as President of the Privy Council. But two years later he was dead.

Politics in Quebec are *different*.

In 1949 Louis St Laurent's government was concerned about

the communists in the Canadian Seamen's Union, so it imported a US ex-con named Hal Banks to come to Montreal and replace the union with the US-based Seafarers' International Union. The replacing would be done with lead pipes and late-night automobile drives. Banks loved playing the role of cigar-smoking thugmeister and friend of governments, claiming that he could buy one anytime he liked. After he had been in the country for five years, the RCMP started a dossier on him. They knew that several Liberals received campaign funds from the SIU, but they got Banks for conspiracy to commit assault. For some inexplicable reason, he was released on a mere $25,000 bail in that wonderful summer of 1964, and skipped the country. When a Canadian newspaperman found Banks smoking a cigar on a yacht in New York, the question of extradition arose. But the SIU was also a big supporter of the Democratic party, so he was allowed to stay in the US.

Erik Nielsen had something to say about Hal Banks, too.

Also in 1964, Paul Martin and some other Windsor-area politicians had gone on record as supporting the immigration of one Onofrio Minaudo, a local baker who had previously done business in Detroit and Sicily. Along the way he had picked up convictions for such peccadillos as armed robbery and murder. Eventually the New Democrats announced that they were going to ask some questions about the support that this Windsor baker was getting. The Conservatives were not raising this issue, because one of Minaudo's supporters was a Tory. Guy Favreau, then the Immigration Minister, had been told by the Ontario Provincial Police that they did not like Minaudo, but the question had slipped Favreau's mind. His successor deported the Mafia man, who later told a Toronto newspaperman that he had bought a few Canadian politicians. A year later Minaudo was found dead with a bullet in his heart.

Yvon Dupuis, a minister without portfolio, was found guilty

of accepting $10,000 for some help in obtaining a licence for a racetrack in 1961. Dupuis wriggled and committed forgery, but was finally ousted from Pearson's government in early 1965. He would get his conviction (one year or $5,000) overturned on a technicality, but now his Liberal friends shunned him for bringing the heat.

There were several other scandals involving criminals during these lively years. The newspapers and the opposition had spies in the civil service. The prime minister did his best to ignore the stories or create distance from them. He had national unity to take care of. But his Quebec cabinet ministers kept screwing up. Maybe they did not know that what passes for normal in Quebec politics can appear as scandalous on the national scene.

Perhaps Immigration Minister René Tremblay and privy councillor Maurice Lamontagne thought that they would be okay if they stayed away from mafia gunmen and union hoodlums. Tremblay purchased $4,000 worth of furniture, and Lamontagne purchased $7,000 worth from the Sefkind brothers, with amazingly easy terms at great savings. Wouldn't you like to be so lucky? When Tremblay had been in Lesage's provincial government, he had approved a million-dollar loan to the Sefkinds, who had a habit of going bankrupt and reappearing with a new business. What luck!

What a sordid little scandal. Diefenbaker loved this one. It gave him a chance to perform one of his greatest mime acts in the House. Tremblay and Lamontange joined three other ministers whose careers were shot, and Lester Pearson slumped in his chair, wishing he had a majority government. He looked in the mirror and saw a man who was getting old and a little fat. His hair was white and thin, and he had jowls with brown spots on them. He looked at the snow falling through the lights outside the Sauce Bottles.

Then he wrote a letter to John Diefenbaker, the moral watchdog. He told his adversary that he had just been glancing at a file about the Munsinger affair that had transpired during Dief's regime. Did you have any information you might want to add to it, he asked.

Diefenbaker did not, as far as we know, reply to Pearson's polite letter, but in the House there were no more Liberal scandals mentioned, until Diefenbaker forgot himself in the spring of 1966.

Gerding their loins

In the spring of 1964 the Greeks and Turks were waving automatic rifles at each other on Cyprus, and the UN decided to send peacekeepers. This was Pearson's business, and he got the Canadian contingent in the air to the Mediterranean even before gathering the parliamentary vote on the issue. President Johnson said I owe you one. Pearson was able to feel good for a day or two in 1964.

But it had been a rotten year for the government, and it did not look as if Diefenbaker was going to calm down or be replaced. The Walter Gordon half of the cabinet advised Mike to call another election for the fall of 1965. Once he had a majority he could put scandal-fighting and flag-waving behind him and get this country unified in time for the centenary.

So they hauled out all the tired election machinery and went at it again, the fifth national election in less than a decade. People jeered Pearson and Diefenbaker wherever they went. Millions of dollars were spent and thousands of pep-pills were consumed, and when the results were in, both leaders had been admonished again. The Liberals lost a percentage point and picked up two more seats. But they were a minority again. At last Walter Gordon asked whether he should leave the cabinet, and his old pal Mike said yes.

The late sixties are remembered as a volatile time of citizen protest around the world, often led by students and other young people, often against the US bombings of three countries in what used to be called Indochina. In Canada, peacemaker Pearson presided over less-violent reconsiderations of the power game. New universities and colleges for baby-boomers were rising from muddy fields, and being filled with teachers and students ready for "revolutionary" social change. "Underground" newspapers and small publishing houses announced the arrival of a wild new Canadian literature. As the centenary year approached, there was a hilarity of expectation in the air.

Quebec was hot. Nationalists in the province saw parallels between their revolt and the paving-stone students in Paris, the Viet Kinder in New York and the Black Power soldiers in Oakland. New Quebec writers portrayed an uprising against colonial power, culminating in two major texts of 1968—Michel Lalonde's angry poem "Speak White," and Pierre Vallières's best-selling book *Nègres blancs d'Amérique (White Niggers of America)*. Rhetoric in Quebec began to repeat the word "nation," and the political parties in the province vied with one another in their claims of nationalism. Terrorist cells played out their dreams of glory. The notion of two founding peoples (while allophones were pouring into all provinces) led to demands for special status. Ideas that came from Ottawa, no matter how progressive, were scorned as *patria potestas*.

Pearson felt squeezed in the old PM-squeezer. In the least-liberal parts of English-speaking Canada, he was portrayed as the man who was selling out to Quebec. Canada was not made of two founding nations—it was made of ten provinces, and

Quebec was just one province. Pearson's flag, his Bi and Bi commission, his "co-operative federalism" and his capitulation to Quebec on the Canada Pension Plan were not going to get him any votes in Alberta. The smarter minds in provincial politics noticed that concessions to Quebec would mean concessions to the other provinces. John A. Macdonald's centrist vision was becoming a nineteenth-century idea.

Of course the old story is this: the Liberal party cannot be the government of Canada unless it holds a lot of seats in Quebec. Canada has two provinces with big populations, and eight other provinces and a territory or two. Whenever there is a Liberal party in government there are a lot of important Quebec cabinet ministries. But Pearson's Quebeckers had been leaving government and trying to stay out of jail. He needed some smart Montrealers, fast. Three glittering magi on foam-flecked horses arrived with the 1965 election. They were Gérard Pelletier, Pierre Elliott Trudeau and Jean Marchand. They were called the "Three Wise Men" from the east, but it was not clear what star they might have been following. They were all three born right *after* the First World War, and they were all radical federalists, enemies of separatism but hopeful architects of a new kind of Canadian union and social justice.

John Diefenbaker had managed to get rid of some of Pearson's Montrealers, and he knew that there were lots of targetable pols left in the city, but there was that blackmail letter from Pearson to consider. Oh heck, he could not help himself. Early in 1966 he went after Guy Favreau's successor, Lucien Cardin, who had made the mistake of attacking Diefenbaker a few years earlier. Cardin had said something on a television show to suggest that the RCMP were keeping tabs on George Spencer, a Vancouver postal clerk who may have been talking to a minor Soviet agent. Diefenbaker shook his jowls and fulminated about Spencer's civil rights. Cardin, who was known for his short temper, shouted that Diefenbaker had reason to keep quiet about security matters: what about his cover-up of the "Monseignor case" when he was temporarily prime minister?

Oops. Diefenbaker had forgotten about the blackmail letter. Maybe he had forgotten about Gerda Munsinger. In all likelihood the parliamentary reporters had too, but it was not long till they were digging up the dirt, and their appetite for scandal was quickened. The Munsinger case was pretty goofy, and was taken seriously only because of the low drama that had played out over the famous British Profumo scandal, a story of spies, whores and cabinet ministers. Now the reporters listened avidly as Cardin gave a riotous press conference.

Gerda Munsinger was a whore who had lived in the interesting country of East Germany. Conservative storytellers circulated the notion that she had recently died. Liberal storytellers said that she had come to Canada and jumped into bed with as many Tory ministers as she could. But Toronto newspapers had the kind of reporters who can track Mafia guys to Sicily and union hoods to New York yachts. One of them found Gerda Munsinger in a West German bar, and came back with a swell interview. She said that she used to have lunch with debonair George Hees, and more serious meals with associate defence minister Pierre Sévigny in the good old days.

Of course a royal commission was set up, and the unsurprising news emerged that Gerda had been conducting her career in bars owned by the mob in Montreal. She had also fooled around with an officer in Soviet intelligence. All the right ingredients were in the bowl. The most damning information was not that she had had a continuous relationship with Pierre Sévigny, but that John Diefenbaker had known about it and neither told his cabinet nor fired Sévigny.

How long had the Liberals known about this? Oh, a year or two. They had gone fishing in RCMP files while the Conservatives were dropping their bombs. If it was so important to national security, why had they waited till now to bring it into the open? Oh, said Davie Fulton, Conservative Justice critic, Guy Favreau told me a while back that Cardin was going to mention Munsinger if we mentioned George Spencer.

Oh, Lord, said the Canadian voters, we elected these guys?

Mike Pearson was not much interested in scandals. He had some important legislation and a centenary to take care of. The Canada Pension Plan, with its concession to Quebec, was introduced in 1966. The Canada-US Automotive Products Agreement (Autopact) was signed in 1965, in an effort to assure businessmen that not only workers were going to be helped by Pearson's legislation. In December 1966, after a vote of 177–2, the Medical Care Act became law, though the government could not afford to implement it yet. "I regarded it as a major triumph," wrote Pearson in his memoirs, and then dropped the subject.

When Pearson decided that Saskatchewan's experiment with public health insurance could not be contained within its straight borders, he had taken up the issue as part of a Canadian democracy that Mackenzie King might have envisioned. The US power-mongers who had managed to get him elected must have wondered whether they had made a mistake, whether Mike might be a "pinko" after all. Profiteers in the US health business had campaigned against Red Saskatchewan, and now they had agents all over Ottawa and elsewhere, trying to alert Canadian Minutemen against this latest attack of the Bolsheviks. It did not work: medicare would come into effect in 1968, and become an important myth for nationalists who want to see essential differences between the North American democracies (the other being handguns).

Buy a hundred candles

Probably the most enduring memory-image of the Canadian centennial year is a very large ball. That was a "geodesic dome" as imagined by the radical old architect Buckminster Fuller. It was a centrepiece at Montreal's extravagant world exposition for 1967, and a kind of logo that appeared on brochures and postcards and billboards advertising "Man and his World." In keeping with the history of Canadian boosterism, it happened to be the US pavilion at the world's fair.

Outside the country, the big exposition was a Canadian event. In the province of Quebec it was generally considered to be another Montreal megaproject, following the subway called Métro, which opened in 1966, and preceding the expected summer Olympics of 1976.

Lester Pearson was not really a megaproject man. He wanted to leave a legacy of international peacekeeping and cooperation. He would oversee a centennial celebration that was whimsical and humorous rather than military and jingoistic. He oversaw the creation of the Company of Young Canadians, a domestic version of the Canadian University Service Overseas organization (which had been set up in 1961). In 1967 he listened to the vigorous advice of Maryon Pearson and the volatile Secretary of State, Judy LaMarsh, and created a Royal Commission on the Status of Women. Maryon had joined the Voice of Women, a national organization that criticized nuclear arms and promoted abortion reform, among other issues. Maryon Pearson was a spiritual and political descendent of Lady Aberdeen, who had helped found the National Council of Women more than seventy years earlier, and led her husband into the ruffled waters of gender politics.

Yes, 1967 was going to be a year in which Canada could congratulate itself for being a progressive democracy. The world's fair was in the heart of French Canada, and the country had never seen or heard so much bilingualism. *"Terre des hommes"* included room for women, of course—that's how the language works. Every community across the country was invited to plan a "centennial project," and to apply for federal funds to bring it off. Elementary school children had to march around singing a children's anthem that left an annoying scrap of melody in their parents' heads. It was understood to be a good sign that the most famous centennial project in Canada was not the erection of some statue but rather the bonfire of biffies as a Manitoba town celebrated its new sewage system by hauling together its outhouses and setting them aflame. A town in Alberta built a landing pad for extraterrestrial spaceships. In a small town in British Columbia a driver named Bomber Lacy painted portraits of all the Canadian prime ministers on his bus, with John A. Macdonald riding outside and up front.

Lester Pearson was looking more and more like a frumpy grandfather who just could not keep his lank hair combed. He wanted a nice centenary. Noise was all right if it was joyful noise. "Caa-naa-daa," he hummed as he walked from bathroom to bedroom. He knew that there were crazies and firebrands in Quebec, but he really hoped that bilingualism and Expo would keep things peaceful. He did not need Chartier and de Gaulle.

On May 18, 1966, the Spence Commission was conducting its hearings on the Munsinger affair, and in the House of Commons Labour Minister Jack Nicholson was standing up and trying to answer some question from the opposition while the usual rude comments were being directed his way. In the visitors' gallery a man named Paul Joseph Chartier asked his neighbour to save his seat while he went to the toilet. Chartier probably did have to go, because he was wearing a bomb, but his primary objective was to get the bomb primed. He was going to come back from the toilet and fling the bomb over the rail.

He never got back: there was a loud explosion in the toilet, the corridors were filled with smoke, and members of Parliament were united for once in their desire to reach the spring air outside. Chartier left a note that begins with proper parliamentary etiquette: "Mr Speaker, Gentlemen, I might as well give you a blast to wake you up. For one whole year I have thought of nothing but how to *exterminate* as many of you as possible. I knew I was to give my life for this." The words appear as centre-text for a large family painting by Greg Curnoe, one of the young painters who were getting hot around centenary time. In 1967 Curnoe would win the national giant birthday cake contest, with a mammoth confection flavoured with Canadian bacon and maple syrup.

That's the spirit.

Chartier seemed to come out of nowhere. Charles de Gaulle was equally demented but very methodical. He would deliver his bomb not from the visitors' gallery but from the balcony of Montreal's sentimental old city hall. His models were the Pope and Mussolini.

Lester Pearson, it was generally felt, had stayed on as prime minister so that he could be the genial host at Canada's big birthday party. During the celebration he welcomed sixty heads of state and government. He was all set to welcome French president Charles de Gaulle. The normal protocol was that the VIP would first land in Ottawa, and then tour Montreal or some other place. De Gaulle said that he was coming by ship, so he would land at Quebec. Rumours of trouble began to circulate around Ottawa. Countries around the world had grown used to his self-regarding antics, and he was not taken seriously in many capitals; but he was coming to a province in which nationalism and troublemaking were waiting for attention.

De Gaulle was seventy-six years old. He liked to wear military uniforms and be called General de Gaulle. Early in the

Second World War he had been made a temporary brigadier-general, and after he left France, the wartime French government had stripped him of the title. He led a conservative government with strong presidential powers, under a constitution he had insisted upon. In recent years he had been trying to reassert France's influence, calling for the desatelliting of the US and Soviet empires. Now he was in Canada to manage something similar for the French Canadians. He started gradually. Though he had landed at Wolfe's Cove, a shore rippled with historical significance, and though his ship was not flying the new Canadian flag, as it should have been, he finished his inaugural speech with three cheers: *"Vive le Canada! Vive le Québec! Vive la France!"*

Then the Union Nationale government of Daniel Johnson took over and tried to make people believe that the president was visiting Quebec province, with the Canadian centenary as a side-visit. There was a glorious motor cavalcade up what they call the north shore of the St Lawrence, with villagers encouraged to come out and wave every kind of flag but the Maple Leaf. By the time that de Gaulle arrived in Montreal, he was surrounded by separatists, many of them waving placards that suggested *Québec libre!* During his speech from the balcony he was full of himself; he declared that his motorcade from Quebec had reminded him of liberation day in Paris, August 1944. Then, as if he had commanded a tank division through massive resistance to get there, he bellowed: *"Vive Montréal! Vive le Québec! Vive le Québec libre!"* The separatists smiled.

The prime minister was ready to throw a fastball at a head. He saw the speech on television. He did not like to hear the separatist slogan spoken by a foreigner, but even less did he enjoy the comparison de Gaulle had made. Later, in the calm of memoir-writing he would write about the analogy he made comparing his procession on that day to his march into Paris during the liberation of 1944. That I found infuriating. That his entry into Montreal should be compared in any way, shape, or form with his entry into Paris following the Nazi occupation was entirely unacceptable. I grabbed a pencil and started to write a reply. (It is always good to get something down on paper that can be torn up later.) Then my phone began to ring.

Protests were pouring in from English-speaking Canada. The governor general wondered whether to quit overseeing the magnificent 120-guest dinner. Pearson, steam shooting from his ears, met in cabinet for three hours. They were not deciding what to do—they were composing a telegram. Pearson made sure that Canadians got to hear it, going on air that night. Among other things he pointed out that

> [T]he people of Canada are free. Every province of Canada is free. Canadians do not need to be liberated. Indeed, many thousands of Canadians gave their lives in two world wars in the liberation of France and other European countries.
>
> Canada will remain united and will reject any effort to destroy her unity.

General de Gaulle never made it to that big dinner. The city of Montreal did give him a farewell show, and Pearson was watching television again. He heard Montreal Mayor Jean Drapeau tell the French president that he was in a Canadian city. Pearson grabbed his pencil again and sent Drapeau a thank-you note. De Gaulle flew back to Paris. When he got there he was met by some worried-looking cabinet ministers, but after a meeting in a closed room at the airport, they all came out sharing a good laugh.

In Montreal the separatist advertisers were ordering de Gaulle posters.

Five months later Expo was over and the last two or three dry maple leaves were twitching on black stems. The red Maple Leaf flags were turning orange as they faded. Everyone knew that Mike Pearson was leaving politics. The Conservatives had finally knifed Diefenbaker and gone with the underwear man from the Maritimes. In December Pearson told his associates he was on his way home, and on April 23, the birthday he shared with the Immortal Bard, he exited without alarums or flourishes, simply came to the first day of the 1968 session and announced dissolution, thereby preventing any laudatory speeches.

On the last day of 1972, his funeral procession slogged through the snow at a cemetery in the Gatineau Hills north of Ottawa. There, under a black sky and a red-and-white Canadian flag, Lester Pearson was buried alongside his youthful diplomat friends, Hume Wrong and Norman Robertson.

In August of 1973 Queen Elizabeth came to Ottawa to attend the Commonwealth conference, and while there she presided at the official opening of the new Department of External Affairs building that stretches along the Ottawa River. Prime Minister Trudeau had insisted that it be known as the Lester B. Pearson Building. It does not have a softball field outside.

CHAPTER 21

Guns and Roses

------◆•◆•◆------

Pierre Elliot Trudeau 1968–79

IN 1978 PRIME MINISTER Trudeau asked all the other small-power countries in the United Nations not to allow testing of nuclear weapons or the platforms that carry them. In 1983 he allowed the USAmericans to test nuclear weapons in northern Canada. In 1984 he won the Albert Einstein peace prize. His favourite achievement was the new Canadian Constitution with a bill of rights that would decrease the government's control over the lives of individuals. But in 1970 he had sent armed federal troops into Montreal to grab dissident poets and throw them into jail. When the Tories pleaded with him to install wage and price controls he mocked the idea. A year later he installed wage and price controls.

He was like that.

Visit Pierre Trudeau's Canada—a land of contrasts.

The citizens of this country responded in kind. In 1968 the members of the press dropped their pens and cameras and clapped hands. Frenzied women of all ages, tears pouring down their faces, struggled past one another in an attempt to touch him, and went home with poster-size photographs of the new superstar. This was all called "charisma," and then "Trudeaumania." But in rural communities of the Canadian west, the term "Trudeau" became a word to spit out when a really bad insult was required—and so it remains today. Go to a small town in B.C., for instance; find an aging man with a fifties haircut, and ask him about Sir John Abbott. He won't know who you're talking about. Ask him about Trudeau. He'll spit.

Wise men from the east

When I lived in Montreal during those amazing years of 1967-71, my front window looked down upon a grubby little gas station with a name I had never seen before. Someone told me it was part of a chain owned by the Trudeaus. That had once been true. Pierre Trudeau's father, Jean-Charles Emile Trudeau, had left the farm and become a wealthy bourgeois, first as a lawyer and then as a businessman. During the Depression, Imperial Oil bought his gas stations and made him a millionaire. His son Joseph Phillippe Pierre Yves Elliott Trudeau was just entering his teenage years at the time. A year later "Charlie" died, and the son learned from his business associates how to build a fortune. Nine years later he would be admitted to the Quebec bar. In a family that had six or seven million dollars, he did not really have to reverse his father's progress and practise law. And he did not really have to look for a job. He decided to quit shaving and see the world.

He had been brought up by a Scottish-Canadian mother on a street with a Scottish name in Outremont. Why bother getting bogged down in Quebec? He would become a free spirit and a citizen of the world. He had shown his restiveness in various ways. During his schoolboy days at Jean de Brébeuf College he raised hell as only a rich kid can, and became an obnoxious nonconformist, but he also learned physical discipline, boxing, skiing, martial arts and diving, discovering how to be a tough and vain individual. Later he drove to his law classes at the University of Montreal on a Harley-Davidson, wearing an old German army helmet. It was a way to demonstrate his anti-conscription sentiments.

After the University of Montreal he spent some time at Harvard, and when the war ended, he sat in political science classes in Paris and at the London School of Economics, where he thought that he had become a socialist. He began to think about going back to Canada and finding some way to promote social justice. But first, there was a world to explore. He had lots of money; he could have hired a limousine and a company of beaters. But he got himself a backpack, and with a very shallow wad of dollars he set off, first through the occupied Germany of 1948, then through eastern Europe, and the Middle East. He went in costume, as he would for the whole of his life. In Palestine he wore a burnoose and no shoes. The Arabs thought he was a Haganah agent. The Israelis thought he was another dopey American kid.

He continued east, usually crossing borders illegally, his chin beard growing longer and sillier. He travelled through newly independent Pakistan into China, where he had to join some USAmericans escaping from the Red Chinese. He scooted across Burma into Viet Nam, where he had to join some French escaping from the Viet Minh. During all these trips he spent as little money as possible, took trains instead of planes, walked when he could, got into trouble for practising his high-school pranksterism where there were border guards instead of Latin masters. He saw wars conducted along lines of race and religion. He saw poor individuals oppressed by colonizers and industrialists. When he got back, finally, to Montreal, Duplessis was running Quebec, and Gérard Pelletier, brilliant son of the working class, was attacking Duplessis in the pages of *Le Devoir*. A hotshot named René Lévesque was in town briefly, between his stints as a war correspondent. He had covered the USAmericans in Europe, and would soon follow their troops to Korea. In the shabby town of Asbestos there was a long and virulent labour battle at the Canadian Johns-Manville mine. A stocky man with thick hair was championing the miners. His name was Jean Marchand.

On his first day back in Montreal, Trudeau phoned Pelletier and asked him to take him along to Asbestos. Louis St Laurent did not know it yet, but the histories of the Liberal party and of Canadian-Quebec politics were about to be shaped by asbestos, a mineral used in defence against fire, a fibre that makes death miserable.

The strike had started, illegally, on Valentine's Day of 1949, and would go on for over four months. Jean Marchand, graduate of Laval and intellectual leader of the 5,000 miners, had a lot of enemies—the US owners of the majority of asbestos mines in the province, the English-speaking managers and the Duplessis government, which sent policemen to act as strikebreakers, blatantly organizing them in company offices. Duplessis had legislated against the unions before; now Jean Marchand, usually called "fiery," was working to gather unified labour solidarity across the province, and lining up the Church against Duplessis for a change.

For Jean Marchand the massive strike was a labour issue that would have to be fought in every political room he could gain access to. He was turning into the smartest organizer the workers could have lucked onto. Compared to him, Hal Banks was a foreign goon with a narrow ambition. For Gérard Pelletier, the strike was a highly symbolic confrontation of the ordinary Quebecker and the fat foreign financier. For Pierre Trudeau, this was a civil rights case like those he had seen in Europe and Asia—the individual was being turned into a beast to send into the huge pits that were gobbling countryside and town's edge.

These three men recognized their differences and the skills they could join to assail their common enemies. They were thirty years old, full of energy and wise as all get-out. Trudeau and Pelletier were intellectuals, of course, one a dilettantish rich boy, the other a worker's son from a big family. They got together with some more anti-Duplessis thinkers and founded the famous philosophical-political magazine *Cité libre*, which would outlast *Le chef* and continue until Pelletier and Trudeau and Marchand entered politics. *Cité libre* is sometimes characterized as a leftist journal. It might better be called humanist, perhaps progressive. Trudeau had, in Paris, come to think of himself as a "personalist," as proposed by the French thinker Emmanuel Mounier and his magazine *Esprit*. In his thin *Memoirs* Trudeau would remember "a philosophy that reconciles the individual and society. The person . . . is the individual enriched with a social conscience, integrated into the life of the communities around him and the economic context of his time, both of which must in turn give persons the means to exercise their freedom of choice." It was a moral philosophy that found room for the rich man. Totalitarianism could be attacked from several angles. Pierre Vallières would meet Pierre Trudeau in the pages of *Cité libre*.

The magazine was in favour of something "universal" in mankind; it was against totalitarian machines, and it was also against the nationalist sentiments that Duplessis had exploited to get his machine working. In his articles Trudeau did not spare the Quebec Liberals, damning them for opportunism, seeming to find honest principles in no party but the NDP, which tried valiantly to get a foothold in old New France.

Trudeau used his legal training here and there. Once in a

while he would do something for the unions. For a year he worked in Ottawa, sorting through paragraphs for the Privy Council. After Duplessis died in 1959 and Lesage's "Quiet Revolution" revved its engines in 1960, Trudeau taught constitutional law at the University of Montreal. It was a place to which he could go to work in his favoured sandals and turtleneck sweaters. In 1962 the Liberals, looking for some Quebec minds to put up against Diefenbaker, hinted and winked, but the Three Wise Men from the east did not see a star.

Nineteen sixty-five was different. The "Quiet Revolution" was showing signs of embracing a respectable separatism as opposed to the Union Nationale's brand. René Lévesque had moved from Radio-Canada to Lesage, and was growing impatient. Some of Lester Pearson's Quebec guys had honey all over their fingers and wrists. Pearson's men begged Jean Marchand to come into federal politics. He said that he would come if he could bring the other two magi. The Pearson people needed Marchand, so they agreed, and began looking for a safe English-speaking riding for this Pierre Elliott somebody who had decided at age fifteen that his spoken French would be *Parisien* from then on. The francophone papers that opposed him called him "Elliott-Trudeau." The candidate must have turned on the charisma for the people of Mt Royal—he would be their MP for the next two decades. For now he would park his sandals under one of the backbenches, and loll like a schoolboy planning a prank. The honourable member for Algoma East noticed his new parliamentary secretary's Mercedes sports car in the parking lot, and wondered what the world was coming to.

The intellectual Trudeau had decided to enter politics as a Liberal because he needed a power base to fight the Quebec nationalism in which he had always seen reactionary politics and base racial emotions. This notwithstanding the recent separatist voices that were trying to combine Marxism and ethnic fantasy. Paul Chamberland, for example, a man twenty years Trudeau's junior, and a poet who had started the hot little magazine *parti pris*, was, around 1964, writing propaganda poems for the self-defined revolutionaries in the FLQ. These poems employed the suspect old calls to the blood:

> your cause is our own and so what
> if today on the English gibbet
> you swing and so what
> if it's our turn tomorrow
>
> the forge is set up in our veins
> the veins of a people
> the enormous land takes breath and shapes in her flesh
> anvil and beetle cordite and gun
> her face takes form in the bomb's opening light
>

Etc. (Translation by Francis Sparshott).

Of course there was no gibbet for the nationalists, and if there had been it would not have been an English one, but in the romance of the revolution in the sixties there was a lot of room for such images by the poets. Trudeau read them, and filed their names. In April 1967, Pierre Trudeau was made Minister of Justice and put in charge of constitutional negotiations with the provinces, including the new Union Nationale government of Daniel Johnson.

Suddenly the curious man who had been in politics for two years was a star. His flamboyant dress and expensive sporty automobile had made for snappy photographs in the newspapers, and once in a while people in British Columbia or Manitoba would wonder: who is this guy? How could such a person make it to the prime minister's circle so fast? There was some confusion about whether he was a politician or a media star. This was the sixties, after all: instant celebrities were appearing as never before. The Beatles could not play extraordinary music, but they were more popular in some circles than Jesus. Hormonal girls all over the globe were vibrating and clutching their faces, and the phenomenon was called "Beatlemania." The most often quoted poet in the world was boxing's heavyweight champion Muhammed Ali, who would have his title yanked in 1967 for refusing to go to Viet Nam and kill the locals. The newspapers and magazines and television stations of the world had learned to become part of the stars' publicity machine. Stars appeared in the firmament awfully quickly. John Diefenbaker, who had had to swallow defeat after defeat before slipping past his own party into the PM's chair, was not happy with Trudeau's nonconformist rise in the Commons. When the new Justice Minister took his front bench, the Chief noted that he had changed his cravat for a tie, but complained that it was too gaudy.

What is this? asked the populace. We are so used to old fuddy-duddies like C.D. Howe. What the heck is blowin' in the wind?

The future

Canada was enjoying its birthday in 1967, and Lester Pearson was coasting. Everyone knew that he just wanted to be around for the party, and it was time to start thinking about a new leader. The old battle between long-time loyalty and party survival would be inevitable. There were some long-time cabinet ministers around, but they had been cabinet ministers during all those failures to catch a majority in the House. These were the sixties—maybe the party needed to cash in on the theme of youth that had been declared by the media. Not dope-smoking, guitar-playing, sit-in youth, but maybe a man who was not afraid to let his hair grow a little and wear a fresh flower (well, not behind his ear, but) in his lapel every morning. Trudeau said that he was born in 1921 rather than 1919.

Not only did Trudeau like to wear a costume for every occasion, but he had the knack for making memorable phrases, some of them X-rated. As Justice Minister he said "The state has no business in the bedrooms of the nation." In his work on the divorce bill and rewriting of the Criminal Code, he could exercise his opinion that the individual should be left alone as much as possible in his moral life. The newspapers of the western world were proclaiming a "sexual revolution," which meant largely that young people would not have to go through so many contortions to get laid, but women were still making the coffee.

Through most of 1967 Trudeau could be seen slowly changing his position on the Constitution, first saying that it should just be respected, then in the fall agreeing that an amending formula should be sought in consultation among Ottawa and the provinces. Then in December, while snow drifted against the dark buildings left at the Expo site, he introduced two innovative pieces of legislation, news that could make or break his political future. On December 4 he brought in the divorce bill that would mean that "marriage breakdown" could be grounds —couples would not have to hire private detectives to photograph staged adulteries any more. On December 21 a wide criminal law revision was proposed. It would decriminalize voluntary sodomy between consenting adults in private, make highly regulated therapeutic abortion possible, legalize lotteries for charities, introduce breathalyzer tests for squiffy drivers and bring in tame gun-control regulations.

What an interesting gamble! On the one hand, there might be enough "concerned parents" in the land to support the blusterings of old-time Conservatives in House debates. For a certainty, there would be rumours in the small-town beer parlours and redeemed-blood-of-the-lamb churches of the western prairies that this guy TROO-dough, or Troo-DOUGH or however you say it was a frenchie commie sodomite antichrist. On the other hand, the buildup to the centenary had been persuading the Canadian people that they were grown up, an adult country that should not be embarrassed by antiquated bumpkin laws in a mod world. We were tired of going across the line for fun.

Was Pierre Trudeau running for the Liberal leadership? Did he know what he was doing? Was he setting a trap for the Conservatives, or was he the humanist idealist he proclaimed himself to be? What about his amazing candour (except about his age)? He was getting famous for using the most colourful and crude anatomical words in his quick answers to challenges by the francophone press.

Mike Pearson was leaning toward Trudeau. He called Trudeau and Jean Marchand into his office and explained that he thought the Liberal party had by now decided to alternate leadership between the founding peoples. Mike had brought in Trudeau in order to get Marchand, now Minister of Citizenship and Immigration. He still wanted Marchand, because of his amazing skill at organizing groups of people. Marchand said that his English was not good enough, and his wife would not put up with a PM for a husband. Trudeau made one of his patented shrugs and pretended his usual reluctance.

Pearson forced the issue, announcing the leadership race for April 1968. Pretty soon the cameras and bright lights were following Trudeau everywhere, jostling with Trudeaumaniacal women to get close enough for a good shot of that handsome bony face and that Roman-senate hair. Trudeau's backers in the party, especially Marc Lalonde and Gordon Gibson, became as expert as any Yippie in acquiring air time. In January Trudeau was sent to the provincial capitals to talk up the coming federal-provincial conference. Then at the end of the month he stole the show at the Quebec Liberal convention. Then at the federal-provincial conference he faced down the challenge of Daniel Johnson, exhibiting a tough and articulate pro-federalism that gathered in votes all over anglophone Canada. Maybe this guy was not wearing devil's horns; maybe he was some sort of hip saviour. On Valentine's Day Trudeau announced his candidature.

During the campaign he appeared cool. He knew how to talk in front of TV cameras. He had a terrific organization, and he had the papers. It took him four ballots to win over Robert Winters and Paul Hellyer and the handsome young John Turner. On April 19 he carried two suitcases into 24 Sussex Drive, and then he called an election for June 25.

You should try to remember what kind of year 1968 was. The Vietnamese launched their Tet Offensive, and thousands of US soldiers came home in body bags. American and Canadian television was full of explosions and bodies in the jungle. Martin Luther King Jr. was shot to death. Bobby Kennedy was shot to death. Bobby Hutton, the Black Panther leader, was shot to death. Black students in the US South were shot to death. There were riots at US universities. There were flames in US cities. L.B. Johnson announced that he would not run for re-election. In Paris the students threw paving stones at the machine guns, and almost brought down General de Gaulle. In Montreal the FLQ was trying to get some time in the news, try-ing to look as dangerous as the Red Brigades and the Viet Cong and the Black Panthers.

In the 1968 campaign in Canada, Pierre Trudeau did not make blustery promises; he spoke like a cool professor or a Gallic Kennedy, and he told Canadians that good government was *their* job. But the women came running for a kiss, and the

TV reporters gushed. His fans called him by his initials, and often one saw photographs of large-breasted women wearing shirts on which could be read the words "PET or bust." This was not so much a campaign as it was a love-in. The Conservatives put up Robert Stanfield the underwear man. He looked like steady old Maritime Gothic. He looked a little like a nineteenth-century Tory in a twentieth-century suit, and he spoke slowly. In 1968 it mattered what you looked like and how long it took you to think before you said anything.

Trudeau did not make a lot of promises during the campaign, but he made it clear that he was opposed to the Quebec nationalists. The Quebec government was trying to get French-speaking countries to pretend that Quebec was a country, too. Trudeau said that Canada would speak with one voice overseas, and warned France to quit fooling around. The nationalists in Quebec got really mad. When Trudeau compared the FLQ bomb boys to Bobby Kennedy's killer, the cry went up in the streets: *"Trudeau au poteau!"* It was difficult to miss the significance of that image—a punishment meted out to heretics in the middle ages. In Quebec, as far as the new prime minister was concerned, it was his modernity against festering out-of-date sentiments.

A lot of festering out-of-date sentiments are displayed in the annual St Jean Baptiste Day parade in Montreal. The marching bands wear medieval costumes, complete with feathers, and civilians amble along in clothes that are normally seen in genre paintings of Old Quebec. In 1968, some of Trudeau's advisers and a lot of his loudest enemies warned him not to sit in the reviewing stand for the St John Baptiste Society parade. Bobby Kennedy's name came up again. But election day was June 25, and St Jean Baptiste Day was June 24. Pierre Trudeau showed up at LaFontaine Park on East Sherbrooke Street, dressed better than anyone else, and shared the reviewing stand with

Mayor Jean Drapeau, Premier Daniel Johnson, the archbishop of Montreal, and a gaggle of local bigwigs.

Trudeau was probably going to win the election anyway, but after this day Robert Stanfield would not have a chance. This day Trudeau had another politician to face. This was Pierre Bourgault, leader of the Rassemblement pour l'indépendance nationale. Bourgault had been invited to the reviewing stand, but he refused, shouting that the prime minister of Canada had no business there and that loyal Quebeckers should follow him into the streets. They did, and so did the police, who grabbed Bourgault and hauled him away. This action led to traditional Quebec politics, and pretty soon the pop bottles were flying through the air, many of them in the prime minister's direction.

Some of the pop bottles had gasoline in them, and the gasoline caught fire, and long-haired fellows naturally threw the flaming bottles away. One or two of them ignited a parked police car. The police had horses, too, and these horses made their white-eyed way among the long hairs, some of whom were swinging baseball bats at them. The band played on. Here and there one could see a small circle of policemen swinging sticks at something on the ground, and occasionally a paddywagon left the scene. This was a very loud holiday.

The mayor and the archbishop and the premier had skedaddled. The reviewing stand was covered with overturned chairs and broken glass. There was one human figure there, standing at the front rail. This was the prime minister, alternately waving, blowing kisses, and when the bottles whizzed by his head, protecting his face. After a while the police set up a little human fence, and the other dignitaries rejoined Trudeau, their feet crunching glass.

All this was on television. The next day the Liberal party, including 56 Quebec members, took 155 of Parliament's 264 seats.

Trudeau had the majority that Lester Pearson wanted, while in Quebec all the political parties were fumbling around, except for the new Parti Québécois, which was trying to gather up all the separatist cults.

Having come into power as the tough guy with a flower in his lapel, he took advantage of his popularity and majority to start remaking the governing process. He told the people that democracy could not wait for a dithering Commons and Senate or a vague civil service; democracy was in the hands of a populace that had to take responsibility for change. "The power of both the federal government and the provincial governments should be restrained in favour of the Canadian citizen," the Justice Minister had said in 1967. Now he built his own structure, which meant what some people called a presidential system; the cabinet was asked to form committees and come up with suggestions, while the Prime Minister's Office, which used to have a staff of thirty unelected people, would soon have three times that number. Trudeau was not going to have trouble with his ministers the way his two predecessors had. He had television, and Canadians loved watching television—they thought that they could watch their government on television. There were still muddy-shoed grumblers out west who suspected that their sudden prime minister was some kind of socialist French-Canadian homo, but in 1968 and 1969 they were inundated by Trudeaumania.

In 1969 Trudeau's government passed the Official Languages Act, and progressive parents outside Quebec started sending their kids to French-immersion schools. The act made both French and English usable in all federal services anywhere in Canada and throughout the National Capital Region. The city of Hull, Quebec, would grow in importance during the next few decades. The federal government would put gentle pressure on the provinces to grant educational rights to their

French-speaking populations. An official languages commission was invented, Keith Spicer the first commissioner.

Of course there were yahoos in Alberta and British Columbia who started putting English-only bumper stickers on their cars: "Bilingual today—French tomorrow!" The yahoo phone-in radio shows welcomed callers (and announcers) who complained that those easterners were trying to force French down the throat of every farmer in western Canada. It was impossible to explain two things to these people: western farms are not federal institutions, and a lot of people are really glad that they can read in two languages. There were unhappy people in Quebec, too. How could the secessionists complain about English Canada's linguistic arrogance now? Maybe it was time to start thinking about language laws in Quebec.

Quebec cabinet ministers and prime ministers have always had to worry about being called *vendu*. Trudeau got called a lot of names, and did his own name-calling in return. But his vision was a Canada that included Quebec, and a Quebecker who was a first-class Canadian. The 1968 campaign slogan had advocated a "Just Society." He called separatism a hoax and he asked Canadians to grow up. He was willing to make enemies as long as he could consider the enemies to be insufficiently educated and disciplined.

Remember that this first Trudeau government reigned during the end of the sixties and beginning of the seventies, when the amateur political violence that occurred on the streets of western Europe had appeared in North America. Trudeau let it be known that he was more interested in Canada than in the rest of the world. He saw the devastation of downtown Montreal when the police went on a one-day strike. He decided to slenderize Canada's representation abroad, cutting the overseas military and the diplomatic corps, and hinting that the UN should look for peacekeepers elsewhere. Lester Pearson did not say a word.

Yes, all this time the bombs were going off in Montreal. Bombs were becoming normal. Liberal and federal buildings were the favourite targets. Poets and politicians sometimes romanticized the secret bombers. Pierre Vallières, who had once edited *Cité libre*, wrote *White Niggers of America* while in prison in New York, then spent a few years in prison in Quebec. He advised Quebec rebels to fight with "placards, then with stones, Molotov cocktails, dynamite, revolvers and machine-guns." There was a lot of revolution-envy in Montreal.

Vallières got out on bail in the summer of 1970, and immediately started predicting FLQ bombs. Some Canadians thought of the FLQ as a comic opera bunch, as PLO wannabees. Others were genuinely frightened of them, especially if they had rich houses in the hills of Westmount. No one knows which way Pierre Trudeau leaned, or what inside information he had, but in public he took the FLQ seriously. There were a lot of FLQ terrorists in jail.

By 1970 the big international terrorist news was usually about hijacked passenger jets or ransom kidnappings of prominent citizens. On October 5, 1970, Canada got its first big terrorist kidnapping. Four young guys with handguns hauled British trade commissioner James Cross from his nice Westmount home and demanded half a million dollars and the release of twenty-three FLQ prisoners. Liberal Quebec Premier Bourassa responded to the crisis by travelling to New York for a round of meetings, leaving his Justice Minister, Jérome Choquette, to take care of things. In Ottawa, Trudeau designated Foreign Minister Mitchell Sharp to look after the Cross business. Both governments absolutely refused to pay the money or release the prisoners. Choquette almost gave in, but after a few telephone calls from Ottawa, reduced his offer to a plane ride to Cuba for the kidnappers. Mitchell Sharp gave permission for a broadcast of the kidnappers' manifesto over the radio. He thought that it was so wildly exaggerated in its complaints that any rational listener would turn against the FLQ. The manifesto ranged all over Quebec history and international politics, and spent a lot of its time insulting Trudeau. It kept calling him a fairy.

Trudeau was browned off at Sharpe for allowing the manifesto, and in his statement to the press announced that he was no chickenshit Latin American president—he would not give in to any demands. He would, though, keep a discussion going.

Then on October 10 another cell of the FLQ grabbed Pierre Laporte. Laporte was Quebec Labour Minister, and deputy premier. This was a different kind of kidnapping. James Cross was a foreigner. His kidnappers were dumb enough to think that grabbing an Englishman would really upset English-speaking Canada. But Pierre Laporte was a former journalist, just like Trudeau and Lévesque and Pelletier and Vallières. These people had known each other all their adult lives. René Lévesque, bless his heart, remained quiet through this whole scenario. Trudeau decided that it was time for a showdown. There were a lot of Montreal policemen looking for the kidnappers, but a person should not bet his life on the Montreal police.

Bourassa was back from New York. He surrounded himself with bodyguards in a suite high atop a downtown hotel. Ottawa is a short drive from Montreal. The city was suddenly filled with young men in combat outfits, carrying machine guns. This was a strange sight for Canadians—young men with machine guns belonged in Europe or whatever country USAmerican troops were currently occupying. There were many politicos who were affronted by machine guns in the houses of Parliament. The peaceful towers had to be militarized because some hoodlums had snatched Trudeau's friend?

But the newspapers were doing their best to spread panic through the land. Newspapers do like violence and confrontation, and for them it was wonderful to be able to publish pictures of helmeted soldiers in doorways. There was one CBC reporter, however, who managed to corner the prime minister and ask him whether it was really necessarily to have guns in the streets. Trudeau, clearly agitated, responded with one of his classic retorts: "Well, there's a lot of bleeding hearts around that just don't like to see people with helmets and guns. All I can say is: go ahead and bleed." When he was asked how far he was prepared to go in this unprecedented situation he said, "Just watch me!"

Guitars twanged in the sky. There was going to be a showdown in the box canyon. Far before dawn on October 16, someone awakened Roland Michener, the governor general. Michener was used to getting up early for his morning run, but now he was asked to sign an order for the War Measures Act. Canada's at war? Trudeau called it an "apprehended insurrection," the last phrase of the act's definition. Now the Montreal and Quebec police could bust down doors and arrest anyone who smelled suspicious. Four hundred Quebeckers wound up in jail, some for three weeks. These people included hard-line separatists and poets. Suspicious books and recordings were stripped from the stores. The streets of Montreal were *dangerous*. There were nineteen-year-olds with automatic weapons at intersections. One day in October I was walking toward Montreal's city hall to pay a parking ticket, wearing my usual stupid clothes and carrying an old briefcase. Businessmen walked out of their way to avoid me.

All across Canada there were newspapers and politicians trying to cash in on the War Measures Act. Across the nation policemen could vent their frustrations on people who bugged them. Vancouver's peculiar Mayor Tom Campbell tried to use it to get rid of his terrible hippie problem. The Vancouver *Sun* printed an editorial suggesting that the kidnappings were just part of Quebec's troublemaking, and when the affair was over, printed another editorial asking what Trudeau was hiding.

Rumours spread that there was a huge FLQ offensive in the works, that there were ammunition caches all over the place. There was supposed to be a second conspiracy—a cabal of important citizens that was preparing to oust Bourassa and set up a provisional government. Meanwhile, the insurrection seemed to have been overly well apprehended. There was one military casualty. Near Ottawa a young soldier accidentally shot himself while jumping out of an army truck.

Even while the newspapers were spreading panic, a lot of citizens wondered whether Trudeau had political reasons for escalating the affair. Or did he know something dire? In Montreal, people such as I just went about our business, more nervous about teenage assault troops than about revolutionary cells. There was more excitement in the papers and on television than on Sherbrooke Street. It did not look as if the hockey season was going to be postponed.

On October 18, Pierre Laporte's body was discovered in the trunk of a ditched Chevrolet. Now the newspapers were filled with lurid photographs, and Pierre Trudeau's Canada was pretty well united. James Cross, under the instructions of his shaggy young captors, began sending letters pleading for his life.

Fall turned into winter. On December 4, the RCMP nabbed some of Cross's kidnappers, and soldiers surrounded the apartment where the rest were living their tiresome drama. A few days later James Cross was flying to London, and his kidnappers were flying to Cuba. Just after Christmas the RCMP hauled Laporte's kidnappers out of a hole in the ground on a south shore farm.

Trudeau had faced up to the extreme separatist threat that

he had been predicting, and most of the country seemed to support his actions. The Quebec Liberal party did not look so good. The young Parti Québécois was staggering a little.

The bloom slips off the rose

Trudeau's first mandate was half over. He had downed the separatists, he thought. Now it was time to get the Constitution going. Despite all his efforts to concentrate powers in the Prime Minister's Office, he was living in a Confederation; there would be no presidential patriation of the Charter; the provinces had to be consulted. And there were some new premiers to face—Conservative Bill Davis in Ontario, NDPer Allan Blakeney in Saskatchewan and Conservative Peter Lougheed in Alberta. They were all flush with victory over old guards. How could a bachelor prince handle this ambitious family? It was time to get married.

In March of 1971 Pierre Trudeau was fifty-one years old. Margaret Sinclair, daughter of a rich west coast Liberal, was going on twenty-three. On March 4 they got married in Vancouver. Canadians, who had started to get used to a flamboyant bachelor as their leader, were taken by surprise. Mackenzie King never did anything like this. They were also a little titillated by the Harlequin Romance aspect of the story—rich exotic prince snags pretty girl from the provinces. Margaret Trudeau was the first erotic figure ever to take up the job formerly held by Olive Diefenbaker and Maryon Pearson. The newspapers went wild again, portraying the lady as a flower-child revolutionary.

Well, in high school Margaret Sinclair had been a teenage model. She went to Simon Fraser University during its first years, when the school had a reputation for nonconformist politics and pedagogy. There she seemed to have studied some journalistic satire of sixties youth and missed the irony. She stuck a flower in her hair and ate organic lunches and mind-altering substances. Later she would tell a journalist that her philosophy had been shaped by "the English Romantic poet Robert Blake." I showed the interview to my friend the SFU Romantics professor, and he grimaced handsomely.

The romance and marriage and breakup of the Trudeaus has been told over and over. No Canadian prime minister has had so many crackpot little books written about him, and no prime minister's wife has so often been photographed—at first in costume with her costumed husband, later gyrating at mod-ish discotheques and performing as a groupie with teenagers' music heroes. In the early seventies she charmed the parlia-mentary journalists, bore three male children, and worked on two of her husband's campaigns. Those rednecks in cow coun-try allowed as to how maybe Trudeau was not a hundred per-cent limp-wristed. She went skiing with Pierre and made charmingly undiplomatic remarks when meeting foreign heads of state. Occasionally she did something ditzy, such as standing up and singing at a state dinner, but she was an asset.

What the country did not see was a severe clash in personal-ities. Both Trudeaus were headstrong and sartorially dramatic, but they were very different in a way that did not depend on the big gap in their ages. Margaret was a butterfly who was attracted by fads, and she never questioned the idea of a "lifestyle," especially the fashionably nonconformist one. Pierre was frugal and disciplined, and while he kept asking his wife what the young people thought about, he still used one tiny lit-tle towel after his morning swim.

With the victory over the FLQ and a wife who was far better looking than Jacqueline Kennedy, Trudeau should have had no trouble in his second election, especially as the Conservatives were still pushing Maritime Gothic. Canada had become the second nation, after France, to recognize the government that had run China for two decades. Canadian envoys were travelling the Pacific Rim, informing Asian and Australian business people that we were a Pacific nation. When the USAmericans started trouble with their ships in Canada's Arctic waters, the government declared a twelve-mile sea zone.

Domestically, the Liberals kept spending money on social programs. Equalization moves had a couple billion dollars delivered from the rich provinces to the "have nots." The youth uprising in the sixties had led to a program called Opportunities for Youth, and growing unemployment led to a program called Local Initiatives. Participatory democracy resulted in lots of nifty initials. In Vancouver we started an anti-establishment softball organization called the Kozmik League, and got a federal grant for equipment. I don't remember whether it was an OFY or a LIP.

But there was another new word, coined to refer to this odd period of simultaneous inflation and unemployment: stagflation. Trudeau had attended the London School of Economics for a semester, but he was not a whiz at economics. It looked as if there was a lot of money to be made in Canada, but an awful lot of it was being made by US corporations, and a lot of federal income was heading south as well. Still, the Grits decided to approach the 1972 election the way Pearson's crowd did all theirs. They came up with this slogan: "The land is strong." They suffered Pearson's usual fate. Once again Canada had a minority government. The Liberals got 109 seats to 107 for the Tories, which meant that if they wanted to carry on they would have to pay attention to David Lewis's NDP, which had 31 seats.

Cannon to the left, cannon to the right

Surprise, surprise, Quebec remained a problem. Trudeau had thought that his 1971 constitutional conference in Victoria would clear the way for superseding the BNA Act, but Premier Bourassa scuttled it with some help from his new friends, the other premiers. Then Quebec brought down its own immigration policies along language lines. Trudeau sort of called Bourassa a racist. Bourassa responded by bringing down a language bill, for the first time legally restricting English in his province. People in Montreal were wearing T-shirts with pictures of the FLQ terrorists on them.

Then Richard Nixon slapped a big tariff along the undefended border, and Canadians lost another 100,000 jobs, bringing the jobless total to 700,000. Not all of them could play softball or design neighbourhood theatricals. When 1973 arrived, so did the international oil crisis, and now Alberta became the problem province. Lougheed and his Energy Minister were called the "blue-eyed sheiks," and when the federal authorities began to insist that the nation should stick together to recover from the OPEC attack, people in Alberta started sporting bumper stickers that suggested "Let the eastern bastards freeze in the dark."

Pierre Trudeau had lost his euphoric dreams about national unity. Reporters and photographers noticed that he was now wearing his hair short and appearing in front of the cameras in expensive dark business suits, complete with shoes.

Who knows what goes on in the mind of the Canadian voter? In the 1970s we saw prices we could not believe. Oil prices had quadrupled, of course, but people were dumbstruck by the unbelievable prices of books and bread and beer. The world market economies that had seemed to suggest universal order since the end of the Second World War began to look as if they were fictions that could be erased at any time. For Trudeau the task seemed obvious—how could he and his government protect Canadians from the world's economic earthquake? Maybe the state had no place in the bedrooms of the nation, but the kitchens were another matter. Encouraged by the necessary NDP, Trudeau's government unscrewed the lids on welfare and pension jars, and with a tip of the cap to Walter Stewart, became more nationalistic than it had been for ages in the trade sphere. Young Brian Mulroney, working for USAmerican outfits in his home province of Quebec, took notes and filed them away. He did not fill his gas tank at the new public service station, PetroCanada.

The Canadian voter has a hard enough time trying to know what goes on in the mind of a federal politician. In the 1974 election Trudeau and Stanfield both planned for victory and defeat. David Lewis would have been happy without a showdown, but he had finally voted against a John Turner budget because people were starting to think of the NDP as a branch of the Liberals. In the desultory campaign, Stanfield started off by promising to pin inflation to the mat—he announced his plans for strict price and wage freezes. As the campaign slogged along Dalton Camp noticed that no one was holding sparklers and yelling "whoopee, wage controls! price controls!" and suggested that Stanfield find something else to talk about.

Trudeau put aside his earlier persona, no longer firing off-the-cuff witticisms, no longer speaking about reason in a normal voice. In 1968 his face showed no emotion, and his head might dip slightly to one side as he performed a Gallic shrug. Now he had his gorgeous young wife on the hustings with him, and sometimes she had two children with her, both born on Christmas Days. Subconsciously people remembered that Mary's husband had been a lot older, too. Now Trudeau gestured toward his wife and announced that she had taught him passion. She smiled adoringly at him and rejoined that he had taught her love. A prime minister in love! Not a Mackenzie King secretly in love with nurses and other men's wives. Openly in love, holding hands and facing the forces of darkness and Toryism together. He opened his eyes wide. He shouted over the heads in front of him. He raised his arms and almost shook them. He was looking for a majority government, and he was trying out the old campaign traditions. But he never did out-Diefenbaker the Chief. Well, he just had to best poor sad-looking Bob Stanfield.

The voters collaborated in the rebirth of Pierre Trudeau, and his enemies assumed that he had made a pact with the devil. In July Pierre won 42.4 per cent of the vote, and 141 seats. Margaret checked herself into a psychiatric hospital. Over the next two years Pierre was to see his popularity plunge, bottoming out at 29-per-cent approval by 1976. During that period he was given a third son, but this one was not born on a saviour's birthday. Then he lost seven cabinet ministers and a wife. He must have known that he was losing a lot of voters, too. Out west more and more guys chatting at the gas station referred to him as That *%#@!* Trudeau.

His old ally Gérard Pelletier left his work on the language policy and got out of the country. Young Turner, whose defeated budget had turned some of his hair white, retired to Bay Street and started acting like a Conservative. James Richardson went to the prairies, grumbling about those uppity French Canadians. Jean Marchand was protecting his head from the fallout of scandals in Quebec, some of them related to the unbelievable boondoggle called Mirabel airport.

A year after the election, inflation showed no signs of losing a wrestling match. In the campaign Trudeau had said of the Tories' plan for wage and price controls that it was "a proven disaster." Now in 1975 he announced that wage and price controls would give the nation time to think while wise people devised a new economic reality for Canada. It had been fifty-seven years since Mackenzie King's *Industry and Humanity* announced that regular capitalism could no longer deliver a viable democracy. Now another Liberal prime minister started making comments about the necessity for state intervention in all aspects of industry and labour, for a redistribution of wealth and power. The Bay Street bankers and the Blue-Eyed Sheiks and the impressionable cowboys grew alarmed: this rich man's son was some kind of Red after all—look at those pictures of Fidel Castro holding little Michel Trudeau in his arms.

If Trudeau and his Liberals were performing an economic about-face, perhaps they were introducing the trend for the last quarter-century in Canadian politics. There would be more to come. Eventually the Conservatives, once the party of the National Policy, would be continentalists, while the old-time free-trade Grits would call for protection, only to reverse that position once they re-achieved power. It did not really matter. In the late age of television and advertising, most Canadians would vote for or against photographs. Think about Kim Campbell's coat hanger.

In 1976 Dalton Camp and Robert Stanfield threw in the towel along with the long-johns, and handed the Tory leadership back to the prairies, where twentieth-century Conservative prime ministers came from. Alberta had been feeling a lot of testosterone in recent years, and it would seem to make sense that the province would hoist one of its own into the saddle. But who was this little thirty-six-year-old fellow with no chin and ears that would not stay up? In fact, that was the name he was given: Joe Who? In the House of Commons the new leader of the opposition complicated the image with a deeeeep baritone voice. He talked like a high-school debater, and he enjoyed discussing Liberal scandals for Hansard. Scotch-guzzlers in the National Press Club opined that Trudeau would send this kid home with a note to his mother. But Trudeau leaned sideways in his parliamentary seat whenever he appeared there, and he seemed to be listening to something only he could hear.

Nineteen seventy-six was the worst year in his life so far. His wife was driving him crazy. Part of the time she was out fulfilling herself by taking pictures for a lowbrow US magazine, or picking up another $10,000 worth of clothes at Creed's in Toronto. In late May they announced that they would live apart. His polls had him just about under the Commons carpet. And his old antagonist was the most exciting and newsworthy politician in the country—in both countries, some people would say. Early in the year Trudeau announced that Quebec separatism was kaput. René Lévesque smoked a million cigarettes, then went out and won a whopping PQ majority in the National Assembly, even denying Robert Bourassa a seat. Lévesque promised a referendum on something he called "sovereignty-association," a system by which Quebec would be independent but still get lots of equalization payments from Ottawa. It would be something like the agreement between the Trudeaus.

This was the best thing that could have happened for Pierre Trudeau as 1977 approached. He doubled his daily lengths in the $200,000 pool an anonymous benefactor had installed at 24 Sussex Drive, and put on his gunfighter duds again. He had a bad hombre to face down. He might have a few soda-pop bottles to dodge in his home province, but he would be a hero for the rest of Canada for a while. His cherished new Constitution might have to wait, but a man has to do what a man has to do.

While Lévesque practised his own shrug and sent messages to English Canada that his plans for Quebec would not be cataclysmic, Trudeau talked as if a civil war was in the offing. He painted the peculiar hodgepodge that was the first PQ government as a kind of tie-wearing FLQ. He told reporters several times that Canadians needed something like the separatist challenge because they were growing soft. It had been a decade since the national euphoria of Centennial '67. The government tried all kinds of devices to raise patriotism. Dominion Day was turned into Canada Day, and July 1st became an occasion to fly flags and explode rockets and sing goofy songs. Canada would try to distinguish itself by acting more like the USAmericans. Parents in Vancouver and Saint John were still sending their kids to French-immersion schools, and official bilingualism was developing a good root system, but national unity was a pipe-dream. The provinces pumped iron, and the Liberals lost by-elections. The Native peoples of Canada had finally taught Trudeau that assimilation was not their idea of nationalism, and now in the seventies they had their own schools on reserves. They were designing their own flags.

Réne Lévesque had raised the prime minister's approval rating to a heady 51 per cent.

But René Lévesque was not just a savvy journalist suddenly dropped into a premier's chair. He started a great strategic battle with the man he used to argue with in Pelletier's kitchen. Sure, he passed another anti-English bill, but then he set out to reform his bailiwick. He gave Quebec its best government in memory. He began to look like a Jean Lesage with a messy comb-over and cigarette ashes on his jacket. He brought in public automobile insurance and agricultural rezoning. He reformed Quebec's notorious electoral process and he ran a clean fiscal house. Other provincial premiers relaxed and even began to cozy up to Lévesque as a possible ally in federal-provincial bun fights.

Trudeau kept the lids on his cannons. Lévesque held an advantage in the numbers game: the prime minister had to seek re-election before he did. It turned out that 1978 was no great improvement on 1977, and it ended pretty badly. For a year or so, Trudeau had been following Liberal tradition by grooming a successor, choosing a bilingual anglophile. Francis Fox was his Solicitor General, and solicitors general are supposed to be honest lawyers, one of the paradoxes that attend high-level government. Fox was good-looking in a kind of unathletic way, and the newspapers liked his curly hair. But he used a fake name to get a former girlfriend an abortion, and Trudeau lost another cabinet minister.

The universe unfolds

Then there was 1979. Trudeau had been putting off the necessary election till a propitious time. When one of those did not show up, he had to call one anyway—it was a feature of the Constitution that he was so much interested in. He had been losing cabinet ministers and by-elections like mad. He had been around for eleven years. There were voters who had never heard of another prime minister. He was an institution with three little boys at home and an estranged wife fulfilling herself with roles in B-movies.

Publishers know about election schedules, too. Quite often quick little puff-biographies have been produced to perform symbiotic relationships with campaigns—the book sells because its subject is on the front page every day, and the campaigner benefits because the book makes him seem more important than he is. John Thompson, R.B. Bennett and Joe Clark, for example, were the subjects of quickie books. Now Margaret Trudeau added a new wrinkle to the game. Well, not really Margaret—her name appears on the cover of an "autobiography" written, it would appear, in a heck of a hurry by an English ghost-writer for an outfit called Paddington Press. It has a terrific title, *Beyond Reason*, and appears to be an amazing self-absorbed story of an unfulfilled prime minister's wife. In it, the prime minister-husband is portrayed as hard-hearted, overscheduled and stingy. He was the kind of husband who made a face if his wife spent more than $5,000 at a time for clothes. (Two decades later, a musician who used to spend a lot of time without clothes also attested that Pierre was stingy.)

The book was published in April of 1979. The election took place in May. The book will be an interesting read for people who like prose such as this: "Is it beyond reason for me to hope for a peaceful life, or has my past put me beyond reach of such a dream?" The classically educated and highly disciplined prime minister must have heard this kind of language for years. There is no way of telling whether the book had any effect on the election; probably it did not. Probably a puff-biography would not have, either.

During the campaign Trudeau harped on national unity, on the need for a patriated Constitution, and on the various threats to those two *desiderata*. He portrayed little Joe Clark as the errand boy for the ambitious provinces. "Who," he asked everywhere on the campaign trail, "shall speak for Canada?" He did not have a young wife by his side this time. He was the lone defender of the nation. His one major promise to the people was that if the provinces kept stalling, he would call a referendum on constitutional reform.

The people of Canada were not much interested in constitutional reform. Maybe one in a hundred knew what the BNA Act said. The defender of the nation lost an election for the first time. Canada earned yet another minority government, as decent Joe Clark took 136 seats and the Liberals took 114. We don't know how much more of this we can enjoy, the voters might have said. Most journalists describing May 22, 1979 point out that Mrs Trudeau was photographed that night gyrating at the trendiest disco in New York.

On June 4, Pierre Trudeau resigned as prime minister. He straightened drawers till November, when he announced that he was quitting politics. It was time to put on his fringed buckskin jacket and point his canoe northward.

CHAPTER 22

THE PARTY FAITHFUL

---◆---

Joseph Clark 1979–80

I N NOVEMBER OF 1993, the Association for Canadian Studies
in the United States was holding its biennial conference in a
big hotel in New Orleans. The main beverage room in the
hotel featured a square bar with tall blonde bartenders inside
the square. Joe Clark walked away from the bar with a glass in
his hand. Douglas Barbour, the Alberta poet, informed the bar-
tender that she had just sold a drink to a man who used to be
prime minister of Canada.

"No shit!" she said, and wiped the surface of her work station
with a white towel. Actually, there wasn't any exclamation mark
in her reply.

Barbour and Bowering exchanged a glance dignifying history.

Learning the joe job

We have plenty of stories about prime ministers who fell into
the job. Charles Joseph Clark got into Conservative politics as a

schoolboy, and started a lifetime of paying his dues, as musicians say. All his life his outlook on Canada would be from a politician's window. He was born in 1939, when Pierre Trudeau was twenty, and raised in the southern Alberta foothills town of High River. What a wonderful small town! There were stores on one side of the main street, and on the other side were grain elevators and railroad tracks. Before Joe's time the most famous denizen was Bob Edwards, the eccentric newspaperman, and after Joe's time the most famous local was novelist W.O. Mitchell, who raised orchids in his greenhouse. If there was no train parked on the tracks you could look east and see the prairie. Look west and see the Rocky Mountains. Just about anywhere you looked you could see a horse. People like Pierre Trudeau do not even know about places like High River, but when John Diefenbaker stopped for a speech in 1958, Joe the hooky player was there to listen.

Joe's grandfather started a weekly newspaper there when Alberta became a province, and in time Joe's father took it over. Joe worked at the paper when he was a boy, but he was not going to be a small-town newspaper editor. At age sixteen he started his political career by winning a speaking contest put on by the Rotary Club. The prize was a trip to Ottawa to watch the Canadian Parliament at work. What bad timing! The parliamentarians were jumping all over each other and shouting inanities during C.D. Howe's famous pipeline debate. But while he was in Ottawa, Joe met John Diefenbaker, and once again the old scene was played: prairie lad meets prime minister (in this case soon-to-be prime minister) and dreams of high office. Teenage Joe Clark began to work on his jowls and his voice.

At the University of Alberta he was not a star student in French, but he diligently applied himself to politics. Off campus he worked on Alan Lazerte's campaign for the leadership of the Alberta Tories. The Alberta Tories at the time were the theoretical opposition to the ruling Social Credit, a lot of chiropractors and farm-equipment salesmen led by fundamentalist preacher Ernest Manning. Compared to them, the Conservatives looked Progressive, indeed.

So Joe Clark spent more time with the student parliament, where he was Conservative leader. Most university students don't even know that there *is* a student parliament, but a young man who wants to get ahead in the game plays the game. The leader of the majority party was a chubby fellow named Jim Coutts. Joe and Jim had staged a lot of debates; Joe never learned to hate his Jim as Arthur Meighen hated Rex King at the University of Toronto, but he did keep running into him. Coutts became Pierre Trudeau's right-hand man, and planned the anti-Clark strategies in 1979 and 1980.

After getting his BA at Alberta, Joe went to Dalhousie to study law. Either he did not like law or law did not like him, but he dived into student politics again, becoming president of the Conservatives' national student organization. In this capacity he was obliged to travel around the country, meeting most of the important Tories, working on his jowls. He worked and worked the smoke-filled rooms, never having a puff himself. Now he decided to try the law school at the University of British Columbia. I probably never laid eyes on him there. I was a grad student in English and working on a poetry magazine. He was spending a lot of his time working for Davie Fulton, who had left Ottawa to revive the B.C. Tories. Once again the Socreds would demolish Joe's party.

Next year Joe went back to the university in Edmonton, to start work on a master's degree in political science. Political science professors scare the hell out of other faculty, but they probably don't bother future prime ministers. It would take Joe Clark a decade to get his MA. He had work to do. He went to work for Peter Lougheed, scion of a well-established Alberta family and the new leader of the Alberta Conservatives. In the 1967 election he ran in Calgary South against the Socred Speaker of the legislature. By this time just about everyone in the various Conservative organizations knew the skinny kid with the ears, but the general populace did not really know who he was. He should have been squashed in the election, but he lost by only 462 votes. Lougheed and five other PCs got elected, and the writing was on the elevator wall for the Socreds.

The old-time Conservatives were finally bouncing John Diefenbaker, and looking for a new leader to run at the arrogant Liberals. Joe Clark went to work for Davie Fulton again, but Fulton lost to sad-go-unlucky Robert Stanfield. So Joe Clark went to work as a speech writer for Stanfield. If you could write a speech for Stanfield, you could do just about anything. Joe sensed that it was about time to train himself for the top job, even if he was only approaching thirty. He studied French as hard as he could. He would need it for his MA anyway.

He filled his spare time as he had done for several years, as a journalist and a traveller in Europe. As a journalist he was no Trudeau; he had even been a sports reporter in Calgary. As a traveller he was no Trudeau, either. He was an Albertan in France. He did not grow a goofy beard, though his chin could have used one. He did eventually grow sideburns, but in the seventies every politician except Flora MacDonald grew sideburns.

What? Where? Who?

In 1972 he was past thirty and he had not held a seat in a real House yet. He set about politicking for the Conservative nomination in Rocky Mountain, an underpopulated hilly riding just west of his hometown. Older Tories told him he was just a kid. But he won the nomination and went after the seat that belonged to the Liberals. When the west went solidly Conservative and came within a wheatstalk of bouncing Trudeau, Joe Clark became a member of Parliament and one of the most attentive backbenchers in the huge opposition. The sixties were pretty well over, but all over the world the old guard were disappearing: de Gaulle had been dead for two years, Salazar was dead and Portugal was hopping toward democracy, and pretty soon the Greek colonels and Haile Selassie would be on their way out. In the USA, however, Richard Nixon got re-elected in 1972. Well, you can't win them all.

In Ottawa, Joe Clark worked as hard as usual, continuing to be as he had always been and would be in years to come, the most decent and loyal member of his party. He was coming to believe that a decent and loyal party man might some day be leader and prime minister. In four years, perhaps, if Robert Stanfield could not get the Tories over the hump, he would throw his hat into the leadership ring, drop out on the second or third ballot, get better known, and four years later pick up all the marbles. If that is what he was thinking, he had joined the vast majority of pols who underestimated Joe Clark.

Another step he made in Ottawa was marriage. Maureen McTeer was only twenty years old when Clark hired her as a research assistant, but she was as smart as a whip. Like Margaret Trudeau, she had been exposed to Canadian politics as a girl, but she had not been distracted by any success as a teenage model. Like her future husband, she had been a young Conservative, president of their youth outfit in eastern Ontario. She was going to go to law school because she wanted to be a politician and most successful politicians were lawyers, like John A. Macdonald and Richard Nixon. She spoke French, too.

Joe and Maureen had a whirlwind romance, and were married before the dust settled. Smart-aleck newspaper journalists later suggested that it must have been Maureen who found their way to the church, because Joe had a habit of getting lost when the roads were not Alberta-straight. It was the early seventies—Maureen decided to keep the name McTeer. Here the reporters could have congratulated the couple for being up-to-date in terms of gender equality. Instead they chose the old hoo-haw route, portraying Joe Clark as a wimp who could not subjugate his own wife. In fact, the press, perhaps embarrassed by its fomenting of unrestrained Trudeaumania, decided to go after Joe Clark, presenting him as a chinless kid with clumsy feet, exaggerating anything that could be turned into yokelism. When some airline lost his luggage while he was on a world tour, the papers said he could not get a grip.

But they knew that he was honest and decent, so they did not hate him. They just made fun of him. The *Toronto Star*'s famous cartoonist Duncan Macpherson always drew him with droopy ears and a head too big for his neck. One got the impression that Canada's newspapers thought we should be embarrassed to have a clumsy tyro for a prime minister. A tyro from the west. The way Joe talked to public gatherings did not help his image. He had that deep voice that accentuated rather than offset his youth and skinniness. It sounded put-on. So did his laugh. When asked questions, he often started with a laugh, but he did not laugh his laugh—it sounded as if he were *saying* ha ha ha. In the House of Commons he had a nearly perfect speaking style, the repetitive, semi-oratorical voice that rose above catcalls and chiselled its way into Hansard. But on a stage in a small Ontario town, or in front of television cameras, he made a bad contrast to Trudeau's wry off-the-cuff remarks.

One got the impression that a kid in Alberta had studied politicians and, deciding to make himself into one, borrowed their tics and talks. It was as if he were going to a wedding in someone else's suit.

In terms of hammering together a political record, he had

not made a mistake since his first nails at age sixteen. Now in 1974 Bob Stanfield had lost to Trudeau a third time, and decided to fall on his own pitchfork. A party convention was called for 1976, and every variety of blue lined up for the leader's job. There was Paul Hellyer, who had run against Trudeau for the Liberal leadership. There was Jack Horner the cowboy, who would become a Liberal later on. There was Sinclair Stevens, the financier. There was Flora MacDonald, who had become an MP after being insulted by Diefenbaker in one of his misogynist rants. There was Claude Wagner, tough-guy judge and ex-Liberal from Quebec. There was a young business hustler from Montreal named Brian Mulroney. And there was the throw-in, little six-foot Joe Clark, who was putting his name in to buy recognition for a contest down the line.

What a lot of candidates! What a lot of backroom deals and insincere statements! Most pundits expected Claude Wagner to win, and he did lead after the first ballot. This bothered some other candidates, who opined that in Trudeau the country already had enough leaders from Quebec. They began looking around for somewhere to hang their votes, but could not bear the sight of one another. Joe Clark began to wiggle up through the middle of the pack. Why not pick Joe for now, and fix things later? What about the feisty Flora MacDonald? It turned out that a lot of buttoned-up Tories felt the way Diefenbaker did about women politicians. She had a wonderful last name for Canadian politics, but her first name was a problem. When she had had enough of the obvious, MacDonald strode across the floor to Joe's group and gave her support to the man who had the nerve and good sense to check into his hotel rooms with Maureen McTeer.

In his memoirs Pierre Trudeau would say that the Conservatives picked their best man at that convention. In the House the new backbencher had perforated some of the PM's gas balloons;

now as leader of the opposition he would be the smiling gun-slinger in town. Trudeau suddenly realized that his days as the young gun were gone. Brian Mulroney was the same age as Joe Clark, and when Joe won the job, Brian said congratulations in his own version of the deep deep voice, then went away and plotted, staying away from election campaigns for a few years. He had us dollars to make. The *Toronto Star* asked the famous question "Joe Who?" and the name would stick for years.

The Ontario Conservatives, becoming known as the "Big Blue Machine," were not altogether happy; they thought that Joe Clark was a leftist with sentimental preference for people over power. When Flora MacDonald, the notorious "Red Tory," embraced him, they knew that it was time to start looking for a candidate who looked good in a dark blue suit and expensive shoes. Meanwhile, the cretinous right wanted to put pressure on ordinary Joe to oppose some of those Liberal conspiracies they had heard about. The good old flag had been gone for a decade—now there were dark forces emanating from Quebec that would force us to speak French at the breakfast table (look at the cornflakes box!) and bring in the metric system. Jumping Pound Creek, Alberta, would have to change its name! That would be the worst meddling with nature since Daylight Saving Time!

But for three years Joe Clark built respect in the House, and as the Trudeau regime sank in a mess of nationalism, Joe stood up for provincial rights, the handle that Trudeau had offered him. He liked to talk about a "community of communities," and lots of alienated voters across the country liked the sound of the phrase. In the election campaign of 1979 he seemed to be the voice for the little guy. There was no such thing as Clark-mania; the voters were exercising their traditional right to turf out a Liberal government that had been in power too long.

If he had carried six more seats he would have had a majority as skinny as himself. With 136 seats he might have had a working majority, if the third party he had to please had not been the NDP.

Bang, you're dead

In a few months Prime Minister Clark was going to set a record he would not like to remember, but when he became PM on June 4, 1979, the man named Who was in the record books for accomplishments that brought satisfaction and wonderment to places such as High River, Alberta, and his new riding of Yellowhead. He was elected prime minister of Canada the day before his fortieth birthday. He was only five and a half months older than Margaret Atwood, who published her novel *Life Before Man* in 1979. Although twentieth-century Conservative prime ministers came from the prairie provinces, he was the first one to be born in the west. And perhaps most spectacular of all, he was the first and only person ever to beat Pierre Trudeau at anything.

He was in no hurry to call Parliament into session. He made a cabinet more or less to his liking, rewarding Flora MacDonald with the post of Secretary of State for External Affairs. She was the first woman in Canada to achieve that lofty position. Clark made Lincoln Alexander Labour Minister and thus the first African Canadian in any federal cabinet. A community of communities, indeed. And he made John Crosbie of Newfoundland his Finance Minister. John Crosbie used to like to entertain reporters with his cod-fishin' Newfie act, but he was a millionaire's son with a PhD. Joe was an ex-sports writer who didn't know how to throw a body-check. He listened to John Crosbie's advice about public monetary policy.

Pierre Trudeau spent August canoeing in the Northwest

Territories, and September growing his beard in the Himalayas. He returned to Ottawa for the fall, and on November 21, three days after Margaret Atwood's fortieth birthday, he told staff and caucus that the Liberals needed to look for a new leader. That afternoon in the House, Joe Clark's sonorous voice extended Canada's thanks for Trudeau's "many years of distinguished service," after which all the members stood and applauded for five minutes while Trudeau sat in his front-bench seat, his face in his hands, tears on his high cheekbones.

Joe Clark had set another record: no prime minister before him had ever let four and a half months elapse between election victory and parliamentary session. Maybe he was hoping that in the interim everyone would forget the Conservatives' campaign promises, the usual stuff about tax cuts and interest-rate reductions. Joe Who was becoming Joe When. Hoping to get some international exposure that might help him get recognized at home, he took off for some foreign jaunts, to Japan and Africa. He was not exactly an innocent abroad, but though the jowls were coming along, he sure looked young.

It was a good thing that he did not head a mission to the east end of the Mediterranean. In Alberta he had never had to hustle up the Jewish vote, so maybe he was a tad impressionable when he came to round up support in the big cities of the east. He promised the shopkeepers of the Spadina riding in Toronto that his government would move the Canadian Embassy from Tel Aviv to Jerusalem. Of course the Israeli government had been trying to get nations to make such a move for years, but most countries were too smart about Middle East politics to do such a thing. Even Jimmy Carter had been persuaded that his tentative promise to do such a thing might be allowed to vanish. Joe Clark did not have such good advisers. He said that the move would go ahead.

Now the oil-rich Arab countries said that they would boycott

Canadian trade and send the Canadian economy into a faster downward spiral. Just what a minority government needed. Flora MacDonald, the External Affairs Minister, persuaded reliable old Bob Stanfield to go to the Middle East and see whether he could bore the sheiks and presidents-for-life into mellowing their threats. The Arabs told Stanfield that they wanted a highly public retraction of the announced embassy shift. Later, later, Clark told Stanfield. Very slowly, Stanfield explained the power held by the Arab oil-producers in the late seventies. At the end of October, Clark announced in Parliament that the embassy move was not going to happen.

He was truly upset that his campaign promises were so hard to fulfil. And he wanted to get some damned legislation enacted. He was afraid of setting any more records. His plurality was thin, and a lot of the Ontario seats he held were held by onion-skin margins. More people had voted Liberal than had voted Conservative on June 4. A Gallup poll that week had shown that only 7 per cent of Canadians thought that he was the country's most effective leader. Meanwhile the Joe Clark jokes were sweeping the nation, and as Thanksgiving neared the jokes involved turkeys.

Joe tried to be a good sport about it. "Ha ha ha," he commented.

But his government passed a total of one bill, a little piece having to do with pensions. "Raise your expectations," he had told Canadians during the campaign. His government did introduce an important measure to provide something that had become popular in the USA, a freedom-of-information bill, but he never had time to enact it, and it would have to be completed by the next Liberal government.

Still, when Trudeau resigned, it looked like relatively clear sailing for the Tories, even for a minority government that needed every Socred vote to win by one. With the Liberals leaderless, the Conservatives could ease up on the voters, build public confidence, allow the press and public to get to know Joe Who, pass a few bills and remember where their parking spots were. Instead, Joe handed things over to John Crosbie.

Crosbie was a rich guy from a poor province. He had never liked Trudeau's lavish spending, all those OFY grants and LIP grants, and hippy poets using public money to publish dirty poems. Dirty jokes were for loud nights in the press club; they weren't culture. He remembered that Trudeau's magazine had usually supported the NDP, and he considered Trudeau to be a rich socialist. Now, with Trudeau's resignation, the tabloid *Toronto Sun* had announced: "Conservatives out of danger." On December 11, Crosbie announced his budget.

The budget was designed to slash the deficit, an idea that would gain currency in years to come, but which had not been attempted in the last sixteen years of Liberal budgets. Taxes were going to go up by $4 billion, a number that public servants can imagine without crossing their eyes. Of special interest was a gasoline surtax of eighteen cents a gallon. Canadians understand that kind of number, because they drive a lot, especially the truckers who haul goods long distances between Canada's widely separated cities.

"Short-term pain for long-term gain," said Mr Crosbie.

"Eighteen cents a gallon?" replied nearly everyone else, including the Quebec farmers who had elected the six Créditistes in the House.

Liberal house leader Allan MacEachern said that his people would have to vote against the budget. The NDP ritually introduced their third non-confidence motion. One of the funniest and most dramatic of three-act plays in Ottawa history was to be performed. Two Liberal MPs were at a NATO meeting in Brussels with Flora MacDonald. They were telephoned and instructed to get back to Ottawa right away, and not to mention this to Flora.

The Conservatives finally remembered to call her, and tried to get her onto the Concord SST, but she missed the plane. Oh oh. Alvin Hamilton was in the hospital, and another MP was halfway around the world in the Pacific. What about the Créditistes? They did not want their farm voters to see them voting for expensive *gaz*. And the Conservatives had not been talking to them—the Conservatives did not have a lot of experience of talking with Quebeckers.

Mr MacEachern was seen with his mouth close to Mr Trudeau's ear. From the gallery people could see Mr Trudeau shrug.

The NDP had thought that this vote would just be a warning to the government. Now on December 13 it looked more exciting than that. An ambulance pulled up to the Commons door, and a man on a gurney was wheeled into the chamber. This was a Liberal MP who had been recovering in hospital from cardiac surgery. Associates helped him to his seat and then helped him to stand and vote. He voted against Mr Crosbie's budget. Associates helped him back to the gurney.

One hundred and thirty-nine members voted against the budget. One hundred and thirty-three voted for it. The margin of six was the same as the number of Créditistes who abstained.

Joe Clark had set two more records. His was the first Canadian government to be brought down by the defeat of its budget. Some previous prime ministers had lasted shorter times, but not after winning a national election.

As the members of Parliament folded their briefcases and walked out of the chamber, they looked tired and maybe disbelieving. John Crosbie's face was red with fury. Maybe he was already vowing revenge.

CHAPTER 23

THE CNA ACT

———◆•◆•———

Pierre Elliott Trudeau 1980–84

W HAT A PECULIAR ELECTION campaign we had in January
of 1980! Joe Clark had called the date: February 18, and
more or less told the Liberals to find a candidate. What were
the Liberals going to do—hold a quick convention while the
Conservatives were out there rounding up votes? Who were
they going to go with—John Turner? Allan MacEachern? Lloyd
Axworthy? They pleaded with Pierre Trudeau to retire from his
retirement, but Trudeau had told them earlier that they would
have to get Queen Elizabeth II to beg on bended knee. Now he
saw his duty. The gas-station czar's son could not tolerate the
Tories' promise of soaring fuel prices. He would lead his party
in the winter campaign.

Ordinary folk across the country wondered what was going
on. A lot of them had always suspected Trudeau of being devious if not devilish—had he orchestrated this whole mess? Was
it the only way he could think of to rule into the new decade?
But then Trudeau announced that he was willing to carry the
Liberal flag this one last time. He was not going to serve a full

term; as soon as things settled down he would ask his party to pick a successor to finish out his term. Oh sure, said the prairie skeptics.

So here was the Liberal leader running on a platform of quitting. What were the Tories offering? Higher taxes on gasoline and cigarettes and booze, all the things that made a Canadian winter worth living through. Given the choice between a young goof and an aging tap-dancer, the people could have gone over massively to the NDP. Oh sure, they said, we really need another minority government.

But as so often happens, the politics of Quebec had a profound effect on the politics of Ottawa. Whatever else Canadians thought he might be, Pierre Trudeau was a profoundly committed federalist, and his old enemies in *la belle province* were at it again. René Lévesque had promised a referendum on quasi-separation, and it was going to be called for late spring of 1980. In the 1979 federal election the Liberals had taken sixty-seven of seventy-five seats in the province, and the Créditistes six; a Conservative prime minister was not going to have much of a base to fight the separatist vote. Trudeau felt that he had to be there to lead the *"non"* forces. Perhaps later he could fight the separatists in Alberta and get the Constitution patriated. He needed such a monument—he hated the idea of ending his political career without a monument.

So Trudeau campaigned. Or at least he went around the country advocating low fuel prices and saying that his party had an energy policy. He did not make quips for the reporters. His handlers tried to make him as bland as possible. Joe Clark's handlers had a problem, too. Their only real hope was that the voters were sick of Trudeau and his one-man show, and would give the new fellow a fair chance. Both parties' television advertising reached a new low, US-style "attack ads" trying to demonize the other guy.

Maureen McTeer had law exams coming up. Margaret Trudeau's publisher went into receivership, and the "author" was not going to get any royalty cheques to pay the enormous bills she had run up. Pierre and Joe nearly disappeared into the arms of their handlers.

On election night Pierre Trudeau had a tidy majority, 146 seats. Now he offered another of his famous lines: "Well, welcome to the eighties." It sounded as if the same man were going to say something like that every ten years. In a few days it seemed as if the Clark interregnum had never happened.

Say no if you love this country

The referendum was set for May 20. Trudeau had three months to prepare for his gunfight with Dead-Eye Lévesque. In the February polls he had taken seventy-four of Quebec's seventy-five seats and the bulletproof Roch LaSalle had taken the other one. LaSalle would later refer to those seventy-four as "wet noodles," but for now they seemed to be a harbinger of good prospects for Trudeau's federalists.

Here is what the referendum question asked for Quebec: "the power to make its laws, levy its taxes and establish relations abroad," while it would "maintain with Canada an economic association including a common currency." It was not about language rights—those were being taken care of by Bill 101. And its language was overly careful in its ambiguity. Trudeau went to Quebec and mocked the Péquistes as cowardly nationalists in contrast to the forthright separatists of the past. Speaking at a rally of 6,000 people in Quebec City, he said "Pride and honour are not on their side with their ambiguity and their equivocation. They are on our side." Lévesque rather surprised people by becoming shrill and petulant, pointing out Trudeau's middle name—this in a province dotted with francophone Johnsons. Trudeau crooned and quipped, and told his people that after they had voted *"non"* he would ask the rest of Canada for a show of appreciation in terms of a new Constitution and a new deal for Quebec within Confederation. He was like a pop star who was making a big comeback.

When the last ballots were counted and just under 60 per cent of the voters had voted *"non,"* Lévesque was seen to droop. He made his usual shrug and moved his cigarette-holding hands in a fretful gesture of resignation. Then he promised that there would be a next time.

This last Trudeau government was going to go for broke on the Constitution. The country may have been going broke in the meantime, as Mrs Trudeau was not the only one who ran up huge bills. The Trudeau years were a time of dizzying jumps in deficit financing. The figures are so alarming that any amateur historian quails at repeating the figures for fear of fainting in his pyjamas.

Having decided that this was to be his last hurrah, Trudeau put on his gunslinger outfit and put all his energy into provoking a showdown on constitutional reform. He dared the provinces to fight, he warned the Brits to back off, and he pointed his six-guns at all those Conservatives who were still flying the Red Ensign in front of their summer cottages.

He was not shy about stating his aim—a patriated Constitution, with a Charter of Rights and Freedoms and an amending formula. He found himself in the OK Corral, in a sense, because in promising Quebec a new federalism, and having always been against radical special status for the province, he was in effect saying that all the provinces could expect greater powers and independence. He was in Joe Clark territory. But he was trying to complete the work of Borden, Laurier and Pearson. How could he make a truly independent country without seeing it fall into virtually independent fiefdoms?

His two-year struggle from spring 1980 to spring 1982 was immensely complex, and the almost innumerable details and chicaneries have been aptly described by real historians such as Christina McCall and Stephen Clarkson. The document itself, as well as events leading up to it and proceeding from it to Meech Lake, can be easily consulted in David Milne's short book about the subject. Or I could add a two-hundred-page chapter right here.

Not withstanding

The leader of the opposition certainly did his job. He filibustered and fired small-bore salvos during question period. He was the champion of the provinces and the people against a nabob who was threatening to go over everyone's head. He insisted that the patriation be delayed until there had been a thorough study, debate and federal-provincial agreement followed by a judicial review. He was a hell of a good opposition leader. Surely the party would see that he was their best hope, and reward him with continued support till he could get the PM job back.

Trudeau had two provinces with him, Ontario and New Brunswick, two places in which Joe Clark's name did not even elicit the courtesy of a joke any more. The other eight provinces forced Trudeau to take his proposition to the Supreme Court. The Supreme Court, being Canadian, came down with an ambiguous decision, one that would put Lévesque's referendum question to shame. The judges ruled that Ottawa's unilateral request to the British Parliament would in the strictest sense be legal. However: since Confederation, all questions having to do with constitutional matters had normally been thrashed out among the national government and the former colonies. Therefore, he could but he should not.

The wrangling continued, and more and more the provinces succeeded in getting Trudeau to make the Charter's language more vague and ambiguous. Justice Minister Jean Chrétien had grown up through Liberal ranks with a preference for fist fights over crooning, but he schmoozed with the premiers, and in November of 1981, at the Ottawa Conference Centre, a group of men made room among their coffee and cakes to lay out a deal. It would include the infamous "notwithstanding" clause, whereby in exigent circumstances a province could override some of the provisions in the Charter of Rights and Freedoms. This compromise was widely seen as a sop to Quebec, but when it came to initialling the two years' work, Quebec refused to sign anyway. Quebec politicians did not like the idea of losing such a valuable British colonialist target as the BNA Act.

On December 2, the House voted 246 to 24 to request that Britain give up on the BNA Act, and permit a Canadian Constitution with a Bill of Rights, an amending formula, and entrenched rights for French and English. Quebec went through the expected theatrics, with fiery speeches and flags at half-mast. In March the British parliamentarians stifled their yawns and approved the move. On April 17 Queen Elizabeth II came to Ottawa, commanded the Canadian winter to tone it down to simple rain and wind, and signed the proclamation in front of the Peace Tower, Canadian premiers gathered round. A small crowd of Canadians, umbrellas dripping on their neighbours, watched the historic event, the dour monarch, the toothy prime minister. Then a horrible rainstorm cleared the area. Oh Canada.

It would be, even without the "notwithstanding" clause, a typically Canadian document. The first clause of the Charter of

Rights and Freedoms reads, "Whereas Canada is founded upon principles that recognize the supremacy of God and the rule of law," and then the first fundamental freedom is listed as "freedom of conscience and religion."

Running out of energy

The Liberals proclaimed two major ambitions when they came to power in 1980. One was the Constitution, and the other was their National Energy Program. Canadians were supposed to patriate their petroleum resources, voluntarily and involuntarily, through private investment and public investment. The government and industrialists of Alberta kind of liked the high oil prices created by the OPEC countries in the seventies, but they hated the eastern Canadians for imposing low domestic prices. Now they really hated the eastern Canadians for deciding that government should have a higher interest in the whole business of yanking oil and gas out of the ground, the ground being largely Alberta ground.

Anyone who could recite all the details of the National Energy Program was probably well qualified to be in the enormous Prime Minister's Office. Anyone who could understand all those details got busy and invested their dollars in some other country. Great hillocks of public money, borrowed from non-public banks, went into exploration, holes in the ground, shale deposits, lawyers' pockets and thin air. Then the international price of oil fell like an Arabian night. Then a dreadful recession welcomed Canadians (and others) to the eighties. Government economists were chased around Parliament Hill by white-suited men with butterfly nets. People who wanted to hang onto a mortgage would eventually be invited to pay 21.5-per-cent interest. Pierre Trudeau's fiscal policies and popularity rate resembled the Olympic Stadium in Montreal. It was time to make tracks.

But not into retirement, not yet. He had more or less promised that he would give way to a new leader once he had dried the ink on the Constitution. Maybe he was waiting till he could see René Lévesque's body in the dust. Surely he was not going to go after Mackenzie King's longevity record?

Most of the tracks he would make would be made outside the country, but he did take a quixotic train trip to the west coast. British Columbia would always hold some sort of fascinating doom for him. He married a woman young enough to be his daughter there, and he would lose his youngest son to its southern mountains. The people in the west had just about had enough of high interest rates and millionaire French Canadians; they waited at railroad stations for his private car, carrying placards and throwing soft fruit and vegetables. People from central Canada usually characterize B.C. folk as whiners. Trudeau had insulted them from time to time, calling them lazy voluptuaries. Now they were waiting at the station in bucolic Salmon Arm, in the Shuswap area just north of the Okanagan Valley. The man in the *haute couture* duds had no idea what these strangers' lives were like, but he knew that they were shouting uncomplimentary epithets. It was lucky for Pierre Trudeau that he was not outside, riding on the cowcatcher as John A. Macdonald had done. If he had been, he might have been able to advise his audience to eat manure, as he had told some unfriendlies in Quebec. But he was inside the glass of his snazzy private car. He settled for the most famous one-finger salute in Canadian history. A thousand cartoons were born. A souvenir industry was resuscitated.

Please retire again, so we can start liking you, his parishioners were saying. But foreigners were not aware of his unpopularity. With the PMO office churning out the press releases,

Trudeau embarked on a world-wide peace mission, trying to persuade the atomic powers to stay cool, and entreating the have nations to act more generously toward the Third World and start thinking about the north-south imbalance of riches. (This while Canadian businesses were doing just fine in apartheid South Africa, for instance.) He was photographed and feted in foreign capitals, and someone nominated him for a Nobel Prize, but the superpowers thought that he just sounded like a more intelligent Margaret Sinclair. He bounced off Margaret Thatcher's solid hair. The Soviet leaders were involved in a parade of funerals. As far as Reagan's USA was concerned, he was just another Beatle. Trudeau recognized that in the emerging world of market thuggery and cruise missiles he might be looked upon as a dreamer, and he did not claim to have waved the wand of world peace. In his memoirs he says simply, "we had put the megaphones away and were talking rather than shouting."

Nineteen eighty-four did not bring with it a brave new world. It looked as if Canadians were going to have to vote pretty soon, and many of them said that they could not afford the bus-fare to get to the ballot boxes. In the polls, the Conservatives looked like the next government, but there were some right-wing central-Canadian Tory thinkers who wanted to improve the odds. They figured that Joe Clark would never get past the ridicule of the media, and that he was altogether too Progressive and not enough Conservative, so they forced a leadership review in 1983. There were Alberta Tories who did not like him, either—they thought that he had cozied up to Quebec, and he had even taken French lessons. Now decent Joe Who did something that puzzled anyone who had ever been exposed to politics. At the Winnipeg convention he called for a vote of confidence, saying that he was looking for two-thirds of the delegates. He got 66.9 per cent. Too close, he said. Despite his years in leadership, Joe thought that he should give honest politics a chance, and called for a convention in a hockey arena in Ottawa in June.

On a regular basis the Conservative party of Canada likes to have a nice *auto-da-fé* for its leader. Now they were going to Diefenbake Joe Clark. Joe Clark campaigned hard in 1983, amazing people with his energy. He was forty-four years old. So was Brian Mulroney, his main adversary. He had to fight Mulroney for the Quebec delegates, putting his seven years of leadership up against Mulroney's cronies. John Crosbie, who did not speak a syllable of French, and who had the unfortunate habit of insulting Quebeckers, would have to look for delegates elsewhere.

The arena was sweltering, and Joe took his jacket off. He borrowed one of those cute little fans with the words "I'm a Joe fan" on them. This was not a community of communities. This was a hot arena containing a lot of ambitious politicians who saw Trudeau fading and wanted an image to run against Trudeau's successor, probably the photogenic John Turner or the two-fisted Jean Chrétien. Joe Who was not the image they wanted. The right wing of the party eventually jumped on Brian Mulroney's back, because they were afraid that John Crosbie would self-destruct somewhere along the way. Mulroney, who was from a Liberal family on the north shore of the St Lawrence, had fallen into Conservative ways, but he was not yet a right-winger, just an opportunist. In fact, he admired Pierre Trudeau, and wished that he could be like him. As the years went by, he would spend a lot of money on clothes, but he could not pull it off—Trudeau always had style; Mulroney dressed in fashion.

So Joe, like Diefenbaker, was embarrassed by his party but stayed in the House of Commons as a member of Parliament. He would continue to serve and continue to hold to his ideals as his jowls grew into maturity. He would work to caulk the cracks in the party. When Mulroney became prime minister he gave Joe the plum Ministry of External Affairs. Later, as Minister of Constitutional Affairs he would lead the drafting of the Charlottetown Accord. In 1998 the bruised rump of the Conservative party would make fifty-nine-year-old Joe Clark their national leader again.

Gone again

On February 28, 1984 there was a famous snowfall in the Ottawa region. The reason that it became famous was that the prime minister was out on the grounds of 24 Sussex Drive, taking a walk and thinking about the near future. The near future presented the image of a prime minister named Mulroney and an opposition leader named Trudeau. He might have enjoyed being opposition leader, firing quotations from George Santayana at Mulroney, whose idea of a European thinker was Aldo Gucci. But, Trudeau says in his memoirs, the challenge would not have been worth it—Mulroney would not have been the worthy opponent Joe Clark had proven to be. He came in out of the snow, sat in his sauna at midnight, and made his decision.

The next day was February 29, leap day. Trudeau leapt.

CHAPTER 24

BEAU LIBERAL

---·•·---

John Turner 1984

WELCOME TO THE EIGHTIES, indeed. In the Canadian federal election race of 1984, the Liberals and the Conservatives were both led by men who thought that the PM was a kind
of CEO. One was a corporation lawyer in Montreal; the other
was a corporation lawyer in Toronto. Both were proud of their
singing voices. The Conservative was an admirer of Pierre
Trudeau. The Liberal had quit Parliament because he could
not get along with Pierre Trudeau. Neither had held a Commons seat when the eighties started. Both came from families
that had scrabbled for a living just two generations before, and
now both handled millions of dollars for a living. Both had
been considered ladies' men when they were young lawyers in
Montreal. Both were on record as being opposed to political
patronage.

The Liberal was John Turner, the first prime minister in ever
so long to have been born in England. That happened in 1929.
His mother, Phyllis Gregory, was a PhD student, and his father,
Leonard Turner, was a mystery. Leonard Turner looks dashing

and wry in the photograph his son keeps in his office, and it is usually hinted that he was an adventurer in the Far East. He was a gunsmith when he began a family in Surrey, but he died when John was two years old, leaving the little family poor. Phyllis would not talk about him with her son, and neither would Leonard's brother and sister, no matter how much they were prodded. They would not even tell him why his middle name was Napier.

Luckily, Phyllis Gregory Turner was a smart and energetic woman. After her husband died, she took John and his sister, Brenda, back to her hometown of Rossland, B.C., where she had grown up. Rossland was a little mining and skiing town in the mountains west of the Rockies. Phyllis Gregory's father was a mine lift attendant, and kept his family well in a small-town way. But Phyllis was smart and energetic: she went to the University of British Columbia, then to the Ivy League, and then to the London School of Economics. She was a scholarship girl, and seemed bound to join the list of mothers who would be good examples for their future-prime-minister sons. In 1934 she hauled her little family to Ottawa, where she entered the civil service and rose steadily in the ranks. She sent her son to a private school, where he excelled. John and Brenda Turner would grow up surrounded by Ottawa. People like Mackenzie King and C.D. Howe and Lester Pearson got used to seeing the good-looking kid around.

When John was sixteen his mother married Frank Ross and moved the family into a completely different kind of Ross land. Frank Ross had come to Canada as a poor boy, and was now a big Vancouver industrialist. Teenaged John Turner moved into his mansion on millionaires' row, Belmont Street. There was a view of the ocean and the mountains and the islands and the sky. The University of British Columbia was a longish run away, and John went to UBC and became a runner. He became a dynamo like his mother. He wrote sports for the *Ubyssey*, the student paper with so many famous alumni. He joined a fraternity that did more singing than drinking. He got good grades. He became a champion sprinter. He was movie-star handsome, and his stepfather was rich. He wrote a graduating thesis explaining why the Canadian Senate should be abolished or reformed. As if following a script (possibly by F. Scott Fitzgerald), he became B.C.'s Rhodes scholar after his fourth year, and headed to Oxford, where the competition was a little harder, but where he joined the track team, and made lifelong friends with Roger Bannister and Chris Chataway. He was always making lifelong friends.

At Oxford he progressed academically and socially (though he asked his mother to send him scads of Velveeta Cheese), then tried the Sorbonne for a while, improving his French, which he used well on his return to Canada. He got a job in a law firm in Montreal. He went to mass regularly, as he had done in Paris, and he often told people that he was halfway decided on becoming a priest. He was strikingly good-looking, and had blue eyes that could penetrate a young woman's libido from across a room of people carrying liquor glasses. A priest, eh? For eleven years he practised law in Montreal, specializing in corporate tax litigation and taking on the government's Department of Revenue. All the while he was slapping backs and trading manly jokes, making use of slang in both languages. He worked on his image as a regular fella.

Then in 1958, when he was twenty-nine years old, the less highbrow newspapers of Canada and the land of his birth provided him with a much more glamorous and slightly titillating image. It happened that his stepfather was now the somewhat corpulent lieutenant-governor of British Columbia, and it had fallen upon him to be the host for Britain's twenty-seven-year-old Princess Margaret. Government House in Victoria had been destroyed by a fire, so she was staying at the Ross mansion. Margaret had been getting the tabloid-paper treatment recently, because the royal family had put the kibosh on her romance with the dashing aviator Peter Townsend. Now the vice-regal family of B.C. put the pressure on a reluctant John to fly to Vancouver and console the unhappy and glamorous Princess.

Turner showed up at Belmont Street, and Margaret glommed onto him. At the fancy ball they sat together, smoked cigarettes together, and danced together, all night long. Whenever anyone in her retinue approached, the Princess would wave him away. Then in early August there was another ball for the Princess, this time in Ottawa, and her Canadian swain was there again, dancing and talking all evening. When the Princess skipped the gala ball in Montreal, rumours had it that she did so under instructions from Buckingham Palace. Her sister, it was said, did not want the romantic lives of the royal family to be played out in the tabloid papers. But the papers later suggested that young Turner, as handsome as any of Margaret's suitors, managed to make secret visits in London. When Margaret married a photographer in 1960, John Turner was the only Canadian guest who was not an official government representative. They would be friends for life.

Harmony Grits

Conservative leaders have to come like a dust storm out of nowhere. The Grits groom their young ones. The power-makers in the Liberal party had known young John since he was a boy, and when he turned thirty they started talking to him as a possible candidate for office. C.D. Howe had been talking such talk for years, and found lots for the kid to do in the campaigns of the late fifties. In the Diefenbuck election of

1962, he ran his first campaign, complete with dancing girls and balloons, and took the St Lawrence-St George riding away from the Tories. He had hired 150 lawyers with walkie-talkies to keep derelicts and dead people from voting for a change.

There were numbers of rich and good-looking women working for the cause, and one of them was a nabob's daughter from Winnipeg, Geills Kilgour. Like Maureen McTeer, she was intelligent and ambitious, and devoted to her party. She was a graduate of Harvard Business School and an expert in computers. She rigged the IBMS to analyze the elections that had taken place in their riding, and steered the candidate away from hopeless polls toward the ones that could be redeemed. This was the first time any politician had worked with the new technology. Turner liked the walkie-talkies and the computers, and found out that he loved Geills Kilgour. A year later they were married, and pretty soon they were raising a Catholic Liberal family.

Turner worked as a backbencher in Lester Pearson's opposition, and then in his minority government of the early sixties. After the stupid election of 1965 he was made a minister without portfolio, and disguised his disappointment with remarks about necessary apprenticeship; he was still, at thirty-six, the youngest person in Pearson's cabinet, and he had always known how to make lifelong friends. He began to find a spot to the right and left of centre in his party, making speeches about necessary changes in the bureaucracy, and voting against the trial ban on capital punishment. He also spoke about the needs of English-speaking Canadians in Quebec, and favoured a fast-track for medicare. Pretty soon he was Minister of Consumer and Corporate Affairs, and the newcomer Pierre Trudeau became Justice Minister. Turner knew that Pearson's office was grooming a francophone prime minister. He would have to wait his turn.

In 1968 he ran against Trudeau in the leadership race, and

even though it was clear that Lester Pearson favoured alternating francophone and anglophone leaders, Turner did not throw his support to Trudeau after the first ballot. It would have been a good idea. In the coming years Trudeau did not make the future easy for John Turner, though Trudeau gave Turner his job as Justice Minister in his first cabinet. In doing so, he gave him several tasks that would bring unpopularity from various directions. Turner had to implement the measures to loosen divorce and normalize homosexuality, two subjects that would bother a Catholic who had often talked about entering the priesthood. Some of the flak was comical. When Diefenbaker got up to ask what the Liberal government had done for the people of Canada, a Conservative member from Cape Breton replied, "Made them all homos." Similar philosophical reasoning came from western voices when Turner brought in the official languages bill.

But the Justice Minister did not take most of the hits. The mossbacks went after the prime minister, and viewed Turner as his facilitator, even though the newspapers were telling them that he was next in line for the top job. So when the October Crisis of 1970 came along, it was Turner who had to call for the troops, but it was Trudeau who took the credit in Alberta and Nova Scotia for standing up to the terrorists. By 1970 most people had forgotten that John Turner had a year earlier let slip that Ottawa was preparing troops to handle a potential riot during a big separatist march on McGill University.

By the time of the 1972 election Turner was a star, widely recognized as a PM-in-waiting. Now Trudeau made him Minister of Finance. It's a prominent position, but one that is sometimes considered punitive—a leader wary of competition inside his cabinet will appoint an uppity colleague as Finance Minister, thus ensuring the enmity of the people, especially in hard times. Times in Canada were looking unpleasant in 1972. All the analysts in all the papers and magazines took note of the appointment, and suggested that Trudeau had evened a score with the handsome guy.

The sixties were over. International financiers were talking about a free market and spending restraints, especially restraints on spending that would see money headed away from the rich. The politicians had not yet scared voters into electing people like Thatcher and Reagan and Mulroney. Augusto Pinochet's murderous government was a year away, and the generals had not yet seized Argentina. But John Turner was attentive to the whispers from the international money market; he did not like the Canadian government's deficit, and he did not like to see the government fiddling with the private-enterprise system so much. Trudeau's profligate spending on social causes was making John Turner a conservative.

When Trudeau started talking wage and price controls, and especially after the post-OPEC national energy policy gyrations, Turner decided that he was not a socialist. He offered Trudeau his resignation from Finance. Make me Foreign Minister, he said inside his head, send me to world capitals. Trudeau said which would you prefer: the Senate or a judge's bench? I am only forty-seven years old, Turner said inside his head. I think I'll go to Bay Street and get really rich, he said.

Lawyers in love

Turner spent just about a decade in his posh exile. He was up high in the Royal Bank building, where the carpet is thick and the power is quick. If the guy behind the fifty-thousand-dollar desk asks for a Tibetan tiger, he will get it within the hour. He gets more work done while cutting his veal at lunch than a cabinet minister can do in an afternoon at some woodsy retreat.

Turner's hair was turning a satisfactory white, and his blue eyes looked good with a really expensive blue suit. Once in a while a lifestyle magazine would run a cute article about genius in exile. When the 1980s started they brought with them the Thatchers and the Reagans. Social Democrat parties all over the map were taking a beating. Suave bank millionaires were demanding that prime ministers and presidents cut programs in public health and education and welfare. In Russia there were apparatchiks getting ready to make the switch to the mafia.

In 1984 Pearson's policy of alternating heroes permeated the leadership race, so it was time for Jean Chrétien to wait his turn. Trudeau never said anything about the Pearson policy. He kept mum about his preference, and showed up at the coronation in a white suit. Paul Anka, the aging-teenage-warbler-turned-Las-Vegas-regular, sang "He did it his way," and the stony-faced outgoing prime minister gave no sign that he was sorry not to have escaped before the time of bad taste. When Turner was announced as the winner, Trudeau clapped his hands but he did not raise one of Turner's. Trudeau was never comfortable with corny rituals.

Prime Minister Turner now looked like a fondly regarded middle-aged matinée idol. The staggering economy and the submarine of debt would now be under the scrutiny of a prince from Bay Street. The Liberals were all of a sudden ahead of the Conservatives in the polls, and Turner's handlers persuaded him to call a quick election while the voters were distracted from their economic fears. Unfortunately, the British Queen was scheduled to make a visit to Canada, and so was the Catholic Pope. Jean Chrétien opined that the Liberals could wait till autumn to do the election. But these were the eighties: the prime minister does not listen to party veterans; he listens to his pollsters and advertising men and spin doctors.

The new prime minister hied himself to England to visit his

old dancing partner's big sister. She, of course, gracefully agreed to postpone her trip, as was custom in such a situation. Turner was ready to stump the country and ask people to follow his white plume. Wilfrid Laurier had no ad agencies—he had the human touch that kept him in office for fifteen years, and he had the good luck to start a long Liberal regime during boom times. John had an ad agency but Turner did not have the good luck to hire a public-relations expert who might tell him that people across the country, especially those who had something to gain from a royal visit, might look upon his snap election as an act of opportunism. They might remember that he used to be Minister of Finance.

Turner had defeated loyal old Liberal Chrétien partly because of his tip of the cap to the "restraint" people in the business community. In the leadership competition he used phrases with the word "accountability" in them. He kept inserting remarks about "business confidence," whether referring to Toronto or New York. He was hinting that he was no Trudeau. He said that he would cut the deficit by 50 per cent within seven years, and at the same time create jobs by creating business confidence. He was talking the language of the coming era.

But John Turner had been a one-hundred-yard sprinter, and now Pierre Trudeau had placed another high hurdle on the track. It had taken Trudeau years and years to start acting like a regular politician, and now in his last days he really overdid the act. He drove to work with his batwing Mercedes crammed with patronage plums. He handed them out to more than two hundred faithful party hacks—Senate seats, diplomatic posts, judgeships, civil service sinecures. Okay, he was not the "homo" he had been called at both hayseed ends of the country, but he was all of a sudden the sugar-plum fairy. And John Turner was going to have to pay the Christmas bills.

Worst of all, for Turner, Trudeau postponed announcement

of some of the Order-in-Council pork-barrelling until after the leadership race, so that the contenders' supporters would not be seen as lame ducklings. During the press conference at which Turner announced the September 4 election, he also had to announce that seventeen MPs were retiring to take up plush jobs. This was terrible: not only does he postpone the royal visit, but now he distributes patronage during the election campaign! The usual Liberal arrogance includes the white-haired boy! Brian Mulroney, adamant opponent of political patronage, wink wink, has just been handed a grenade to toss during the upcoming television debate.

Television should have been a friend to such a handsome man as John Turner. Maybe voters like handsome men in the movies, but are suspicious of them in serious politics. How else to explain the success of Gene Whelan? Maybe television-watchers were disconcerted by the disparity between Turner's looks and his voice. He spoke gruffly, like a hearty jock trading banter in a locker room, and between phrases he gruffly cleared his throat. Sometimes while he was doing that, his eyes would bulge. With that voice he should have looked like a cigar-chewing wrinkled but beefy gnome in a loud suit.

It was the first Canadian election to be decided in front of television cameras. Canadians were being further USAmericanized, urged to vote for an individual to head the country. Turner may have welcomed walkie-talkies and computers, but he would have reason to regret television cameras. One of them, for instance, caught him patting the bum of Iona Campagnola, national president of the Liberal party. Campagnola, from northern British Columbia, had been cooperating with the press, who promoted her as sexiness in politics, but she had her limits. Turner cleared his throat and tried to justify himself as a team player—jocks are always patting bums. "I'm reaching out to people," he said. The reporters on the campaign trail told a thousand bum jokes.

But it was the TV debate that did him in. In the French-language session the first night, Brian Mulroney spoke in the lingo he had learned growing up way to hell and gone out on the north shore of the wide St Lawrence. It was as if he were turning from side to side and grinning at his pals while Turner spoke in his pretty good half-Parisian sentences. Ed Broadbent the NDP leader did not gather a lot of votes that night. Then came the English-language debate. Turner had gone into the debate with lots of advice from his corner men. One of them told him to go after Mulroney aggressively. Another told him to appear statesmanlike and calm. For some reason he mentioned the issue of patronage. Mulroney's eyes looked like rolling dice made of crystal. He brought up the seventeen appointments that Turner had made, knowing that Turner was complying with instructions in a secret letter from Trudeau. "I had no option," said the prime minister.

Now the Conservative leader turned from his podium and stood as tall as he could in his expensive suit made east of the Atlantic. With beautiful indignation and outraged moral gallantry he uttered the words that would win him the election: "You had an option. You could have said this was wrong. Instead, you said yes to the old system and the old attitudes. You could have done better." Those sentences were played in CTV's summary and on all the news programs the next day. The people of Canada were delighted. At last, here was a spokesman for all that is decent and righteous! Here at last was a champion of principle above politics! Let us elect this man and put an end to sleaze!

A Southam/Carleton poll asked citizens who would make the best leader. In early July Turner led Mulroney 37 per cent to

22 per cent. By late August Turner trailed 19 per cent to 38 per cent. Those figures leave a lot of room for other people, such as Paul Anka and Guy Lafleur, of course, but they suggest that something drastic happened to the prime minister's image over the summer—and in 1984, image was nearly everything.

It was the new age. Millionaire playboys in the USA were going to prove that they could buy a baseball team and get into the World Series by luring star players away from the small-market cities. Just before starting his campaign, Brian Mulroney made a little trip to Washington, dressed up perfectly, and schmoozed with an Irish accent among the Reaganites. The days of Trudeau hobnobbing in Cuba will be over once I am in the PM's chair, he told the US head office. Twinkle twinkle, said Reagan's eyes. Oh boy, said Canadian big business, on instructions from the south. They looked forward to the end of interference from state activism.

Mulroney was running in his hometown of Baie-Comeau. John Turner, who had represented a Montreal riding and then an Ottawa riding, was the candidate in my riding in Vancouver. I did not see him once during the campaign, though I understand that he had to reach out to people all across the country. Turner's suit looked rumpled from time to time. Mulroney took two dozen outfits with him on his plane. He always looked like the CEO from Gucci. His campaign featured endless well-coiffed women purring among the caviar.

As the summer raced too quickly toward Labour Day, the Turner handlers turned into Mulroney bashers, and the advertising campaign a late-warning system that hardly ever mentioned the prime minister's name. But it looked more and more as if the saviour of morality in Ottawa was going to deliver the latest spanking to the arrogant Grits.

On September 4, Mulroney took 58 seats in Quebec, proving that the famous Liberal machine there had been running on myth. In the west the Liberals held onto 2 seats—one in Manitoba and one in Vancouver Quadra, where the new leader of the opposition would remain a rumour. In all, the Tories now had 211 seats, the most seats ever gathered by a prime minister. The Liberals had only 40, and the NDP had 30. Mulroney had fashioned the truly national party that Joe Clark had been unable to rally. He had all those Quebec voices that should cool separatism for a while. John Turner did not like the huge gap between the numbers, but he would remain as Liberal leader for the rest of the eighties. Someone else would have to say "Welcome to the nineties."

CHAPTER 25

WHEN IRISH EYES ARE GRINNING

———•◆•———

Brian Mulroney 1984–93

I SENT A FAX TO my publisher. Look, I said, I have tried this out on some of my friends, and they think it is a great idea. How would it be if the whole Mulroney chapter consists of this quasi-sentence: "The less said about that the better"? My publisher said no, we have to give Mulroney his pages, but you can mention the fact that you put such an enquiry to me.

There are almost as many books about Brian Mulroney as there are about Pierre Trudeau. Part of the reason for that is that by the eighties and nineties in Canada, there was a great expansion in the publishing of political non-fiction. (Never mind the quibbles about the use of the term non-fiction in this instance.) Another part of the reason may be that during and especially after Mulroney's two terms in office, just about everyone wanted to stomp on his expensive Italian shoes. No Canadian prime minister had ever been the target of so much negative criticism. The books had titles such as *The Politics of Ambition* and *On the Take*. When, in 1998, a defence of Mulroney was finally published, it was first excerpted in a magazine run by Conrad Black, and then reviewed by Conrad Black in a number of newspapers owned by Conrad Black. Another of the earlier books about Mulroney had been titled *Friends in High Places*.

When the agents of Canada's first prime minister, Cardinal Richelieu, came to look over his New World holdings, their sails bent their way up a wide river whose banks were edged with millions of medium-sized trees. The forest that met the so-called north shore stretched thousands of leagues toward an imagined Arctic, presenting an ambiguous prospect for future farmers—lots of work clearing the land, lots of wood from which to make farm buildings and fences. What else could you do with all those medium-sized trees?

In the twentieth century you could make newsprint from them. Well before the fourth decade of the twentieth century the largest city in the United States was entertained by a right-wing tabloid paper called the New York *News*, and the second-largest city in the United States was informed by a right-wing paper called the Chicago *Tribune*. Both papers, and a great deal more, were owned by a tall good-looking and immensely wealthy Irish-American woodpecker named Colonel Robert Rutherford McCormick. These newspapers were so successful that they required shiploads of paper at short and regular intervals. Colonel McCormick owned lots of ships, and had the rights to many square miles of medium-sized trees along the so-called north shore of the St Lawrence River. In the fourth decade of the twentieth century he built the world's biggest pulp mill on the edge of the wide river, and created a town called Baie-Comeau. One wonders about the colonel's sense of humour: the town was built on the forty-ninth parallel.

Colonel McCormick was used to acting like a kind of Cardinal Richelieu. Would-be US presidents wanted to get next to him. He could make or break anyone in Chicago, except Al Capone, against whose criticism he protected himself with an armoured car. His uncle Cyrus McCormick invented the mechanical reaper. When the colonel decided to reap the Quebec forest to print the jingoist US news, he considered no half-measures. He built his town on the river, built schools and a hospital and a fabulous hotel called the Manoir, high on the hill overlooking the wide St Lawrence estuary. It was at the Manoir that he would stay during his annual fishing vacation, to which he would bring famous Irish Americans, such as former heavyweight champion Jack Dempsey. From the Manoir he could watch his fleet carrying paper up the river to New York and Chicago.

Brian Mulroney's father, Ben, had worked in Baie-Comeau since the muddy beginning of the town. Here was a booming community in the middle of the Great Depression, and here in 1939 Brian Mulroney was born. He spent his first fourteen years in Colonel McCormick's fiefdom, going to school in both French and English. Almost everyone in Baie-Comeau worked for the Quebec North Shore Paper Company. They may have been Canadians and/or Quebeckers, but their paycheques and ideas came from the Chicago *Tribune*.

Young Irish-Canadian Brian Mulroney once told his classmates that he would grow up to be the prime minister of Canada, but his role model was Colonel Robert McCormick, the man who came in once a year on his private plane, and stayed in a castle on top of the hill. Like the young John Turner, Brian liked to sing. Eventually he would stand on a stage in Quebec City and sing with Irish-American Ronald Reagan, but the first time he ever got paid for singing to the USAmericans occurred in Baie-Comeau, when he sat on the piano and sang Irish songs for the colonel. The colonel gave him a crisp USAmerican fifty-dollar bill. Later in life, Mulroney liked to tell this story, despite the throat-clearing and arm-waving of his handlers.

For his last three years of high school, young bilingual Mulroney went across the river to a Catholic private school in Chatham, New Brunswick, and then to St Francis Xavier University in Antigonish, Nova Scotia. There he became a big man on a small campus. He could not run like John Turner the sprinter, but he could talk: he was a mover and shaker in debates and drama and student politics. He joined the young Conservatives because the place was full of Liberals, and he was not about to wait his turn. By the time that John Diefenbaker came in a dust cloud out of the west, Mulroney was his youth chairman in Nova Scotia. He went to law school for a year at Dalhousie, then returned to Quebec, to study law, in French, at Laval. He figured rightly that the Conservatives were going to need all the help they could get in Quebec.

And if the boy from Baie-Comeau was some day going to be prime minister of Canada, he had to develop some skills. Let that western fellow Joe Clark spend a career in politics—Brian would become a lawyer and businessman like R.B. Bennett. But he would do it in three languages: English, French and USAmerican. He spent ten years with a Montreal outfit aptly called Ogilvy, Renault. His main job was to dress up and talk smoothly, and avoid labour unrest for his business clients. The waterfronts in the big Quebec cities were not peaceful places, but young Mulroney had the stuff to pour oil on the waters. As the years went by his cases grew in prominence, and he became a star in labour negotiations. In Quebec in the fifties and early sixties you would not want your mother to see what went on behind the scenes in Quebec government and business and labour. But Brian Mulroney came out of the swamp with a well-pressed suit and gleaming shoes.

From time to time he took a drive up the hills of Westmount, looking over the palatial stone manors at the top. He liked to use the word "class" in the slightly mistaken way that people who do not quite have it use the word. He glad-handed his way into Anglo-Montreal society, resting his seat in boardrooms, tasting the famous martini at the Ritz-Carleton, acting relaxed at the Mount Royal Tennis Club. That's where he saw a teenager named Mila Pivnicki.

Here is how he narrated the event to his admiring biographer L. Ian MacDonald: "I was sitting there reading the *New York Times* [Colonel McCormick's tabloid would be the wrong paper in that setting] before having a swim, and Mila goes by. Bikini, what have you. Well, so I arranged to get myself an introduction, and by that I found out that Thursday was her birthday. She was just turning nineteen, for heaven's sake."

He was thirty-three and, like certain other Montreal lawyers, well known as a ladies' man. Maybe he was thinking oh boy, another bikini. Maybe a signal in his head told him that this was his Daisy Buchanan. In any case, she was soon to become his sole mate. She, too, liked really nice shoes, and turned out to be the kind of person who would be photographed wearing really expensive fur to a funeral. Her parents lived in Westmount, and she was really good looking. She had come to Montreal from her native Bosnia at age five, her father immigrating to Canada and a top job in the psychology business, becoming head psychiatrist at Royal Victoria Hospital. Among his élite patients would be Margaret Trudeau. Montreal society was like that.

Mila Pivnicki was not just a classy babe in a minimal bathing suit. She had attended a swank Westmount private school and then started studying engineering at Sir George Williams University just about the time I was leaving the English department there. She said that she wanted to become an architect. Perfect. She had a classy family, she was beautiful, she was intelligent, and she had an ambition to climb to the top of the social mountain. She was also a French-speaking virgin when he met her, a feature that Mulroney did not hide from his friends. The future parliamentarian wanted to be more than first minister.

She was also, of course, a Westmount Progressive Conservative. That sealed it; they were married a year after the young lawyer got his introduction, and set out to arrive. In 1976, without ever having held any political seat, Mulroney jumped into the Tories' enigmatic leadership race. Having worked with Joe Clark on Davie Fulton's doomed ambition, and having worked on Quebec during Robert Stanfield's slow-motion years, he now faced off against Joe Clark and Claude Wagner for the top job. Having finished second in the first ballot, he could have gone to Wagner, finessing the hand for the Quebec Conservatives, but he hung on, and Joe came up through the middle. Mulroney was really pissed off. At a party for the retiring Stanfield everyone got drunk and started making jokes. Mulroney just got more and more pissed off, and finally flipped, shouting insults and wailing that the party had stabbed him in the back and ruined itself by picking the wrong thirty-seven-year-old. Someone took him outside for air.

A few years later the powerhouse lawyer politician showed the kind of restraint and discipline he would urge for the nation: he quit drinking and he quit smoking, and pretty soon he could walk right up a mountain without running out of breath.

After the events of 1976 Joe Clark moved into the opposition leader's house and took a nice livable salary. Brian Mulroney, rebuffed but planning for his future, went after big money. He had lots of offers that would pay him more than his law firm did, but he was interested in a position that had been offered before the leadership race. He put in a call to Cleveland, saying that he was still interested if they were. They were the Hanna

Mining Company, and they were. The Hanna Mining Company handled things for several other mining companies, and they ran the biggest show in eastern Canada. This was the Iron Ore Company of Canada. They had open-pit mines in downriver Quebec and Labrador, big hydroelectric plants, a railroad, a massive shipping terminal—the works. Nobody did more business up the St Lawrence and into the US ports of the Great Lakes. Brian Mulroney became the president of the Iron Ore Company of Canada, and now he had more ships going upriver than Colonel McCormick had ever dreamed of.

He would now make five times his salary as a Montreal lawyer, and there was an important bonus—his company would help him buy a big stone house right on the top of Westmount. Now, that's class!

During the campaign of 1983 Mulroney put out a little book called *Where I Stand*. In the introduction he said that during his years with the Iron Ore Company of Canada, he was "constantly reminded of the unique relationship Canada has with the United States."

In 1981 the boy from downriver managed a $125-million profit for the IOC. A number of big-business types, who imagine that a country is really a big business, started telling each other that the Conservative party could use this kind of president. They were not happy with the Alberta fellow with the receding chin. Now, this Mulroney fellow has enough chin for a whole cabinet. And above it he has a peculiarly small mouth. He dresses a little flashy, but you have to consider where he came from.

And though he had a habit of singing syrupy songs, he was not sentimental when it came to business. In his little campaign book he would refer to the IOC as an outfit that provided Canadian jobs, but when his US companies faced a downturn in 1982, the president of the IOC shut down the huge open-pit mine at

Schefferville, Quebec. During his presidency, jobs had been reduced from 7,500 to 2,700, and now he was closing down a whole town. Mulroney knew that this action could have an undesired effect on his coming PC leadership bid. He flew to Florida and worked on a settlement bid, and then in cold February flew to Schefferville and dazzled everyone, including the Quebec government and the press. As things turned out, he made things sound a lot better than they were, and inspired the conservative newspapers to hail him as a genius of international labour relations. It looked as if 1983 would be in the bag.

Although the Quebec Conservatives had only one member of Parliament, there were suddenly so many voting Conservative delegates that Mulroney breezed into the party's leadership. When he became prime minister he would show some real class by appointing Joe Clark foreign minister. For now he had to go after his first political seat, and though his big promise was to deliver Quebec to the Conservatives, he dropped his Louis Vuitton parachute into a safe Nova Scotia riding, making much of his college days in the province. So while Pierre Trudeau sank in the polls, and while John Turner missed every puck that was fired in his direction, Mulroney looked around for the power outlets on Parliament Hill.

He knew the outlets in Quebec as well as anyone, and he continued to work the front rooms and the backrooms. A lot of jokes were made about the patronage that people could expect when Brian got control, and he himself made some of the jokes. He made a lot of promises, and he was deft enough to make plenty of them in idiomatic French. During the campaign against John Turner, he made that wonderful speech against patronage, and seemed to be promising the television nation that when he got into power the days of patronage would be over. But then he also said that he would never agree to US requests for free trade. He said that the free-trade idea had been ended for good in the election of 1911, when Robert Borden had put an end to an earlier Liberal regime.

Canada (Canada) Inc.

On September 4, 1984 Martin Brian Mulroney delivered Quebec for the Conservatives. He knew that his landslide was not entirely a message that Canadians wanted to add Mulroneyism to Thatcherism and Reaganism; he knew that it was in part at least an anti-Liberal avalanche. So for a while he swam along the centre lane, using patronage appointments to get rabid neo-conservatives out of his sleek hair. He was looking for respect. He had made it to the top of yet another mountain, but he was smart enough to know that old money still looked on him as new money. What was the use of no longer being Duddy Kravitz if you were now Jay Gatsby?

Pierre, he knew, was going to be thought of as a retired sage now that he was no longer That #@&!*!# Trudeau. Mulroney had always admired and envied Trudeau. Somehow, even though Trudeau had never taken over a failing iron company and turned it into a billion-dollar performer, he was respected as some sort of natural genius around the world. According to Trudeau's *Memoirs*, the new prime minister called the former prime minister to his office and asked him whether he would advise him on international matters from time to time. Sure, said Trudeau, and my first piece of advice is to make friends with the USAmericans but don't suck up to them, because Canadians want them as friends, not as masters. Mulroney then made a public announcement that Trudeau would advise him on international matters. According to Trudeau, this action would cause trouble between Trudeau and John Turner, the new leader of the Liberals. Trudeau would not play that game any more. In fact, the next time he gave Mulroney any advice, it would be about Meech Lake.

So Brian Mulroney had to manage what the dilettante Trudeau could not. At the beginning of his mandate he let it be known that he was interested in his place in history, and he wanted to be remembered for bringing Quebec into a consti-tutional agreement once and for all. His background was not politics—it was business and it was especially the settling of dis-putes in order to keep business moving ahead. He looked around and decided that any constitutional agreement would depend on a Quebec that felt empowered. He also understood that the other provinces would say that if Quebec was going to feel empowered, they wanted to feel empowered too. Politi-cians in Quebec held the position that Canada was made of two parts—Quebec and not-Quebec. Politicians in Saskatch-ewan and Nova Scotia held the position that Canada was made up of ten provinces and maybe a couple of territories.

Mulroney's chief adviser and speech writer from Quebec was a man named Lucien Bouchard. Bouchard had been in Mul-roney's year at Laval, and in 1980 he spent half a year working on René Lévesque's team in its battle against the public ser-vants' union in Quebec. Now the PQ was heading toward defeat, and Bouchard was working as a gradualist separatist in the federal capital. Old-time fans of Canadian politics were get-ting confused: here was the party of John A. Macdonald pro-moting provincial power, and here was the party of Sir Wilfrid Laurier defending Trudeau's centralism. The world was upside down. If you did not watch out, the Conservatives would soon be on the side of continental free trade and the Grits would have to support protectionism. No, that would be exaggerat-ing, wouldn't it?

We would see. In their first year the Mulroneyites did away with Trudeau's national energy program and made the Albertans a little happier. Then of course, the Newfoundlanders started getting excited about their own oil future, and the feds danced a jig with them. Mulroney had worked all his life for big businesses in Quebec, and now big business in Quebec felt pretty good about their future. Mulroney and his people understood business and were not that sure about organizations that were not dedicated to potential profit. There would be no more LIPs and OFYs. If the artists and daycare workers wanted to live a better life, they should get under the corporate framework and let the wealth trickle down on them. However, despite his campaign remarks about cutbacks and restraint, Mulroney's government was ready to spend just as fast as the Trudeau crowd.

Participatory democracy was still around; it was just that you had to have an abstract company name in order to participate. Here is an example. Mulroney's government forwarded a lot of the people's money to Domtar. Domtar is such a big Quebec chemical company that it used to leave a centimetre of soot on the windowsill of my Montreal apartment and supply wonderful baseball facilities to its workers' team that played against my York Street Tigers every Saturday morning. "Domtar" is short for the Dominion Tar and Chemical Company. It was managed by Argus Corporation Ltd., a giant Toronto investment company founded by E.P. Taylor. Argus had its hands on the Dominion Stores chain, and Hollinger Mines, and Massey-Ferguson, and Standard Broadcasting, and the Crown Trust Co., etc. etc. This is the kind of world that was a complete mystery to a small-town Saskatchewan Diefenbaker voter, but which people like John Turner and Brian Mulroney could walk around in.

So much for Canadian corporate giants, as they say. Mulroney had always thought of the mighty St Lawrence River and seaway as a conduit for USAmerican giant corporations. Canadians across the country had not even had time to remember his name before he was down across the line, telling politicians and investors that Canada was open for business again. The trouble with saying such a thing to US businessmen is that they really would like to own the store.

Still, if a government was going to reduce the deficit and maybe even the debt, it had to make spending cuts. These are the familiar phrases of the Reagan-Thatcher years. Right-wing governments usually do not make cuts that affect big corporations, and they usually give out a lot of talk about heroic small business. So where can you make cuts that will not alienate your usual sources of power? Well, you can ask the Canadian Broadcasting Corporation to remove jobs and reduce "regional" programming and quit shelling out royalties to long-haired filmmakers. And you can nibble away at "universal" welfare handouts. Surely the more comfortable Canadians did not need the baby bonuses and old-age pensions that the Liberals had brought in during the middle of the century? In 1985 the unfortunate Finance Minister Michael Wilson started talking about doing away with such unneeded monthly cheques. He ran right into Grey Power.

The sixties had taught television viewers that you could express your concerns about social and political matters by making placards and telephoning the TV stations, and appearing as a group on the walkway in front of the Parliament Buildings. Now it happened that Mulroney, in his usual romantic language, had made a promise to leave pensions alone, calling them a Canadian "sacred trust." But here on June 19, 1985, he was standing in front of some television cameras, listening to a tough little old Ottawa lady named Solange Denis. Solange Denis weighed half as much as the superbly clad prime minister, and was two-thirds his height, but she had a gaze that would dissolve diamonds. Solange Denis called the prime minister a liar and promise-breaker on national television. "I am listening, madame," he said in his basso whisper. "Well, madame is damned angry," said this little poet of Parliament Hill.

This was a tremendously important moment for Mulroney's ministry. Across the country people were beginning to experience a sliver of doubt. Could this man be a plutocrat with underdeveloped concern for the little people? A week later Mulroney said that the pension cuts would not, after all, be in Wilson's budget, but the doubts were out there. The *Globe and Mail*, not an enemy to big business by any means, printed a headline that started "Mulroney called liar." Most people had forgotten, and probably never knew, that as far back as his 1976 leadership campaign, Mulroney had given an interview to Standard Broadcast News (one of the outfits, remember, run by the Argus Corp.) in which he said that universality was a waste of money and bureaucracy. Living at the top of Westmount, he certainly did not need it, for instance.

A lot of little people like Solange Denis had ideas about ways in which the government could save money, including a less lavish lifestyle for ministers, prime and otherwise. And a working mother could not be blamed for becoming a little cynical when she heard that the restraint-minded prime minister had more pairs of Gucci loafers than her entire family had had shoes since the last year of the second Macdonald government. In any case, the Tories in the eighties amassed more public debt than all the Liberal governments since Mackenzie King.

But what the hell, Canada was open for business. Mulroney appointed Simon Reisman as head of his negotiating team for the new free-trade talks with the USAmericans. Some patriotic Canadians were made a little nervous by the news that Reisman was involved in a proposed megaproject that would send fresh Canadian water to Arizona. The trade talks went on and on, getting nasty at times, illustrating the power and arrogance of the USAmerican negotiators, who felt as if they were interviewing their debtors. The Canadian newspapers were filled with ads for and against free trade. The business community, as the press likes to call them, and the Conservative party, if that is not a redundancy, tried to seduce Canadians into thinking about their personal interests, and assuring them that with free trade they would soon be buying US-made stuff a lot cheaper.

Brian Mulroney wanted to show the world that the US suspicion of Canadian prime ministers was a thing of the past. He made much of his chumminess with Ronald Reagan, and in March 1985, the Reagans and Mulroneys stood on the stage in Quebec and warbled "When Irish Eyes Are Smiling," one of the songs that the tad Brian had sung for Colonel McCormick. The FTA would be signed in October 1987 and ratified in Parliament early in 1989. Soon the orchards of the South Okanagan Valley would have FOR SALE signs nailed to the trees, as Washington State apples and peaches, ripened a week or two earlier, beat B.C. fruit into the supermarkets. Two years later the average Canadian was still looking around for the cheap US goods, but found instead a new federal sales tax. This was the 7-per-cent goods and services tax, to be added to their provincial sales taxes. When people were told to pay GST on the duty they paid on US books they had bought in the States, they asked themselves: which was that, a good or a service?

This was not the only tax reform brought in by Finance Minister Wilson. Over the years of the Mulroney government, the rightist ideologues often promoted the nice simple notion of a "flat tax." But if Solange Denis would not let him index the old-age pension, Mulroney was not going to take the chance of de-indexing the income tax and hearing from her again. The job would have to be done slowly. Over the years of the Mulroney government, low-wage earners would pay a little higher percentage of their earnings, and high-income people, especially with the availability of retirement savings plans, would pay a little lower percentage. The GST, too, worked like a flat tax: it was, Wilson said, introduced to replace the tax previously laid on manufacturers. We are spreading the wealth, said the Tories. Where can I go to have a look at this wealth, asked the minimum-wage earner who was now paying 7-per-cent more for her fast-food burger.

Meech me in Charlottetown

The various provincial premiers had been having unpublicized meetings with one another for two years, planning some kind of semi-unified front, fretting about Quebec's idea that Quebec somehow deserved rights that the rest of the provinces did not need. Now the prime minister invited everyone to a private meeting at a retreat called Meech Lake. Someone started talking about the conclave as a "first ministers' meeting," as if international heads of state were convening.

North of Ottawa, Meech Lake (called Lac Meach in French) is a little bit north of a former prime minister's Kingsmere, and not quite as far as Harrington Lake, the summer residence of current prime ministers. It used to be the site of a research station, where Thomas Willson figured out how to manufacture calcium carbide. Calcium carbide is useful because you can make acetylene from it by adding water, which can be nice for a place that has lots of water and not enough petroleum. Now the federal government has a little retreat there, and at the end of April 1987, eleven "first ministers" met there to consider ways to amend the Constitution and get Quebec to sign.

They talked and eyed each other and ate some pretty good food, and after ten hours came out of their meeting with tears of joy on their faces. They had loosened Ottawa's grip, welcomed the errant son back into the family, and given the prime minister a chance to walk around with his chest stuck out—he had outdone Trudeau at last. He was the first prime minister ever to have brought ten provincial leaders into a constitutional agreement. Hell, he had even outdone Macdonald!

He knew that Canada had been right to elect a brilliant labour-relations lawyer to its top post. Who else could have pulled off such a deal? So what if the meeting had been attended by eleven executives and no union representatives? Quebec was onside—all it had taken was some serious bowing by ten men to the one who had now acquired recognition of a "distinct society." Here was another of those terms, like "sovereignty association," that had been acquired at the expense of a wheelbarrowful of money and a desensitizing of that part of the brain that loves definition and accuracy. Quebec's demands had been satisfied. Hah hah hah.

Would anyone in Canada snot on the prime minister's designer hankie? Yes, Pierre Trudeau would. Trudeau would later compare his actions to those of Abraham Lincoln, although he said that he would not use federal troops to keep Canada together. In 1987 and 1988 he put on his suit and attacked Meech Lake in the press, in front of the joint Senate-Commons committee, and in the Senate itself. He called the provincial leaders a bunch of stupid wimps who would let the country be blackmailed apart. He mourned the one bilingual Canada that a century of Liberal prime ministers had fought for, and he questioned the nerve of the present office-holder.

Aw, he thinks he's still running the show, said the present office-holder, and called a meeting in early June to solidify the accord. This time the "first ministers" took off their jackets and worked for nineteen hours. They came out exhausted, but they had an agreement, and they were ready to go to the provinces with it. Quebec was first to ratify the accord, on June 23. In August the premiers met and decided not to reopen the accord despite Trudeau's speeches. Saskatchewan ratified on September 23. The Commons approved the accord in October. Alberta ratified in December, and in May Prince Edward Island and Nova Scotia came aboard. In June so did British Columbia and Ontario. In July Newfoundland joined up. That made eight.

The trouble was that during this time, odds would have it that there would be a couple of provincial elections, and if there were provincial elections, the voters in those provinces might treat them as referenda about the accord. They might elect new premiers who had campaigned against the accord. Other events might take the gleam off the prime minister's teeth. Alberta and Saskatchewan might try to overturn the old Northwest Territories law that made French education available on the prairies. If the Supreme Court struck down Quebec's law about unilingual French signs, Quebec might invoke the notwithstanding clause in the Constitution. This might lead to second thoughts across Canada, and might even lead to small towns in bilingual northwest Ontario declaring themselves officially English-only. It might lead to resolutions from some areas that the notwithstanding clause should be scrapped. Old-time federalist Jean Chrétien was contesting the Liberal leadership, and he announced that the deal should be scrapped and a new one figured out. Meech Lake was getting pretty muddy by 1989.

By 1989 New Brunswick and Manitoba had new governments, and these two provinces began to hold hearings about ratification of Meech. New Brunswick Premier Frank McKenna had the province with the second-highest French-speaking percentage in its populace, and he was, coincidentally, an anti-Meecher. In Manitoba there was a Native member of the legislature named Elijah Harper. Elijah Harper often wore a feather in his hair, and was serious about his responsibility not only to his provincial riding but also to his national constituency.

From the time of the earliest white immigration until the latest adventures of the federal Department of Northern and Indian Affairs, white people had not been well known for distinguishing among the nations that existed on the lands they wanted to move into and across. Now Elijah Harper wondered why he and his people should be expected to notice a "distinct society" among the white people. Would it not have been more logical to entrench distinction for the federation of First Nations in Canada?

Meech Lake was another of those issues that is seen variously by the two founding nationalisms: the politicians in the rest of Canada saw it as a step toward unity; the Quebec politicians saw it as a step toward sovereignty.

The feds had set June 23, 1990 as the deadline for all provincial ratifications. McKenna finally came in under the wire, but the new government of Newfoundland reneged on the province's earlier ratification, and now it looked as if the youngest province might not get there in time. In Manitoba, the legislature was bogged down, and the pro-Meech forces were trying to expedite matters. Elijah Harper pointed out that the legislature would have to break its own rules in order to get the debate finished in time.

Mulroney tried to get an extension on the date. Trudeau scoffed. He could spot some trembling in that big chin, he said. On June 22, Elijah Harper held a feather up for the newspaper cameramen to see, and he would not drop it. The Manitoba legislature could not cut off debate and ratify in time. That evening Premier Clyde Wells of Newfoundland announced that he was cancelling the vote in his assembly. Meech Lake was just another pond full of acid rain.

On June 23, "Prime Minister" Bourassa of Quebec announced that his province would henceforth negotiate with Canada bilaterally.

On that same day Jean Chrétien became the new leader of the Liberal party of Canada.

By the middle of the week, there would be eight independent MPs who had been sitting Tories when all this business started. The most prominent was Lucien Bouchard, who was talking about Réne Lévesque all the time again. He would be one of the many Quebec politicians who blamed the death of Meech Lake on anti-French-Canadian sentiment in Canada. He did not say anything about the aspirations of Native peoples and their distrust of eleven white men huddled at a Gatineau hideaway. Quebec was having enough of its own problems with Native peoples.

Brian Mulroney had been re-elected in 1988. He got a smaller majority, 170 seats, but it was still a majority. His personal popularity was not doing as well as his party was, but he had won a mandate to formalize the Canada-US Free Trade Agreement, and he could start thinking about further benefits for his voters in the business "community." Mulroney had always been a success in the boardroom. He knew how to get powerful men onside. His own cabinet and upper civil service did not hassle him—except by resigning, or pitching face-first into greasy scandals. In the US, Reagan and George Bush were "streamlining" the economy, as for instance when ketchup was declared a vegetable to comply with federal standards in school cafeterias. Reagan and Bush were the great leaders, along with the steel-haired Mrs Thatcher, in privatizing essential services and deregulating big businesses, such as the airlines. They would explain to the people that such measures were taken in order to benefit the ordinary citizen. People sleeping on sidewalk grates in front of bank buildings grimaced their thanks.

Deregulation and privatizing became a reality in Canada

during the eighties and early nineties. Some influential Tories even wanted to privatize the Canadian Broadcasting Corporation, which had been invented by a previous millionaire Conservative prime minister. The yahoo branch of the Tories, who had not created their own national party yet, looked at the CBC as a nest of commie pinko homo freeloaders with no respect for "family values" and honest competition. Literate Canadians felt the cold wind of future fear when the CBC was threatened. Then the bottom-line right started talking about privatizing Air Canada, and Macdonald's railroad, and health plans, and schools. A few on the far fringe wanted to privatize the Senate and the House of Commons.

Mackenzie King had understood the present and the future; he knew that Canada's semi-welfare system made the country different from the cowboy state to the south. Canadians came to expect their country to care for them, and after the public health-care system came in despite the vigorous input by the American Medical Society, Canadians regarded their public health system as sacrosanct. The average Canadian's fear was that when she travelled to the US she might be gunned down and then taken to a private hospital where the radios played country music and McDonald's commercials.

CEO Mulroney knew that you got things done by listening to the people with the big expense accounts, and talking persuasively with the men who were used to dining under chandeliers. He did not really know how to talk to the little guys, and he had been riding in limousines too long to know what they were thinking. Hardly any of them had been given fifty dollars US for singing "Danny Boy" when they were tykes. Mulroney did not understand that the little guy struggling through a nagging recession could come to resent a prime minister who strutted around in expensive European suits and shoes. Especially after he had laid the GST on them. In a 1998 *Maclean's* survey citizens were asked which kind of tax pissed them off, and the GST was there ahead of income tax and property tax.

A year or so into his second term, his advisers were wondering how to tell him not to run a third time. He may have burnt away more Grits than even Diefenbaker's firestorm had, but his popularity fell faster than Dief's, and reached levels lower than any previous PM's. The look on his face in his last days in office showed incomprehension of this fate.

But I brought them NAFTA.

Exactly.

But I'm wearing my power tie.

Diefenbaker wore a lumpy Indian sweater for photo opportunities.

When Meech did not make it, Quebec said never again, then said well, we will give you one more chance—but if we do not get a constitutional package, we are going to hold a referendum on independence in 1992.

At least Mulroney knew that this time the future of the Constitution had better not be engineered by a small group of executives at some retreat no one had ever heard of, and that the voters of Canada had better be persuaded that they had some say in the matter. He guessed that a fair percentage of them would have heard of the Fathers of Confederation and their historic meeting in Charlottetown. He was savvy enough to perceive that it might look better to the citizens if he were not handling this new action from a throne. So he asked loyal party man Joe Clark to take some time off his job at External Affairs and set up a constitutional session in Charlottetown, and to find some way to consult his subjects—I mean the masses.

By now, the premiers of the provinces were used to being called "first ministers," and they liked it. They liked the new sense of Canada as an alliance of independent states. That's what they were looking for at Charlottetown. First, though, the feds organized a televised citizens' forum, and invited spokesmen for special interests to let off steam and narrate dreams. During this forum it became clear to television audiences and federal poobahs that there were a lot of people out there who had innovative ideas on democracy in the late days of the twentieth century. Pierre Trudeau's invocation of participatory democracy brought thinkers and zealots out of the woods.

You'd better hurry up, said Quebec, we can feel a referendum coming on. In August of 1992 the "first ministers" closed the high doors in Charlottetown and they huffed and they puffed. When they came out into the Maritime air they were waving a document that was notable for its inclusivity and its vagueness. Quebec would still be a "distinct society," but the Native peoples would have a right to form some sort of self-government. The other provinces would still get to protect themselves against interprovincial trade and thought. There would be some sort of reform of the Senate, though it would not be privatized. Quebec Premier Bourassa was not smiling, but he was not foaming at the mouth, either. One clause of the agreement would give Quebec eighteen more seats in an enlarged Commons, and guarantee the province at least 25 per cent of the Commons seats.

That's a start, said the prime minister, thinking of the election that he might just run in.

I can live with dat, said the leader of the opposition, because he was a man of the people.

Now the vague proposal would be taken to the people on October 26. It would have to be passed by a majority of voting Canadians, and it would also have to be passed by the vote in each of the provinces. Provincial rights would be decided by provincial rights. John A. Macdonald's bones shifted perceptibly in his Kingston grave.

In an early poll the majority of Canadians were ready to vote yes. What a relief it would be when Quebec quit bitching! What a relief it would be when Canada's bony grip on the habitant throat was loosened! The "yes" forces crossed the nation(s), smoothing rough spots. Unfortunately for the Conservatives, Brian Mulroney was an active member of the "yes" forces. On one occasion, referring to separatist agitators in Quebec, he referred to the "no" voters as "enemies of Canada." A lot of potential "yes" voters thought he sounded as if he were identifying himself with Canada, and became enthusiastic "no" voters. Recognizing the fact, Mulroney urged voters to put aside their animosity toward him and vote for the accord.

Then Doctor No made his appearance. Having been out of office for eight years, Pierre Trudeau was now a statesman, while Brian Mulroney was definitely a politician. Trudeau was, of course, defending his Constitution, and at the same time interested in slapping down the *arriviste* who was so clearly trying to make his own image in history. Trudeau stood up in a pretentious Chinese restaurant in Montreal and called the Charlottetown accord a "mess." It was vague and divisive, he said, and patriotic Canadians, despite what the prime minister might say, could with good conscience vote "no."

It would also, he did not have to hint, be an opportunity to vote against Mulroney. Preston Manning, the son of the preacher man, and now leader of a new party that called itself Reform, kept referring to the accord as "Mulroney's deal." The graffiti was on the wall: on referendum day 54.4 per cent of the voters said "no." Most people were saying "no" to a specific clause: they were against Quebec, or against Indians, or did not think that women had been listened to enough, or liked the Senate the way it was. It was such a stupidly presented referendum question—if there is a flavour in here that you want, it said, you have to take all the others as well.

Mulroney had fought the 1988 election on free trade, and beaten a disorganized Liberal bunch. Now, how was he going to win an election against Jean Chrétien? With two failed unity accords?

Privatizing Imelda

Maybe Canada is lucky that it did not have a career policeman or a novelist as prime minister. We may have had a top honcho who looked at the country as a bunch of perpetrators, or as a plot that needed fleshing out. Lawyers tend to pay attention to legal arguments, and generals are interested in strategy. Mulroney the CEO was a power-broker. While many people look on the Constitution as a guarantor of rights and freedoms, Mulroney thought of it as a deal. He was ready to make concessions to the provinces as a way of keeping peace for a company, Canada (Canada) Inc., which he wanted to get back into the black.

He was used to rewards, a crisp US fifty, a huge bonus, a slap on the back, a big new office with gorgeous furniture and en-suite facilities, a big promotion. Lots of formal congratulations. At cabinet meetings and caucus gatherings and PMO sessions he said a few words in his deep voice, and his operatives were always with him. The ones who had not jumped ship were loyal throughout his descent, and he was, by all accounts, decent to them. In Washington he was the most popular Canadian prime minister in memory. Now after nearly two terms in office he was the least-liked prime minister in history. He could not understand his unpopularity, because he was used to extended hands and boardroom chairs. He had a big house on the very top of the hill in Westmount. Who had soured the Canadian people on him—That &*%$#@! Trudeau?

Rumours circulated that Brian Mulroney was lobbying for one of the most respected positions in the world—Secretary-General of the UN. All over Canada columnists and farmers could be heard snickering in disbelief. Why doesn't he just run for Pope, some people asked.

In 1992 the US people dumped market-oriented President Bush after one term, and replaced him with a Rhodes scholar populist Democrat from the South. Canadians had a habit of paralleling the Yanks: when a Democrat gets in, you can soon expect a Liberal north of the border. Sensing the climate of the times, Mulroney's government had made numerous moves toward a market economy. The trouble with a market economy is that the market in question is the US market (even if the market building is owned by some corporation based in Japan).

Mackenzie King the Liberal had worked for some powerful USAmericans, but he turned out to have a vision that would make Canada different from the US. Richard Bedford Bennett paid a lot of attention to the planet of the stock exchange, but he dreamed up national institutions that would make east and west listen to one another's aspirations. Mulroney made it to the top of the hill, but he thought that his visible success was enough to make Canadians admire him. Now even his two main sources of support were looking elsewhere, as the Bloc Québécois arose in his home fiefdom, and the Bloc Albertois, officially the Reform party, appeared in the cowboy province.

Mulroney, by the onset of 1993, had succeeded in uniting the country—just about everyone was against him. Worse, it began to appear that he was dragging the Conservative party down with him. The right-wingers were preaching a new no-nonsense kind of conservatism, in which fancy suits and expensive haircuts did not figure. In January an Angus Reid poll announced that the Liberals were liked by 46 per cent of Canadians, and the once-mighty Tories were at 18 per cent. The good news for the Tories was that the Liberal leader, Chrétien, was far behind his party at 27 per cent; the not-so-good news was that Mulroney scored 14 per cent. The solution to the problem was obvious but not a sure thing: they had to find a new leader who could eclipse Chrétien, dazzle the voters, and suggest that the Tories were serious about popularity.

Mulroney in 1988 had been the only Tory in the twentieth century to win back-to-back majorities. Now in 1993 he would be the first sitting Tory prime minister to pass the torch to a successor before an election. The party would hold its first leadership contest in a decade. They did not want another Diefenbaker ejection seat, and they did not want another Joe Clark downpipe. This would be an orderly and dignified succession. If there were any Conservative delegates left in the country.

On February 24, the prime minister announced that he was leaving politics. Soon the big companies would be lining up to hire him and his influence and his rich low voice. He would leave office on June 25. He got into that office by saying shame on you to John Turner for following Trudeau's patronage appointments. He said that Canada was sick of that sort of practice. Now in his last half-year, Mulroney made four hundred more appointments than Trudeau and Turner had. Presumably Canadians were now nearly three times as sick.

Then there was the famous departure from the prime minister's much-refurbished residence. People across the country forced exhausted smiles when they heard garbled stories about Mila Mulroney's attempt to sell the furniture to the government. She finally put an end of sorts to that escapade with a letter of cancellation sent from the European home of one of the more fortunate patronage recipients. This money business gets more and more complicated, and one's heart shrinks as one's imagination spirals. Most people do not know anyone who shops in Montreal every week and New York every month and stays in $1,600 hotel rooms while doing so. Most people do not have offspring staying at $30,000-a-year universities, and mortgage payments of $90,000 a year. For a detailed report of the Mulroneys' lifestyle, a reader can check out Stevie Cameron's best-selling book *On the Take.* It is worth pointing out that Ms Cameron has not been sued about this book, even though Conrad Black does not like it. As for me, I am not going to say anything about national airlines or European-made jetliners.

One day three moving vans showed up in front of 24 Sussex Drive. They say that one of them was for the shoes.

CHAPTER 26

INTO THE LIFEBOAT

———◆•◆•———

Kim Campbell 1993

. . . it did not seem likely that there was much promising material for celebrities in Avonlea school; but you could never tell
what might happen if a teacher used her influence for good.
Anne had certain rose-tinted ideals of what a teacher might
accomplish if she only went the right way about it; and she was
in the midst of a delightful scene, forty years hence, with a
famous personage . . . just exactly what he was to be famous for
was left in convenient haziness, but Anne thought it would be
rather nice to have him a college president or a Canadian premier . . . bowing low over her wrinkled hand and assuring her
that it was she who had first kindled his ambition, and that all
his success in life was due to the lessons she had instilled so
long ago in Avonlea school.

THUS IN *Anne of Avonlea* A red-haired girl fancies her place in
the education of a male celebrity, maybe a political leader.
Kim Campbell had sort of red hair too, except when it was
blonde, and she too dreamed of ambition and celebrity, but

she did not want to be a muse. She wanted to be a Canadian premier.

Canadian semiotician Frank Davey was the first to note the similarity between Kim Campbell and Anne of Green Gables, that other island girl who defined herself before anyone else could. It is a delicious irony that in the 1993 rush to publish instant books about Kim, Davey's leading entry should take naming, reading, signing and meaning as its subject. All political celebrities have to invent themselves more or less, but Kim Campbell did so in an age when advertising-bombarded voters thought that they knew something about the process. Image-making in an age of irony and the instant transmission of "information" is a challenging task.

It is not simply a matter of her name. In 1993, when the newspaper columns and television minutes were trying to explain the sudden apparition of a brash woman from the left coast, the most often repeated factoid was that she had, as a twelve-year-old, changed her name from Avril Phaedra to Kim, a name that could be female or male, Korean or Kiplingesque. In the late fifties a current Hollywood babe was Kim Novak, and you can bet that that was not her name, either. An ancestor of Wilfrid Laurier had made up the family name, and his mother had got his first name from a Scottish romance. An ancestor of Louis St Laurent had chosen the name of a great river. John Turner could have been John Ross. Joe Clark could have been Charlie or Joseph. So it goes.

No, the successor to Martin B. Mulroney had been inventing herself all her wakeful life; she knew that a rose by any other name will smell different.

Avril Campbell descended from connected Scottish families that found their way early in the twentieth century to Nanaimo and then Port Alberni on Vancouver Island, in the province that not long before had had a premier who had changed his name from Bill Smith to Amor de Cosmos. There was a lot of coming apart and reinventing in her family background, as parents died young or separated, leaving children to make up their own lives. Kim's own mother got her and her sister into a Catholic boarding school in Victoria, and then ran off to Europe with a married man. At that juncture, Kim's father, whose wife had made him change his name from George to Paul, changed it back to George. Ringo, apparently, was never an option. But what is it with all these names, asked the press. Kim's sister got the names Alix Paula Bernadette, and she was tagged Avril Phaedra Douglas. Why Phaedra, asked the reporters who had taken the time to look up what happened to that unfortunate young woman in ancient Athens. Lissa Campbell replied that she did not know what the Greeks did—she just thought that the name sounded nice. In the coming years Kim would get married and divorced twice, and she would not have any children to name.

She was a bright little redhead. Everywhere she went to school —Port Alberni, Victoria, Vancouver—she created theatricals and costumes, and a personality. The Protestant girl in the Catholic school was the smartest kid they had ever seen. At Prince of Wales high school on Vancouver's west side she decided that she was going to be the first female person who had ever done what she was going to do. She told friends that she was going to be prime minister and maybe head of the UN. Prince of Wales was apparently a pretty conservative school— she would become, in Grade 12, its first female president of the students' council. She was also the valedictorian for her class and a member of the school's "Reach for the Top" team in that popular television quiz show.

When she got to UBC, where John Turner had been a popular young runner and frat lad, she ran for the position of president of the freshman class, deciding not to waste any political time. I had left the campus half a year earlier, unaware that there was such a position. She won the election, becoming the first female person to hold the position. While she was pursuing a BA in political science, she spent her years in student politics, a conservative during those tumultuous sixties on a campus swarming with hippies and student communists. "Most of the young people I knew who were movers and shakers were Liberals, because that was the party in government," she would remember in her memoirs. There must have been several untouching circles at UBC in those days—I spent six years there and never met a Liberal.

By 1969 she would have her BA, having produced a fairly good transcript, despite all her hours in politics. Her political record was interesting: more a Libertarian than a Tory, she bothered some of her doctrinaire associates by defending the rights of the radicals when they ran into an Alma Mater Society wall.

Her father was busy reinventing his life, going to law school, and marrying a woman almost as young as his daughters. Now Kim would fall for an enigmatic man old enough to be her father. This was Nathan Divinsky, a math professor and demi-renaissance man, chess fanatic and gourmet. His marriage was deteriorating, and his wife had a private detective on him. He had persuaded many students and colleagues that he was a genius intellectual, and he certainly captivated young Kim's intellect and ambition. He was also a notorious right-winger, a fan of Ayn Rand's writings, and upholder of many pre-liberation views on women and the poor. He often went out of his way to praise real-estate developers as models of social behaviour.

Kim lived with Divinsky in Oregon the summer after her graduation, taking an undergraduate course while he taught two graduate courses. In the fall she started working on an MA at UBC, but dropped it, and the next year got a grant to attend the London School of Economics and start on a PhD. There she started work toward a thesis on Stalin's mistakes, but she would never finish that degree either. She married Divinsky shortly after her father acquired his third bride, and checked out the political and musical life of London.

A decade later, when she was a cabinet minister in Mulroney's government and looked upon as a possible successor, the press started to portray her as an intellectual, perhaps a female Trudeau. Somehow, when she was Justice Minister it appeared that she had acquired a post-graduate degree or two, and the magazines repeated it. Canadians also began to hear of her proficiency in languages, that she spoke perfect French and good Russian and German, for example. When they were put to the test, the French wasn't bad. When she applied for a teaching job at Simon Fraser University and the job went to a USAmerican man, she opined that universities were generally sexist, but a spokesman of the university said that they also like to hire teachers who hold post-graduate degrees.

She did get some teaching jobs, as a sessional appointee at UBC and Vancouver Community College, and lived with her husband Divinsky in their house on the university grounds. It happened that Divinsky had for four terms held a seat on Vancouver's school board, and had decided to run for a seat on city council. Kim decided to run for the position that he was vacating, and, of course, to run as a member of his party, the Civic Nonpartisan Association. The NPA, as it is known, is a right-wing party with strong connections to the world of real-estate developers. Husband and wife were both elected, but had to sit in opposition to a left-leaning administration called COPE.

But Kim Campbell had made a successful move from school politics to grown-up politics, and looked ahead to loftier things. In the meantime she decided to go back to school. Recognizing that law is a traditional stepping stone to public office, she enrolled as a law student at UBC in 1980. In the meantime she joined her husband in some real-estate development. By 1982 the marriage was over, and Kim was ready for the next step in right-wing politics.

Vancouver city council and school board are traditional farm teams for provincial elections. The COPE members become NDP folk, and the NPA members become Socreds. In British Columbia, Social Credit candidates usually claim to be non-partisan, once refusing even to call their organization a party, and often decrying politics altogether. Politics, they feel, is a word meaning anything that threatens to slow down the real-estate developers. In 1980 the party asked Kim Campbell to run for them in a riding in downtown Vancouver. Now those people and journalists who portrayed her as an "intellectual" wondered whether she would be able to swallow her pride and carry the Socred banner. Among Social Credit organizers, most of whom worked in suburban and rural ridings, an intellectual is someone who finishes high school.

The Progressive Conservative party in British Columbia had nearly disappeared. There were plenty of Tories who wore their suits to Socred conventions and explained to themselves that it was worth getting a little cow manure on one's heel if that would keep the socialists out of power.

By 1983 Kim Campbell was chair of the school board, where she was best known for her unconsidered insults of colleagues and school groups and concerned parents. Inner-city schools, Native students, women's groups did not make much progress while Campbell sat. She was most interested in programs for "gifted students," for individuals rather than groups. According to Phil Rankin, a fellow board member, Campbell intimidated the less powerful, who thought she must be an intellectual with little patience for things such as affirmative action.

In 1983 she got her law degree, and applied for an articling position with a prestigious law firm that was suitably conservative and corporation-oriented. They wondered whether she would be committed to a long-term law career or whether she planned on politics. She told them that she would quit her job on the school board. A couple weeks later she was a Socred, and there was an election to be held in May. Bill Bennett's Socreds won, but Kim could not get elected in downtown Vancouver. She bided her time now, while the slick Conservative handlers from Ontario turned Bennett's bunch from his father's glorious hayseeds into another blue machine to work for international corporations. Campbell would serve the cause on the school board, facilitating the Socred government's policy called "restraint," laying off thousands of teachers, for example.

In 1985 she said goodbye to her law firm and moved into Bill Bennett's office as a policy adviser. A year later Bennett mysteriously stepped down as premier. Kim had been a Socred for three years, and she had lost her only bid to become an MLA; but she was almost forty years old. Joe Clark had become prime minister before he was forty years old. She entered the Socred leadership race. Her one memorable line during the campaign was her warning about the eventual winner Bill Vander Zalm: "Charisma without substance is a dangerous thing." She was getting public exposure and establishing her credentials as an outspoken newcomer and red-headed promise of change. She received fourteen votes and finished twelfth out of twelve. Bill Vander Zalm never quite finished high school, though his spin doctors tried to plant information that he had. He became premier of British Columbia, and Kim Campbell would never get a job with him.

In 1986 Kim Campbell celebrated her second marriage, this time to a lawyer who fought for the Social Credit government against Native land claims. And she finally made it into the B.C. legislature, winning a seat in the UBC area. In the legislature she could not be a Vander Zalm person. Vander Zalm, though he made things easy for the megacorporations, played the old shit-kicking Socred role, so Kim went Tory all the way, snobbily looking down even on her party leader now. She would never be anything but a backbencher in a Vander Zalm government. So she was able to apply her famous dismissive remarks to the premier. When he called on his Catholic heritage and announced that his government would always be against abortion, for instance, she just called him a bigot.

If she wanted to look for an opportunity in politics she had better look beyond the Social Credit outfit.

Onward and upward and downward

Kim decided to become a federal Tory. She used her growing public recognition in her home province to join Brian Mulroney's call for free trade and to ridicule Liberals and any others who did not have her intellectual perspective on Canada's future. In 1988 she was running in downtown Vancouver again, this time in a federal election. It was a loud and pretty dirty campaign. Campbell escalated from sarcastic remarks to outright yelling. At all-candidates meetings she encouraged the rich lawyers and other blueshirts in the audience as they shouted down the Liberal and NDP candidates, then bellowed "What are you people afraid of?" at her own opponents. At the time free trade was favoured by 28 per cent of B.C.ers in a poll. When media interviewers questioned some of her remarks, she would reply "You don't know what you're talking about."

But Brian Mulroney swept the west, and Kim Campbell was elected by ten votes in downtown Vancouver. It was a riding that always sent somebody into cabinet. There were plenty of B.C. members to choose from now, but Mulroney was not all that much impressed by them. When in December Mulroney asked Campbell to respond to the speech from the throne, she did so—in both languages. In January she became Minister of State for Indian and Northern Affairs, and was appointed to three of the fifteen cabinet committees. Now she had a limousine and a staff and $130,000 a year. The Native people of B.C. were not ecstatic, especially when she responded to their complaints thus: "Why must there always be this litany of negativism?"

In February of 1990 Mulroney elevated her to the position of Minister of Justice. Some critics, especially among Canadian women, said that this was her reward for lending a female voice to the Tory bill to return abortion to the Criminal Code. But here she was again: the first woman ever to become Canada's attorney general. She was forty-two years old, eight years younger than the prime minister. Women's groups were upset that she had compromised her pro-abortion stance in favour of her ambition. Knuckle-draggers on the right were not happy about the appointment, either—they grunted that the feminists were taking over everything.

The abortion bill said that women had to consult doctors rather than their own consciences, and that doctors could support abortions only for the health of the mother. Justice Minister Campbell said that it was the only possible compromise, that without it the provinces might bring in harsh anti-abortion legislation. Pro-life and pro-choice people were both mad at her. Political insiders watched her with keen interest—if she could persuade voters that the legislation was a paradoxical sort of pro-choice measure, we just may have a future prime minister here.

The bill was finally defeated in the Senate, where eight Tory senators had voted against the government. The Senate vote was a 43-43 tie. Campbell had proven her loyalty to her chief, but she had narrowly lost her first big bill, and she had lost a lot of her female constituency across the nation. Marc Lepine gave her a chance to win some back when he killed fourteen young women at Montreal's École Polytechnique two months before she got the Justice portfolio. During the election campaign Mulroney had mentioned tightening Canada's gun laws. Campbell's predecessor had been working on a rather toothless bill, banning the importation of Uzis and AK-47s, but not clamping down on semi-automatic weapons and handguns.

Campbell looked at the huge piles of anti-gun petitions, and went to the École Polytechnique where she told the students that it was "simplistic" to ban semi-automatic weapons. She told the students that since they were future engineers they should know that a handy person could upgrade a rifle. They pointed out that they could turn a semi-automatic weapon into a fully automatic one, but no one could turn a bolt-action rifle into a semi-automatic one. Then Campbell said that people were killed by people, not by guns. It was often pointed out to her that she was repeating the cliché offered by the gun lobby.

As the year wore on, Campbell had to listen to the gun lobby explain that rural folk needed assault rifles to protect themselves against snakes and badgers. There were lots of Tory MPs who had been elected by gun-loving ranchers and owners of pickup trucks. When the anniversary of Lepine's massacre came around, the weapons bill had been shelved, but the federal government led the nation in a tribute to the fourteen slaughtered women in Montreal. It would be another year before a diluted law was passed and nearly another year before it would begin to come into effect. Now owners of AK-47s and other mass-killing weapons would have to pay a fifty-dollar fee for a special certificate. The gun that Lepine had used was a Sturm Ruger. It was still available over the counter.

Mulroney's candidate

Campbell may have been having a rough go with Canadian women who did not like being raped and shot at and unhappily pregnant, but she did gather a lot of helpful publicity in the early nineties. She was becoming a kind of smart-talking celebrity with a blondish-red bouffant and a huge white smile. When the public saw her bare shoulders they caught a whiff of Trudeau-like impertinence that they liked. The photograph by Barbara Woodley showed Campbell holding her legal robes on a coat hanger in front of her bare shoulders, and it had been hanging on a Vancouver bank wall for two years before it appeared in the *Ottawa Citizen* and then just about everywhere else. Cruel wags might have made a comment about the coat hanger and the minister's abortion legislation, but most Canadians, apparently, just said "whoopee!" They liked her because in that picture she showed everyone how unlike Brian Mulroney she was. Wouldn't it be neat to have a bare-naked prime minister, some Canadians thought. They may be getting all excited about this youngster Clinton down south, but the USAmericans would never have the nerve to elect a bare-naked president.

Meanwhile, Brian Mulroney was planning his retirement. He knew that he could not get re-elected in 1993, and he knew that the party was in trouble. Jean Chrétien was not much of an opponent, but the Tories were not much in the way of champions. On the third day of 1993 Mulroney came back from his luxurious Florida retreat and announced a big and surprising cabinet shuffle. Fifteen ministers were moved around or turfed out, and Kim Campbell was the new Minister of Defence. The dumber newspapers interpreted this as a demotion for Kim. The smarter newspapers figured it out: Mulroney had chosen her as his favoured successor. If she were to stay in Justice, she would be associated with abortions and gun control and gays, and the fundamentalist right would flock to the Reform party. What ministry would give her the best opportunity to show off her conservative nature? In defence she would have more guns than anyone, even the Alberta ranchers worried about snakes.

Two weeks later Defence Minister Campbell, in one of her more famous quips, showed that she understood the situation: "Who needs a leadership race? I'll just stage a military coup. Don't mess with me. I have tanks."

On February 24 Mulroney announced his resignation, and the sky over Canada turned blue. Nine years earlier Pierre Trudeau had resigned when Liberal fortunes looked bleak, and the first national opinion poll showed that John Turner would slap down the upstart CEO from Baie-Comeau. Now Mulroney the unpopular had quit, and the first three national opinion polls showed that of all the Conservative hopefuls, Kim Campbell looked like a waltz-in, and that she would flatten Jean Chrétien and everyone else. The Gallup poll was the most dramatic, showing the Campbell Tories taking 50 per cent of the vote.

How could the Tories nominate anyone else? People like Michael Wilson and Don Mazankowski had been carefully building support for years, and now the bankers and feedlot managers were scrambling after the Campbell bandwagon. I quit, said Wilson in March. Most of the others followed suit right away. Oh oh, said Mulroney and other Tory bosses, we have to have some sort of contest. People started talking to Jean Charest, the beautifully bilingual Environment Minister, and the prime minister, though he did not think that another Quebec man had a chance, was relieved to see that a convention would be necessary.

One comical event transpired in May. Joe Clark, worried by the idea of a party led by this puffy-haired flake from the coast, declared that if anyone wanted to draft him he might stand for leadership again. No one took him up on it, and Joe got the message that he was an ex-leader.

Campbell was Mulroney's candidate, but she knew that she had to run against him. In her leadership campaign and then her election campaign she kept offering this seeming bromide, knowing that it was code language: "I want to change the way people think about politics in this country by changing the way we do politics in this country." This was supposed to make potential voters think that she was a breath of fresh Pacific air, and not the supporter of Bill Bennett and Brian Mulroney that she had been. She wanted the public to elect an emperor in new clothes. For the campaign she adopted the colour pink. She could be cute and spunky at the same time. In his leadership campaign Charest liked to point out that Mulroney kept showing up in pictures with Kim Campbell.

The Tories had a convention just like their other conventions. The new leader was going to be someone dropped at their feet by a gust of wind. Why was it that they could not bring their leaders up through the ranks the way the Liberals usually did? Who were these people? How could the delegates vote for anything but the show? Kim Campbell put on a hell of a show, though she continued her old habit of making unconsidered comments during all the heat and noise. She resorted to a Mulroneyism, referring to people who disagreed about the deficit as "enemies of Canada." Damn it! Back in January she had given an interview to a Vancouver magazine, and said this about people who did not support a political party: "To hell with them!" Photocopying machines buzzed all over Ottawa. She made a lot of reckless asides and ironic quips, and readers such as I found that to be her only attractive feature, but there are always reporters out there, busy stripping away context and irony, and Kim's "candour" and liveliness were turned into political shortcomings, as is depressingly common. Pierre Trudeau had been able to pull it off, but while Trudeau sounded like a condescending patrician, Kim Campbell sounded more like an upstart smart-ass.

So much so that by the beginning of the convention she had squandered her big lead and was neck and neck with Charest, according to the polls. But she won 48 per cent on the first ballot, and gathered 307 votes from friendly Jim Edwards to win the leadership. The public liked Charest but the party machine was impressed by Campbell. These two candidates had turned out to be unfriendly toward one another, but when Kim Campbell became leader her people persuaded her to make a stab at party solidarity by offering Charest the job of deputy prime minister.

So here she was again. This time she was the first woman ever to become prime minister of Canada. She would be party leader for exactly half a year, and prime minister for four months and nine days.

What a prize she had won! She had inherited Canada's oldest political party, some people would point out. Others would say that that party had disappeared with the arrival of Brian Mulroney nine years earlier. Kim Campbell did not have any leeway—she had to call an election for 1993, and she had to ask the Canadian people to show their confidence in an outfit that had brought the free-trade agreement, initiated work on the coming North American agreement, introduced the GST and failed at Meech Lake and Charlottetown. There was a lot of hostility floating around, and a lot of resentment. The Tories in 1984 and 1988 had promised that their economic theories would bring good times.

The Tories in 1984 and 1988 had also derived a lot of their strength from Alberta and Quebec. Now there were temporary Tories traipsing to the latest separatist group, the Bloc Québécois, and Tories of convenience strutting to the latest fundamentalist right party, the Reformers. Maybe Mulroney and Campbell should have called them the "enemies of Canada." They had clearly borrowed their "philosophy" and even their name from a USAmerican splinter party headed by a jug-eared little Texan with piles of virtual money. Most Reform voters and candidates had never heard of the nineteenth-century Reform party whose political position was exactly opposite theirs.

In the 1993 campaign the public was very highly aware that image would be the Conservatives' focus. Surely Kim Campbell was right for the new age, and surely Jean Chrétien represented the bad old ways. "Yesterday's man," the Tory ads called him. Campbell's campaign Boeing 737 had her first name written in big letters on the fuselage. The colour pink kept showing up. Her trademark lapel brooch appeared in hundreds of photographs. So what if it now appeared that her "fluency" in French was an exaggeration? The Liberal leader sounded less than mellifluous in both languages. In Quebec the Conservative team took the notion of image a little too far, creating an attack ad for television that exaggerated and demonized Chrétien's sideways mouth, a relic of a childhood illness. It seemed to take forever before the prime minister found out about the ad and had it pulled.

She went through all the normal late-twentieth-century election stuff, flying and busing all over the country, debating the other leaders on television, being photographed eating unhealthy food, and discussing the issues. Well, in fact, she spent most of her time discussing Kim Campbell, as usual. An election campaign, she said, was the worst possible time to talk about complex issues such as medicare and the economy. The media people loved that one, but she was only repeating what she had said in her Social Credit campaign a few years ago. The people got the message—they were too stupid to follow issues, so they needed images. Well, she had said that the

Charlottetown accord went down because of the ignorance of Canadian voters.

The desperate Conservatives had not noticed that Canadians in the nineties had long ago learned how to read television and especially advertising. There will always be a number of poor souls who think they are going to become millionaires because they got an exciting envelope from the Publishers Clearing House. But by 1993 there were millions of amateur semioticians in Canada, and they knew that they were being offered the "new improved Kim." Some of them voted against her; others voted against Brian Mulroney, the man who invented the take-a-penny-give-a-penny bowl you see on convenience store counters.

The Liberals knew better. They did not construct attack ads that might jump all over Campbell's obvious liabilities. Instead they went back to Mackenzie King's staid tactic, publishing a detailed platform. Sign here, they said. They were drifting to the right as conservative voters in the country slid ahead of them. They spruced their candidate up a little, but everyone in the country had known him for years. It would have been difficult to substitute an image.

A lot of people just did not have the energy to go to the polling stations and vote against the Tories. Sixty-nine per cent of the voters turned out, the lowest percentage since the sleepy 1953 re-election of Louis St Laurent. But the 1993 election will never be forgotten.

The Progressive Conservative party, which in 1984 won 211 seats, won 2 seats on October 25, 1993. They finished ahead of the Rhino party, the Greens, and the Christian Heritage party. Neither half of their caucus would be Kim Campbell. Elsie Wayne would represent the party for Atlantic Canada, and Jean Charest the Eastern Townships. The Progressive Conservatives became the first party to achieve sexual parity in the House of Commons.

The Liberals more than doubled their numbers to 177 and took 41 per cent of the vote. The Conservatives got 16 per cent. The NDP fell far to 7 per cent. Manning's maverick Reformers took 19 per cent and 52 seats. The Bloc Québécois managed 13.5 per cent and 54 Quebec seats.

So now the electoral map, as they say, had changed into Laurier's nightmare, a number of regions standing up against one another. Now when any USAmericans who knew that there was a country north of them asked about our governmental system, we had some explaining to do.

"You see, we have a majority of Liberal members. They form the government. Then the party with the second-highest number of seats is called the Official Opposition. We call them 'the loyal opposition,' and as of 1993 that would be the Bloc Québécois. The Bloc? Well, these are the people whose platform consists largely of not recognizing the government of Canada."

The true north strong and strange.

CHAPTER 27

AUTOMATIC PILOT

———◆•◆•◆———

Jean Chrétien 1993–

J UST CALL ME JOE, said Mr Clark from Alberta. You can refer to me as Your Eminence, suggested the manner of Mr Mulroney from downriver Quebec. I am calling myself Kim, said Ms Campbell from Vancouver Island. Then along came the veteran pol who referred to himself as "the little guy from Shawinigan."

Jean Chrétien is about as much different from Cardinal Richelieu as you can be and still be prime minister of Canada. He calls his short breezy memoir *Straight from the Heart,* and on the cover he is shown wearing an open-collared denim shirt. Just in case he might be going too low-scale, the publisher Key Porter prints "The Right Honourable Jean" in small print above the author's surname. The prose is regular-guy stuff, with phrases such as "so I told my wife . . ." and "I got shafted on the first ballot." Chrétien is a lawyer by profession, but even when he is wearing a suit and tie he contrives to look as if he could be hanging around a gas station talking about hockey.

He was born in 1934 in La Baie Shawinigan, a tough indus-trial town in old Quebec in the middle of the Depression. His mother gave birth to nineteen children in twenty-six years, and only nine of them lived to be two years old. He was the third of Marie Boisvert Chrétien's sons to be named Jean. In that village next to industrial Shawinigan, you had to fight to stay alive and you had to fight the other working-class children who stayed alive. Ti-Jean was a big-headed kid with a bad ear and a crooked mouth from a childhood disease he had managed to survive. So he had to learn riverfront survival techniques.

His mother, despite her constant pregnancy, had ambition. She did not hang around with the neighbourhood wives gos-siping and shelling peas. They thought she was a snob in a small town. She lived in a new mill town up in the hills back of Trois-Rivières, the second-oldest city in Canada. Her children were going to be something, doctors, lawyers. But she was not thinking of prime ministers: Ti-Jean went to a French-only boarding school at age five. He came from a *rouge* family, though, and his father, a machinist in a mill, was a Liberal organizer, so Ti-Jean was delivering Liberal pamphlets as soon as he could keep up to Wellie Chrétien's walk. In his memoir, he points out the deep political differences of nineteenth-century Quebec, when Conservatives were mixed up with the priests and Liberals were anti-clerical freethinkers, and could be ex-communicated for their politics. The bishop, he remembers, explained that heaven is *bleu* and hell is *rouge*. In the late thirties twentieth-century rural Quebec was still nineteenth-century political Quebec.

Like Joe Clark and Brian Mulroney, Jean Chrétien got in-volved in campus politics, becoming president of the Liberal club at Laval University, where he studied law. In the late fifties John Diefenbaker's version of the Conservatives ran Ottawa, and Maurice Duplessis was handing out all the goodies in Quebec, so Chrétien still had to be a battler with the odds against him. The priests backed Duplessis because, like him, they wanted as few Trudeaus and Chrétiens around as possible. Education and appointment of intellectuals and liberals were not good for corrupt regimes or privileged hierarchies. Duplessis came from Trois-Rivières, and Laval is in Quebec City, so young Chrétien had lots of opportunities to watch the Union-Nationale in operation. In Quebec City he did lots of the usual student politics, sometimes pranks, sometimes demonstrations. On one occasion he organized a thousand protestors who encamped in front of the National Assembly, and some of them were sipping whisky (Chrétien did not drink or smoke or chase women), and some of them were throwing the traditional eggs and tomatoes at the government building. The National Assembly was protected by provincial police, but they were not dressed up as science-fiction terrorists, like the riot(ing) cops that would attack protestors in Vancouver forty years later, while Prime Minister Chrétien was inside a posh hotel speaking to party financiers.

When law school would recess for the summer, young Chrétien came home and worked in the mill as a "broke hustler." That meant that when the machines broke down, as they often did, he went and gathered up the chunks of massacred trees and threw them into the pulper. The mill was hot as hell and full of Liberals. And it was very loud—it must have seemed a dangerous place for a young man with only one working ear. When he was not working, he was usually with Aline Chainé, the young woman he had sparked at college in Trois-Rivières, and the reason why he did not chase babes in Quebec. When he was not with Aline, he was being used as a warm-up act by various area Liberal politicians, whipping up the crowd with his animated attacks on everything *bleu*.

Halfway through law school he married Aline. He was twenty-three years old, and had been seeing her since he was seventeen. They stuck. They became the closest married couple in Quebec, and they would support one another in their ambitions, she to learn English and music, he to learn the law. When he made it to the PM's chair, he was half of the tightest team since the St Laurents. In their early days the rest of the world did not see much of the Chrétiens—they were each other's planet.

In January of 1958 Jean Chrétien was president of the Young Liberals of Quebec, and so a delegate at the convention to choose St Laurent's successor. The Tories had recently picked Diefenbaker, and even younger delegate Brian Mulroney was often seen grinning beside Dief. Lester B. Pearson looked like a shoo-in for the Grit leadership, and Chrétien left for the convention prepared to lead his group in a show of support for the Anglo from Toronto. But on the first day he met Paul Martin, the candidate without a hope, and felt a rush of sympathy simply because Martin was an underdog, an outsider. The little guy from Shawinigan was a sucker for underdogs and outsiders. He persuaded his entourage to give their first-ballot votes to Martin.

While he was at the convention Chrétien made some speeches, attacking Duplessis's nepotism and demanding university access for poor people. He also visited all the offices he could, meeting Liberals young and old. He had told Aline that he did not plan to enter politics until he was forty, but he had been a Liberal organizer since the age of five. When he got back to school he managed to get himself elected vice-president of the Canadian university Liberals and president of his law class for the third year in a row. Next he ran for president of the whole law faculty, and ran up against a Union Nationale candidate for the first time. Chrétien rallied a lot of workers around him, but

Duplessis had his youngsters working hard at Laval, and the vote ended in a tie. In a run-off election Chrétien lost to the UN candidate by a few votes. It was his first defeat.

In 1959 he was admitted to the bar, and joined the oldest law firm in Shawinigan. The firm was full of Duplessis men and Quebec nationalists, so here was Jean Chrétien where he would always want to be—an outsider on the inside. In his very first case he won $5,000 for one of his neighbours, and the man tried to stiff him when the lawyer asked for a measly 5-per-cent fee. Welcome to the legal world. But in his first few years he proved to be a good local lawyer, and he managed to put some money away, living frugally and wearing inexpensive suits. He would always be a fiscal conservative. He was earning a reputation as a guy who looked after details and left the flashy stuff for other people. He also had a reputation as a tough guy, both inside and outside the law courts. Two years into his career he decked another lawyer who made catty remarks at a lawyers' party.

A rough *rouge*

Jean Chrétien had never stopped thinking about politics, though he had told Aline that he could put off running till he was forty and they were really well set up. He thought about provincial politics. He had one of his big ears open to the separatist breezes. But his family tradition was all about Laurier federalism. He did not speak a lot of English, and he had hardly ever been far away from the St Lawrence River, but when the 1962 election came along he managed to be seen in the right places. The trouble was that his riding, St-Maurice–Laflèche, had been represented since 1949 by a Liberal named J.A. Richard. As Richard was now seventy-two years old, and as he had never been known to stand up and say something in the

House, the young Liberals around Shawinigan started mentioning twenty-eight-year-old Chrétien as a new candidate. But Richard decided that he would like to sit in Ottawa for another term. He never got the chance: one of Réal Caouette's Social Creditors lambasted the old man, as the funny-money party took twenty-six seats in the province.

Chrétien had warned the quiet old guy that it would happen. When another election was called for the following year, Chrétien decided to run against the Social Creditor who had won by 10,000 votes. He would have no chance of winning, of course, but he would get lots of publicity, and if he could cut into his opponent's lead, people would pay attention to him. His first campaign was a tough and dirty one, as was to be expected in that place. He had to run against the Social Credit and the local priest. With his deep shadow-circled eyes and crisp hair that shot up and back, he sometimes looked possessed as he fired off his fast vernacular French in halls and on porches. But he had something new to politics in this region—whereas it was normal for the candidate to stand in front of veteran politicos and venerable public figures, Chrétien surrounded himself with an athletic youth brigade who worked all hours and exhibited boundless and focused energy. While the old guard smiled and patted their candidate's head, Chrétien's troops did their best to imitate John Kennedy's famous team.

But they did not abandon normal Quebec politics. Chrétien insulted his opponent with every speech, and his organizers attacked Social Credit as funny-money buffoons who would have Quebeckers wheeling barrows of banknotes through rubble. Money and alcohol changed hands according to ancient patterns. Fists were held in front of noses. The Social Creditors' campaign resembled sc campaigns elsewhere: called nutcakes and morons by more educated people, they countered that the intellectuals were the ones who always got the ordinary people into a mess. There were not a lot of intellectuals in the area of Shawinigan and Grand-Mère, but on April 8, the Liberals were back in power there and across the country, and Jean Chrétien was on his way to Ottawa.

He was the new member for St-Maurice–Laflèche, which constituted an irony that he appreciated and determined to erase. Monsignor Louis-François Laflèche had been the Trois-Rivières bishop who would not absolve Jean's grandfather for the common sin of handing out alcohol during the 1896 election campaign. Whether he had anything to do about it or not, Chrétien expressed satisfaction when in 1968 his riding's name was shortened to St-Maurice.

Here was a young man from the (relative) sticks, who had turned around 12,000 votes in one year, walking under the Peace Tower in the country's capital, finally making his family proud of him, and sure to make an impression on Lester Pearson, the new minority prime minister. He told his brother that he would do this for ten years and then become a judge, but he never said that to his party leadership. He was a cocky young fellow, not yet thirty, and almost unilingual (there were those detractors back home who said that he had not mastered French yet, either) in a government city where nearly everything was still done in English. There were a lot of new MPs from Quebec, but none of them had the drive and desire that the little guy from Shawinigan would soon show.

Soon he was making himself known and useful to the English-Canadian Liberals, though he could not read their letters and reports, and it was not long until the newspapers painted him as an intellectual lightweight who knew how to work people and get the details done. His first significant legislative triumph occured in 1964, when he got the name of Trans-Canada Airlines changed to Air Canada. There were several good reasons for the change, but a backbencher's motion did not have much of a chance of making it through the severe time restraints laid on it. Chrétien had prepared himself by meeting with people from all parties and asking them for quick assent. He made a quick proposal, got his quick "I agrees," and won congratulations from Lester Pearson for solving one of his own problems so handily. The young man made sure that Mike saw pictures of him in his Shawinigan baseball uniform.

This was the period of tumbling ministers, as Quebec Liberals got caught with their pants down and their hands full of folding money. Eventually the prime minister's parliamentary secretary joined the legion of the disgraced, and looking for another French Canadian for the job, Pearson picked Jean Chrétien. The Quebec provincial Liberals, on the recommendation of René Levésque, had been urging Chrétien to join them, but now it looked as if he had a future in Ottawa.

Naturally he thought that when he was returned in the 1965 election, he was prime material for a cabinet post, but that was the year of the Three Wise Men. Quebec intellectuals were in and detail-men would have to wait a bit. Pearson told Chrétien that he was saving him for the Finance portfolio in the future, and did not want to get him sidetracked in some less important ministry. Then in April of 1967 he got his toe in, being appointed minister without portfolio and attached to Finance. Early in 1968, just before Pearson left office, he appointed Chrétien Minister of National Revenue.

For the 1968 leadership race, Chrétien lent his services to Mitchell Sharp, the Finance Minister and the party's chief anti-nationalist. Jean Marchand was trying to get everyone to back Pierre Trudeau and show the country that the party was unified behind his man. But for one thing, Trudeau had a snotty habit of insulting the brainpower of the guy from the sticks, and for another, Jean Chrétien had a habit of his own, of backing the underdog. Ten years earlier it had been Paul Martin; now it was Mitchell Sharp. Slowly but surely, Chrétien was letting English Canada know that they had someone they could trust in Quebec.

When Sharp had a good look at his probable vote total he decided to go over to Trudeau, and gave Jean the job of carrying the news to Pierre. As usual, Chrétien made himself useful and did what was right for the party. He was a kind of Liberal Joe Clark.

Everyone's second choice

Trudeau made Chrétien his Minister of Indian Affairs and Northern Development, a job that would last for six years. Trudeau had the idea that Native peoples should be integrated into the population as a whole rather than continuing their special relationship with the federal government, and Chrétien was supposed to persuade them that it was a good idea. Chrétien was finally getting a chance to see the Canada that lay outside Quebec and distant from Ottawa. When he flew north and west and told the people that they were going to become normal citizens, many of them dealing with provincial governments, he was at first puzzled to learn that the people were not enthusiastic about his news. As time went by he could not help but disagree with Trudeau's vision. I have been hung out to dry, he began to tell anyone who would listen.

Aline travelled with him during many of his flights north and west. She had had some very bad luck in her attempts to create a big Quebec-type family. She had two miscarriages and two surviving children, daughter France and son Hubert. When she had difficulty with Hubert's birth and suffered a long sickness after it, she was told not to get pregnant again. Hubert, it would turn out, suffered dyslexia. Partly to make a larger family, and partly to illustrate Chrétien's commitment to the underdog, the Chrétiens adopted another son, Michel, who had been selected from an orphanage in Inuvik by Chrétien's brother Michel, a volunteer medical worker among northern Natives. Michel would become a troublesome and expensive son for the Chrétiens, running away from school, refusing to smile or talk, drinking beer in his room, and eventually getting into serious trouble with the police. Hubert, meanwhile, would drift away from his father and his father's politics, eventually working at car dealerships.

The dyslexia that plagued Hubert was a family problem. Jean Chrétien himself has a version diagnosed by his brother Maurice the doctor as dyslalia. "I stumble over words," says the prime minister, putting it as simply as possible. Sometimes, while reading from a prepared speech, he will miss a word, or say a word twice, or say a long word incorrectly. It was this kind of difficulty with articulation that reporters or candidate Trudeau would represent as inarticulate. Put dyslalia together with Bell's palsy and hearing difficulties, and see whether you can become the most popular politician in the land.

Gathering votes, maybe

During his years in Trudeau's cabinet Chrétien forgot about his ten-year limit. He wanted to see how far he could rise. He looked good in a lot of photographs. His skill in managing people made him a valuable friend inside and outside his ministry. Trudeau was hanging on a long time, though, and there were times when Chrétien could not hold back his disagreement. When Trudeau started talking about invoking the War Measures Act to fight the "apprehended insurrection" in Montreal, Chrétien vociferously opposed it. Typically, when the measure was decided on, he joined in the government's action, and even took hits for his chief.

His frustrating tenure at Indian Affairs was finally over in 1974, when a cabinet shuffle got him the presidency of the Treasury Board. During the next decade he would also be Minister of Industry, Trade and Commerce, then the first ever French-Canadian Minister of Finance, then Minister of Justice and attorney-general as well as Minister of State for Social Development, then Minister of Energy, Mines and Resources. When John Turner fulfilled the Pearson policy and became the English-Canadian Liberal prime minister in the summer of 1984, he made Jean Chrétien his deputy prime minister and Secretary of State for External Affairs.

Jean Chrétien's year as Finance Minister was the worst year in his political career. The Canadian economy was in dismal shape, and the Liberals did not have a clue about what to do about it. He got double-crossed by Pierre Trudeau, squeezed between the Quebec government and the Canadian government, and loudly criticized by a bankers' lawyer named John Turner. When Trudeau called the 1979 election, Chrétien had to fight for his seat against his record in Finance; his foes were now stagflation and government debt rather than Church and Duplessites, but the new Quebec voters knew him, and liked him. He enjoyed his short time in opposition, and he continued his attacks on the separatists when Trudeau returned to office. Trudeau did not return him to the Finance portfolio, and he refused to give him the External Affairs job. He wanted him to stay in Canada and fight the separatists and their referendum. A lot of other Quebec members would have liked the

Justice portfolio and its main task of keeping Quebec in the country, and when Chrétien got the job, his colleagues called him Trudeau's "yes man."

He was Trudeau's bulldog. During the referendum campaign he exhibited all the skills that a century of Chrétien mill-town politics had developed. Now the whole country enjoyed the image of a tough scrapper with scarred knuckles and a suit that was sometimes used for sleeping in. He was not afraid to shout corny patriotic remarks: over and over he declared that he wanted the beautiful Canadian Rockies for his children and grandchildren. He would throw his typed speech away and talk "straight from the heart," over and over. His prose resembled a chicken in a tornado, but his uncomplicated passion would define him for the rest of his political life. He's no Trudeau, people would decide. I like him, they would decide. I have reason to hate him and fear him, the separatist strategists would admit to themselves while they mocked him aloud.

When the referendum vote was in, and Canada was kind of saved, Chrétien, exhausted and criss-crossed with emotions, went straight to see his boss. Grab a clean bunch of shirts, Trudeau told him, you are taking a plane this afternoon. There was a new Constitution to prepare. Trudeau might be in the habit of insulting his yes-man and hanging him out to dry, but he also knew that Chrétien was his number-one fixer. Whenever anyone in the organization came to Trudeau with a desperate cry for help, Trudeau told him to see Jean.

So between the Quebec referendum and the patriation of the Constitution, Jean Chrétien was everywhere in the country, saving Trudeau's ass and earning points with that largest group of outsiders, the Canadians who lived outside Ottawa and were not civil servants or elected officials. In the meantime, as he did the work of a dozen people, his family continued its troubled ways. His father died. His nephew went to jail in South America.

His sons never communicated with him. He did not see Aline enough. She joked that he might have trouble with his own restive Quebec.

He used his rough charm with the provincial premiers, served as a brawl-settling linesman in the Quebec-Ontario hockey showdowns, sat at his desk while Trudeau slept at night, and made his place in history as the husband of Confederation. In the photograph taken while the Justice Minister was signing the new Constitution, one can see Queen Elizabeth II smiling despite the bad weather. Pierre Trudeau had managed to break the tip of the pen, and Chrétien was worried that people in the future would react to his handwriting the way that reporters in the past had reacted to his speech.

Snakes and ladders

By the time of the 1984 leadership campaign, Jean Chrétien had been a party worker for 90 per cent of his fifty years, and a great help to a great number of cabinet members since his first election twenty-one years earlier. He had held eight or nine cabinet posts, depending on how you count. He was due. John Turner was a high-priced lawyer in Toronto's money canyon.

But Lester Pearson's idea was alternating leaders, and it was an anglophone's turn. Chrétien would be the only francophone in the race. But could he get the Quebec establishment onside? His mentor Mitchell Sharp warned him about that, and he thought about quitting. Then Pierre Trudeau brought up the Pearson idea at a caucus meeting. Was I chosen because I was a francophone, or because I was good, he asked his Liberals. Chrétien was in the race.

But people kept defaulting on the markers he had out. Friends lined up at his door to apologize and explain why they had to support John Turner. Jean Chrétien added to his record as the most often shafted Liberal. Even Trudeau, who had shafted him a few times earlier, could not help him much now. The country was tired of Trudeau, and John Turner was known to have stood up to him and to have sat out his second reign. As the campaign narrowed down to two candidates, fans of Canadian politics watched with awe as Turner and Chrétien fell all over their own feet. Could either of these guys beat baritone Brian Mulroney?

One of Chrétien's worst mistakes was to promise that he would serve in a Turner government. The party knew that if Chrétien won the nomination, Turner would skedaddle back to his steaks and cigars in Toronto. So more and more of his pals went to Turner, figuring that they would be keeping Chrétien too. Chrétien congratulated the winner and the party, but there were dying shorebirds in his eyes. He would go into a funk that would last for years.

Nevertheless, he ran in the 1984 election. The Mulroney Conservatives had one of those Tory landslides, but Chrétien was the first declared winner of a seat in Quebec. Then he watched the western returns on a television set. When Turner won the Vancouver Quadra seat to become the only sitting Liberal west of Winnipeg, the member for St-Maurice had an unhappy look on his face—maybe he was mourning the party's wipeout in the west. For the next two years he would sit in opposition, not far from a chastised Turner, who had for some reason stayed on as leader.

There were now forty Liberals in the House, and they began to act more like the Conservative party, splitting into Chrétien and Turner factions, quarrelling and scheming, and putting up little opposition to the grinning Irish eyes across the room. Meanwhile, Chrétien's salary was cut in half, so he took a one-day-a-week job in a Toronto law firm. Considering that he had made some unpleasant cracks about Turner's Bay Street home, he must have had to offer quite a few shit-eating smiles on that one day a week. In the House he was the external affairs critic, and spent most of his air denouncing Mulroney's cozying-up to the USAmericans. He also set to work writing his folksy *Straight from the Heart*, along with journalist Ron Graham. People in political and publishing circles wondered whether Key Porter Books had lost their mind—this was a guy who had just lost a leadership race for a party that was in the dumpster. But when it was published—in English— in 1985, it became a stampeding best-seller. People lined up around the block at signings. Chrétien signed a copy for John Turner, thanking him for winning the leadership and giving him time to become an author.

The book made him the most prominent Liberal in the country again. The media gobbled him up, and the party's most recent prime minister became nervous about his chances in the 1986 leadership review. Chrétien had a surprise for him, though. On February 27, he went to Turner's office and told him that he was dropping out of any leadership race, and—wait for it—dropping out of politics. Turner was flabbergasted. For a while he probably did not figure out what was happening. Aline Chrétien played her part, telling reporters that her husband was not going to take any more shit from his colleagues. Her husband almost gave the plan away when a reporter asked him whether he had been pushed out. "Have you ever tried to push out Jean Chrétien?" he asked. "Don't try it."

There was a lot of caterwauling in 1986. Columnists composed encomia for the faithful war-mule. The day after his announcement, Jeffrey Simpson of the *Globe and Mail* called him the soul of the party, and lamented that now, "no one speaks for humour in Liberal discourse, for patriotism, for generosity of spirit."

Jeffrey Simpson is a pretty smart political-historian; he probably knew what was going on. Brian Mulroney had a huge majority, and it was going to take a while for the Canadian people to come to their senses. Jean Chrétien, still only fifty-one years old, was not retiring—he was making a strategic retreat. *Straight from the Heart* was going to be revised and updated and republished in the nineties.

Look! It's alive!

It would have been wise for any pundit or ambitious pol to remember that Jean Chrétien had a sentimental attachment to the outsider. So did a lot of other people—polls have a habit of favouring outsiders over incumbents, especially for a party in opposition, and now in the late eighties the polls were showing that the self-styled "little guy from Shawinigan" was more popular than the other guy from Bay Street. Not that Chrétien had disappeared from the scene—he was everywhere, involving himself in provincial Liberal goings-on, lending his popularity to provincial candidates around the country, getting his picture taken a lot.

The animosity between Turner and Chrétien probably delighted the Tories. It was certainly no secret from anyone who bothered to read the dull parts of the newspaper. The Liberals doubled their representation in the 1988 Parliament, but the Mulroneys still had a big majority. What would the Liberals do now, and what was Chrétien doing? Well, Chrétien the little guy from the mill town was out in the real world becoming a millionaire, sitting on boards, acting as an adviser, cashing in on his popularity and influence. He was working half as hard and making ten times as much moolah as he had been in

Ottawa. Maybe politics was not the only interesting trip. But he did not sell his house in Ottawa.

In his hometown he bought the golf course that had discriminated against French Canadians. The deal would come undone early in 1999. He owned stocks all over the place, including a west coast mining company called Viceroy Resources, which enjoyed a big gold strike in California. Its director, Ross Fitzpatrick, had always liked gold. When he was a year ahead of me in high school in Oliver, B.C., he had a gold corner on one of his front teeth. Those were the days of pegged pants and chains that looped from belt to pocket. My chain was ripped off an old bathtub plug. His was made of his name in gold letters. Now he was a gold and golf buddy of Jean Chrétien, who often visited the links in Kelowna. Ross says that Chrétien likes to hang with powerful business people, but never forgets the mill in Shawinigan. He still likes to watch baseball on television.

The polls suggested that Chrétien could have won the 1988 election. The day after that election he leaked the news that he was available just in case the party was thinking that Turner should head back to the legal life. Pretty soon some of the big-deal Liberals who had betrayed and deserted him in 1984 began to drop by and try to make amends. Pretty soon the makeover crew was moving in. They smoothed his English. They taught him how to read a speech without stumbling. They buffed and polished and tucked and smoothed. How dumb can you be? The Canadian people did not want a Mulroney-style Chrétien. They wanted an honest guy with mustard on his tie.

Sure, he was the ultimate establishment man in federal politics and in the boardrooms. But he was popular, damn it! He was popular because he talked like a guy who might strike up a conversation at a hot-dog lineup. Now he was in a position to call in his markers from all the guilt-ridden Grits who had jumped over his body and given John Turner to the nation in 1984. Turner announced his resignation in 1989, and Jean Chrétien was back in federal politics. Some people, notably the provincial establishments, ran Sheila Copps and Paul Martin Jr. against him. But really: how could the Liberals pick anyone other than the wrinkled fellow with the Damon Runyan voice?

So the day after Meech Lake dried up, Jean Chrétien was the old new leader of the Liberal party. Of course he became very unpopular in Quebec, at least with the newspapers and politicians who blamed him for the defeat of the accord. He was just as glad when Mulroney called a by-election in the New Brunswick riding of Beauséjour, where he could campaign in French and English. In 1990 he had a new seat in the front bench, and quietly set to work normalizing the situation. For the next couple of years he watched the restraint-promising Conservatives build a fantastic deficit, and kept track of all the patronage and lobbying he saw going on. To hell with the spin doctors and makeover people: during the next election he was going to lead a raucous caucus.

In the meantime he would be the details man. His strength had always been in cajoling, uniting, clearing away debris and making alliances within the organization. He raised money and arm-twisted confederates. He was not interested in a party philosophy—problems came along one by one, and you fixed them with the tools on your bench. If there was going to be a policy it would be this: promise to reduce the deficit while maintaining precious social programs.

When the 1993 election finally came around, the party offered its version of Canada in a 112-page "Red Book," a platform that promised a Kennedyish action plan and the notion that these Liberals were a fresh new idea at the end of a tedious Gucci regime. They probably didn't need it; they had the arithmetic. They were expecting the Progressive Conservatives to lose a lot of seats. They knew that they were running against the Quebec Bloc and the Alberta Bloc, and that the turncoat and the chipmunk would gather in a number of seats lost by Gucci and out of the reach of Anne of Green Gables.

What a strange new political map Canadians unrolled on October 25, 1993! Nine years earlier Brian Mulroney had reduced the Grits to two seats west of Ontario. Now the Tories themselves were reduced to two seats west of Greenland. The normal government party was back in power with a pretty good majority, the anti-Canadians were the loyal opposition, and the right-wing party with the left-wing name was close behind them. Sir Wilfrid Laurier's nightmare of a regionalized Parliament had been realized at the end of the century he had been so rosy about.

How could things ever get back to normal? And how could things change much unless the Chrétien government could satisfy all partialities? There was a finite number of Quebec members, so the BQ could never become the federal government they wanted to estrange. The fundamentalist Reform could never make inroads in the sophisticated cities of central Canada. The NDP had been squeezed out in the rush toward either the extremes or the popular new old PM. The Bay Street suits would take a long time to figure out whom they could buy.

The prime minister had come back to his riding of St-Maurice and knocked off the separatists there. He was surrounded by his grandchildren when he woke up to the official news that he had carried the country. He got a telephone call from the US president, and he held the phone to his working ear. He would listen, but unlike his predecessor, he might not sing along. On November 4, he was sworn in as Canada's twentieth postConfederation prime minister. But he had already been working at his desk in Ottawa for a week and more. His first signal to the Canadian people was a smaller cabinet. It could mean

(a) he was going to cut costs and trim the budget, and (b) the PMO was going to become even more powerful.

In his spare time he wrote two new chapters for the 1994 edition of his book. It ends with his optimistic federalist philosophy: "Canada is the best!"

Minding the store

"Tell me," said the curious Australian, "what big things has your man Chrétien done since he took control?"

"Say," I replied, "did I ever tell you about the time John A. Macdonald . . . ."

The twentieth president of the United States, James A. Garfield, spent most of his tenure in sleep. While the twentieth post-Confederation prime minister of Canada has been in power, the people of his country have taken a rest from federal politics. Jean Chrétien understood that Mulroney's obsession with a post-Trudeau Constitution had led to sore feelings that may never be mollified. He understood that people would welcome deficit-trimming until it threatened their health care dramatically. Chrétien had always been a details man, not an idea man, not a dreamer. For him the best government is a quiet government.

In the nineties Canadians would be hard-pressed to come up with the names of Chrétien's cabinet ministers, with the exception of his mooted successor, Paul Martin, the Finance Minister who claims to have achieved a budget surplus. While Reform candidates call for such reforms as bringing back the hangman, the Liberals have been trying to find ways to trim here and tuck there, to make adjustments to public institutions, to— oh dear, I'm a little sleepy myself.

The "underdog" prime minister has, for instance, charged a

committee to find out ways to make backbenchers' work more meaningful, probably remembering the backbencher's bill he himself had worked so hard to put through. He would also like to find a way to fix or dump the Senate, but he does not want to risk any foofaraw about the Constitution to do it. He has operatives from his caucus and PMO out there finding ways to improve the RCMP and the RCAF without spending too much. His government is a very busy one, but it is busy at work that is not glamorous enough for competitive television news programs.

There have been a few moments of excitement. Halfway through Chrétien's first term the provincial government of Quebec, led by a man who dressed like a British toff and spoke English like a stuffy retired major in a British comedy, held another referendum on independence. The prime minister decided to keep pretty well out of the campaign leading to the vote, and watched as a majority of francophones voted "*oui*," and the province as a whole rejected the move by a sliver of a percentage point, leading to the recriminations and accusations of fraud that usually attend Quebec politics.

A couple of years later Chrétien ran into one of those picturesque demonstrations that characterize the west coast. In 1997 it was Canada's turn to host the annual meeting of the Asia Pacific Economic Cooperation countries, their heads of state and the bodyguards of their heads of state. When these people appeared on the University of British Columbia campus on the last day of the meetings, they were greeted by students and other activists who objected to any kind of cordiality extended to Indonesia's loathsome strongman Suharto. There was a rumour that Canada had allowed Suharto's bodyguards to carry machine pistols. Whether that was true or not, the RCMP were carrying pepper spray, and they were quick to use it—on the Canadians.

When he heard about the event, Chrétien tried to make what he must have considered a witticism: "For me, pepper, I put it on my plate." He was a lot more careful a year later, when he spoke at a Liberal fundraising dinner in an expensive downtown Vancouver hotel. While the ins were inside eating expensive fish, there were seven hundred APEC protesters outside the hotel, including several who had been pepper-sprayed at UBC. Chrétien, alluding to the people in the street, said "Sometimes democracy is noisy, and it's messy." He said that he strongly supported the right of those young people to express their views. He then reminded his audience that he had led student protests against the Duplessis regime in Quebec.

It was pouring rain where the outs were, outside the doors of the Burrard Street hotel. Between the people and the hotel were 115 Vancouver police officers. Down the street were 60 RCMP officers under the command of a man known to the APEC protesters as "Sergeant Pepper" because of his favourite condiment. Once in a while there was a little surge in the wet, cold crowd, but the hotel looked as if it would stand. A dozen of the protesters sat down on the wet pavement and linked arms. All at once 54 frightening creatures emerged fast from inside the hotel. These were the Vancouver police riot squad. They wore helmets and costumes that made them look like a cross between science-fiction samurai and black metallic robots from a futuristic terror regime. They were banging long cudgels against their transparent shields, and advancing upon the wet people.

These creatures were easy to fear but difficult to respect. When their work was done a fifty-nine-year-old female antipoverty worker was hurled through the air and later treated for a broken tailbone. Several of the seated people had blood on their faces. The Vancouver police spokeswoman said that the riot police were trained to swing their clubs at people's lower legs, and that the protesters had screwed up the works by deliberately placing their heads at leg level. Television footage would show police sticks lifted high.

The feds instituted an inquiry into the APEC adventure, and protesters were invited to hire all the lawyers they could afford to oppose the position taken by the six lawyers paid by the taxpayers. It began to look like an inquiry that would not end in the twentieth century. It was not long before Chrétien's solicitor-general, Andy Scott, was forced to resign for chatting about the inquiry while relaxing on an airplane. Then the head of the inquiry panel, Gerald Morin, resigned after being accused of pre-judging the findings. Then the other panelists resigned, and early in 1999 a new panel was somehow found. A lot of cynicism was generated by the long process. Demonstrators said that they would like the inquiry to investigate the PMO as well as the RCMP. They wanted the prime minister implicated. They made posters to portray Chrétien as a kind of Suharto. Such inflammatory symbolism is not all that uncommon in the regular protest business in Vancouver.

All this kafuffle was supposed to sour people on the popular preem, according to the newspaper and magazine analyzers. Earlier they had run a blurry photograph pinched off television and showing Chrétien with his hands around the neck of a goofy protester who pushed himself into the prime minister's path. The prime minister's popularity went up a notch. One may suppose that Canadians pined for the days when John A. Macdonald would cross the stage to hurl himself on an opponent. The newspapers and magazines, whether Conrad Black's right-wing group or the various cities' weekly alternative CD-and-movie rags, would carry on a campaign of attack, portraying the prime minister as a power-hungry one-man gang, an oldster clinging to his privileges, a former populist become remote, a federalist who cannot face up to the devious premier of Quebec, and a long-time parliamentarian in semi-retirement. *Maclean's*, which was not yet directly controlled by Conrad Black, had a columnist who wrote weekly anti-Chrétien columns, carefully insinuating that the PM is a bully and a manipulator, among other things.

A criticism that comes up regularly in the press is the jibe that Chrétien has gone even further toward a USAmerican presidential-style rule. It would be hard, though, to imagine the US president's undergoing the Chrétiens' experience during the early hours of 1995. That night a loony store clerk from Montreal managed to enter the prime minister's residence at 24 Sussex Drive in Ottawa, and holding a pocket knife in his hand, advance nearly to the door of the first couple's bedroom, before security police managed to spot him and take him away. The loony store clerk was probably lucky: Jean Chrétien was waiting for him with an Inuit sculpture in his hands, and assuming a classic batting stance. The scene was so reassuringly Canadian that the prime minister's popularity went up again.

In spring of 1997 the Liberals had a leadership review, and gave Jean Chrétien 90 per cent of their backing. Then, after only three and a half years in power, Chrétien went to the people and won a second majority. In 1999 he would be sixty-five years old. A lot of those unsatisfied people in the news media suggested that he might retire before his mandate is over in 2002, even before the millennium is over on the last day of 2000. Did you ever try to push Jean Chrétien? Don't try.

CHAPTER 28

CENTURY'S END

As the last decade of the twentieth century AD slipped by, there were lots of Canadian prime ministers around. One day in 1994, there was a prime ministers' ceremony conducted at the National Archives in Ottawa, and plenty of commemorative photographs taken. The gorgeous group enlargements would hang in colour on the Archives' walls, and a nifty black-and-white postcard would be published by the Friends of the National Archives of Canada. Five of our living prime ministers stand together, each with his or her particular kind of smile. Pierre Trudeau has the best suit. They all have high foreheads, Jean Chrétien's the highest. John Turner and Joe Clark and Kim Campbell are there. Only one living ex-prime minister is missing from the pictures.

There were ugly rumours and accusations swooping around the capital and across the Atlantic Ocean. The government was probing, as the newspapers like to put it, the possibility that Brian Mulroney had a fat numbered bank account in Zurich, and that the contents of the account had something to do with a supply of European aircraft purchased by Air Canada. These rumours would persist, and add to the public's low regard for Mulroney, until he decided to sue the government he had left. By 1998 he would look like a rich honest guy, and there would be a book published about his wounded dignity and innocence. An extract would be published in a magazine owned by his old friend Conrad Black, who would also write a long review praising the book and its subject, and publish the review in some of the newspapers he controlled. Now the people who felt uneasy about flying across the country in an Airbus could enter the plane without a troubled conscience. Meanwhile, Mulroney was still advancing his US career: he was appointed chairman of *Forbes Global Business and Finance* magazine.

Just before the 1997 election, another magazine, not yet owned by Conrad Black, would publish a ranking of the twenty post-Confederation prime ministers. *Maclean's* asked twenty-five professors of Canadian history to consider success in leadership and legislation, and then pooled the results. Here is their ranking:

1. William Lyon Mackenzie King
2. Sir John A. Macdonald
3. Sir Wilfrid Laurier
4. Louis St Laurent
5. Pierre Elliott Trudeau
6. Lester Pearson
7. Sir Robert Borden
8. Brian Mulroney
9. Jean Chrétien
10. Sir John Thompson
11. Alexander Mackenzie
12. R.B. Bennett
13. John Diefenbaker
14. Arthur Meighen

15. Joe Clark
16. Sir Charles Tupper
17. Sir John Abbott
18. John Turner
19. Sir Mackenzie Bowell
20. Kim Campbell

One assumes that our historians base their decisions on historical principles, and that it is history that has decided that the Liberal prime ministers seem to have occupied, in general terms, the top half of the column.

A year later a research outfit conducted a poll of non-academics to find out who was the most highly trusted living politician in Canada. Prime Minister Chrétien finished second as 40 per cent of the respondents called him trustworthy. He was edged out by seventy-nine-year-old Pierre Trudeau, who got 42 per cent. Seventh, and last, came Brian Mulroney, at 12 per cent

One criterion that the scholars in the *Maclean's* list were not invited to employ was a prime minister's ability to keep a secret. During the grand debate between Diefenbaker and Pearson regarding the deployment of atomic weapons on Canadian soil or snow, most of us lowly airmen in the RCAF assumed that there were already A-missiles at such places as Comox and Val d'Or. In 1998 John Clearwater, a young military analyst at the Department of Defence, published a report that announced that the weapons were put into place as early as 1963, and were not removed until two decades later, if then. Pearson and Trudeau and Clark and Turner knew about them, but they did not have a little box with push-buttons to fire them at the enemy. During the great Canadian nationalist fervour of the late sixties, the atomic push-buttons were at Norad headquarters under a mountain in Colorado.

Still, Canada has always prided itself on not being nuclear-scary. Chrétien's Foreign Affairs Minister, Lloyd Axworthy, would carry on a campaign to readjust NATO's policy about atomic weapons. Canada was still an active member of NATO, and hence committed to its strategic policies, which include nuclear threatening. He would lobby member countries to forswear the first use of nuclear weapons. In Germany he would make some inroads with the centre-leftist government that had replaced old warhorse Helmut Kohl. Axworthy wanted the issue to be openly discussed among NATO members, but stood little chance of making a dent on the bellicose USAmericans, who considered him just another of those pesky Canadians they had to brush off from time to time.

Kim Campbell, meanwhile, did pretty well with the USAmericans she met daily in her new job as consul-general in Los Angeles. She even returned to the show-business activities she had shown such promise in during her schoolgirl days. With her "partner in life and arts," the twenty-nine-year-old Montreal-born composer Howard Felder, she created a musical about the Holocaust and called it *Noah's Ark*. It was work-shopped at the UCLA Center for the Performing Arts, and the co-authors were thinking of rewriting it and looking for another stage. Meanwhile, the consul-general would be quite busy in Lala-Land, where an inordinate number of Canadians reach for the brass ring.

Her successor as Tory leader, Jean Charest, would become leader of the Liberal opposition in the Quebec legislature, and would not fail during his election campaigning to offer up one of those quotable conundrums that (former) Tory hopefuls are famous for: "The *status quo*," he said, "does not mean that there will not be change."

While Charest left the rubble of the federal Conservative caucus for provincial politics, one of his former colleagues went to jail. Young lawyer Carole Jacques had been elected to Parliament from east-end Montreal at age 24 in the Mulroney landslide of 1984. She was re-elected in 1988, but in 1993, Kim Campbell refused to sign her nomination papers, and she ran as an independent. She lost her seat, and then the police had a good look at her record. It appeared that she and her aide had demanded $90,000 in bribes from two Montreal business-men in 1991. You see, some Montreal Liberals pointed out, it is not just we who get caught in scandals in this city. A judge would fine Carole Jacques $11,000 and sentence her to sixty days, to be served on weekends. The Quebec bar association would disbar her for two years. The people of Canada would continue to pay her MP's pension, which she started collecting in her early thirties.

A much more honest Conservative MP, John G. Diefenbaker, has been disinterred yet again, this time on the Internet. A young Carleton University journalism student, Glen Gower, cre-ated a Diefenbaker site on the Web, to which surfers could advance, where they would be treated to a journey through the life of the Chief. The story is pretty rosy, another proof that Diefenbaker's firestorm of forty years earlier was still keeping true believers warm. Visitors who enter the site can leave their comments behind. The address is: *http://diefenbaker.ottawa.com/*.

Another Diefenbaker fan, a Toronto lawyer named John Medcof, bought the Chief's childhood home in Neustadt, Ontario. The seven-room house had stood empty for two decades, and after its most recent owner died, it was put on the market for $159,000. No one was interested at that price, and when Dief fans asked the federal government to make a bid, they were rebuffed; the Diefenbaker home in Saskatchewan was already a museum, for goodness' sake. All right, said the fans, what about a plaque or a sign that might inform passersby that the young Diefenbaker had mowed the lawn around here?

Not interested, said the government. When the price came down to $59,000, Mr Medcof bought the house and started talking to the local history society and some service clubs about making it a museum.

The Canadian government has never been much interested in dead prime ministers, and the country is lucky that there are history cranks like John Medcof around. When a clump of letters from Wilfrid Laurier to his law partner's wife were offered at auction in 1972, the starting bid was supposed to be $25,000, but they were withdrawn from sale when the top bid turned out to be $4,500. Despite the enduring rumour that Émilie Lavergne's son Armand was Laurier's son as well, the letters sat for another twenty-five years in a vault in Bermuda. Finally, in 1998, they were auctioned again, and this time they went for $12,000 and came to rest in the National Archives. Perhaps the extra-marital adventures of the current US president had inspired the romantic or salacious envy of Canadian officials.

Though prime ministers' birth sites arouse no interest in the Canadian government, perhaps now their final resting places will. In 1998 the *Ottawa Citizen* published a feature article about the sorry state of some of the graves. Alexander Mackenzie, for example, was resting under a tangle of weeds and broken masonry in his hometown Sarnia. Jean Chrétien read the newspaper and made a few angry telephone calls. At the next cabinet meeting there was unanimous assent to his call to develop a national plan to renovate his predecessors' graves. No longer would they be decrepit and forgotten. They would become national monuments and kept tidy, and there would be signposts to identify them for tourists and graveyard buffs. "Holy cow," a future passerby may one day say, "we used to have a prime minister named Mackenzie Bowell!"

But what about R.B. Bennett? He is the only former prime minister of the post-Confederation period who is not buried in

Canada. When he left the country in a huff to become Viscount Bennett of Mickleham, *etc.*, not many of his Depression-era compatriots complained. But half a century after Bennett's death, an MLA in New Brunswick, Liberal Harry Doyle, started agitating to have the bones of the old Tory brought home for reburial at his birth site of Hopewell Hill, N.B. Although Bennett had no offspring to consult, a nephew, William Herridge, allowed as to how he would take the repatriation under consideration. But there are some Canadians whose memories are older than they are. An Ottawa management consultant named Peter O'Mally, who was born three years after Bennett died, has created an Internet Web site to oppose Doyle's reinterment plan. Anyone who cannot forgive Bennett for getting tremendously rich during the drought can reach the site at *www. omalco.com/bennett-rip.htm*

But as the twentieth century and the second millennium come to an end, anyone with a sense of history and order experiences a yearning for some kind of tidy closure. It would be patriotically comforting to have all our dead prime ministers in Canadian soil, under well-tended national monuments. Once we have R.B. Bennett back, we can go after the remains of Armand-Jean du Plessis, *cardinal et duc de* Richelieu. He was buried in the chapel of the Sorbonne. Surely we can strike a deal with the French authorities and bring our very first prime minister to the banks of the river named after him, where his word was law, and where he invested some of his personal fortune. At the magnificent reinterment ceremony our current prime minister could exclaim: *Vive l'Éminence Rouge libre!*

BIBLIOGRAPHY

Axworthy, Thomas S. and Pierre Elliott Trudeau, eds. *Towards a Just Society*. Toronto: Viking, 1990.

Ayre, W. Burton. *Mr Pearson and Canada's Revolution by Diplomacy*. Montreal [self-published], 1966.

Beal, John Robinson. *The Pearson Phenomenon*. Toronto: Longmans, 1964.

Beer, Donald R. *Sir Allan Napier MacNab*. Hamilton: Dictionary of Hamilton Biography, 1984.

Bergin, Joseph. *Cardinal Richelieu: Power and the Pursuit of Wealth*. New Haven: Yale University Press, 1985.

Bliss, J.M., ed. *Canadian History in Documents. 1763–1966*. Toronto: Ryerson, 1966.

Bliss, Michael. *Right Honourable Men: The Descent of Canadian Politics from Macdonald to Mulroney*. Toronto: HarperCollins, 1994.

Borden, Robert Laird. *Letters to Limbo*. Edited by Henry Borden. Toronto: University of Toronto Press, 1971.

Bothwell, Robert. *Pearson: His Life and World*. Toronto: McGraw-Hill Ryerson, 1978.

Bowering, George. *West Window*. Toronto: General Publishing, 1982.

Broadfoot, Barry, ed. *Ten Lost Years: 1929–1939*. Toronto: Doubleday, 1973.

Brown, George W., ed. *Readings in Canadian History*. Toronto: Dent, 1940.

Brown, Robert Craig. *Robert Laird Borden: a Biography*. Toronto: Macmillan, two volumes, 1975 and 1980.

Butler, Rick, and Jean-Guy Carrier, eds. *The Trudeau Decade*. Toronto: Doubleday, 1979.

Cahill, Jack. *John Turner: the Long Run*. Toronto: McClelland & Stewart, 1984.

Cameron, Stevie. *On the Take: Crime, Corruption and Greed in the Mulroney Years*. Toronto: McClelland–Bantam Seal, (revised) 1995.

Campbell, Kim. *Time and Chance*. Toronto: Doubleday, 1996.

Careless, J.M.S., and R. Craig Brown, eds., *The Canadians, 1867–1967*. Toronto: Macmillan, 1967.

Careless, J.M.S. *The Union of the Canadas*. Toronto: McClelland & Stewart, 1967.

Carter, Charles A. *The Gallant Knight*. Hamilton: The MacNab Circle, 1969.

Chodos, Robert, Rae Murphy, and Eric Hamovitch. *Selling Out: Four Years of the Mulroney Government*. Toronto: James Lorimer, 1988.

Chrétien, Jean. *Straight from the Heart*. Rev. ed. Toronto: Key Porter, 1994.

Christiano, Kevin J. *Pierre Elliot Trudeau: Reason Before Passion*. Toronto: ECW Press, 1994.

Coleridge, Samuel Taylor. *Poetical Works*. Edited by Ernest Hartley Coleridge. London: Oxford University Press, 1967.

Colquhoun, A.H.U. *The Fathers of Confederation*. Toronto, Glasgow: Brook & Co., 1921.

Creighton, Donald. *Canada's First Century, 1867–1967*. Toronto: Macmillan, 1970.

Creighton, Donald G. *John A. Macdonald: the Young Politician*. Toronto: Macmillan, 1952.

Creighton, Donald G. *John A. Macdonald: The Old Chieftain*. Toronto: Macmillan, 1955.

Davey, Frank. *Reading "Kim" Right*. Vancouver: Talonbooks, 1993.

Dawson, R. MacGregor. *William Lyon Mackenzie King: a Political Biography*. Toronto: University of Toronto Press, 1958.

Dent, John Charles. *The Last Forty Years: Canada Since the Union of 1841*. 2 Vols. Toronto: George Virtue, 1881.

Diefenbaker, John G. *One Canada: Memoirs of the Right Honourable John G. Diefenbaker*, Vol. 1: *The Crusading Years, 1895–1956*. Toronto: Macmillan, 1975.

Dobbin, Murray. *The Politics of Kim Campbell*. Toronto: James Lorimer, 1993.

Donaldson, Gordon. *Eighteen Men: the Prime Ministers of Canada*. Toronto: Doubleday, 1985.

English, John. *Shadow of Heaven: The Life of Lester Pearson, Volume One: 1897–1948*. Toronto: Lester & Orpen Dennys, 1989.

English, John. *The Worldly Years: The Life of Lester Pearson, Volume Two: 1949–1972*. Toronto: Knopf, 1992.

Esberey, Joy E. *Knight of the Holy Spirit: A Study of William Lyon Mackenzie King*. Toronto: University of Toronto Press, 1980.

Ferns, H.S. and B. Ostrey. *The Age of Mackenzie King*. Toronto: British Book Service, 1955.

Fife, Robert. *Kim Campbell, the Making of a Politician*. Toronto: HarperCollins, 1993.

Frizzell, Alan, and Anthony Westell. *The Canadian General Election of 1984*. Ottawa: Carleton University Press, 1985.

Frizzell, Alan, Jon H. Pammett, and Anthony Westell. *The Canadian General Election of 1988*. Ottawa: Carleton University Press, 1989.

Frizzell, Alan, Jon. H. Pammett, and Anthony Westell. *The Canadian General Election of 1993*. Ottawa: Carleton University Press, 1994.

Gollner, Andrew B., and Daniel Salée, eds. *Canada Under Mulroney: an End-of-Term Report*. Montreal: Véhicule, 1988.

Granatstein, J.L. *Mackenzie King: His Life and World*. Toronto: McGraw-Hill Ryerson, 1977.

Graham, Roger. *Arthur Meighen: A Biography*. Vol. 1. *The Door of Opportunity*. Toronto: Clarke, Irwin, 1960.

Graham, Roger. *Arthur Meighen: A Biography*. Vol. 2. *And Fortune Fled*. Toronto: Clarke, Irwin, 1963.

Graham, Roger. *Arthur Meighen: A Biography*. Vol. 3. *No Surrender*. Toronto: Clarke, Irwin, 1965.

Gratton, Michel. *"So, What are the Boys Saying?": An Inside Look at Brian Mulroney in Power*. Toronto: McGraw-Hill Ryerson, 1987.

Gratton, Michel. *Still the Boss: A Candid Look at Brian Mulroney*. Scarborough: Prentice-Hall, 1990.

Gray, James H. *R.B. Bennett: The Calgary Years*. Toronto: University of Toronto Press, 1991.

Gwyn, Richard. *The Northern Magus: Pierre Trudeau and the Canadians*. Toronto: McClelland & Stewart, 1980.

Hardy, H. Reginald. *Mackenzie King of Canada*. Toronto: Oxford University Press, 1949.

Hopkins, J. Castell. *Life and Work of the Rt. Hon. Sir John Thompson, P.C., K.C.M.G., Q.C., Prime Minister of Canada*. Brantford: Bradley, Garretson, and Co., 1895.

Hoy, Claire. *Friends in High Places: Politics and Patronage in the Mulroney Government*. Toronto: McClelland & Stewart, 1988.

Humphreys, David L. *Joe Clark: A Portrait*. Toronto: Deneau & Greenberg, 1978.

Hutchison, Bruce. *The Incredible Canadian: A Candid Portrait of Mackenzie King*. Toronto: Longmans, Green and Co., 1953.

Hutchison, Bruce. *Mr. Prime Minister: 1867–1964*. Toronto: Longmans, 1964.

Johnson, J.K. *Affectionately Yours: The Letters of Sir John A. Macdonald and his Family*. Toronto: Macmillan, 1969.

Johnston, James. *The Party's Over.* Don Mills: Longmans, 1971.

King, W.L. Mackenzie. *The Message of the Carillon and Other Addresses.* Toronto: Macmillan, 1927.

Lalonde, Michelle. *Défense et illustration de la langue Québécoise.* Montreal: L'Hexagone, 1980.

LaPierre, Laurier L. *Sir Wilfrid Laurier and the Romance of Canada.* Toronto: Stoddart, 1996.

Laxer, James and Robert Laxer. *The Liberal Idea of Canada.* Toronto: James Lorimer, 1977.

Lee, Dennis. *Civil Elegies and other poems.* Toronto: House of Anansi, 1972.

MacDonald, L. Ian. *Mulroney: The Making of the Prime Minister.* Toronto: McClelland & Stewart, 1985.

MacLean, Andrew D. *R.B. Bennett, Prime Minister of Canada.* Toronto: Excelsior Publishing, 1935.

MacMechan, Archibald. *The Winning of Popular Government.* Toronto, Glasgow: Brook & Co., 1921.

MacQuarrie, Heath, ed. *Robert Laird Borden: His Memoirs.* Toronto: McClelland & Stewart, Carleton Library, two volumes, 1969.

MacRae, Marion. *MacNab of Dundurn.* Toronto: Clark, Irwin, 1971.

Martin, Lawrence. *Chrétien: The Will to Win.* Toronto: Lester Publishing, 1995.

McCall, Christina, and Stephen Clarkson. *Trudeau and our Times, Vol. 1: The Magnificent Obsession.* Toronto: McClelland & Stewart, 1991.

McCall, Christina, and Stephen Clarkson. *Trudeau and our Times, Vol. 2: The Heroic Delusion.* Toronto: McClelland & Stewart, 1994.

McDonald, Marci. *Yankee Doodle Dandy: Brian Mulroney and the American Agenda.* Toronto: Stoddart, 1995.

McInnis, Edgar. *Canada: A Political and Social History.* New York: Rinehart, 1956.

McLaughlin, David. *Poisoned Chalice: The Last Campaign of the Progressive Conservative Party?* Toronto: Dundurn, 1994.

Meighen, Arthur. *Unrevised and Unrepented: Debating Speeches and Others*. Toronto: Clarke, Irwin, 1949.

Milne, David. *The Canadian Constitution*. Toronto: James Lorimer, 1991.

Montgomery, L.M. *Anne of Avonlea*. Toronto: Ryerson, 1942.

Mulroney, Brian. *Where I Stand*. Toronto: McClelland & Stewart, 1983.

Munro, John A. ed. *The Wit & Wisdom of John Diefenbaker*. Edmonton: Hurtig, 1982.

Murphy, Rae, Robert Chodos, and Nick Auf der Maur. *Brian Mulroney: the Boy from Baie-Comeau*. Toronto: James Lorimer, 1984.

Murrow, Casey. *Henri Bourassa and French-Canadian Nationalism*. Montreal: Harvest House, 1968.

Neatby, H. Blair. *William Lyon Mackenzie King: A Political Biography*. Vol. 2. *The Lonely Heights*. Toronto: University of Toronto Press, 1963.

Neatby, H. Blair. *William Lyon Mackenzie King: A Political Biography*. Vol. 3. *The Prism of Unity*. Toronto: University of Toronto Press, 1976.

Newman, Peter C. *The Distemper of our Times*. Toronto: McClelland & Stewart, 1968.

Newman, Peter C. *Renegade in Power: The Diefenbaker Years*. Toronto: McClelland & Stewart, 1963.

Nicholson, Patrick. *Vision and Indecision*. Don Mills: Longmans, 1968.

Nolan, Michael. *Joe Clark: The Emerging Leader*. Toronto: Fitzhenry & Whiteside, 1978.

Ondaatje, Christopher. *The Prime Ministers of Canada, 1867-1967*. Toronto: Canyon Press, 1967.

Pearson, Geoffrey A.H. *Seize the Day: Lester B. Pearson and Crisis Diplomacy*. Ottawa: Carleton University Press, 1993.

Pearson, Lester B. *Mike: the Memoirs of the Right Honourable Lester B. Pearson*. Vol. 1. *1897–1948*. Toronto: University of Toronto Press, 1972.

Pearson, Lester B. *Mike: the Memoirs of the Right Honourable Lester B. Pearson*. Vol. 2. *1948–1957*. Toronto: University of Toronto Press, 1973.

Pearson, Lester B. *Mike: the Memoirs of the Right Honourable Lester B. Pearson*. Vol. 3. *1957–1968*. Toronto: University of Toronto Press, 1975.

Pearson, Lester B. *Words and Occasions.* Toronto: University of Toronto Press, 1970.

Pickersgill, J.W., and D.F. Forster. *The Mackenzie King Record.* Vol. 1. *1939–1944.* Toronto: University of Toronto Press, 1960.

Pickersgill, J.W., and D.F. Forster. *The Mackenzie King Record.* Vol. 2 *1944–1945.* Toronto: University of Toronto Press, 1968.

Pickersgill, J.W., and D.F. Forster. *The Mackenzie King Record.* Vol. 3 *1945–1946.* Toronto: University of Toronto Press, 1970.

Pickersgill, J.W., and D.F. Forster. *The Mackenzie King Record.* Vol. 4 *1947–1948.* Toronto: University of Toronto Press, 1970.

Pickersgill, J.W. *My Years with Louis St Laurent.* Toronto: University of Toronto Press, 1975.

Quinn, Magella, and Claude Marcil. *Louis S. St-Laurent.* Ottawa: Parks Canada, 1982.

Radwanski, George. *Trudeau.* Toronto: Macmillan, 1978.

Reynolds, Louise. *Agnes: the Biography of Lady Macdonald.* Toronto: Samuel Stevens, 1979.

Richardson, B.T. *Canada and Mr. Diefenbaker.* Toronto: McClelland & Stewart, 1962.

Robertson, Barbara. *Sir Wilfrid Laurier: The Great Conciliator.* Kingston: Quarry, 1991.

Robinson, H. Basil. *Diefenbaker's World: A Populist in Foreign Affairs.* Toronto: University of Toronto Press, 1989.

Robinson, J.H. *Readings in European History,* two vols. Boston: Ginn, 1906.

Sawatsky, John. *Mulroney: The Politics of Ambition.* Toronto: Macfarlane Walter & Ross, 1991.

Schull, Joseph. *Laurier: The First Canadian.* Toronto: Macmillan, 1965.

Simpson, Jeffrey. *The Anxious Years: Politics in the Age of Mulroney and Chrétien.* Toronto: Lester Publishing, 1996.

Simpson, Jeffrey. *Discipline of Power.* Toronto: University of Toronto Press, 1980.

Smith, Cynthia M., and Jack McLeod, eds. *Sir John A.: An Anecdotal Life of John A. Macdonald.* Toronto: Oxford, 1989.

Smith, Denis. *Rogue Tory: The Life and Legend of John G. Diefenbaker.* Toronto: Macfarlane Walter & Ross, 1995.

Snider, Norman. *The Changing of the Guard.* Toronto: Lester & Orpen Dennys, 1985.

Spencer, Dick. *Trumpets and Drums: John Diefenbaker on the Campaign Trail.* Vancouver: Douglas & McIntyre, 1994.

Stacey, C.P. *A Very Double Life: The Private World of Mackenzie King.* Toronto: Macmillan, Laurentian Library, 1977.

Stewart, Walter. *Shrug: Trudeau in Power.* Toronto: New Press, 1971.

St Laurent, Louis. *The Foundations of Canadian Policy in World Affairs.* Toronto: University of Toronto Press, 1947.

Stonechild, Blair, and Bill Waiser. *Loyal Till Death: Indians and the North-West Rebellion.* Calgary: Fifth House, 1997.

Stursberg, Peter. *Diefenbaker: Leadership Lost, 1962-67.* Toronto: University of Toronto Press, 1976.

Stursburg, Peter. *Lester Pearson and the American Dilemma.* Toronto: Doubleday, 1980.

Stursburg, Peter. *Lester Pearson and the Dream of Unity.* Toronto: Doubleday, 1978.

Sullivan, Martin. *Mandate '68.* Toronto: Doubleday, 1968.

Thomson, Dale. C. *Louis St. Laurent: Canadian.* Toronto: Macmillan, 1967.

Thordarson, Bruce. *Lester Pearson: Diplomat and Politician.* Toronto: Oxford, 1974.

Troyer, Warner. *200 Days: Joe Clark in Power.* Toronto: Personal Library, 1980.

Trudeau, Margaret. *Beyond Reason.* London: Paddington, 1979.

Trudeau, Margaret. *Consequences.* Toronto: McClelland & Stewart, 1982.

Trudeau, Pierre Elliott. *Memoirs.* Toronto: McClelland & Stewart, 1993.

Van Dusen, Thomas. *The Chief.* Toronto: McGraw-Hill, 1968.

Vastel, Michel. *The Outsider: The Life of Pierre Elliott Trudeau.* Toronto: Macmillan, 1990.

Waite, P.B. *The Man from Halifax: Sir John Thompson, Prime Minister.* Toronto: University of Toronto Press, 1985.

Watkins, Ernest. *R.B. Bennett.* London: Secker & Warburg, 1963.

Werthman, William C., ed. *Canada in Cartoon: A Pictorial History of the Confederation Years 1867-1967.* Fredericton: Brunswick Press, 1967.

Westell, Anthony. *Paradox: Trudeau as Prime Minister.* Scarborough: Prentice-Hall, 1972.

Weston, Greg. *Reign of Error: The Inside Story of John Turner's Troubled Leadership.* Toronto: McGraw-Hill Ryerson, 1988.

Wilson, Garrett, and Kevin Wilson. *Diefenbaker for the Defence.* Toronto: James Lorimer & Co., 1988.

Wrong, George M. *The Rise and Fall of New France.* 2 vols. Toronto: Macmillan, 1928.

Zolf, Larry. *Just Watch Me: Remembering Pierre Trudeau.* Toronto: James Lorimer, 1984.

INDEX